Carnegie Commission on Higher Education

Sponsored Research Studies

TEACHERS AND STUDENTS:
ASPECTS OF AMERICAN
HIGHER EDUCATION
Martin Trow (ed.)

THE DIVIDED ACADEMY:
PROFESSORS AND POLITICS
*Everett Carll Ladd, Jr. and
Seymour Martin Lipset*

EDUCATION AND POLITICS
AT HARVARD
*Seymour Martin Lipset and
David Riesman*

HIGHER EDUCATION AND EARNINGS:
COLLEGE AS AN INVESTMENT AND A
SCREENING DEVICE
Paul Taubman and Terence Wales

EDUCATION, INCOME, AND
HUMAN BEHAVIOR
F. Thomas Juster (ed.)

AMERICAN LEARNED SOCIETIES
IN TRANSITION:
THE IMPACT OF DISSENT
AND RECESSION
*Harland G. Bloland and
Sue M. Bloland*

ANTIBIAS REGULATION OF
UNIVERSITIES:
FACULTY PROBLEMS AND
THEIR SOLUTIONS
Richard A. Lester

CHANGES IN UNIVERSITY
ORGANIZATION, 1964—1971
Edward Gross and Paul V. Grambsch

ESCAPE FROM THE DOLL'S HOUSE: WOMEN
IN GRADUATE AND PROFESSIONAL SCHOOL
EDUCATION
Saul D. Feldman

HIGHER EDUCATION AND
THE LABOR MARKET
Margaret S. Gordon (ed.)

THE ACADEMIC MELTING POT:
CATHOLICS AND JEWS IN
AMERICAN HIGHER EDUCATION
Stephen Steinberg

LEADERSHIP AND AMBIGUITY:
THE AMERICAN COLLEGE
PRESIDENT
*Michael D. Cohen and
James G. March*

THE ACADEMIC SYSTEM IN
AMERICAN SOCIETY
Alain Touraine

EDUCATION FOR THE PROFESSIONS
OF MEDICINE, LAW, THEOLOGY,
AND SOCIAL WELFARE
*Everett C. Hughes, Barrie Thorne,
Agostino De Baggis, Arnold Gurin,
and David Williams*

THE FUTURE OF HIGHER
EDUCATION:
SOME SPECULATIONS AND
SUGGESTIONS
Alexander M. Mood

TUITION: A SUPPLEMENTAL
STATEMENT TO THE REPORT
OF THE CARNEGIE COMMISSION
ON HIGHER EDUCATION ON
"WHO PAYS? WHO BENEFITS?
WHO SHOULD PAY?"

THE GREAT AMERICAN
DEGREE MACHINE
Douglas L. Adkins

The following reprints are available from the Carnegie Commission on Higher Education, 2150 Shattuck Avenue, Berkeley, California 94704.

ACCELERATED PROGRAMS OF MEDICAL EDUCATION, *by Mark S. Blumberg, reprinted from* JOURNAL OF MEDICAL EDUCATION, *vol. 46, no. 8, August 1971.**

SCIENTIFIC MANPOWER FOR 1970–1985, *by Allan M. Cartter, reprinted from* SCIENCE, *vol. 172, no. 3979, pp. 132–140, April 9, 1971.*

A NEW METHOD OF MEASURING STATES' HIGHER EDUCATION BURDEN, *by Neil Timm, reprinted from* THE JOURNAL OF HIGHER EDUCATION, *vol. 42, no. 1, pp. 27–33, January 1971.**

REGENT WATCHING, *by Earl F. Cheit, reprinted from* AGB REPORTS, *vol. 13, no. 6, pp. 4–13, March 1971.*

COLLEGE GENERATIONS—FROM THE 1930s TO THE 1960s, *by Seymour M. Lipset and Everett C. Ladd, Jr., reprinted from* THE PUBLIC INTEREST, *no. 25, Summer 1971.*

AMERICAN SOCIAL SCIENTISTS AND THE GROWTH OF CAMPUS POLITICAL ACTIVISM IN THE 1960s, *by Everett C. Ladd, Jr., and Seymour M. Lipset, reprinted from* SOCIAL SCIENCES INFORMATION, *vol. 10, no. 2, April 1971.*

THE POLITICS OF AMERICAN POLITICAL SCIENTISTS, *by Everett C. Ladd, Jr., and Seymour M. Lipset, reprinted from* PS, *vol. 4, no. 2, Spring 1971.**

THE DIVIDED PROFESSORIATE, *by Seymour M. Lipset and Everett C. Ladd, Jr., reprinted from* CHANGE, *vol. 3, no. 3, pp. 54–60, May 1971.**

JEWISH ACADEMICS IN THE UNITED STATES: THEIR ACHIEVEMENTS, CULTURE AND POLITICS, *by Seymour M. Lipset and Everett C. Ladd, Jr., reprinted from* AMERICAN JEWISH YEAR BOOK, *1971.*

THE UNHOLY ALLIANCE AGAINST THE CAMPUS, *by Kenneth Keniston and Michael Lerner, reprinted from* NEW YORK TIMES MAGAZINE, *November 8, 1970.*

PRECARIOUS PROFESSORS: NEW PATTERNS OF REPRESENTATION, *by Joseph W. Garbarino, reprinted from* INDUSTRIAL RELATIONS, *vol. 10, no. 1, February 1971.**

*The Commission's stock of this reprint has been exhausted.

. . . AND WHAT PROFESSORS THINK: ABOUT STUDENT PROTEST AND MANNERS, MORALS, POLITICS, AND CHAOS ON THE CAMPUS, *by Seymour Martin Lipset and Everett C. Ladd, Jr., reprinted from* PSYCHOLOGY TODAY, *November 1970.* *

DEMAND AND SUPPLY IN U.S. HIGHER EDUCATION: A PROGRESS REPORT, *by Roy Radner and Leonard S. Miller, reprinted from* AMERICAN ECONOMIC REVIEW, *May 1970.* *

RESOURCES FOR HIGHER EDUCATION: AN ECONOMIST'S VIEW, *by Theodore W. Schultz, reprinted from* JOURNAL OF POLITICAL ECONOMY, *vol. 76, no. 3, University of Chicago, May/June 1968.* *

INDUSTRIAL RELATIONS AND UNIVERSITY RELATIONS, *by Clark Kerr, reprinted from* PROCEEDINGS OF THE 21ST ANNUAL WINTER MEETING OF THE INDUSTRIAL RELATIONS RESEARCH ASSOCIATION, *pp. 15–25.* *

NEW CHALLENGES TO THE COLLEGE AND UNIVERSITY, *by Clark Kerr, reprinted from Kermit Gordon (ed.),* AGENDA FOR THE NATION, *The Brookings Institution, Washington, D.C., 1968.* *

PRESIDENTIAL DISCONTENT, *by Clark Kerr, reprinted from David C. Nichols (ed.),* PERSPECTIVES ON CAMPUS TENSIONS: PAPERS PREPARED FOR THE SPECIAL COMMITTEE ON CAMPUS TENSIONS, *American Council on Education, Washington, D.C., September 1970.* *

STUDENT PROTEST—AN INSTITUTIONAL AND NATIONAL PROFILE, *by Harold Hodgkinson, reprinted from* THE RECORD, *vol. 71, no. 4, May 1970.* *

WHAT'S BUGGING THE STUDENTS?, *by Kenneth Keniston, reprinted from* EDUCATIONAL RECORD, *American Council on Education, Washington, D.C., Spring 1970.* *

THE POLITICS OF ACADEMIA, *by Seymour Martin Lipset, reprinted from David C. Nichols (ed.),* PERSPECTIVES ON CAMPUS TENSIONS: PAPERS PREPARED FOR THE SPECIAL COMMITTEE ON CAMPUS TENSIONS, *American Council on Education, Washington, D.C., September 1970.* *

INTERNATIONAL PROGRAMS OF U.S. COLLEGES AND UNIVERSITIES: PRIORITIES FOR THE SEVENTIES, *by James A. Perkins, reprinted by permission of the International Council for Educational Development, Occasional Paper no. 1, July 1971.*

FACULTY UNIONISM: FROM THEORY TO PRACTICE, *by Joseph W. Garbarino, reprinted from* INDUSTRIAL RELATIONS, *vol. 11, no. 1, pp. 1–17, February 1972.*

MORE FOR LESS: HIGHER EDUCATION'S NEW PRIORITY, *by Virginia B. Smith, reprinted from* UNIVERSAL HIGHER EDUCATION: COSTS AND BENEFITS, *American Council on Education, Washington, D.C., 1971.*

ACADEMIA AND POLITICS IN AMERICA, *by Seymour M. Lipset, reprinted from Thomas J.*

The Commission's stock of this reprint has been exhausted.

Nossiter (ed.), IMAGINATION AND PRECISION IN THE SOCIAL SCIENCES, pp. 211–289, Faber and Faber, London, 1972.

POLITICS OF ACADEMIC NATURAL SCIENTISTS AND ENGINEERS, by Everett C. Ladd, Jr., and Seymour M. Lipset, reprinted from SCIENCE, vol. 176, no. 4039, pp. 1091–1100, June 9, 1972.

THE INTELLECTUAL AS CRITIC AND REBEL: WITH SPECIAL REFERENCE TO THE UNITED STATES AND THE SOVIET UNION, by Seymour M. Lipset and Richard B. Dobson, reprinted from DAEDALUS, vol. 101, no. 3, pp. 137–198, Summer 1972.

COMING OF MIDDLE AGE IN HIGHER EDUCATION, by Earl F. Cheit, address delivered to American Association of State Colleges and Universities and National Association of State Universities and Land-Grant Colleges, Nov. 13, 1972.

THE NATURE AND ORIGINS OF THE CARNEGIE COMMISSION ON HIGHER EDUCATION, by Alan Pifer, reprinted by permission of The Carnegie Commission for the Advancement of Teaching, speech delivered Oct. 16, 1972.

THE DISTRIBUTION OF ACADEMIC TENURE IN AMERICAN HIGHER EDUCATION, by Martin Trow, reprinted from THE TENURE DEBATE, Bardwell Smith (ed.), Jossey-Bass, San Francisco, 1972.

THE POLITICS OF AMERICAN SOCIOLOGISTS, by Seymour M. Lipset and Everett C. Ladd, Jr., reprinted from THE AMERICAN JOURNAL OF SOCIOLOGY, vol. 78, no. 1, July 1972.

MEASURING FACULTY UNIONISM: QUANTITY AND QUALITY, by Bill Aussieker and J. W. Garbarino, reprinted from INDUSTRIAL RELATIONS, vol. 12, no. 2, May 1973.

PROBLEMS IN THE TRANSITION FROM ELITE TO MASS HIGHER EDUCATION, by Martin Trow, paper presented at an Organization for Economic Co-operation and Development conference on mass higher education, June 1973.

Nossiter (ed.), IMAGINATION AND PRECISION IN THE SOCIAL SCIENCES, *pp. 211–289, Faber and Faber, London, 1972.*

POLITICS OF ACADEMIC NATURAL SCIENTISTS AND ENGINEERS, *by Everett C. Ladd, Jr., and Seymour M. Lipset, reprinted from* SCIENCE, *vol. 176, no. 4039, pp. 1091–1100, June 9, 1972.*

THE INTELLECTUAL AS CRITIC AND REBEL: WITH SPECIAL REFERENCE TO THE UNITED STATES AND THE SOVIET UNION, *by Seymour M. Lipset and Richard B. Dobson, reprinted from* DAEDALUS, *vol. 101, no. 3, pp. 137–198, Summer 1972.*

COMING OF MIDDLE AGE IN HIGHER EDUCATION, *by Earl F. Cheit, address delivered to American Association of State Colleges and Universities and National Association of State Universities and Land-Grant Colleges, Nov. 13, 1972.*

THE NATURE AND ORIGINS OF THE CARNEGIE COMMISSION ON HIGHER EDUCATION, *by Alan Pifer, reprinted by permission of The Carnegie Commission for the Advancement of Teaching, speech delivered Oct. 16, 1972.*

THE DISTRIBUTION OF ACADEMIC TENURE IN AMERICAN HIGHER EDUCATION, *by Martin Trow, reprinted from* THE TENURE DEBATE, *Bardwell Smith (ed.), Jossey-Bass, San Francisco, 1972.*

THE POLITICS OF AMERICAN SOCIOLOGISTS, *by Seymour M. Lipset and Everett C. Ladd, Jr., reprinted from* THE AMERICAN JOURNAL OF SOCIOLOGY, *vol. 78, no. 1, July 1972.*

MEASURING FACULTY UNIONISM: QUANTITY AND QUALITY, *by Bill Aussieker and J. W. Garbarino, reprinted from* INDUSTRIAL RELATIONS, *vol. 12, no. 2, May 1973.*

PROBLEMS IN THE TRANSITION FROM ELITE TO MASS HIGHER EDUCATION, *by Martin Trow, paper presented at an Organization for Economic Co-operation and Development conference on mass higher education, June 1973.*

$17.50

Teachers and Students

edited by *Martin Trow*

The largest and most complete survey
to determine attitudes of students
and faculty members in colleges and
universities was undertaken in 1969
by the Carnegie Commission on
Higher Education with the cooperation
of the American Council on Education
and the support of the U.S. Office of
Education. The survey yielded data
about the opinions of faculty, graduate
students, and undergraduates in the
whole universe of American higher
education: colleges and universities,
two-year and four-year, public and
private.

This collection of essays was written
by the members of the research team
that designed and administered the
survey. Using survey data, the authors
are able to explore distinct segments
and activities of the academic
population. These selected studies are
concerned with faculty research,

Teachers and Students

the extent and effect of religious
commitment of faculty,
undergraduates in sociology,
undergraduate peer influence and
group norms, and academic women
and blacks.

The authors, all sociologists, interpret
the data in the light of social and
academic conditions and expectations
—and thus give us an enlarged
understanding of the relationship
between higher education and society.
The result is a multifaceted portrait of
our system of higher education and
the people who study and teach on the
campuses.

Martin Trow, professor of sociology
in the Graduate School of Public
Policy at the University of California
at Berkeley, is the editor of *Teachers
and Students*.

McGraw-Hill Book Company
1221 Avenue of the Americas
New York, New York 10020

Teachers and Students

ASPECTS OF AMERICAN HIGHER EDUCATION

edited by *Martin Trow*

Professor of Sociology
Graduate School of Public Policy
University of California, Berkeley

A Volume of Essays Sponsored by
The Carnegie Commission on Higher Education

MCGRAW-HILL BOOK COMPANY
New York   St. Louis   San Francisco
Düsseldorf   Johannesburg   Kuala Lumpur   London   Mexico
Montreal   New Delhi   Panama   Paris   São Paulo
Singapore   Sydney   Tokyo   Toronto

The Carnegie Commission on Higher Education,
2150 Shattuck Avenue, Berkeley, California 94704,
has sponsored preparation of this report as part
of a continuing effort to obtain and present
significant information for public discussion.
The views expressed are those of the authors.

TEACHERS AND STUDENTS
Aspects of American Higher Education

This book was set in Palatino by Black Dot Computer Typesetting
Corp. It was printed and bound by The Maple Press Company.
The designer was Elliot Epstein. The editors were
Nancy Tressel and Michael Hennelly for McGraw-Hill Book Company
and Verne A. Stadtman and Sidney J. P. Hollister for the
Carnegie Commission on Higher Education. Audre Hanneman
edited the index. Milton J. Heiberg supervised the production.

Library of Congress Cataloging in Publication Data

Main entry under title:

Teachers and students: aspects of American higher
education.

"A volume of essays sponsored by the Carnegie
Commission on Higher Education."
1. College students—United States. 2. College
students' socio-economic status—United States—
Statistics. I. Trow, Martin A., 1926-ed.
II. Carnegie Commission on Higher Education.

LA229.T42   378.73   74-17388
ISBN 0-07-010070-5

1 2 3 4 5 6 7 8 9 MAMM 7 9 8 7 6 5

Contents

Contributors

Ted K. Bradshaw
Assistant Research Sociologist
Institute of Government Studies
University of California, Berkeley

Saul D. Feldman
Assistant Professor of Sociology
Case Western Reserve University

Oliver Fulton
Assistant Research Sociologist
Survey Research Center
University of California, Berkeley

Judy Roizen
Postgraduate Research Psychologist
Survey Research Center
University of California, Berkeley

Stephen Steinberg
Assistant Professor of Sociology
Graduate School and University
  Center
The City University of New York

Martin Trow
Professor of Sociology
University of California, Berkeley

Joseph Zelan
Director of Research and
  Evaluation
University of California
  Consortium for the Extended
  University

Foreword

The 1969 Carnegie Commission Survey of Faculty and Student Opinion was designed and administered by a remarkable team of scholars. Under the direction of Martin Trow, they gathered statistics on almost two hundred thousand faculty, graduate students, and undergraduates in the higher education community. Respondents provided personal data on their age, sex, race, marital status, socioeconomic background, academic field, and so on. They also answered questions about their views on current social and political issues, about their education, and even about potential personal problems.

These data have given us an unparalleled opportunity to study the characteristics and opinions of a large sample of participants in higher education in the context of diverse college and university settings, as well as in relation to the population as a whole.

The results of the survey have informed the deliberations of the Commission, itself, and were the basis for many of our recommendations. Our reports *Reform on Campus, Dissent and Disruption,* and *Governance of Higher Education,* in particular, benefited greatly from these data.

The data also have helped others engaged in higher education research. And some of those most familiar with the survey—the group that administered the questionnaires—have, in this volume, given us some samples of the kinds of social and cultural analyses that can be made using the survey data. Examining such diverse phenomena as faculty research activity and the effect of college attendance on the values of undergraduates, this collection of essays provides a broad portrait of American higher education at one moment in history. It is our hope that further research into this body of data will illuminate other aspects of this portrait and that future scholars will refer to it as they chronicle the changing character of our colleges and universities.

The Carnegie Commission is deeply appreciative of the work of the scholars contributing to this volume, and particularly to Martin Trow for his wise and energetic leadership that has guided this remarkable and valuable study.

Clark Kerr

Chairman
Carnegie Commission
on Higher Education

May 1975

Introduction and Acknowledgments

The essays in this volume were written by members of the research group that designed and carried out the National Survey of Faculty and Student Opinion for the Carnegie Commission on Higher Education between 1968 and 1972. The survey was sponsored by the Carnegie Commission and the American Council on Education and financed in roughly equal parts by the Commission and the U.S. Office of Education.[1] This survey, the largest ever carried out in American colleges and universities, had several purposes:

First, it was designed to gather information that would be useful to the members of the Commission and its staff in their deliberations and preparation of reports and recommendations on various aspects of American higher education. For this reason, the survey included questions on a variety of issues central to the Commission's concerns: the attitudes of teachers and students toward student activism and militancy; their attitudes toward a variety of educational reforms or proposals; their feelings about their own education, or the education offered in their institutions; their attitudes toward collective bargaining in colleges and universities; their attitudes toward a variety of social and political issues—for example, race relations and the war in Vietnam—that clearly were having large repercussions on campus. Many of the findings of the survey were in fact used by the

---

[1] This is perhaps the appropriate place to note that the interpretations put forward in this volume do not necessarily reflect the position of the Office of Education, and no official endorsement by the Office of Education should be inferred.

Commission to inform and provide supporting evidence for their recommendations.[2]

Second, the survey was designed to provide a base line for regular and recurrent surveys of faculty and students. The survey gained information for the first time on a variety of academic and related issues from a large, representative sample of American college students and teachers. It clearly would be useful, both to scholars and to policy makers, to be able on the basis of this and future related surveys, to learn something of the trends of attitudes and sentiments toward the matters explored by the survey. Obviously no single survey can cover all the issues on which future scholars and educators might wish to be informed, nor could researchers in 1969 anticipate all the issues that may be salient in five or ten or fifteen years. Nevertheless, on many questions, and especially in matters affecting education policies and decisions, the attitudes and behaviors of participants in higher education at any one time are much more meaningful in light of knowledge about the direction and character of change. Already, parts of the faculty survey have been replicated by S. M. Lipset and Everett Ladd in their studies of faculty attitudes toward political issues and toward collective bargaining, by the American Council on Education,[3] and by other scholars as well.

Third, the survey was intended to provide a rich source of data for secondary analysis by scholars interested in a wide variety of problems and topics. The size of the sample and the scope of the questions have made it potentially useful to educators and social scientists interested in specific subgroups within the American academic community: to people interested in the characteristics of teachers of engineering or social work, for example, or in the role of women or minority groups in American academic life. For this reason, and with appropriate protection of the anonymity of individual respondents and institutions, the data were made

---

[2] See, for example, *Dissent and Disruption* (June 1971), *The More Effective Use of Resources* (June 1972), *Reform on Campus* (June 1972), *College Graduates and Jobs* (April 1973), *Governance of Higher Education* (April 1973), *The Purposes and the Performance of Higher Education in the United States* (June 1973), and *Opportunities for Women in Higher Education* (September 1973). All published by McGraw-Hill Book Company, New York.

[3] See Everett C. Ladd, Jr. and Seymour M. Lipset: *The Divided Academy*, McGraw-Hill Book Company, New York, forthcoming, and Alan E. Bayer: "College Faculties: Le Plus Ça Change . . . ," *Change*, vol. 6, p. 49ff., March 1974.

generally available on tape, at nominal cost and with full documentation, through the Data Library of the Survey Research Center at Berkeley, shortly after they were collected and processed. Since then, the library has had numerous inquiries, and has sent the whole or parts of the data tapes to some 20 scholars or groups of scholars throughout the country. The present volume, which includes the main survey questionnaires and a full technical report as appendixes, is in part intended to suggest the variety of questions to which this survey lends itself and to encourage scholars to use this body of data for further studies of their own.

Finally, this survey was also intended to provide data for analysis by members of the research group that designed, administered, and carried out the survey. The present collection provides a sample of this work. The survey has also provided the basis for a number of other books and monographs by members of the group, some of them completed, others still in progress.[4]

S. M. Lipset was associated with the project from the beginning in the planning and design of the questionnaires. He and Everett Ladd have since carried out several analyses of the data, particularly in the areas of faculty politics and collective bargaining, and have already carried out one partial replication.[5]

This volume provides a welcome opportunity to acknowledge the help of some of the many people who have contributed to it.

The survey was conceived and commissioned by Clark Kerr, chairman of the Carnegie Commission, as part of the Commission's broad efforts to extend our knowledge about American higher education as well as to make recommendations for its future. Throughout our work, Dr. Kerr gave the research group his warm encouragement and generous support, both moral and

---

[4] See, for example, Ted Bradshaw: *The Impact of Education on Leisure*, unpublished Ph.D. dissertation, University of California, Berkeley; Saul D. Feldman: *Escape from the Doll's House*, McGraw-Hill Book Company, New York, 1974; Oliver Fulton: *Men and Women Faculty in American Higher Education*, forthcoming Ph.D. dissertation, University of California, Berkeley; Oliver Fulton and Martin Trow: *The American Academics*, forthcoming; and Stephen Steinberg: *The Academic Melting Pot*, McGraw-Hill Book Company, New York, 1974.

[5] See, for example, Everett C. Ladd, Jr. and S. M. Lipset: "The Politics of American Sociologists," *American Journal of Sociology*, vol. 78, pp. 67–104, July 1972; *Professors, Unions, and American Higher Education*, Carnegie Commission on Higher Education, Berkeley, Calif., 1973; and *The Divided Academy*, McGraw-Hill Book Company, New York, forthcoming.

material. We could not have wanted a more generous and supportive sponsor.

Virginia Smith, former associate director of the Commission, worked closely with us on a range of difficult administrative and financial problems. She was especially helpful in our negotiations with the U.S. Office of Education for a major supporting grant and in helping us develop policies for the protection of the anonymity of participating institutions and individuals. The study had delicate and complex relations with many other organizations: the firm to whom we contracted the mailing and processing of our questionnaires;[6] the over three hundred participating colleges and universities; the research division of the American Council on Education; and government agencies. I came to value and depend heavily on Ms. Smith's judgment and wisdom in our relations with these organizations.

Other members of the Commission staff (happily for us, based nearby in Berkeley) were helpful in many ways throughout the survey. Special thanks go to Gloria Copeland and Verne Stadtman.

The survey was housed and administered at the University of California's Survey Research Center in Berkeley. The director of the center, Charles Glock, and William Nicholls, acting director during the last phases of the work, are both experienced survey researchers. They gave us their professional advice as well as the invaluable facilities of SRC. Eleanor Stevenson carried a major administrative responsibility for our project with skill, patience, and good humor.

No project of this kind can be carried out without the help and advice of numerous colleagues around the country—advice ranging from the broadest questions of survey coverage to the most technical issues of sample design. We can thank them here if not name them all. But David Riesman deserves special thanks for his supportive interest and thoughtful comments at various stages in our work.

The members of the research staff, professional and administrative, are listed alphabetically in Appendix A as coauthors and contributors to the technical report. They were the best of colleagues and friends. They know, though it is perhaps appro-

[6] Mr. Vern Koch of National Computer Systems in Minneapolis was especially helpful in designing the layout of the machine-processed questionnaire forms.

priate to say here, that I am very grateful for their devotion to our common work, often under difficult circumstances and pressures. The survey was conducted during turbulent times, at Berkeley as at other American colleges and universities. All of us were deeply involved in these events, and not always with the same views about them. Tear gas coming off Sproul Hall Plaza gave a certain acrid urgency and relevance to our research into the state of American higher education. But personal and professional loyalties enabled us to complete our work in the face of major strains and distractions, both on and off campus. The fact that we could carry on our work without compromising either our own views or the integrity of the research is itself a datum worth recording.

Finally, this study depended on the cooperation of hundreds of administrators, faculty members, and students in our participating institutions, and nearly two hundred thousand students and teachers who responded to our questionnaires. It is to them, and to their institutions, that these essays are dedicated.

Martin Trow
Berkeley, California

Teachers and Students

1. Students and Teachers: Some General Findings of the 1969 Carnegie Commission Survey

by Oliver Fulton and Martin Trow

The Carnegie Commission National Survey of Faculty and Student Opinion had as its chief purpose to gather new and uniquely comprehensive data from a broad sample of teachers and students in higher education. The information sought falls into three types: first, the basic demographic characteristics of the respondents, their backgrounds, and their educational careers; second, the respondents' styles of work or study, their interests and pursuits on campus, and their involvement in a variety of academic activities; and third, their opinions on various aspects of higher education and on problems in the larger society. The aggregate picture that emerges here should serve both as a useful baseline and as a corrective to some of the simplified and distorted images of university activities and university opinion that were current in some quarters in the late 1960s. But if the Carnegie survey had any one overarching purpose, it was to document and illuminate the enormous diversity of American higher education. No brief statement can do justice to 7 million students, 500,000 faculty members, and 2,500 institutions of higher education. A brief summary of a large study and much data runs the risk of replacing one set of stereotypes with another or of introducing new distortion.

The purpose of this essay, then, is not to provide an exhaustive portrait of American higher education. Rather, it is to present in summary form basic descriptive data and selected opinions held by faculty and students at a variety of types of institutions. These data offer a broad description of American higher education at one moment in history and will provide useful information for the study of change in the higher education system. In addition, they may be more immediately useful in providing a general context within which to interpret the detailed analyses presented in the main body of this book and in illustrating the diversity of institutions that make up the system. (All responses are given by institutional type and quality and for the universe as a whole. For a description of our quality classification, see Appendix A.)

DISTRIBUTION OF INSTITUTIONS, FACULTY, AND STUDENTS

In the academic year 1968–69, there were 2,836 accredited higher education institutions, according to Office of Education figures.[1] Their numbers and—leaving aside the 228 institutions ineligible for our survey[2]—their distribution across type and quality categories as well as the proportion of faculty and students that they employ or enroll are shown in Table 1-1. Also shown is the proportion of institutions in each category that are private. As can be seen, just over half of the elite universities are private, but large majorities of universities lower in quality are public. Roughly three-quarters of four-year colleges are private; two-thirds of junior colleges are public. However (although the figures are not shown here), public universities and colleges tend to be considerably larger than their private counterparts, and so enroll a larger proportion of students than the figures here suggest. One of the most noticeable points in this table is the difference in size between types of institutions. This is illustrated by the 43 leading universities in the country; these comprise only 2 percent of the total number of eligible institutions, but they enroll 6 percent of undergraduates and 17 percent of graduate students, and employ 13 percent of all faculty. Universities of other types are similarly large, while higher- and medium-quality colleges contain faculty and students roughly in proportion to their numbers. Over one-third of all higher education institutions, however, are junior colleges, and well over another third are low-quality colleges. These two types enroll more than half of all undergraduates, and the junior colleges alone enroll 38 percent of all freshmen, but the two types combined employ only

[1] This number is somewhat arbitrary, in that it is contingent on how the constituent campuses of geographically or administratively divided units are counted. See Appendix A.

[2] Eligibility is explained in Appendix A. The major categories of institutions excluded are those with no undergraduate enrollment, institutions founded after 1966, and a handful of very small institutions.

TABLE 1-1   *Distribution of institutions and of faculty, graduate students, and undergraduates, 1968–69*

	Quality level and type							
	Universities			Four-year colleges			Junior colleges	
	High (I)	*Medium* (II)	*Low* (III)	*High* (IV)	*Medium* (V)	*Low* (VI)	*All* (VII)	*Total*
Institutions (number)†	43	141	176	110	248	997	893	2,608
Institutions (percent)	2	5	7	4	10	38	34	100
Percentage of institutions that are private in each category	56	14	20	71	77	73	30	55*
Faculty (percent)	13	18	16	6	11	22	15	101
Graduate students (percent)	17	26	22	7	12	17	—	100
Full-time undergraduates, 1969–70 (percent)‡	6	12	14	6	11	29	23	101
Entering freshmen, Fall 1969 (percent)§	4	9	13	3	10	23	38	100

* All institutions.

SOURCES: †Number of institutions from National Survey files, using data on the universe of higher education supplied by the U.S. Office of Education and the American Council on Education in 1969. A further 228 institutions were ineligible for the survey. For further details see Appendix A. ‡Percentage of full-time undergraduates computed from figures supplied by 2,350 institutions to the U.S. Department of Health, Education, and Welfare, Office for Civil Rights (*Chronicle of Higher Education*, Mar. 29, 1971). §Entering freshmen from American Council on Education (*National Norms for Entering College Freshmen—Fall 1969*, 1969). All other data in this table and following tables are from the Carnegie Commission National Survey of Faculty and Student Opinion.

37 percent of the faculty. A final observation: just over a third (36 percent) of all graduate students are enrolled in "four-year colleges," by the U.S. Office of Education definition—institutions, that is, that either do not award the Ph.D. at all, or do so only in a few specialized fields.

CHARACTERISTICS OF FACULTY Table 1-2 shows the background characteristics of the faculty. Of these, their educational qualifications are perhaps the most important differentiating features. If one uses one of the standard measures of an institution's prestige—the proportion of Ph.D. holders on its staff—there is, at first glance, very little difference between different quality levels of universities or between universities and high-quality colleges. Quality levels I and II are identical (59 percent); level IV colleges have 58 percent; level III universities have 51 percent, but thereafter a sharp drop occurs, down to 5 percent at junior colleges. The rest of this table, however, shows that even among the first four levels there are real differences among their faculty. The leading universities have the largest professional schools, particularly in the older and more prestigious areas of law and medicine, and corresponding proportions of their staff hold the appropriate professional degree rather than the Ph.D. Thus, except between levels III and IV, the proportion of faculty who are "underqualified" by the formal standards of elite universities—that is, who hold a master's degree or less—rises steadily from 16 percent (quality I) to 30 percent (quality III), from 28 percent (quality IV) to 50 percent (quality VI), and to 79 percent, or about four-fifths at junior colleges.[3]

"Quality" or at least prestige differences are shown even more sharply in section B, Table 1-2: the proportion of faculty who earned their degrees from large, high-quality universities[4] drops

---

[3] This table shows that the level of degree attainment of the faculty is a valid indicator of institutional quality—or at least that it corresponds with the overall measure of quality that we have constructed. (However, our quality typology is not entirely independent of Ph.D. proportions. See Appendix A.) But it makes clear that the best guide to institutional quality is not the conventionally used measurement of the proportion of faculty holding Ph.D.'s—unless this is confined to the "academic" (i.e., nonprofessional) departments of the institution. A better single measurement would be the proportion of faculty holding master's or lower degrees.

[4] Owing to space constraints in the questionnaire, it was possible to list only the large high-quality institutions; percentages in this table are therefore lower than the true figures for faculty recruitment from this type of institution.

off very sharply as institutional quality declines. The level of "self-recruitment"[5] at the elite universities is extremely high; indeed, obtaining a degree from one of them is nearly essential if one wishes to teach there. What is interesting, however, is that the elite four-year colleges have more staff with degrees from leading universities than even the medium-quality universities. In part, this is another aspect of self-recruitment: institutions in quality levels II and III give Ph.D.'s and so can hire their own students, but (except in a few subjects at a handful of institutions) teachers at level IV could not have obtained their doctorates at their present institutions, and had to be recruited from outside. Nevertheless, those who have earned their degrees from graduate schools of the elite, high-quality institutions command the highest prestige (and the highest salary). By this standard the staff of the four-year colleges are extremely well qualified, and compare very favorably with the staff in medium-quality universities.[6]

Section D of Table 1-2 shows that there is no appreciable difference in the average age of teachers in different parts of the system—an interesting discovery, since the growth rates of these sectors have been quite different in recent years. This suggests that institutions may well recruit their staff at different ages and have different degrees of receptivity to those who have worked outside academia: here again is a subject for further research. Section C shows quite sharp differences in the proportion of women faculty at different levels, ranging from 10 percent at high-quality universities to 17 percent at low-quality universities, from 16 percent at high-quality colleges to 29 percent at low-quality colleges, and to 26 percent in the junior colleges. Some of the difference is associated with the larger number of single-sex

---

[5] True self-recruitment—that is, the appointment of faculty to the actual institution from which they obtained their doctorate—is a separate issue. Both topics are investigated in full in Trow and Fulton, *The American Academics* (forthcoming).

[6] We report responses to the question "Where did you obtain your highest degree?"—not "your doctorate." It might be suspected that a disproportionate number of the alumni of quality level I who teach in level IV colleges do not hold the doctorate, whereas faculty in level IV who do hold the Ph.D. earned it at lower-quality universities than level I. In fact this is not the case: Even among Ph.D. holders, more of the staff at quality IV institutions have earned their doctorates at quality I universities than have the staff even of quality II institutions. The whole question of educational careers and recruitment will be explored in future work.

		Quality level	
		Universities	
	High (I)	*Medium* (II)	*Low* (III)

TABLE 1-2
Background information on faculty

A. *Highest degree attained (percent)*

	High (I)	Medium (II)	Low (III)
Ph.D.	59	59	51
Professional (law or medicine)	15	11	4
Other professional	10	10	14
Master's	11	16	26
Other or none	5	4	4
	100	100	100

B. *Percentage whose highest degree was earned at a large, high-quality university* — 70 / 40 / 34

C. *Percentage who are male* — 90 / 87 / 83

D. *Average (mean) age* — 42 / 42 / 42

E. *Father's occupation:* percentage whose fathers are/were manual workers* — 15 / 19 / 24

F. *Average (mean) hours per week spent in classroom teaching (includes part-time staff)* — 5.4 / 6.4 / 7.9

G. *Percentage of faculty teaching less than 25 students in courses this term* — 40 / 30 / 22

H. *Percentage who teach exclusively undergraduates* — 17 / 24 / 36

I. *Percentage whose interests lie primarily in research rather than teaching* — 50 / 40 / 28

J. *Number of professional writings published or accepted for publication in last 2 years (percent)*

	High (I)	Medium (II)	Low (III)
0	21	29	42
1–4	52	51	47
5 or more	27	20	11
	100	100	100

K. *Percentage who have worked outside the academic profession for at least a year since obtaining their bachelor's degree.* — 57 / 62 / 67

L. *Average (median) salary (thousands of dollars)* — 14.5 / 13.9 / 12.3

*The response categories for this question varied slightly between samples. Comparisons between types of institutions are valid, but comparisons between faculty, graduate students, and undergraduates may be misleading.

and type

	Four-year colleges			Junior colleges	
	High (IV)	Medium (V)	Low (VI)	All (VII)	All institutions
	58	38	28	5	40
	2	1	1	2	5
	12	18	21	14	15
	22	39	45	63	33
	6	4	5	16	6
	100	100	100	100	99
	49	29	24	18	35
	84	78	71	74	80
	42	41	41	42	42
	19	27	30	30	24
	8.1	10.3	10.9	13.4	9.0
	22	15	16	12	22
	61	69	78	99	55
	26	12	10	5	24
	47	63	73	87	53
	44	33	25	12	36
	9	4	2	1	11
	100	100	100	100	100
	62	69	72	80	68
	12.6	10.6	9.7	10.1	11.5

(mostly female) institutions among the colleges, especially at the lower end, but besides this there is a persistent relation between a high proportion of women and low status, which can be found within as well as between institutions (see Chapter 6). Sharp differences are also found in the social origins of academics, as measured by their fathers' occupations (section E): the junior colleges and low-quality four-year colleges contain twice as many faculty whose fathers were manual workers as do the elite universities.

Sections F through J of Table 1-2 can be taken together: they show in clear outline the division of academic labor with which Chapter 2 is chiefly concerned. Section F underestimates the number of classroom-teaching hours per week that the universities require of a faculty member with a full teaching load, since our respondents include part-time staff and those on "released time" for research, but it shows that the actual number of hours per week faculty members spend in formal instruction varies very substantially, from $5^1/_2$ to almost 8 in the universities, from 8 to almost 11 at four-year colleges, and to $13^1/_2$ at junior colleges. Similarly, 40 percent of the teachers at the leading universities and 30 percent at the medium-quality universities have fewer than 25 students enrolled in all their courses. Below this point the differences are smaller: even in the junior colleges 12 percent of our respondents taught only this number of students. (Again, at the research universities, the percentage may include faculty members who are temporarily engaged in full-time research. Our sample was designed to exclude permanent full-time administrators.) The balance between graduate and undergraduate teaching also varies in predictable ways between types of institutions; at the junior colleges (for obvious reasons) virtually all staff teach only undergraduates; at the four-year colleges between three-fifths and four-fifths do so; the proportions are much lower (17 percent to 36 percent) in the universities. What is more interesting than the variation, perhaps, is that even in the high-quality universities 17 percent of the staff have no contact with graduate students, from whose presence the elite nature of the institution largely derives. The average level of interest in research or teaching expressed by respondents (section I, Table 1-2) given a forced choice between the two, corresponds with the average number of hours that faculty spend teaching at different types of institutions.[7] Half of all respondents at the elite universities are primarily, if not exclusively, interested in research; at the other extreme this drops to as low as 5 percent at junior colleges. And the rates at which faculty members publish articles or books vary correspondingly (section J): at quality level I one-quarter of the faculty have five or more publications to their credit in the last two years, and three-quarters have published something. These figures drop fairly gently till quality level IV (where one-tenth have published five or more articles, and over half have published something), and more sharply thereafter until in the junior colleges almost nine-tenths have not recently published at all.

Two other background items are of interest. Since obtaining their bachelor's degree, two-thirds of all current faculty have been employed for at least one year outside the academic profession; the lowest proportions are found at the higher end of the quality spectrum, and the highest (80 percent) at junior colleges. This is a consequence partly of the more predictable and straightforward career line of the full professional at the top end of the system, and partly of the especially high growth of the lower end in recent years, which has forced these institutions to recruit from outside the profession. Finally, average salary levels differ substantially at different types of institution. Comparing the two extremes, the median annual salary ranged (in 1969) from $14,500 at quality I to $10,000 at quality level VII (see section L of Table 1-2). While these figures have, of course, changed since the survey was done, the differential undoubtedly persists.

CHARACTERISTICS OF GRADUATE STUDENTS

Turning now to graduate students, we show that in the system as a whole, more than half (54 percent) are working for master's-level degrees (see section A, Table 1-3). This proportion varies from one-third at quality I institutions to three-quarters at quality level VI. The proportion working for the Ph.D.—22 percent overall—ranges from 42 percent at quality I to 21 percent at quality III among the universities, with 30 percent of graduate students at quality IV working for this degree. There is a sharp

---

[7] This is not to imply that the preferences of individuals necessarily correspond to their personal teaching loads. See Chapter 2.

TABLE 1-3
Background information on graduate students

	Quality level		
	Universities		
	High (I)	Medium (II)	Low (III)
A. Degree for which students are currently working (percent)			
Ph.D.	42	31	21
Law degree	6	6	7
Medical degree	8	8	4
Other doctorate	4	4	5
Other professional	7	6	6
Master's	31	42	54
None	2	2	3
	100	99	99
B. Percentage who expect Ph.D. as highest degree	60	53	45
C. Percentage who are male	74	71	75
D. Age (average age)	28.0	28.9	29.9
E. Father's occupation:* percentage whose fathers are/were manual workers	17	22	23
F. Expected occupation (percent†)			
College or university teaching	44	39	32
Junior college teaching	4	6	8
Elementary or secondary school teaching	5	9	8
Research (university or nonprofit organizations)	14	10	9
Research (industrial)	9	8	9
Professional practice	26	27	26
Executive/administrator (government or education)	7	9	10
Executive/administrator (industry)	7	7	10
All others (including self-employed business, military service, clerical, or manual occupations)	2	2	3

*See note to Table 1-2.
†Percentages do not add to 100 because of multiple response.

break, however, between colleges in quality level IV[8] (which broadly resemble the universities except for the virtual absence of

[8] Quality level IV includes some schools with Ph.D. programs in a restricted number of fields—which disqualifies them from classification as universities although these programs may be comparable in standard even to programs in the elite universities. Most graduate students in quality-level IV institutions are enrolled in these schools, rather than in the elite liberal arts colleges that are also found in this category.

and type				
Four-year colleges			*Junior colleges*	
High (IV)	*Medium* (V)	*Low* (VI)	*All* (VII)	*All institutions*
30	2	2		22
3	3	0		5
1	0	1		4
2	4	2		4
8	7	12		7
53	77	76		54
2	6	6		3
99	99	99		99
55	30	24		45
74	57	59		69
29.0	31.0	33.9		29.4
19	31	29		23
33	28	24		35
9	10	23		9
14	23	29		13
10	4	2		9
15	4	3		8
21	18	15		23
6	12	13		10
10	11	7		8
4	4	2		3

law and medical students) and those in quality levels V and VI. (A very large proportion of graduate students at levels V and VI are working for master's degrees in education.) Section B of Table 1-3 shows the ultimate degree ambition of the graduate student sample: 45 percent, overall, are aiming for the Ph.D., with 60 percent doing so in quality level I, and 24 percent in quality level VI, the latter presumably expecting to transfer elsewhere. The lower-quality institutions contain somewhat older students on average (section D); again, many of those at levels V and VI have returned from schoolteaching for a higher certification in education. At these levels over 40 percent are women (section C), whereas in the Ph.D.-granting institutions only about a quarter are women. The social origins of graduate students vary among institutions as much as those of their faculty, with the children of manual workers being better represented lower in the system, especially in the colleges.

Section F of Table 1-3 shows the occupations that the graduate students in the sample expect to enter. The proportions mentioning university or college teaching are remarkably high—nearly half (44 percent) at elite universities, one-third or more at the other Ph.D.-granting institutions, and a quarter even at the medium- and lower-quality colleges. Junior college teaching, however, is not an ambition of many students except at the lowest-quality four-year colleges (23 percent); at these and at the medium-level colleges, as we suggested above, a fairly large number of students look toward elementary or secondary school teaching as their future career (23 percent and 29 percent, respectively). The proportions mentioning academic (or non-profit) research are smaller than, but correspond to, those anticipating a university teaching career; industrial research, however, was mentioned disproportionately by those in high-quality colleges.[9] Prospective professional practitioners are found, not surprisingly, at the universities with professional schools; government or educational administrators are drawn slightly more from the low end of the quality scale (again, most of these are education students). Other occupations are mentioned in small numbers, and indiscriminately from across the board.

CHARACTERISTICS OF UNDER-GRADUATES Finally, Table 1-4 shows that the undergraduates[10] (like the other groups) are more likely to be older, to be female, and to come from working-class families in the lower-status institutions—except for those in junior colleges, who are sharply older than elsewhere, but more likely to be male than in low- or

---

9 Some of these are highly specialized, science- and technology-oriented universities: see footnote 8.

10 Our undergraduate sample is composed only of students who entered college as freshmen in the years 1966 through 1969. They do not include people who had entered earlier, dropped out, and returned.

TABLE 1-4 *Background information on undergraduates (entering freshmen, 1966-1969)*

	Quality level and type							
	Universities			Four-year colleges			Junior colleges	All institutions
	High (I)	Medium (II)	Low (III)	High (IV)	Medium (V)	Low (VI)	All (VII)	
A. Percentage who are male	61	68	53	68	45	40	58	53
B. Age: percentage who are 19 or over	6	12	12	8	12	17	27	18
C. Father's occupation:* percentage whose fathers are/were manual workers	15	21	22	13	25	32	31	27
D. Expected long-run employment (percent)								
Professional (self-employed or salaried)	26	22	18	21	13	11	18	17
Business (self-employed or salaried)	22	25	25	30	19	15	26	23
Government (except education)	5	7	7	8	6	6	6	7
Elementary or secondary school teaching	10	17	21	9	32	37	19	25
College or university teaching (including junior college)	12	10	8	12	10	11	10	10
Nonprofit organization (including research institutes and medical institutions)	17	11	13	13	12	12	11	12
Other	7	6	7	7	7	7	8	7
	99	98	99	100	99	99	98	101

*See note to Table 1-2.

medium-quality colleges, or even than in low-quality universities. The higher-quality universities are more likely than average to be teaching future professionals; the low- or medium-quality colleges are less likely. Graduates of the latter are also less likely to expect to enter business occupations and much more likely to intend to become schoolteachers. But in most other respects, undergraduates from all types of institutions look remarkably alike. For those who obtain second degrees, their graduate school has much more power than their undergraduate institution to determine where in the occupational structure they will end up, and for this reason future occupational differences show up less sharply among undergraduates than in the graduate population. It is also possible that undergraduates have less realistic expectations than graduates: those who are obtaining their degrees in institutions low in the system may not yet have learned to lower their sights accordingly.

CHARACTERISTICS OF INSTITUTIONS

Before turning to the attitudes and opinions of faculty and students, it may be useful to summarize some of the differences among types of institutions. We can do this best by describing the portrait of each type that emerges from our data so far. The elite universities (quality I), a slight majority of which are private institutions, are few in number (a mere 2 percent of the universe of institutions), and they enroll few undergraduates, but they enroll one-sixth of the graduate students and have on paper the highest ratio of staff to students (with the possible exception of the leading four-year colleges). Three-fifths of their staff hold Ph.D.'s, and another quarter hold professional qualifications. Probably at least three-quarters of their faculty earned their degrees at institutions of equal prestige to the one which now employs them. A higher proportion are male than at any other type of institution and fewer come from working-class families. On the average, staff members spend $5^1/_2$ hours in classroom teaching, and have published two or three articles or books in the past two years; half of them are more interested in research than teaching. Among the graduate students in quality I institutions, three-fifths expect eventually to obtain a Ph.D., and two-fifths are currently working toward that degree. They are slightly younger than students at other institutions; fewer of them are from working-class families; and three-quarters of them are male. Nearly half of them expect to become academics themselves in due course. The undergraduates, too, come from comparatively middle-class backgrounds; they are comparatively young, on average; three-fifths of them are male; a higher than average proportion expect to enter professional careers other than school or college teaching or to work for a nonprofit organization.

Quality level II (medium-quality universities) is both like and unlike quality level I. It is almost entirely public; it is larger—containing 141 institutions—and as a whole it enrolls twice as many undergraduates and half again as many graduate students. The faculty is not proportionately larger, however, since the staff-student ratio is worse. Proportionately as many faculty hold Ph.D.'s as in quality level I, but not from such prestigious institutions; the faculty teaches slightly longer hours and more students, of whom more are undergraduates, and it publishes very slightly less. Almost as many faculty are male and come from middle-class families as faculty in quality level I. Fewer graduate students in these institutions are currently working for Ph.D.'s, though nearly as many expect to obtain them eventually as those in level I. Somewhat more of them have fathers in blue-collar occupations. Their job aspirations, however, are not very different. The undergraduates in quality level II universities are somewhat older than at quality I; more of them are male, more come from working-class families, and somewhat more expect to enter schoolteaching.

The low-quality universities (level III), 80 percent of which are public, comprise almost as many institutions as high- and medium-quality universities put together; they enroll more undergraduates than institutions of quality II, and more freshmen than levels I and II combined, but they have fewer graduate students and fewer faculty than quality II alone. Their faculty are less well qualified, compared not only with other universities, but also with the elite four-year colleges. Their faculty look very similar to those in the latter quality level in the number of hours and the number of students they teach and in research interest but many more (almost one-third) have no contact with graduate students. More than half of the graduate students in these universities are working for their master's degree—a proportion again comparable with that in the elite four-year colleges. Fewer of them than at institutions in quality levels I, II, or IV expect to enter university teaching or research. Finally, again compared with levels, I, II, and IV, considerably more (almost half) of their undergraduates (though not of their graduate students) are female; their students are also somewhat more likely to be aiming for schoolteaching as a career and less likely to expect to enter one of the other professions, including college teaching.

The elite four-year colleges (level IV) are something of a mixture, containing both the elite pure liberal arts colleges and some institutions with Ph.D. programs in certain areas (notably science and technology). Like all the four-year colleges they are mostly private institutions. They are few in number, enroll relatively few students and employ few faculty. Only 3 percent of all freshmen entered them in 1969, although they enroll 6 percent of all undergraduates. Their faculty are almost as likely to hold Ph.D.'s as those at the elite universities, and almost half of them earned their degrees from these universities. But in other respects, they look more like the lowest level of universities, especially in the preferences and involvement of their staff in research and teaching. For faculty and students alike, their social composition is more middle class than at any but quality I institutions (in the case of undergraduates, even more than the latter). One-third of the graduate students that they enroll are working for the Ph.D., and 55 percent (more than anywhere except in quality level I) hope to earn it eventually. A fairly high proportion of them, though fewer than at the universities, expect to enter academic life; fewer intend to become professionals, and more to enter schoolteaching; and a very high proportion, comparatively, expect to enter research posts in industry.[11] Their undergraduates are relatively young and disproportionately male, as well as being middle class, and a rather high proportion aim for careers in business.

Levels V and VI can, for our purposes, be looked at together. Level V contains roughly 10 percent of all institutions of higher education, and also of faculty, graduates, and undergraduates; level VI comprises over one-third of all institutions, about a quarter of the faculty, 17 percent of the graduate students, and nearly one-third of the undergraduates. Both levels are predominantly private. The faculty are conspicuously less well qualified than at the universities or other colleges—less again at level VI

---

[11] Many of these are presumably the engineers from technological institutes of whom we spoke earlier.

than at level V; they teach more than 10 hours a week; three-fifths of them have no contact with graduate students; they publish very little; very few (just over one-tenth) are interested in research in preference to teaching. Over three-quarters of their graduate students are working for master's degrees, and most of the rest are studying for qualifications in the newer professions. A fairly high proportion of the faculty and students are the children of manual workers; at least two-fifths of the graduate students are female (compared with one-quarter elsewhere); their undergraduates, too, are much more likely to be female. A high proportion of graduate students and still higher (over one-third) of undergraduates expect to become schoolteachers, and almost a quarter of the graduate students at quality VI institutions expect to enter junior college teaching.

The junior colleges constituted in 1969 just over one-third of all higher education institutions; they enrolled about two-fifths of entering freshmen, and employed 15 percent of all faculty. One-third of them are private and, as in other sectors, the private colleges are on average much smaller than their public counterparts. Almost four-fifths of junior college faculty hold master's degrees or less; they teach 13 hours a week on average, and are almost wholly uninvolved and uninterested in research. Their staff are not more likely to come from blue-collar backgrounds than the staff in institutions of quality levels V and VI, but their students are much more working-class in origin. The students are likely to be male and noticeably older than undergraduates elsewhere but, perhaps surprisingly, their career ambitions closely resemble those of the undergraduate population as a whole.

ATTITUDES AND OPINIONS
We turn now from a description of faculty and students to an examination of their views on matters on and off the campus (Table 1-5). We have selected certain items from the wide range of opinions elicited by the questionnaires to illustrate both the general trends of campus attitudes and the considerable diversity in the system. We have also chosen questions, for the most part, that were asked in more than one survey, to show the extent of agreement or disagreement between faculty, graduate students, and undergraduates. Many of the items are not specifically discussed, and readers are asked to consult the tables and draw their own conclusions. A few words of caution are in order, therefore, especially as regards questions dealing with political

TABLE 1-5 Attitudes and opinions (in percentages)

				Quality level and type					
		Universities			Four-year colleges			Junior colleges	All institutions
		High (I)	Medium (II)	Low (III)	High (IV)	Medium (V)	Low (VI)	All (VII)	

A. Political and social issues

How would you characterize yourself politically at the present time?

		High (I)	Medium (II)	Low (III)	High (IV)	Medium (V)	Low (VI)	All (VII)	All institutions
Left	F	8	6	4	8	4	3	2	5
	G	13	6	4	6	3	2		5
	U	15	7	6	12	4	3	4	5
Liberal	F	51	45	40	45	38	39	30	41
	G	48	40	34	35	32	26	35	37
	U	50	44	42	45	39	40	35	40
Middle-of-the-road	F	23	25	28	24	28	30	31	27
	G	20	27	28	27	27	32		27
	U	22	32	34	26	36	37	41	37
Moderately conservative	F	17	23	26	21	27	26	34	25
	G	16	24	30	28	35	35		27
	U	10	15	17	16	18	17	17	17
Strongly conservative	F	2	2	3	3	3	3	3	3
	G	2	3	4	4	4	5		4
	U	2	2	2	2	2	2	2	2
	F	101	101	101	101	100	101	100	101
	G	101	100	100	100	101	100		100
	U	99	100	101	101	99	99	99	101
Meaningful social change cannot be achieved through traditional American politics.	F	29	30	31	29	31	40	34	33
	G	39	36	35	42	39	36		37
	U	51	49	51	46	50	57	54	53

The main cause of Negro riots in the cities is white racism.	F	53	48	43	48	45	47	37	46
	G	54	41	36	37	33	30		39
	U	58	50	45	51	44	48	43	46
Marijuana should be legalized.	F	49	39	32	52	31	26	24	33
	G	58	52	31	35	23	20		36
	U	73	62	53	67	47	41	40	47
In the United States today there can be no justification for using violence to achieve political goals.	F	69	72	74	71	73	71	76	71
	U	63	71	75	68	75	76	78	75
B. Political/academic issues									
Opportunities for higher education should be available for all who want it.	F	65	67	68	67	68	71	86	71
	G	87	85	87	84	89	92	⋯	87
	U	94	94	96	95	96	97	97	96
Scientists should publish their findings regardless of the possible consequences.	G	60	63	62	61	66	66		63
	U	64	63	60	60	63	59	56	59
A man's (a professor's) teaching and research inevitably reflect his political values.	F	34	33	36	38	41	42	45	39
	U	45	47	46	44	49	48	54	49
C. Campus political issues									
Faculty members should be free to present in class any idea they consider relevant.	F	88	83	82	84	82	83	77	83
	G	91	85	82	82	76	74		80
	U	95	93	91	93	93	91	89	91
Classified weapons research is a legitimate activity on college and university campuses.	F	34	43	46	38	44	42	46	42
	G	41	51	55	50	45	54		50
	U	37	45	50	44	48	48	50	48

NOTE: Unless otherwise indicated, figures represent percentages of respondents who agree strongly or agree with reservations: F = Faculty, G = Graduate students, U = Undergraduates.

TABLE 1-5 (continued)

		Universities			Four-year colleges			Junior colleges	All institutions
		High (I)	Medium (II)	Low (III)	High (IV)	Medium (V)	Low (VI)	All (VII)	
Faculty members should be free on campus to advocate violent resistance to public authority.	F	31	23	21	27	21	19	15	22
	G	37	24	19	23	12	15		22
	U	55	38	36	45	33	31	29	33
Campus disruptions by militant students are a threat to academic freedom.	F	81	82	82	82	83	83	86	82
Students who disrupt the functioning of a college should be expelled or suspended.	F	74	78	80	77	80	81	85	80
	G	57	69	75	73	84	81		72
	U	42	58	61	55	60	61	69	62
What do you think of the emergence of radical student activism in recent years? (percentage approving with or without reservations)	F	51	46	42	46	42	42	33	43
	G	54	40	32	35	28	25		36
Has your campus experienced any student protests or demonstrations during this academic year? (percentage "Yes")	F	83	79	65	55	40	29	28	53
	G	84	78	60	47	32	31		60
How would you character-ize your attitude toward									

Quality level and type

the most recent demonstration? (Asked of those on campuses which had experienced student protest or demonstration during the year):

1. Percentage approving the demonstrators' aims.	F	52	44	54	55	57	57	49	51
	G	54	43	44	46	41	39		46
2. Percentage approving both their aims and their methods	F	18	19	30	27	38	31	21	24
	G	21	18	22	19	17	18		20
Student demonstrations have no place on a college campus.	F	20	23	28	27	32	33	42	30
	G	20	30	38	38	45	51		36
	U	10	18	22	19	22	29	36	28
Political activities by students have no place on campus.	F	11	13	15	14	15	17	23	16
	U	5	7	10	8	9	12	19	13
Most college officials have been too lax in dealing with student protests.	G	44	58	67	64	74	75		63
	U	29	40	46	40	45	44	54	47
College officials have the right to regulate student behavior off campus.	F	12	14	19	14	21	24	18	18
	G	8	13	18	15	21	24		16
	U	2	4	4	5	6	7	6	6
Most rules governing student behavior here are sensible.	F	82	80	75	80	77	78	85	79
	U	85	80	74	76	71	77	89	77

D. *Unionization*

Faculty members/graduate students/students should be more militant in defending their interests.	F	55	57	55	53	56	54	53	55
	G	51	45	40	42	34	29		41
	U	28	19	20	24	19	22	22	22

TABLE 1-5 (continued)

		Quality level and type						Junior colleges	
		Universities			Four-year colleges				
		High (I)	Medium (II)	Low (III)	High (IV)	Medium (V)	Low (VI)	All (VII)	All institutions
Faculty unions have a divisive effect on academic life.	F	54	52	51	54	51	51	56	53
	G	33	38	44	47	48	51		43
Teaching assistants' unions have a divisive effect on academic life.	F	52	50	50	54	48	49	53	51
	G	32	36	41	44	44	51		40
Do you feel there are circumstances in which a strike would be a legitimate means of collective action for faculty members? (Responses: definitely yes and probably yes)*	F	47	46	44	46	46	46	47	46
	G	74	67	61	62	58	61		64
	U	71	64	61	66	62	66	59	62
Do you feel there are circumstances in which a strike would be a legitimate means of collective action for TAs. (Responses: definitely yes and probably yes)	F	51	46	41	45	41	39	38	43
	G	70	61	52	56	48	49		57

E. *Campus governance*

What role do you believe undergraduates should play in decisions on the following:

	Control	Voting power on committees	Formal consultation	Informal consultation	Little or no role	Total
1. Faculty appointment and promotion						
F	†	6	15	25	54	100
G	1	10	20	26	44	101
U	1	22	24	28	25	100
2. Undergraduate admissions policy						
F	†	13	24	28	34	99
G	1	12	24	28	35	100
U	1	23	28	25	22	99
3. Bachelor's degree requirements						
F	†	14	30	25	31	100
G	1	15	32	24	28	100
U	2	28	33	21	16	100
4. Provision and content of courses						
F	†	15	35	37	13	100
G	1	24	38	27	10	100
U	5	39	34	17	6	101
5. Student discipline						
F	15	49	24	9	4	101
G	11	42	26	13	7	99
U	26	48	17	6	3	100

*Undergraduates: "A strike would be a legitimate means of collective action for faculty members under some circumstances."

† Less than 0.5 percent.

TABLE 1-5 *(continued)*

What role do you believe graduate students should play in decisions on the following? (Response: little or no role)		Quality level and type							
		Universities			Four-year colleges			Junior colleges	All institutions
		High (I)	Medium (II)	Low (III)	High (IV)	Medium (V)	Low (VI)	All (VII)	
1. Faculty appointment and promotion	F	51	55	54	49	53	53	60	54
	G	32	42	46	46	47	52		44
	U	14	19	22	14	21	26	30	25
2. Undergraduate admissions policy	F	33	34	37	31	34	32	36	34
	G	26	33	38	37	36	42		35
	U	17	19	24	18	22	23	23	22
3. Bachelor's degree requirements	F	28	30	31	32	32	30	39	31
	G	19	25	31	30	27	37		28
	U	7	11	14	10	13	16	22	16
4. Provision and content of courses	F	10	13	14	12	14	13	16	13
	G	5	8	11	11	10	13		10
	U	2	4	4	3	4	5	9	6
5. Student discipline	F	4	4	4	4	3	3	6	4
	G	4	7	8	10	8	10		7
	U	2	2	2	1	2	3	4	3

What role do you believe graduate students should play in decisions on the following:		Control	Voting power on committees	Formal consultation	Informal consultation	Little or no role	Total
1. Faculty appointment and promotion	F	†	10	20	26	43	99
	G	1	19	27	25	28	100

(table continued from previous page)

		High (I)	Medium (II)	Low (III)	High (IV)	Medium (V)	Low (VI)	All (VII)	All institutions
2. Departmental graduate admissions policy	F	†	16	27			28	28	99
	G	1	21	32			26	20	100
3. Provision and content of graduate courses	F	1	23	41			27	8	100
	G	4	39	38			15	4	100
4. Student discipline	F	19	42	22			10	7	100
	G	16	38	24			13	9	100
5. Advanced degree requirements	F	1	20	34			24	21	100
	G	2	27	37			19	15	100

What role do you believe undergraduates should play in decisions on the following? (Response: little or no role)

		Quality level and type							
		Universities			Four-year colleges			Junior colleges	All institutions
		High (I)	Medium (II)	Low (III)	High (IV)	Medium (V)	Low (VI)	All (VII)	
1. Faculty appointments and promotion	F	42	46	45	42	44	40	43	43
	G	18	25	29	32	30	35	25	28
2. Departmental admissions policy	F	28	30	30	29	28	25	25	28
	G	15	19	22	23	19	26		20
3. Advanced degree requirements	F	19	21	22	25	22	19	21	21
	G	9	12	15	16	15	25		15
4. Provision and content of graduate courses	F	4	6	7	8	9	8	11	8
	G	2	3	4	4	5	9		4
5. Student discipline	F	5	7	8	8	9	6	10	7
	G	5	8	10	13	11	13		9

TABLE 1-5 *(continued)*

		Quality level and type							
		Universities			Four-year colleges			Junior colleges	All institutions
		High (I)	Medium (II)	Low (III)	High (IV)	Medium (V)	Low (VI)	All (VII)	
F. Campus educational issues									
Undergraduate education would be improved if:									
1. Course work were more relevant to contemporary life and problems	F	65	69	74	67	75	82	83	75
	U	87	89	93	87	91	92	91	91
2. More attention were paid to the emotional growth of students	F	62	65	70	68	71	78	79	71
	U	79	81	83	82	84	86	83	83
3. Grades were abolished	F	29	30	33	31	32	36	37	33
	U	69	57	61	60	60	59	56	59
4. All courses were elective	F	20	19	18	24	21	20	22	20
	U	56	52	55	49	54	53	51	52
5. Students were required to spend a year in community service in the United States or abroad	F	50	53	53	52	56	61	62	56
	U	51	49	50	50	52	52	44	48
6. The colleges were governed completely by their faculty and students	F	41	40	40	42	39	41	33	39
	U	61	64	66	62	63	65	62	64

Statement	Code								
7. *There were less emphasis on specialized training and more on broad liberal education*	F	56	54	55	60	60	62	50	57
	U	47	41	40	52	42	40	38	40
Most American colleges reward conformity and crush student creativity.	F	45	49	53	49	52	55	52	51
	U	58	52	54	55	52	56	49	53
Genuine scholarship is threatened in universities by the proliferation of big research centers.	F	28	30	35	33	35	38	37	34
	G	34	35	36	34	38	36	.....	35
The typical undergraduate curriculum has suffered from the specialization of faculty members.	F	52	52	52	49	47	51	49	51
	G	44	40	38	34	35	32		38
Teaching effectiveness, not publication, should be the primary criterion for the promotion of faculty.	F	51	62	74	75	88	90	96	77
	G	81	87	91	97	97	95		89
	U	95	69	97	97	98	95	95	96

G. Satisfaction with institution

Statement	Code								
Most undergraduates at my college are satisfied with the education they are getting.	U	68	68	69	74	73	70	74	72
Most undergraduates here are basically satisfied with the education they are getting.	F	63	68	72	71	75	72	84	73
I am basically satisfied with the education I am getting.	G	76	75	76	73	81	82		77
Most graduate students in my department are basically satisfied with the education they are getting.	F	73	77	77	79	80	83		77

TABLE 1-5 *(continued)*

			Quality level and type							
			Universities			Four-year colleges			Junior colleges	All institutions
			High (I)	Medium (II)	Low (III)	High (IV)	Medium (V)	Low (VI)	All (VII)	
In general, how do you feel about this institution?‡										
It is a very good place for me (U: very satisfied)	F		58	47	44	52	46	45	56	49
	G		57	48	47	42	49	55		51
	U		37	21	19	29	22	17	18	20
It is a fairly good place for me (U: satisfied)	F		36	45	46	40	45	45	36	43
	G		38	45	46	49	44	41		44
	U		42	49	45	42	46	48	47	47
It is not the place for me (U: dissatisfied and very dissatisfied)	F		6	8	10	8	9	10	8	9
	G		5	6	7	9	6	4		6
	U		7	11	13	12	11	12	13	12
On the fence	U		13	18	22	17	21	23	22	21
	F		100%	100%	100%	100%	100%	100%	100%	101%
	G		100%	99%	100%	100%	99%	100%		101%
	U		99%	99%	99%	100%	100%	100%	100%	100%
Most faculty here are strongly interested in the academic problems of undergraduates.	F		48	54	57	68	71	69	77	63
	U		54	54	53	68	63	61	63	61
Much of what is taught in my department (U: at my college) is irrelevant to the outside world.	G		42	37	34	37	36	32		36
	U		42	47	46	43	46	43	37	43
Rating of the intellectual environment (Response to:										

"How would you describe it in your department?"								
Excellent	F	28	15	10	16	10	8	8	13
	G	25	13	10	11	11	8		13
Good	F	46	50	47	48	50	47	54	49
	G	41	43	41	33	48	52		44
Fair	F	20	27	33	27	30	34	30	29
	G	24	31	35	39	33	30		31
Poor	F	6	8	10	9	10	11	9	9
	G	9	12	12	14	8	9		11
Do you find yourself bored in class these days?§								
Almost all the time/almost always true	G	6	5	5	4	4	3	9	5
	U	7	10	9	7	8	8		9
Fairly often/usually true	G	21	21	19	23	16	14	30	19
	U	32	34	34	30	35	36		33
Occasionally/usually false	G	39	44	45	41	48	42	50	44
	U	52	49	50	53	49	48		49
Almost never/almost always false	G	16	19	22	21	26	32	11	22
	U	9	7	7	10	8	8		9
I don't take classes	G	17	10	9	11	6	8	9	10
If you were to begin your career again, would you still want to be a college professor? (Response: definitely or probably not)	F	9	9	9	10	9	10	9	9
I think I would be happier if I had not entered graduate school/college.	G	7	8	7	11	10	5	7	7
	U	5	5	6	5	5	7		6

‡ Undergraduates: "What is your overall evaluation of your college?"

§ Undergraduates: "I find myself bored in class. . . ." Graduate responses are given first.

activity and with campus reform and innovation. While the surveys can throw light on the attitudes of faculty and students in these areas, they do not explain how or why changes occur on college and university campuses. On such issues, numerical majorities are not generally crucial: as in most other social institutions, the political process is more responsive to concerned and active minorities. On many campuses, moreover, small proportions can mean large absolute numbers. On a campus of 30,000 students, for example, the tiny proportion of 5 percent amounts to 1,500 people—who, if organized, can be an important force in campus politics. And 30 percent, still a minority, constitutes nearly 10,000 people.

Furthermore, the possibilities for change always depend on the peculiar political situation on any given campus, and especially on the character of student and faculty leaders and administrators and their relations with one another. This, of course, is not revealed in the marginal distributions of a broad national survey. Clearly, the situation on specific campuses or in specific departments will differ greatly from the overall picture.

Political and social issues

While both faculty members and students could be found at all points along the political spectrum (section A, Table 1-5), from left to strongly conservative, about 9 out of every 10 respondents of each status in the system as a whole placed themselves in one of three middle positions—liberal, middle-of-the-road, or moderately conservative. But there were sharp and interesting variations between institutions. Taking the extreme political categories first, the proportions calling themselves "strongly conservative" are very small at every type of institution, but the proportions describing themselves as "left" are appreciable, at least in the elite institutions, both universities and colleges. Here 8 percent of the faculty, 13 percent of the graduate students (at the universities), and 15 percent of the undergraduates at the universities and 12 percent at the colleges describe themselves as "left." Moreover, even within the three central categories there are quite sharp variations. At the leading universities, half of the respondents at each level describe themselves as "liberal"; this drops to one-third or less at the lower end of the quality scale; the proportions in the "middle-of-the-road" group rise, correspondingly, from one-fifth to one-third; and those in the "moderately conservative" category rise, in the case of faculty and graduates, from one-sixth to one-third (undergraduates move from one-tenth to one-sixth). Faculty and undergraduates look fairly similar at each type of institution (except that somewhat more undergraduates tend to prefer the "middle-of-the-road" to "moderately conservative" label), but the graduate students are somewhat to the right of the other two groups in the lower half of the system. (As we noted earlier, graduate students here tend disproportionately to be older persons improving their qualifications in education and other professional fields.)

Not many questions relating to specific social and political issues were asked of all three groups, but a few are given in section A. Skepticism about the capacity of "traditional American politics" to achieve meaningful social change was expressed by a third of graduates and faculty, and over half of the undergraduates. This skepticism somewhat qualifies our suggestion in commenting on the previous item (on political self-identification) that most respondents fit within the mainstream of the American political system. Moreover, all three groups agreed to a surprisingly large extent—especially at the upper levels—with the diagnosis of "white racism" as a primary cause of urban riots in black areas; but the extent of the agreement varies across institutions parallel with the variation in basic political disposition. Finally, the proposal to "legalize" marijuana—presumably taken to mean at a minimum the decriminalization of possession and use—was endorsed by one-third of the faculty and graduate students, and almost half of the undergraduates, though again variations across types of institutions are substantial. At the elite universities half the faculty and almost three-quarters of the undergraduates endorsed legalization, while only a quarter of junior college faculty and two-fifths of their undergraduates would endorse it.

These findings are somewhat contradictory. On the one hand, the large majority of students and teachers described themselves as fitting into the more central categories of the political spectrum; on the other, there was fairly widespread disbelief, especially among the undergraduates, that the American political system could respond to urgent social needs, and a willingness to define those needs in terms ("white racism") that would not have been endorsed by centrists in the larger adult population. Indeed, a substantial minority of 30 percent (more at the leading institutions) of teachers and undergraduates could, in 1969, imagine situations in the United States that might justify the use of violence to achieve political goals. Undoubtedly, such feelings and sympathies help to explain both the high incidence of campus disturbances and the even more widespread approval and support of protest which we shall illustrate below.

Political and academic issues

Section B of Table 1-5 groups together three questions on issues basically concerned with the higher education system and with the role of the academic. All three are issues on which broad political views might be expected to make a difference. Interestingly, however, insofar as the opinions of most of our respondents vary by type of institution, they do so in the opposite direction from that which the prevailing political sentiment of those institutions would lead one to expect. The principle of open access to higher education[12] was endorsed by large majorities of all three groups, led by the almost universal agreement of the undergraduates; considerably more faculty than students had reservations, however, especially at schools above the junior college level. In general, respondents at the lower end of the system, where access is in fact least restricted, were most in favor of such a policy. Responses to the two questions on the limits of an academic's (strictly, a scientist's) duty to publish the results of research, and on the possibility of a scholarly objectivity independent of political ideology—both areas in which a New Left point of view was being strongly expressed at that time—show how broadly such skeptical views were held, and by many who would not think of themselves as members or supporters of New Left political movements. This raises interesting questions as to the relation between leftist ideology and scholarly commitment at times when the two are perceived to be in conflict. How are such apparently conflicting pressures dealt with both by individual students and scholars and by their institutions? Our data will allow us to explore the first question in future work, and the late 1960s will undoubtedly provide historians with intriguing institutional case studies.

---

[12] It should be noted that the amount of such education and the type of institution that should provide it were not specified.

Campus political issues

On campus political issues, the basic political differences between types of institutions (section A) tend to assert themselves,
if to varying extents in different areas. On most of these issues
there is a remarkably high degree of consensus between faculty
and students at different levels. In the area of academic freedom,
there is very strong support for the principle of complete faculty
autonomy in choice of teaching material right across the quality
levels; there is nearly an even split between those who would
permit and those who would forbid classified weapons research
on campus, with the opponents in a majority, especially among
the faculty at the leading universities (the group most likely to be
involved in such research); and in the area of the limits of free
speech on campus, less than one-quarter of faculty and graduate
students (though more at quality level I, and more undergraduates) agreed that it should extend to cover the advocacy by the
faculty of violent resistance to public authority.

When asked directly about on-campus political activity and
disruptions by students, the academic community again gave
answers that, while not necessarily contradictory, provide am-
munition for several different interpretations. On one hand,
more than four out of five of college and university teachers
agreed that "campus disruptions by militant students are a threat
to academic freedom." About the same proportion of faculty
members agreed that "students who disrupt the functioning of a
college should be expelled or suspended." This statement was
also agreed to by substantial majorities of graduate and undergraduate students. When asked, "What do you think of the
emergence of radical student activism in recent years?" only
about 3 percent of the college teachers and graduate students
indicated unreserved approval. In the leading colleges and universities, where student activism has been most visible, the
proportions were a little higher: 5 percent of the faculty and 8
percent of the graduate students gave the radical movement
unreserved support.

These findings, however, should not be interpreted to mean
that there was little sympathy on the nation's campuses for
student activists. Forty-three percent of the faculty and 36
percent of the graduate students expressed at least qualified
approval of radical activism. Of those faculty on campuses which

experienced student demonstrations, about half approved of the aims of the most recent demonstration, and half of these approved of the methods of the demonstrators as well. In addition, the overwhelming majority of all faculty and students agreed that student demonstrations have a place on college campuses. Less than one-third of the faculty and students surveyed disagreed with this, and one-half of even these disapprovers of demonstrations believed that other forms of campus political activity were appropriate.

Unionization

In this area we report the specific attitudes (as of the time of the survey) of faculty and graduate students toward unionization and strike action, and also responses to a general question on the issue of increased "militancy" in defense of their interests (see section D, Table 1-5). It seems likely that the latter question was interpreted differently by faculty and students. The former probably defined their "interests" in terms of their conditions of employment—pay, hours of work, etc.—while students may well have been thinking of more generalized political activity. Be this as it may, it is clear that large majorities of the undergraduates, and never less than half the graduate students, were satisfied with the (arguably high) level of militancy they saw expressed in 1969, while a bare majority of faculty would have favored increasing militancy. In specific terms, however, just over half of all faculty and from one-third to one-half of all graduate students felt that the effects of faculty and teaching assistants' unions were "divisive."[13] Views on unions for the two groups were almost identical. In 1969, as today, moves toward unionization of faculty were more common lower in the system; for teaching assistants, however, such unions were largely confined to the leading and medium-quality universities. Graduate students, therefore, appear to be somewhat more likely to favor teaching assistants' unions if they have had experience with them. Turning to specific forms of collective action, slightly more than

13 "Divisive" should not be equated with "bad." Most of those who agreed with this statement probably meant to condemn unions by doing so; but some at least would probably argue, with some union leaders, that the notion of an academic "community" is outdated in the mass higher education system, that there are real conflicts of interests that divide its members, and that unions provide a rational mechanism for coping with these conflicts.

half of all faculty could not imagine circumstances that might justify striking, either for themselves or for graduate student teaching assistants, compared with two-thirds or more of the students who could imagine such circumstances.

Governance

Differences in the views of faculty members, graduate students, and undergraduates on the question of student power and decision making were large. Section E shows both the overall distribution of views on participation in governance by undergraduates and graduate students respectively, for a variety of decision-making areas, and the distribution within quality categories of those who are opposed even to "informal consultation" with students in these areas. Almost one-quarter of all undergraduates believed that undergraduates should have at least voting power on faculty promotion and appointment committees. Another quarter of them believed that they should at least be formally consulted in appointments and promotion; only 6 percent of faculty, however, would give voting power in this area, and only 21 percent would agree that undergraduates should even be formally consulted in these matters. Less pronounced differences were found with respect to undergraduate admissions policy, bachelor's degree requirements, and course curriculum, although faculty members were still dubious about expanding the role undergraduates play in those areas. Only in the rather different area of student discipline were a majority of all three groups prepared to give undergraduates at least voting rights. In most areas, graduate students' views on undergraduate consultation fall somewhere in between the views of faculty and undergraduates.[14]

Differences over the proper role of graduate students in academic decision making were almost as sharp. Nineteen percent of the graduate students believed that they should have formal voting rights on faculty appointments and promotions, and another 27 percent believed they should be formally consulted on them. Only 10 percent of the faculty would grant graduate students voting rights, and another 20 percent would allow them formal consultation in this area. On other issues, the

[14] But in some cases graduates are as likely to be restrictive of undergraduates' rights as the faculty—an interesting example, perhaps, of anticipatory socialization.

differences are less pronounced. Twenty-one percent of the graduate students want voting rights, and another 32 percent would like to be consulted concerning graduate admissions policies. The proportions of faculty with similar views are 16 percent and 27 percent, respectively. Thirty-nine percent of the graduate students want formal voting rights on the provision and content of graduate courses, compared with less than a fourth (23 percent) of the faculty who would extend those rights. A further substantial proportion of the graduate students (38 percent) would like formal consultation on graduate student courses; 41 percent of the faculty would agree to that procedure. These issues are still being fought out in many graduate departments all over the country, and the results will be highly consequential for the character of graduate education and for graduate student (and faculty) morale.

Educational issues

Although faculty members and students were in many respects satisfied with their institutions, they agreed on several ways in which undergraduate education could be improved. To the statement, "Undergraduate education in America would be improved if: (followed by a list of suggestions)" they responded as shown in section F of Table 1-5.

Particularly significant is the fact that 9 out of 10 undergraduates (and three-quarters of the faculty), with very little variation across institutions, would like course work to be "more relevant to contemporary life and problems," and nearly as many agreed that more attention should be paid to students' emotional growth. Clear majorities of undergraduates would also like to see grades abolished (to which only one-third of faculty agree) and all course work made elective. All these possible changes fall within the domain of curricular structure and the conduct of instruction that has traditionally been controlled by the faculty. On the latter two proposals, which are both more radical and more specific, student and faculty views were sharply in opposition to one another, especially at universities.

On a variety of other issues, however, faculty and students were much more closely aligned: for instance, in seeing American colleges as "crushing creativity" in favor of conformity—to which half of each group agreed—or in seeing research and specialization as threats to teaching and scholarship.[15] And clear and substantial majorities, ranging from 75 percent of the faculty to 96 percent of undergraduates, felt that teaching effectiveness rather than publication should be the primary criterion for faculty promotion. (Among the faculty there were very sharp differences by quality on this issue.)

Satisfaction and discontent

In spite of the considerable turbulence on American college campuses at the time this study was conducted, most respondents expressed satisfaction with their campuses in general, with the general quality of the educational experience within them, and even with the various rules by which they were governed (see section C, Table 1-5). As section G of Table 1-5 shows, 72 percent of all undergraduates agreed (with or without reservations) with the statement, "Most undergraduates in my college are satisfied with the education they are getting." An almost identical proportion of the faculty—73 percent—answered the same way.[16] Moreover, among the students these sentiments appeared in similar proportions across the board from the biggest universities to the smallest liberal arts colleges and junior colleges. Only 7 percent of the undergraduates in all institutions strongly disagreed with that statement. The graduate students' satisfaction, as reported by themselves and the faculty, was even higher.

When asked, "What is your overall evaluation of your college?" only 4 percent of our sample of undergraduates said they were "very dissatisfied" and another 9 percent said they were "dissatisfied." Fully 67 percent of the undergraduates said they were "very satisfied" or "satisfied"; the remaining 21 percent said they were "on the fence." At the leading universities (where campus protests occurred most frequently) the proportion who said they were "satisfied" or "very satisfied" was 80 percent—higher than the national average. With the more pointed statement, "Most faculty are strongly interested in the academic

[15] In the latter case, however, the faculty—regardless of their institutional location—were more likely to agree than graduate students.

[16] This statement describes respondents' perceptions of their campus atmosphere, rather than their personal views, but their own views are similar (see below).

problems of undergraduates," nearly two-thirds (61 percent) of the undergraduates agreed; the proportion of faculty members agreeing was only slightly higher. Both faculty and students at universities, however, expressed considerably more disagreement with this statement than did those at four-year colleges and junior colleges. Finally, however, extremely small proportions of students felt they would have been happier if they had not entered college or graduate school, and equally few faculty had second thoughts about their choice of career.

CONCLUSION: DIMENSIONS OF DIVERSITY

This brief chapter has provided summaries of answers to selected questionnaire items from the three surveys. In presenting figures specified by the type and quality of respondents' institutions, we have incidentally shown how large are some of the differences that might have been concealed within a single figure summarizing all institutions combined. This procedure serves to document and illustrate some of the diversity within the higher education system. It also serves as a warning. Even within these institutional categories there are variations—between subject fields, between men and women, between faculty and students of different ages, ranks, and statuses—which are as large or larger than any we have seen thus far. An enormous range of individual orientations, attitudes, and feelings, interconnected in complex patterns, are lumped together here, still in aggregate forms. In the following chapters, the authors of this volume describe these and other variations in more detail. In analyzing their interconnections, they begin to explain the structures and mechanisms that create or support the diversity that is central to American higher education.

2. Research Activity in American Higher Education

by Martin Trow and Oliver Fulton

by Martin Trow and Oliver Fulton

INTRODUCTION The roughly 2,500 universities and colleges of higher education in the United States perform an enormously wide variety of functions for their society. The existence of this diversity among institutions is fully recognized, and its roots and sources in American history and social structure are increasingly well understood. (For recent analytical essays on American higher education, see Ashby, 1971; Ben-David, 1971.) What is much less clear is how these diverse functions are performed by the system as a whole and by its component institutions: where (and how) they are located; how (and to what extent) they are institutionalized in the system; and how far they are complementary or competitive. What needs to be done is to spell out in greater detail the nature of the division of labor within American higher education, both among and within its colleges and universities.

The 1969 Carnegie Commission Survey of Faculty and Student Opinion, which includes academic men and women teaching in institutions ranging from junior colleges through the big multiversities, allows us to begin this more detailed mapping of the functional division of labor among American institutions. This paper is the first of several based on this survey to be addressed to the subject of research activities in American colleges and universities.[1] Research—by which term we also refer to the

---

[1] In this essay we confine our attention to the research activities of academic men and women, that is, the men and women who hold regular academic appointments or whose appointments also involve responsibility for graduate or undergraduate teaching—"all those other than graduate teaching assistants actually carrying the burden of instruction in their institution" (see Appendix A). We are not here considering the work of full-time or part-time professional research workers who do not have academic appointments but are, for the most part, attached to research centers or institutes in universities. A separate study of these professional research workers was done as part of the Carnegie survey; its findings will be reported elsewhere.

scholarly work of nonscientific disciplines—is one of the core functions of American higher education. Despite the fact that it is not carried on by all American academics, nor even encouraged in all institutions, its influence is felt in every academic institution, both through its effects on the growth of knowledge (and thus on the content of higher education everywhere) and through its role in providing the basis of institutional prestige.

American universities and colleges are, for the most part, intensely competitive: the prize they seek is institutional prestige. Universities, but not undergraduate colleges, have a formal obligation to carry on research and graduate instruction—the two are closely related—and at least part of their regular faculty (at the leading institutions, nearly all of it) is appointed with research promise and achievement in mind. And there is plenty of evidence that universities judge themselves, and are judged by others, on the basis of their research productivity (see, for example, Cartter, 1966). University departments, the institutional arms of academic disciplines, organize graduate training and largely determine faculty appointments and promotions. Insofar as departments accept the preeminence of the research function, they also compete intensively for a disciplinary prestige that is partly related to and partly independent of their universities (Hagstrom, 1971). Similarly, academic scientists and scholars, through their research, compete as individuals for personal prestige in their disciplines, though this, too, is related to and affected by the prestige of their departments and universities.

Although universities and university teachers have a broad obligation to further the growth of knowledge across a broad range of fields and disciplines, there is not only considerable variation in the success with which institutions, departments, and individuals meet this obligation, but perhaps an even wider variation in the intensity with which they enter the competitive arenas of science and scholarship. As we shall see, over half of all academic men and women in our survey had not published a single research or scholarly paper in the two years preceding the survey, while 3 percent had published 10 or more such papers during that time. In our category of "high-quality" universities,[2] over 20 percent had not published in the last two years, while in the "weaker" universities over twice that many had not pub-

---

[2] For the definition of these categories, see Appendix A.

lished anything recently. This variation in research activity and commitment[3] will be the center of our attention in this essay.[4]

Our focus on research activities has several broad purposes. First, it aims to extend our knowledge about the distribution of research itself: where it is done, how much is done, by whom, and at what costs (or benefits) to other activities of academic men and women. For example, there is a widespread but underexamined belief that research is carried on at the expense of teaching in the leading research universities—and this belief is now generating demands that the structure of rewards be modified to redress the balance or that other more coercive action be taken.[5] But at the same time we shall be looking at research activity for the light it can throw on the whole structure of American higher education—that is, on the division of academic labor, both among institutions and among individuals.

We begin by reporting the distributions of interest and activity in research within seven broad categories of colleges and universities. We then look at variations in research activity by subject field, academic rank, and age within these broad institutional

---

[3] Although publication—the means by which research findings are communicated to all but an academic's closest professional associates (and the means by which prestige is usually, and promotion almost always, gained)—is our chief indicator of what we call "research activity," it is not our only interest. Research work that is not published does not become part of science or scholarship. Nevertheless, unpublished research activities by academics may be communicated through teaching or other means and may affect the climate in which research is carried on, or the recruitment and training of young scientists, and therefore is relevant to our general concerns. Research activity that may not eventuate in publication is reflected in our study through expressions of interest in research and through the opportunity to report that one is "currently engaged in research" or scholarly work, even though the respondent is not currently publishing (and may never publish) the results of his or her work.

[4] Parsons and Platt (1968a) stress the integration of research with teaching in the "full" university, and the importance of this integration both for American society and for the rest of the academic system. Our evidence supports Parsons and Platt in their general finding of the integration of these activities in the leading institutions. But our interests are in broad variations both throughout the system and in those parts, even of the leading universities, that stress one or the other of these core functions almost to the exclusion of the other. That, we propose, may create strains that are obscured by imputing to the whole of an institution or a system characteristics that apply only to parts of it.

[5] For example, several states are now attempting to control or increase by legislation the number of "contact" hours of teaching that academic men and women in state universities must meet (see "Public Funds for . . .," 1972, pp. 1, 4).

categories. Finally, we examine a wide range of correlates of research activity, with special attention to the competitive demands of other academic activities, such as administration and teaching, and to the differential rewards associated with research activity as opposed to these other activities of academic men and women.

There are obvious limitations to assessing research activity primarily through reports of the amounts and rates of publication. Apart from the problem of research that is not published (or even intended for publication), this procedure cannot take into account either the enormous variations in the quality of published research or its significance for the body of knowledge to which it is meant to contribute. Our aim, however, is not to study the internal processes of academic science or scholarship, for which judgments of quality and importance are crucial, but rather to explore the connections between research as an institutionalized activity and function and the colleges and universities in which much of it is done.

TEACHING OR RESEARCH: ORIENTATIONS AND ACTIVITY   In 1969, in answer to the question, "Do your interests lie primarily in teaching or research?" only 4 percent of a large national sample of teachers in American universities and colleges were prepared to say "Very heavily in research," while another 20 percent answered, "Both, but leaning to research." Under one-quarter, therefore, tended to favor research over teaching; just over one-third preferred teaching, but expressed some interest in research; and 43 percent said that their interests lay very heavily in teaching (Table 2-1). It is immediately clear, therefore, that judged by its staff's self-conceptions, the American academic system as a whole is *primarily* a teaching system. Any notion that teaching generally takes second place to research is certainly not borne out—though it is true that as well as universities, the sample includes four-year institutions (whose teachers constitute 39 percent of all academic faculty) and junior colleges (15 percent).[6]

In any event, Table 2-2 shows the diversity with which the different functions of teaching and research are spread across the American educational system. On the one hand, the high-quality universities contain about twice as many men and women

[6] These percentages are based on the Carnegie Commission Survey's own figures for 1968–69, collected for weighting purposes (see Appendix A).

TABLE 2-1 *"Do your interests lie primarily in teaching or research?"* **United States, 1969 (in percentages; not answered omitted; weighted totals in parentheses)**	

Primary interest	All institutions
Very heavily in research	4⎫
Both, but leaning to research	20⎭24
Both, but leaning to teaching	34
Very heavily in teaching	43
	101%*
	(432,482)

*Totals may add up to 99 or 101 percent due to rounding error.

NOTE: For a description of the survey, of weighting procedures, and of conventions used in the tables, see Appendix A.

SOURCE: 1969 Carnegie Commission Survey of Faculty and Student Opinion. Sample: all faculty respondents ($N = 60,028$). In subsequent tables in this chapter where this sample is the source, it will be referred to as the all-respondents sample ($N = 60,028$).

devoted to research (that is, whose interests lie "very heavily" in research) as does the system as a whole; and half of all teachers in these leading American universities describe their interests as lying at least primarily in research, compared with little more than a quarter in the weaker universities. At the other extreme, the junior colleges contain only 5 percent of faculty who claim any interest in research,[7] and three-fourths of the junior college faculty say, not surprisingly, that their interests lie very heavily in teaching. The diversity between the two extremes should come as no surprise; not only is it commonplace in descriptions of the American system, it is generally written into legislative distinctions between public universities and colleges. It is noteworthy, however, that there is no sharp differentiation of function between colleges and universities. While all the four-year colleges show a primary commitment to teaching, the high-quality colleges have about as many "researchers" on their faculties as do the weaker universities.[8]

A closer look at Table 2-2, however, shows very clearly that despite the variations, teaching still plays a crucial part in all levels of the system: even in our high-quality (quality I) universities only half of the respondents defined themselves as primarily

[7] Some of these may be young graduate students holding temporary jobs in junior colleges while they complete their qualifications to teach higher in the system.

[8] The proportion of researchers in this category of "high-quality four-year colleges" is slightly inflated since it includes a few small but high-prestige technical institutions (such as the California Institute of Technology), which might more logically be found with the universities; for an explanation see Appendix A.

TABLE 2-2 "Do your interests lie primarily in teaching or research?" by type and quality of institution (in percentages; weighted totals in parentheses)

Primary interest	Quality level and type							All institutions
	Universities			Four-year colleges			Junior colleges	
	High (I)	Medium (II)	Low (III)	High (IV)	Medium (V)	Low (VI)	All (VII)	
Very heavily in research	9 }50	7 }40	4 }28	4 }26	1 }12	1 }10	1 }5	4 }24
Both, but leaning to research	41	33	24	22	11	9	4	20
Both, but leaning to teaching	35	37	39	39	37	34	18	34
Very heavily in teaching	15	23	33	35	51	56	77	43
	100%	100%	100%	100%	100%	100%	100%	101%
	(54,161)	(78,242)	(68,246)	(24,553)	(47,408)	(96,844)	(63,028)	(432,482)

SOURCE: All-respondents sample ($N = 60,028$).

researchers.[9] Even in the largest state universities (many of which are in this quality I category), where for years the doctrine of "publish or perish," large semiautonomous research "empires," excessive student numbers, and poor faculty-student ratios have been criticized, only a very small minority of faculty are uninterested in teaching, while half the total faculty claim to be more interested in teaching than research. An important first conclusion, therefore, is that although the variation among institutions, in type and in "quality," is partly responsible for the division of labor, it far from totally accounts for that division. In the junior colleges, admittedly, there is almost no variation in devotion to teaching, but in the universities there is an *internal* division; to explain it, we must look much more closely at their internal workings. Secondly, the reader should know at the outset that, leaving aside all questions of the amount of research actually done, and the extent to which American universities facilitate and reward it, the *normative* climate in the United States, as reflected in academics' personal preferences, is far more favorable to teaching than most observers would have predicted. (This is consistent with the findings of Parsons and Platt, 1968*b*.)

Turning now from expressions of interest to actual behavior, we show in Table 2-3 how research activity[10] varies in the

[9] An interesting comparison is provided by the data on British university teachers from Halsey and Trow (1971). In answer to the identical question in 1964, almost two-thirds of British teachers (64 percent) stated that they at least leaned toward research. This is the more surprising since British universities are thought, by members and observers alike, to have a strong ideology of devotion to undergraduate teaching. Indeed, to judge by comparative descriptive accounts of the two systems, and by much of the rhetoric used by British academics, one would expect British universities to look, in their emphasis on teaching, more like American liberal arts colleges. (The British-American comparison will be pursued in another publication of the authors.)

[10] The "typology of research activity" is constructed from two variables: first, the number of "professional writings" of all kinds that a respondent has published or had accepted for publication in the past two years: five or more publications we have called "many," and one to four, "few." Those who answered "none" we subdivided on a second variable—according to whether they were currently engaged in any research or scholarly work that they expected to lead to publication ("active, no recent publications") or not ("inactive . . ."). Although this measure obviously underestimates the research and scholarly activity of men and women in fields where the book is a fairly common form of publication, we have compared the typology with measures of lifetime publication of books and articles, and find that, even in fields such as the humanities, those who publish most books do also publish large numbers of articles (and vice versa); the typology does not do them a serious injustice. (For further details, distributions etc., see Fulton and Trow, 1972, pp. 31–35.)

TABLE 2-3 Research activity by type and quality of institution (in percentages; weighted totals in parentheses)

| | Quality level and type | | | | | | | |
| | Universities | | | Four-year colleges | | | Junior colleges | All institutions |
Research activity	High (I)	Medium (II)	Low (III)	High (IV)	Medium (V)	Low (VI)	All (VII)	All (VIII)
Inactive, not currently publishing	9	14	21	23	37	48	70	33
Active, no recent publications	12	15	23	23	26	24	16	20
Few current publications	51 ⎱79	52 ⎱72	46 ⎱57	45 ⎱54	34 ⎱37	26 ⎱29	12 ⎱14	37 ⎱48
Many current publications	28 ⎰	20 ⎰	11 ⎰	9 ⎰	3 ⎰	3 ⎰	2 ⎰	11 ⎰
	100%	101%	101%	100%	100%	101%	100%	101%
	(54,189)	(77,012)	(67,414)	(24,206)	(46,720)	(93,525)	(61,114)	(424,180)

SOURCE: 27,000-case sample of faculty from the 1969 Carnegie Commission Survey of Faculty and Student Opinion. This sample, which is used in most tables, is a reweighted, stratified sample of 27,191 cases, containing all respondents at four-year and junior colleges, and a systematic 1:4 sample of all those at universities, where the original numbers were very large. Base figures in the tables are population estimates: the numbers in each quality category in the 27,000-case sample are I, 3,481; II, 3,868; III, 3,595; IV, 4,648; V, 4,801; VI, 4,658; VII, 2,140. In subsequent tables in this chapter where this is the source, it will simply be referred to as the 27,000-case sample.

different types of college and university. In high-quality universities, almost four-fifths of the population have published in the past two years, and over one-quarter have more than five publications to their credit. At the other extreme, in junior colleges, only 2 percent have published more than five pieces and not much more than one-eighth have published any. This table, in general, shows the obverse of our finding about interest in teaching (Table 2-2). Once again the division of labor is clear, but it is striking that even in low-quality institutions, which we have described as allowing for research only in their faculty's spare time, a noticeable amount of research is in fact carried on and published. Although practically no one beyond quality IV has published more than five pieces in the past two years, a substantial number have published at least one. On the other hand, a majority of all faculty in each four-year category and one-third even in junior colleges are at least "active" in research by their own definition. Although the amount of research (and surely its character and quality, which we cannot assess) varies enormously, some research activity, and publication, can be found almost everywhere.[11]

Time Spent in Classroom Teaching

Table 2-2 showed the extent of interest in research among faculty members across different types of institutions. As we have suggested, these differences are strongly reinforced by the nature of the institutions themselves. Specifically, teaching loads may vary from a norm of as little as three courses per year in the "academic" departments of high-quality universities to five or six courses per term at junior colleges. (The norm itself at high-quality institutions applies only to those carrying a "full teaching load"; the widespread use of "released time" permits academics to reduce this load very substantially if they wish, by paying part of their own salaries out of research grants.) The effect on time spent "in class"—i.e., on all but the most informal teaching—is strikingly seen in Table 2-4, which shows, for example, that less than one-fifth of those at high-quality universities spent over nine hours per week in class, compared with four-fifths at junior colleges. It would seem that these enormous differences would

[11] But again, we shall have to ask whether this demonstrates the integration of the two roles or whether there is also an internal division of labor within each institution, with pockets of research activity at the bottom and pockets of full-time teaching at the top.

TABLE 2-4 *Hours per week in class, by type and quality of institution (in percentages; weighted totals in parentheses)*

| | Quality level and type | | | | | | | |
| | Universities | | | Four-year colleges | | | Junior colleges | |
Hours/week	High (I)	Medium (II)	Low (III)	High (IV)	Medium (V)	Low (VI)	All (VII)	All institutions
None	11	13	9	7	4	3	3	7
1–4	34	24	15	16	8	8	6	15
5–6	24	22	19	15	9	8	6	14
7–8	13	14	12	14	12	7	3	10
9–10	8	13	17	21	18	16	5	13
11–12	3	6	15	14	28	28	12	16
13–16	3	5	8	9	14	20	38	14
17–20	2	3	4	3	5	6	20	6
21+	2	1	2	2	2	4	8	3
	100%	101%	101%	101%	100%	100%	101%	98%
	(55,520)	(79,988)	(69,884)	(25,157)	(48,374)	(98,185)	(64,610)	(441,719)

Bracketed subtotals:
Inner (None + 1–4): 46, 37, 24, 22, 12, 11, 9, 23
Outer (None + 1–4 + 5–6): 70, 58, 43, 37, 22, 19, 14, 37
Inner (13–16 + 17–20 + 21+): 6, 9, 13, 14, 20, 30, 66, 24
Outer (9–10 … 21+): 17, 28, 45, 49, 66, 74, 82, 53

SOURCE: 27,000-case sample.

be enough by themselves to explain the differences in research interests that we have seen.

The actual link, however, between research preferences and freedom from formal teaching requirements can be seen in Table 2-5. In fact, we find that despite the very great differences in time available, academics in higher-quality institutions are still far more likely to be interested in research than those in lower-quality colleges, even with roughly the same amount of formal classroom instruction. Interest in research, in other words, does not only increase to fill the time available; it is something encouraged by high-quality institutions at least partly independently of teaching requirements. Indeed, an important facet of institutional quality is not so much that the better institutions provide more time for research as that research there is integrated with, not seen as incompatible with, teaching.

Although it is true that for any given number of hours spent in formal teaching, the higher the quality of their institutions, the more likely academics are to be researchers, it is also true (reading the table vertically instead of horizontally) that within quality categories, the more hours unused by teaching, the more academics are interested in research—down through quality IV.[12] Beyond this point, there is essentially no difference in research orientation even between those with very high and very low teaching loads.[13] This suggests that while reduced teaching loads in universities are intended to provide extra time for research, in small colleges they are a function of time spent on administration or on other kinds of instruction. Research at these colleges (for the few who do it) is a spare-time activity, for which the institution makes no provision. In this respect, at least, research is something quite different in the weaker colleges (level V and below) from the kind of activity that researchers at universities would recognize.[14]

[12] There is one exception: In the leading universities, there is practically no difference among the three groups with the lightest teaching loads (six or fewer hours per week). These are "standard" teaching loads in leading universities; it is somewhat fortuitous whether an academic teaches less than that in any given semester, and need not reflect differences in research orientation.

[13] This is an important finding about the character of American higher education— a "fault line" between levels IV and V, which shows itself, as we shall see, in many other institutional and individual characteristics.

[14] Hereafter, in many tabulations concerned with actual research behavior, we shall respond to this fact by analyzing research orientations and behavior for institutions in quality levels I through IV— those places where research is a legitimate and integrated activity. (All such table sections are specifically marked "Quality levels I–IV.")

TABLE 2-5 *Percentage whose interests lie heavily in, or lean toward, research, by type and quality of institution and hours per week spent in class (base totals omitted)**

		Quality level and type						
		Universities			Four-year colleges			Junior colleges	
	Hours/week	High (I)	Medium (II)	Low (III)	High (IV)	Medium (V)	Low (VI)	All (VII)	All institutions
	None	56	56	49	44	18	18	4	44
	1–4	59	52	40	43	9	13	7	43
	5–6	54	45	37	36	17	12	12	38
	7–8	40	35	29	24	15	10	7	25
	9–10	33	26	20	22	12	11	7	18
	11–12	31	19	14	14	10	10	6	11
	13–16	26	18	10	11	11	8	2	7
	17+	19	20	11	7	15	8	4	9
	All categories	50	40	28	26	12	10	5	24

*The smallest unweighted base for any cell is 63 (junior colleges, 7–8 hours per week.)

SOURCE: All-respondents sample (N = 60,028).

We are beginning to see emerging here some of the central themes that we discussed earlier. First of all, there is the "division of labor," the extreme differentiation of the American system of higher education: there are whole sections of the system where the teaching function is dominant, largely to the exclusion of research; and there are other areas where research has an equal claim on an academic's time and energies, and where teaching is much more closely integrated with it. Second, we have seen one of the mechanisms whereby the functional division is encouraged—the assignment of teaching loads. This mechanism seems to operate both at an individual level—faculty with lower teaching requirements do more research—and, significantly, at an institutional level: as we pointed out above, in institutions with generally lower teaching loads (i.e., those of higher quality) academics tend to be more interested in research,[15] even if their personal teaching loads are heavier. (Again, teaching requirements are only the most obvious mechanism: we shall, in due course, be looking at others, e.g., the different availability of funds and facilities for research, and the different structures of rewards for research and for teaching.)

RESEARCH ORIENTATION AND ACTIVITY COMPARED Before looking further at the distributions of research and teaching roles and functions, it may be worth asking what the relation is between our two indicators: how closely do expressions of interest correspond to actual behavior? In Table 2-6 we see that while the relation between activity and orientation, measured by our index,[16] is quite strong, it is by no means perfect. For example, only two-thirds of those whose orientation is "exclusively" to teaching are totally inactive in research—and almost one-fifth of them have in fact published at least one piece in the past two years. The proportion who have published rises

---

[15] And to do more, though we do not show this table.

[16] The "index of research orientation" is constructed from two items: (1) respondents' interest in teaching or research (see Table 2-1) scored from 0 ("Very heavily in teaching") to 3 ("Very heavily in research"); and (2) respondents' rating from 1 to 4 of the "importance to you personally" of "to engage in research," "to train graduate or professional students," "to provide undergraduates with a broad liberal education," and "to prepare undergraduates for their chosen occupation." Responses were scored from 0 (research rated fourth) to 3 (research rated first in importance): the two scores were added and the results combined: a score of 0 was called "exclusively teaching," 1 or 2 "primarily teaching," 3 or 4 "both teaching and research," and 5 or 6 "strongly research." (For further details, distributions, etc., see Fulton and Trow, 1972, pp. 23–31.)

TABLE 2-6
*Research activity
(typology) by
research
orientation
(index)
(in percentages;
weighted totals
in parentheses)*

Research activity	Orientation				
	Exclusively teaching	Primarily teaching	Both teaching and research	Strongly research	All
Inactive, not currently publishing	66	38	10	3	33
Active, no recent publications	15	23	22	12	20
Few current publications	18	34	57	53	37
Many current publications	1	5	17	32	11
	100%	100%	100%	100%	101%
	(83,307)	(181,092)	(96,766)	(52,378)	(424,180)

SOURCE: 27,000-case sample.

almost to two-fifths for "primarily teachers" and to over two-thirds for those whose orientation is to "both teaching and research." At the other "deviant" corner of the table, 10 percent of the category labeled "both" are totally inactive in research, and 32 percent have not published at all in the past two years, while the latter is true even of 15 percent of the "strong researchers."[17] It is clear that although orientation and activity correspond moderately closely in the majority of cases, for a substantial number of academics the fit is less good—in other words, they define themselves differently from the way an observer who saw their research behavior would be likely to label them.

At this stage, the reader may be tempted to question the validity of one or both of these measures—most likely the subjective index of "orientation." But rather than discarding it as inaccurate, we suggest that there may be good and significant reasons for the lack of fit, and interesting questions to be raised as to why one who does no research might wish to call oneself a researcher, or one who does a great deal might call oneself a teacher. First, it might be that there is a degree of "slippage" in

[17] Table 2-6 presents the relationship for the whole sample in all quality categories combined. It is not increased within specified quality categories: overall, gamma = .58: partial gammas are as follows: quality I, .50; quality II, .49; quality III, .53; quality IV, .58.

conceptions of research orientation; some academics who are in fact relatively very inactive may still see themselves as researchers (perhaps in relation to still more inactive colleagues around them), whereas others with a much higher research output may not think this entitles them to call themselves researchers, compared with colleagues who are still more active; in other words, standards of self-assessment may not be universal, but may be determined by the "significant others" in the context in which academics actually work. Second, the two activities may not be seen as mutually exclusive to the extent that we have defined them. For example, researchers with heavy output may define themselves as more interested in teaching than research, without giving up their research work; there may also be a number of older academics who are no longer active or interested in research but are still publishing the results of their earlier work. Third, and perhaps most likely or most common, the two measures may both be realistic, their lack of equivalence resulting from constraints that prevent academics from fulfilling what they see as their primary role.[18] Young would-be "researchers," for example, may have teaching loads that simply prevent them from doing publishable research in any quantity,[19] whereas untenured would-be "teachers" may find it essential to publish in order to achieve promotion and job security. No doubt each of these explanations holds for some of those whose answers seem paradoxical; indeed, in another publication we shall be exploring at length this very important question of the fit between orientation and activity, which seems to us to exemplify one of the central problems of American higher education. For the moment, however, it is enough to note that the two measures are far from identical and that on the whole, we shall be concentrating on *activity* in our analysis from now on; its objective meaning is clear,[20] whereas orientation alone raises

---

[18] Moreover, not all research that is done is ever published—although promotion committees and the world at large tend to equate research with visible research, i.e., publication—and therefore, for operational purposes, so do we (to some extent, but see footnote 3).

[19] Or they may have inadequate funds. See footnote 28.

[20] There are still problems, caused especially by taking quantity of publication as an implicit index of quality (see Hagstrom, 1971, and references there); but the two are fairly strongly correlated, and the measurement of quality is beyond the scope of our study.

more acutely all the questions alluded to above. Most of our analysis, therefore, will be concerned with those academics who do, and publish, research rather than those who wish to, or who believe that they do.

THE STRUCTURAL LOCATION OF RESEARCH ACTIVITY

Subject field

Tables 2-7 and 2-8 show the variation in research activity by subject fields. Table 2-7, first, gives the complete distribution of the research activity typology by field,[21] for quality levels I through IV combined; while Table 2-8 shows only the proportions of the appropriate category that have published at all in the past two years—by subject field and institutional quality simultaneously. In Table 2-7 the variation among subjects is striking, especially considering the relatively homogeneous nature of the institutions concerned. Leaving aside for the moment the question of the absolute number of publications (since there may be conventions, or constraints, inherent in the nature of disciplines that lend themselves more or less favorably to frequent brief publication[22]), more than twice as many academics in the biological sciences as in the fine arts have published at all in the past two years—and if we ignore fine arts, which may have special definitional problems, we still find a 25 percentage point difference between the proportions who have published in biology and those who have in the humanities. Likewise, over one-quarter of those in education are totally uninvolved in research, while this is true of almost no one in biology. (Again, it is worth repeating that these figures are for teachers in universities and elite colleges and *exclude* the weaker less research-oriented colleges and all the junior colleges.)

Table 2-8 (which reports research activity in light of both subject and institutional type) begins to show us the character of a highly differentiated system of higher education. We see first that within each category of institutions (at least quality levels I to IV) there is a broadly similar rank ordering of fields (compare Table 2-7). For instance, except in junior colleges, where they fall to second place, the biological sciences consistently show the

---

[21] The reader should note that the category here labeled "new and semiprofessional fields" is essentially an "all other" category, containing such fields as agriculture and forestry, architecture, home economics, journalism, library science, nursing, and social work.

[22] For a brief discussion of this problem, see Fulton and Trow (1972, pp. 35–36).

TABLE 2-7
Research activity by subject field (in percentages); quality levels I–IV (weighted totals in parentheses)

Research activity	Subject				
	Biological sciences	Medicine and law	Social sciences	Physical sciences	Engineering
Inactive, not currently publishing	5	10	8	12	13
Active, no recent publications	11	8	18	14	16
Few current publications	53 ⎫	52 ⎫	56 ⎫	51 ⎫	56 ⎫
Many current publications	30 ⎭ 84	30 ⎭ 82	19 ⎭ 75	23 ⎭ 74	15 ⎭ 71
	99%	100%	101%	100%	100%
	(18,593)	(16,787)	(26,448)	(29,518)	(19,767)

SOURCE: 27,000-case sample.

TABLE 2-8
Percentage who have published at least one article in the last two years, by subject field and type and quality of institution (base totals omitted)*

Quality and type		Subject				
		Biological sciences	Medicine and law	Social sciences	Physical sciences	Engineering
Universities						
High	I	91	83	87	86	85
Medium	II	89	81	80	81	73
Low	III	81	75	68	67	63
Four-year colleges						
High	IV	73	—	59	60	65
Medium	V	55	—	42	39	53
Low	VI	36	—	35	28	29
Junior colleges						
All	VII	15	—	20	10	12
All institutions		67	80	55	50	60

*The smallest unweighted base for any cell is 97 (biology, junior colleges).
SOURCE: All-respondents sample (N = 60,028).

Business	Humanities	Education	New and semi-professional fields	Fine arts	All subjects
19	13	26	26	31	16
19	28	14	15	25	17
48 ⎱ 62 14 ⎰	47 ⎱ 59 12 ⎰	45 ⎱ 60 14 ⎰	44 ⎱ 59 15 ⎰	37 ⎱ 44 8 ⎰	49 ⎱ 67 18 ⎰
100% (10,636)	100% (35,565)	99% (18,237)	101% (31,672)	101% (12,954)	100% (222,821)

Business	Humanities	Education	New and semi-professional fields	Fine arts	All subjects
75	75	70	67	55	79
66	63	63	61	52	71
50	48	53	53	34	58
48	50	38	29	42	53
35	36	34	26	28	37
18	30	25	20	25	28
9	15	15	13	12	13
36	41	38	35	31	47

highest rates of publication of any subject group; and physical science and social science (which are within one point of each other until quality level V), along with the professional schools of law, medicine, and engineering, show rates of publication that are always higher than the mean for their quality stratum, down through quality level V. The humanities and business are a little lower than the mean, followed, except in quality level III, by education and the new and semiprofessional fields, and lastly fine arts.

Second, the variations in range of publication in different types and quality levels of institution that we saw in Table 2-3 still hold for nearly every broad field of study. The only exceptions to a consistent if not regular decline are in three subjects— engineering, humanities, and fine arts—which show slightly higher rates of publication at high-quality four-year colleges than at low-quality universities.[23] But most other subjects, evidently, require something that universities, however low in quality, can supply better than even high-quality four-year colleges: perhaps large scale, perhaps easier access to grants or to research assistants, perhaps a relative absence of distraction by under- graduates. Research in the humanities, by contrast, is more susceptible to variations in quality within universities and seems to be fostered as much by an atmosphere emphasizing high- quality undergraduate teaching as by the presence of less well- qualified Ph.D. students. (Biology and engineering, on the other hand, are noteworthy for fostering a substantial emphasis on research even further down in the educational system—over half the academics in these subjects have published, even when they teach in medium-quality colleges.)

The question of differences among fields and disciplines is a large one; it deserves much fuller discussion,[24] and it is certainly not possible to do justice to it using such crude groupings as we have here. But if Table 2-8 cannot adequately characterize disciplines, it does, in fact, neatly encapsulate the functional diversity that American higher education comprises: a system that permits within its boundaries rates of participation in one of

---

23 None of these are hard to understand. Engineering is largely explained by our definition of four-year colleges, which includes specialized technical institutes (see footnote 8, this chapter), while the humanities and fine arts are the subjects in which "liberal arts" colleges are by definition strongest.

24 This subject will receive more detailed analysis in a later publication by the authors.

its core activities ranging from 9 percent to 91 percent is undeniably well differentiated. At the same time, it is important to remember that although all higher education institutions teach and only some do research, it is research that confers elite status on an institution and a discipline: and the fields where research is done dominate the universities intellectually and politically (though not always numerically). Even in the large land-grant public universities, where professional and service functions have always had a special place, the research-doing faculty embody the norms and carry on the activities that determine the character of their institution and are chiefly responsible for its public image. This group of active researchers dominates the leading institutions just as in many ways the research-oriented institutions dominate those lower in the system.[25] For example, the research enterprise carries with it, controls or influences, and confers vicarious status on, a whole range of other activities, notably professional and undergraduate teaching in universities, and liberal education and vocational training in four- and two-year colleges. Moreover, although the latter have very different tasks to perform, they are staffed, and to some extent governed, by the products of the more elite institutions, and for better or worse they emulate many of the latter's methods and ambitions. But we have run ahead of our data.

We shall have to return to the question of field differences at a later time: but the diversity in Table 2-8 demonstrates that for an understanding of the dynamics of research behavior, we shall need to look not only at individual "active researchers" but also at the "research climate" in which they operate, and whether they constitute, at a minimum, a minority or a majority of the academics in their specific institutional and departmental contexts. If we speak of researchers in the humanities, for example, three-quarters of their colleagues may be frequent publishers (quality I) or only half (quality IV); if we speak of research at high-quality four-year colleges, it may be in a discipline where it is the prevailing norm (biology) or where it is the exception (education). Indeed, one of the chief problems in this study is to take account of the diversities of higher education in the United States; there is a real danger that any generalization may be the spurious result of adding together a series of quite different,

---

[25] But a central interest of our inquiry is how far down in the system, and through what mechanisms, this influence travels.

sometimes contradictory relationships derived from a great variety of contexts. In further work, therefore, we shall begin to look at research and teaching according to its context, not as now by controlling simultaneously for a whole series of structural variables, but by grouping the single departments in which our respondents work according to their "research context." But this must come later; meanwhile, we shall look at another variable—academic rank—and how men and women in different ranks, and different age groups, divide their time between teaching and research.

Academic rank

It is not easy to predict what the effect of rank might be; there are a variety of possible countervailing pressures, some of which we can guess at, without assessing their relative weight. Professors, presumably, if the "publish or perish" maxim holds true, should be the most successful, and hence the most prolific researchers; but they also carry more administrative responsibilities and have less incentive to publish, once established and promoted. Of the career grades, assistant professors have more incentive, but probably also have the highest teaching loads. Those pressures may very well cancel each other out.

Sections A and B of Table 2-9 show the distribution of research activity by rank.[26] It is clear that in high-quality universities, and overall, research activity does not change sharply after academics reach the tenured rank of associate professor; rather, the crucial difference comes between the temporary rank of instructor and

[26] In this case (and in several other tables hereafter) rather than presenting such a complex table as 2-8 above, we show research activity by rank, first of all (section A, Table 2-9) for quality level I alone, and then (section B, Table 2-9) for quality levels I through IV. Although this does not show the whole diversity, it gives a sense of the variation by quality without asking the reader to assimilate so many relationships, some of which we have already covered or anticipated. (And it omits quality levels V through VII, in which, as we have seen, not much research is done or published, and what research there is is probably different in character.) A more conventional table would show first quality level I and then "all others," i.e., quality levels II through IV, especially when in the text we are contrasting one group with the other. By including quality level I in both halves, we are in fact weakening any assertions we may make about differences by quality. But given limited space, we wish to give the reader an overall picture of the whole world where research is carried on; while the tables for quality level I alone show both the special characteristics of the elite universities, and some of the diversity within the research-doing institutions as a whole.

TABLE 2-9 Research activity by rank (in percentages; weighted totals in parentheses)

Research activity	Full professor	Associate professor	Assistant professor	Instructor	Lecturer	Other	All ranks
				Rank			
A. Quality level I							
Inactive, not currently publishing	4	5	7	25	16	40	9
Active, no recent publications	5	8	13	28	18	33	12
Few current publications	50 ⎫91	57 ⎫87	60 ⎫80	41 ⎫47	49 ⎫66	25 ⎫27	51 ⎫79
Many current publications	41 ⎭	30 ⎭	20 ⎭	6 ⎭	17 ⎭	3 ⎭	28 ⎭
	100% (18,665)	100% (10,080)	100% (13,971)	100% (4,605)	100% (3,742)	101% (2,405)	100% (54,189)
B. Quality levels I–IV							
Inactive, not currently publishing	9	12	14	37	24	37	16
Active, no recent publications	9	13	21	32	27	28	17
Few current publications	52 ⎫82	54 ⎫74	53 ⎫66	29 ⎫31	40 ⎫49	30 ⎫35	49 ⎫67
Many current publications	29 ⎭	20 ⎭	13 ⎭	2 ⎭	9 ⎭	5 ⎭	18 ⎭
	100% (64,908)	99% (52,879)	101% (64,578)	100% (25,423)	100% (8,596)	100% (5,579)	100% (222,821)

SOURCE: Quality I, all-respondents sample ($N = 13,924$); quality I–IV, 27,000-case sample.

the career rank of an assistant professor.[27] Within the top three career grades, there is a tendency for research activity to increase with rank. Whether this reflects increasing opportunity for research,[28] increasing experience, or the operation of the "publish or perish" rule can best be explored when we look at the reward structure that surrounds research activity.[29] For the moment, it is enough to look at the differences among the three grades of professor. At the ranking universities (quality level I), the proportion publishing over five pieces within the previous two years more than doubles—from one-fifth to two-fifths—with seniority; the same pattern, at lower levels of activity, can be seen in the wider range of institutions (quality levels I through IV). If we look at the two highest levels of activity (active and publishing), we see a bigger variation by rank in levels I to IV combined—almost inevitably, since at leading universities four-fifths of even assistant professors have published something. Because publication is almost a condition of the job at the quality level I institutions, we cannot expect much variation on our index here. As for the remaining two categories, the number in all three professorial ranks who are not publishing currently is very small at leading universities, while the number totally inactive is practically negligible. There are still substantial numbers of nonpublishing faculty in the nonprofessorial ranks, however, of whom nearly half are currently quite inactive—a further structural division of labor within the quality I institutions. On the other hand, when the leading universities are combined with weaker institutions (quality levels I to IV), the "inactive, not publishing" category is the largest single category for instructors and other ranks; and it is at least one-eighth for all but full

[27] The title "lecturer" means very different things at different ages and in different contexts. It is hard to generalize, but lecturers' collective position in research activity midway between the instructor and the professor ranks probably reflects the fact that they are found through the whole age distribution of academics and exhibit the characteristics of their age (and status) categories.

[28] A recent survey (1971) of department chairmen in 82 academic institutions (weighted to represent 218 institutions that grant Ph.D.'s in science and engineering) showed that a quarter of them believed that junior faculty members in their departments are getting "an inadequate share of research funds" (Jacobson, 1972, p. 3). The proportions varied from 39 percent in physics to 16 percent in chemistry.

[29] The mechanism that operates as "publish or perish" among nontenured ranks comes to function as "publish or flourish" among associate and full professors. See below, pp. 75–78.

professors. Even in elite research institutions, in other words, there are niches not only in particular subjects but in special, if underprivileged, ranks regardless of subject, where those who do no research are accommodated (at least temporarily).

Before leaving the topic of rank differences, it may be interesting to look at sections A and B of Table 2-10, the parallel tabulation for research orientation. We see in quality I (section A) that within both halves of the table (i.e., professorial and nonprofessorial ranks), there are little or no internal differences. Whatever it is that distinguishes full professors from assistants in research output—whether opportunity, energy, or expertise—it is clearly not different preferences. A distinction similar to that in activity can still be found between all professor ranks and the other grades; but it seems considerably weaker: whereas 25 percent of quality I instructors are inactive in research, only 13 percent have an "exclusively teaching" orientation—and similarly for the other junior grades.[30] This somewhat confirms our suspicions, voiced above, that the discrepancy between activity and orientation may be caused by constraints in job requirements; instructors may simply have no time for research they wish to do. We shall return to this question later.

Age

Tables 2-11 and 2-12 show research activity and orientation by age, in five-year intervals. The simplest explanation of these tables, which we shall follow, regards them as *changes* in disposition with increasing age, although the possibility of generational differences cannot entirely be ruled out on internal evidence.[31] We find (Table 2-11) that, in quality level I and in

---

[30] On the whole, the same generalizations hold true for section B, especially on the left-hand side (the professorial ranks); but the other ranks are a little more differentiated from each other.

[31] The general question of age difference in the values and behavior of academic men and women is explored elsewhere. It should be at least noted here that (as can be deduced from the raw numbers given as bases in Table 2-11) the expansion of higher education since the Second World War has vastly increased the proportion of academics in the younger age grades, and *may* have had the effect of reaching further down into the available "pool" and thus recruiting faculty with different attitudes from those of the earlier elite percentage. Standards of recruitment, however, have not been falling, as measured by the qualifications of new appointees (see Cartter, 1971), and to argue this point successfully, one would need to argue that Ph.D. standards have changed or at least that a different type of person now reaches the Ph.D.

TABLE 2-10 Research orientation by rank (percent; weighted totals in parentheses)

A. Quality level I

Orientation	Full professor	Associate professor	Assistant professor	Instructor	Lecturer	Other	All ranks
Exclusively teaching	4	5	5	13	11	15	7
Primarily teaching	24	26	24	39	34	40	27
(combined, braced)	28	31	29	52	46	55	34
Both teaching and research	41	36	35	31	30	30	36
Strongly research	32	33	37	17	25	15	30
	101%	100%	101%	100%	100%	100%	100%
	(18,138)	(9,933)	(13,858)	(4,524)	(3,601)	(2,293)	(52,972)

B. Quality levels I–IV

Orientation	Full professor	Associate professor	Assistant professor	Instructor	Lecturer	Other	All ranks
Exclusively teaching	9	10	10	21	18	15	11
Primarily teaching	33	37	35	45	41	35	36
(combined, braced)	42	47	45	66	60	50	48
Both teaching and research	36	31	31	24	23	29	31
Strongly research	22	22	25	10	17	20	21
	100%	100%	101%	100%	99%	99%	99%
	(64,445)	(52,258)	(64,384)	(25,414)	(8,325)	(5,274)	(221,020)

SOURCE: Quality I–IV, 27,000-case sample; quality I, all-respondents sample (N = 13,924).

TABLE 2-11 **Research activity by age (in percentages; weighted totals in parentheses)**

A. Quality level I

Research activity	25 or under	26–30	31–35	36–40	41–45	46–50	51–55	56–60	61 or over	All ages
Inactive, not currently publishing	48	11	7	6	7	8	9	11	13	9
Active, no recent publications	35	24	12	9	8	9	10	8	9	12
Few current publications	16 }17	51 }64	56 }81	55 }86	53 }85	49 }83	50 }81	52 }81	51 }78	51 }79
Many current publications	1	13	25	31	32	34	32	29	27	28
	100%	99%	100%	100%	100%	100%	100%	100%	100%	100%
	(1,252)	(6,430)	(9,754)	(9,359)	(7,737)	(6,351)	(4,834)	(3,902)	(4,135)	(54,189)

B. Quality levels I–IV

Research activity	25 or under	26–30	31–35	36–40	41–45	46–50	51–55	56–60	61 or over	All ages
Inactive, not currently publishing	51	19	12	10	12	14	20	19	28	16
Active, no recent publications	31	30	18	15	15	13	13	17	14	17
Few current publications	18 }19	41 }51	52 }70	54 }75	53 }73	52 }73	47 }67	44 }64	43 }58	49 }67
Many current publications	1	10	18	21	19	21	20	20	15	18
	100%	100%	100%	100%	100%	100%	100%	100%	100%	100%
	(3,405)	(27,364)	(39,313)	(37,569)	(34,119)	(29,361)	(19,578)	(14,313)	(16,831)	(222,821)

SOURCE: Quality I–IV, 27,000-case sample; quality I, all-respondents sample ($N = 13,924$).

TABLE 2-12 Research orientation by age (in percentages; weighted totals in parentheses)

	Age									
Orientation	*25 or under*	*26–30*	*31–35*	*36–40*	*41–45*	*46–50*	*51–55*	*56–60*	*61 or over*	*All ages*
A. Quality level I										
Exclusively teaching	14 ⎫52	6 ⎫30	4 ⎫25	4 ⎫26	6 ⎫33	5 ⎫35	8 ⎫41	10 ⎫43	10 ⎫46	7 ⎫34
Primarily teaching	38 ⎭	24 ⎭	21 ⎭	22 ⎭	27 ⎭	30 ⎭	34 ⎭	33 ⎭	36 ⎭	27 ⎭
Both teaching and research	29	32	37	39	35	38	35	40	34	36
Strongly research	20	38	38	35	33	27	24	17	20	30
	101%	100%	100%	100%	101%	100%	100%	100%	100%	100%
	(1,221)	(6,297)	(9,595)	(9,139)	(7,529)	(6,188)	(4,829)	(3,803)	(4,049)	(52,972)
B. Quality levels I–IV										
Exclusively teaching	21 ⎫59	11 ⎫44	7 ⎫38	8 ⎫42	11 ⎫46	11 ⎫51	14 ⎫56	15 ⎫60	19 ⎫63	11 ⎫48
Primarily teaching	37 ⎭	32 ⎭	31 ⎭	34 ⎭	35 ⎭	40 ⎭	43 ⎭	45 ⎭	45 ⎭	36 ⎭
Both teaching and research	27	32	34	33	32	31	31	28	25	31
Strongly research	14	24	29	25	22	18	13	12	12	21
	99%	99%	101%	100%	100%	100%	101%	100%	101%	99%
	(3,400)	(27,158)	(38,829)	(37,236)	(33,757)	(28,839)	(19,576)	(14,411)	(16,863)	(221,020)

SOURCE: Quality I–IV, 27,000-case sample; quality I, all-respondents sample (N = 13,924).

levels I to IV taken together, there is no substantial difference in publication rates by age after the age of 30, except for a slight drop for those over 60. In all "research" institutions[32] combined, though not appreciably in quality level I alone, the proportion of "inactives" who are not publishing begins to rise after age 50—from a low point of 10 percent for the 36-to-40 age group, to 20 percent for those between 51 and 60, to 28 percent for those over 60. A certain proportion of older academics, evidently, turn altogether away from research with increasing age. There was no corresponding decline from associate to full professors in the previous tables, and there is no evidence, therefore, to say whether they do so in satisfaction at their own success, in resignation to their relative failure, or what seems most likely, as a result of an increasing load of administrative responsibility. It is notable, however, that this phenomenon does not occur to any substantial extent in quality level I: whatever their preferences, older faculty in elite institutions continue to do research. In the leading universities, apparently, the research norm is so strong that older professors cannot retire gracefully into academic administration, even if they do a lot of it.

Curiously enough, however, we find something rather different when we turn to orientation (Table 2-12). In the case of rank, all three professor grades had virtually identical levels of preference for research, but the senior ranks outdid the junior in actual publication rates. With age, however, we find rather the reverse. Ignoring the extremes, all groups have much the same rate of activity, but, as we see here, the peak of interest (both in the ranking universities and overall) comes as early as the first half of the thirties—and thereafter there is a steady and slow decline: the percentage of "exclusive teachers" doubles and that of "strong researchers" halves between the ages of 31 to 35 and 56 to 60. There is evidently a fairly subtle interplay between rank and age in relation to orientation and activity:[33] academics' own interests and values seem to turn away from research and toward teaching with increasing age—and begin to do so fairly early in their careers; but they are not altered by promotion to higher rank. As to behavior, on the other hand, increasing rank brings

[32] We occasionally use this name to describe the institutions in quality levels I through IV: to be more accurate, we mean those institutions in the quality levels where most research is published.

[33] In a forthcoming paper on the relation of orientation and activity, we shall, of course, examine closely the effects of age and rank.

(or rewards and perpetuates) an increase in research output and increasing age does not substantially reduce it.[34]

In the previous section, we began to show (in preliminary form) the structural location of research and teaching activities. Apart from the topics that we have mentioned for future research, there are two possible areas for immediate investigation. First, to refine and elaborate on the structural location, that is, to describe the division of labor more fully. Table 2-8 shows how complex this quickly becomes, and it seems appropriate to leave it for the development of more refined combinations of subjects and for better measurement of contexts. Secondly, one might look at some of the correlates of involvement in research, and so explore, in different contexts, the mechanisms that support and perpetuate the division of labor. The rest of this paper addresses the latter topic—again, in a preliminary way: we have space here only to look at some of the correlates of varying degrees of research activity for individuals within the broadest possible context—institutional quality. But this will shed light both on the ways in which different institutions support and reward research activity and on the way in which research in turn has consequences for its practitioners and their departments and institutions.

RESEARCH IN RELATION TO OTHER ACTIVITIES In Table 2-13 we present a series of items from our questionnaire showing the frequency of certain specific academic activities for each of our four categories of research involvement. The same tabulation is given three times: first for high-quality universities alone; second, for the other "research" institutions; and third, for all institutions where research is an important activity—that is, quality levels I through IV.

We see first of all that highly active researchers are much more likely to be involved in the administrative processes of their department and their institution (section A, Table 2-13). For example, in leading (level I) universities, over half of the highly active researchers (who have many recent publications) spend more than 10 percent of their time on administration (row 1), compared with one-third of the "inactives." At lower-quality levels, too, the inactives are less likely to be involved, but the

---

[34] We do not directly show the combined effects of rank, quality, and age on publication, but we do present below tables showing the *effect* of research activity on promotion for different age groups.

difference is less sharp than at the leading schools; those publishing most are as likely to be doing administration as at level 1, but low activity is less of a disqualification. Interestingly enough, when we look at higher levels of administrative involvement, we find that the academics who spend more than 20 percent of their time on administration (row 2) are almost equally drawn from researchers and nonresearchers, whereas those who approach full-time administration (60 percent time or more (row 3) are drawn disproportionately from the inactive end of the scale (inevitably so, since they would scarcely have time to do research concurrently). To take one specific example of formal administrative activity, we find that at leading universities a frequent publisher is almost twice as likely to be or to have been head of the department as are inactives (row 4). In levels II through IV the difference is much reduced: in both cases about one-quarter of the most productive researchers have been or are department heads, but as before, the proportion of inactives is higher outside the leading universities. The other items on administrative activity all show a very similar pattern: active researchers are substantially more likely to describe themselves as much more active than average in their departments' affairs (row 5) and more active in their institutions' governmental process (row 6), and correspondingly less likely, especially in quality I, to call themselves much less active than average (row 7).

In all these tables, the level of administrative activity for those with a high publication rate is stable over different institution levels (at least I to IV). At the other extreme, those in elite institutions who are inactive in research tend also to be inactive in administration, whereas in lower-quality institutions, they are much more likely to be involved in administration. It seems likely that at the ranking research universities, research publication is almost a prerequisite for holding power in the institution; elsewhere, there may be other ways to reach positions of influence.[35] In other words, where research is almost the sole

[35] This conclusion is not strictly entailed by Table 2-13, which shows not how research publication *leads* to power, but how much those holding power are concurrently involved in research. A more minimal statement would be that at elite universities, some administrators continue to do research, whereas lower in the quality scale, research is less compatible with administration. In fact, however, the relation between administrative activity and publication over a lifetime is also much stronger at high-quality universities—which bears out our statement about roads to power.

	Quality level	Inactive, not currently publishing	Active, no recent publications
A. Administration			
Percentage who—			
(1) spend more than 10 percent time on administration	I II–IV	33 46 } 44	39 38 } 38
(2) spend more than 20 percent time on administration	I II–IV	21 30 } 29	18 20 } 19
(3) spend more than 60 percent time on administration	I II–IV	9 12 } 11	3 5 } 5
(4) are now or ever have been department chairman	I II–IV	14 21 } 20	11 16 } 16
(5) much more active than average in departmental affairs	I II–IV	17 25 } 24	22 26 } 25
(6) more active than average in institutional affairs	I II–IV	13 19 } 18	14 20 } 19
(7) much less active than average in institutional affairs	I II–IV	49 31 } 33	42 28 } 30
Totals (vary slightly): 100 percent = approx.[†]	I II–IV	(4,700) (30,300) } (35,000)	(6,200) (31,800) } (38,000)
B. Teaching			
Percentage who—			
(8) spend 4 hours or less in class per week	I II–IV	44 24 } 27	36 19 } 22
(9) teach under 25 students this term	I II–IV	37 21 } 23	37 17 } 20

TABLE 2-13
Correlates of research activity: quality level I and quality levels II to IV

ty

	Few current publications	Many current publications	Δ

$\left.\begin{array}{l}48 \\ 51\end{array}\right\}$ 50 $\left.\begin{array}{l}54 \\ 52\end{array}\right\}$ 53 $\left.\begin{array}{l}21 \\ 6\end{array}\right\}$ 9

$\left.\begin{array}{l}23 \\ 25\end{array}\right\}$ 25 $\left.\begin{array}{l}27 \\ 26\end{array}\right\}$ 26 $\left.\begin{array}{l}6 \\ -\end{array}\right\}$ —

$\left.\begin{array}{l}5 \\ 7\end{array}\right\}$ 6 $\left.\begin{array}{l}5 \\ 4\end{array}\right\}$ 5 $\left.\begin{array}{l}4 \\ 8\end{array}\right\}$ 6

$\left.\begin{array}{l}18 \\ 22\end{array}\right\}$ 21 $\left.\begin{array}{l}26 \\ 24\end{array}\right\}$ 25 $\left.\begin{array}{l}12 \\ 3\end{array}\right\}$ 5

$\left.\begin{array}{l}26 \\ 34\end{array}\right\}$ 32 $\left.\begin{array}{l}31 \\ 41\end{array}\right\}$ 37 $\left.\begin{array}{l}14 \\ 16\end{array}\right\}$ 13

$\left.\begin{array}{l}22 \\ 30\end{array}\right\}$ 28 $\left.\begin{array}{l}27 \\ 32\end{array}\right\}$ 30 $\left.\begin{array}{l}14 \\ 13\end{array}\right\}$ 12

$\left.\begin{array}{l}30 \\ 21\end{array}\right\}$ 23 $\left.\begin{array}{l}21 \\ 19\end{array}\right\}$ 20 $\left.\begin{array}{l}28 \\ 12\end{array}\right\}$ 13

$\left.\begin{array}{l}(26,600) \\ (81,400)\end{array}\right\}$ (108,000) $\left.\begin{array}{l}(14,600) \\ (24,900)\end{array}\right\}$ (39,500)

$\left.\begin{array}{l}44 \\ 31\end{array}\right\}$ 34 $\left.\begin{array}{l}53 \\ 44\end{array}\right\}$ 47 $\left.\begin{array}{l}9 \\ 20\end{array}\right\}$ 20

$\left.\begin{array}{l}38 \\ 27\end{array}\right\}$ 30 $\left.\begin{array}{l}46 \\ 37\end{array}\right\}$ 41 $\left.\begin{array}{l}9 \\ 16\end{array}\right\}$ 18

TABLE 2-13
(continued)

	Quality level	Inactive, not currently publishing	Active, no recent publications
(10) discourage undergraduates outside office hours	I II–IV	7⎫ 12⎭ 11	11⎫ 13⎭ 13
(11) see undergraduates informally 2 to 3 times a month or more	I II–IV	27⎫ 29⎭ 29	31⎫ 30⎭ 30
(12) teach graduate students only this year	I II–IV	24⎫ 11⎭ 12	24⎫ 8⎭ 10
(13) teach undergraduates only this year	I II–IV	47⎫ 64⎭ 61	38⎫ 48⎭ 47
Totals (vary slightly): 100 percent = approx.†	I II–IV	(4,700)⎫ (30,300)⎭ (35,000)	(6,200)⎫ (31,800)⎭ (38,000)

C. Research

Percentage who—

	Quality level	Inactive, not currently publishing	Active, no recent publications
(14) spend 4 hours uninterruptedly on professional reading, writing, or research once a week or more often	I II–IV	30⎫ 25⎭ 26	56⎫ 46⎭ 48
(15) have working association with a research center	I II–IV	10⎫ 9⎭ 9	20⎫ 15⎭ 16
(16) have graduate research assistants on a project	I II–IV	* *	19⎫ 17⎭ 17
(17) work with postdoctoral fellows	I II–IV	* *	5⎫ 2⎭ 2
(18) work with full-time professional researchers	I II–IV	* *	20⎫ 10⎭ 12

ity	Few current publications	Many current publications	Δ
	$\left.{12 \atop 14}\right\}$ 13	$\left.{13 \atop 12}\right\}$ 12	$\left.{6 \atop -}\right\}$ 1
	$\left.{27 \atop 26}\right\}$ 26	$\left.{23 \atop 24}\right\}$ 24	$\left.{4 \atop 5}\right\}$ 5
	$\left.{33 \atop 18}\right\}$ 22	$\left.{38 \atop 30}\right\}$ 33	$\left.{14 \atop 19}\right\}$ 21
	$\left.{13 \atop 25}\right\}$ 22	$\left.{6 \atop 13}\right\}$ 10	$\left.{41 \atop 51}\right\}$ 51
	$\left.{(26,600) \atop (81,400)}\right\}$ (108,000)	$\left.{(14,600) \atop (24,900)}\right\}$ (39,500)	
	$\left.{56 \atop 51}\right\}$ 52	$\left.{69 \atop 65}\right\}$ 67	$\left.{39 \atop 40}\right\}$ 41
	$\left.{29 \atop 28}\right\}$ 28	$\left.{42 \atop 39}\right\}$ 40	$\left.{32 \atop 30}\right\}$ 31
	$\left.{39 \atop 43}\right\}$ 42	$\left.{60 \atop 60}\right\}$ 60	$\left.{41 \atop 43}\right\}$ 43
	$\left.{13 \atop 6}\right\}$ 8	$\left.{38 \atop 25}\right\}$ 30	$\left.{33 \atop 23}\right\}$ 28
	$\left.{21 \atop 20}\right\}$ 20	$\left.{36 \atop 37}\right\}$ 37	$\left.{16 \atop 27}\right\}$ 25

TABLE 2-13
(continued)

	Quality level	Inactive, not currently publishing	Active, no recent publications
(19) have published any books	I II–IV	13⎫ 16⎭ 16	23⎫ 19⎭ 20
(20) have published more than 10 articles (ever)	I II–IV	4⎫ 2⎭ 3	7⎫ 4⎭ 5
(21) do some consulting	I II–IV	59⎫ 54⎭ 54	51⎫ 50⎭ 50
Totals (vary slightly): 100 percent = approx.†	I II–IV	(4,700)⎫ (30,300)⎭ (35,000)	(6,200)⎫ (31,800)⎭ (38,000)
D. Salary and tenure			
Percentage who—			
(22) earn over $20,000	I II–IV	7⎫ 5⎭ 6	7⎫ 3⎭ 4
(23) earned 10 percent or more above basic salary last year	I II–IV	45⎫ 42⎭ 42	43⎫ 46⎭ 46
(24) are full professors	I II–IV	15⎫ 18⎭ 17	14⎫ 15⎭ 15
(25) are tenured	I II–IV	32⎫ 46⎭ 44	27⎫ 38⎭ 36
Totals (vary slightly): 100 percent = approx.†	I II–IV	(4,700)⎫ (30,300)⎭ (35,000)	(6,200)⎫ (31,800)⎭ (38,000)

*Excluded in questionnaire.

†Weighted totals: totals vary slightly from one question to another.

SOURCE: 27,000-case sample.

criterion of academic status (i.e. in quality level I institutions), the status gained through research is transformed into, and legitimates, researchers' power in the institution—whether in departmental chairmanships, committee memberships, or higher administrative positions. But there is more to consider than access to power, for our findings clearly conflict with the conventional view of a researcher as isolated in a study, or at a laboratory bench. Despite demands on their time that are surely

vity

	Few current publications	Many current publications	Δ
	51 / 45 } 47	67 / 60 } 63	52 / 44 } 47
	35 / 28 } 30	81 / 76 } 78	77 / 74 } 75
	63 / 59 } 60	77 / 73 } 74	18 / 19 } 20
	(26,600) / (81,400) } (108,000)	(14,600) / (24,900) } (39,500)	
	20 / 11 } 14	40 / 28 } 33	33 / 23 } 27
	57 / 54 } 55	69 / 60 } 63	24 / 18 } 21
	33 / 31 } 31	52 / 46 } 48	37 / 28 } 31
	48 / 56 } 54	66 / 68 } 67	34 / 22 } 23
	(26,600) / (81,400) } (108,000)	(14,600) / (24,900) } (39,500)	

at least as hard to meet as those made by heavy teaching loads, many of even the most active researchers still shoulder an administrative burden—and there is no question that, whatever power it brings with it, administration is frequently burdensome and a potential distraction from research activity.

In section B of Table 2-13, we find that, in the leading universities at least, there is surprisingly little difference between researchers and nonresearchers in their level of teaching activity.

Over half of the most frequent publishers at quality level I spend less than four hours in class in the spring term of 1969 (row 8), but the same is true of more than two-fifths of the inactives;[36] while as to the number of students they teach, the difference (Δ) between the extremes of the typology is just nine percentage points (row 9). When we look at the other institutions, however, the differences are considerably greater ($\Delta = 20, 16$): the frequent publishers in the weaker institutions do a little more teaching than at leading universities, but the nonpublishers do much more. Moreover, researchers are not much more likely to discourage undergraduates from seeing them outside office hours (row 10); and scarcely less likely to see undergraduates informally (row 11). There is a marked difference in teaching patterns, however: the most frequent publishers (especially in the weaker universities) are more likely to teach graduate students and much less likely to teach only undergraduates.

Section B complements section A in demonstrating a particularly significant difference between high-quality universities and other universities. In the others there is, apparently, a separation between research and other roles, whereby those who are not involved in research are much more likely to be teaching and relatively more likely to be administrators; but at elite institutions, the researchers are also the administrators, and are hardly less likely to be teachers than nonresearchers. Even the separation of graduate and undergraduate teaching is more strongly related to research activity at the lower-quality institutions than at the elite universities. We have already noted, when discussing the effect of teaching hours on research orientation, that there is a difference between quality levels IV and V, in that below the elite four-year colleges research seems to be a spare-time activity, whereas above this point it is recognized and fostered by the institution. But we now find a further distinction: below quality I institutions, research and teaching are distinct and alternative activities, carried out by different academics in different balancing time allocations. At the highest level, however, they are no longer separate activities; those who do more of one thing do more, or as much, of other things. This is a principle captured, in the leading universities, by the saying, "If you want something

---

[36] Some of the "inactives," as we saw above, are those with very high administrative loads.

done promptly, ask the busiest person to do it." And the busiest person is usually a highly active researcher. It seems broadly true that the principle "the more, the more," holds in academic life as elsewhere. There is surely a factor of simple energy level that allows people who are active in one area to be active in other areas, too, beyond the average. But it is also a matter of how people organize their time—or have it organized for them. For example (row 14, Table 2-13) there are huge differences in the amount of undisturbed time available for private work.

Those with higher levels of research activity are more likely also to be working with graduate research assistants (row 16), with postdoctoral fellows (row 17), and, though to a lesser extent, with full-time professional researchers (row 18)—and to be associated with research institutes or centers in their institutions (row 15). When we look at their publication of books and articles (rows 19 and 20) throughout their careers, we find predictably strong relations with current activity and current publication rates. Current publication (that is, within the last two years) relates especially strongly to past article publication (only a few who have not published recently, whether inactive or active, have published more than 10 articles during their career): the relation to book publication, though weaker, is still one of the strongest in these tables. Lastly, section C of Table 2-13 shows that the relation between publication and consulting activity (row 21) is relatively small: in quality I universities we find that even three-fifths of the totally inactive devote some of their time to consulting.[37]

Finally, section D shows that salaries vary quite sharply by research activity both at quality I universities and overall: over five times as many frequent publishers as inactives earn more than $20,000 per year (row 22); and twice as many frequent publishers do so than do less-frequent publishers. Whether or not the "publish or perish" mechanism operates, "publish and flourish" clearly does. There is no question that publication sharply enhances an academic's chances of high salary, and also of earnings outside the university (row 23), whether they be royalties or consulting fees. It is possible, however, that this simple relation conceals a more subtle one between publications

---

[37] In a later essay, where we examine disciplinary differences, we shall look more closely at rates of publication and of consulting differentially by field.

and promotion to higher ranks, on the one hand, and between rank and salary on the other, since it is clear (rows 24 and 25) and we have already seen in reverse (Table 2-9) that there is a strong positive relation between current publication and attaining one of the professorial ranks (especially a full professorship).

RESEARCH ACTIVITY AND THE STRUCTURE OF REWARDS

In order to examine this matter of academic rewards more fully, we show in Table 2-14 the proportions of full professors and of tenured faculty, by age as well as by research activity, for quality I (section A) and quality levels I to IV (section B); and in Table 2-15, we show the proportion who earn especially high salaries by rank and research activity simultaneously. Looking first at the rank distribution by age for quality I (section A, Table 2-15), we see that research activity makes an enormous difference to one's prospects for either full professorship or tenure. For example, of the inactive unpublished group, only three age groups have more than half of their members tenured—namely, the over-50 groups; and no age group has more than half of its members full professors. In the active but unpublished group, the majority of those over 55 are full professors, and the majority of those over 45 have tenure. In the next column—few publications—the majority of those over 45 are full professors, and the majority of those over 40 have tenure. In the high-publication group, a majority of those over 40 are full professors, and a majority of all age groups over 35 have tenure. Put slightly differently, for almost every age group over 35, those who have high publication rates in the last two years are several times (at a minimum, $2^{1}/_{2}$ times) more likely to be professors than those who are inactive and unpublished. Or from yet another perspective, a higher proportion of active researchers are tenured at age 35 to 39 than are inactive men or women 20 years older. This is indeed a visible reward for research. Turning now to section B, we see that the same relation holds, though it is somewhat muted; for while high publication continues to increase the chances of early promotion, especially to full professorship, low publication, or none, does not diminish an academic's chances of tenure to the same extent as in the elite institutions alone. We see once again that researchers in elite institutions visibly constitute the leading cadre, whereas lower in the quality scale they are not so sharply distinguished from their less-productive colleagues.

Table 15 shows how salary is affected by research activity,

TABLE 2-14 *Percentage of full professors and percentage tenured* by age and research activity (base totals omitted[†]).*

Age	Research activity				
	Inactive, not currently publishing	Active, no recent publications	Few current publications	Many current publications	All
	A. Quality level I				
60 or over	48 [78]	64 [77]	87 [91]	93 [91]	85 [85]
55–59	29 [53]	59 [72]	74 [81]	93 [92]	77 [82]
50–54	35 [51]	40 [57]	66 [80]	87 [89]	63 [75]
45–49	25 [42]	32 [54]	58 [72]	80 [84]	56 [68]
40–44	10 [35]	16 [40]	39 [65]	65 [79]	42 [66]
35–39	4 [22]	1 [18]	16 [44]	28 [62]	16 [44]
30–34	1 [10]	1 [7]	3 [20]	7 [32]	3 [20]
25–29	0 [5]	1 [3]	1 [3]	0 [10]	0 [4]
Under 25	0 [4]	0 [10]	0 [2]	— [—][‡]	0 [4]
All ages	15 [32]	14 [27]	33 [48]	52 [66]	34 [49]
	B. Quality levels I–IV				
60 or over	48 [78]	71 [87]	81 [90]	92 [88]	71 [85]
55–59	35 [75]	51 [81]	71 [86]	91 [91]	64 [83]
50–54	37 [70]	39 [68]	64 [83]	80 [88]	58 [79]
45–49	19 [63]	29 [70]	53 [73]	73 [88]	49 [74]
40–44	14 [49]	11 [47]	36 [70]	59 [79]	34 [66]
35–39	2 [30]	4 [31]	14 [52]	27 [65]	14 [49]
30–34	0 [13]	0 [11]	2 [23]	7 [33]	2 [21]
25–29	0 [7]	0 [4]	0 [5]	0 [15]	0 [6]
Under 25	0 [9]	0 [10]	3 [3]	— [—][‡]	0 [7]
All ages	17 [44]	15 [36]	31 [54]	48 [67]	29 [52]

*Percentage tenured shown in brackets.

[†] The smallest unweighted base total (except for the two cells omitted) is 35 (quality levels I to IV, under 25, few current publications).

[‡] Base totals too small for reliability.

SOURCE: Quality levels I to IV, 27,000-case sample; quality level I, all-respondents sample ($N = 13,924$).

within specified academic ranks. Once again (compare section D of Table 2-13, row 22), high publication leads to a much greater chance of high salary. In the leading universities, nearly two-thirds of full professors who are active researchers earned $20,000 a year at the time of the survey, as compared with fewer

TABLE 2-15 *Percentage who earned over $20,000 and over $17,000* by rank and research activity (base totals omitted†)*

Rank	Inactive, not currently publishing	Active, no recent publications	Few current publications	Many current publications	All
			Research activity		
	A. Quality level I				
Professor	23 [55]	31 [65]	51 [77]	63 [86]	55 [79]
Associate professor	1 [6]	9 [20]	10 [21]	19 [30]	12 [21]
Assistant professor	5 [7]	3 [5]	5 [11]	8 [16]	6 [13]
All ranks	7 [11]	7 [15]	20 [34]	40 [56]	23 [36]
	B. Quality levels I–IV				
Professor	23 [45]	18 [45]	35 [64]	55 [81]	38 [65]
Associate professor	5 [8]	2 [8]	7 [17]	14 [26]	7 [16]
Assistant professor	1 [4]	1 [3]	2 [5]	10 [17]	3 [6]
All ranks	6 [11]	4 [10]	14 [26]	33 [51]	14 [25]

*Proportions earning over $17,000 shown in brackets.

† The smallest unweighted base total is 158 (quality level I, full professor, inactive not currently publishing).

SOURCE: Quality levels I to IV, 27,000-case sample; quality level I, all-respondents sample (N = 13,924).

than a quarter of the inactive full professors and fewer than a third of those actively doing research who had not recently published. As before, the relation of research activities to salary is stronger than in all research institutions combined; but even looking at the wider spectrum of institutions, the relation is very strong: for example, if we look at full professors in quality I to IV institutions (section B of Table 2-15), we see that about one-quarter of the inactive earned over $20,000 per year (in 1969) and two-fifths earned over $17,000 per year; whereas, of full professors with high publication rates, the corresponding proportions are one-half and four-fifths. In general, there can be no question but that it is research that is rewarded by the salary and promotion structures of universities, especially high-quality ones.

CONCLUSION   In this preliminary paper we have begun to map the distribution of research activities in American colleges and universities. Rather than summarize all our findings in detail, we might recall one theme in our introduction: the division of labor, or of functions, between and within the institutions of American higher education.

One finding that bears on that theme is the relatively high level of research activity in the high-quality four-year colleges. Without much graduate work or many postdoctoral students, or the array of research centers and facilities that mark the full-fledged university, these colleges show levels of research activity by their regular staff that in sheer rate of publication are close to those of the lesser universities, and markedly higher than those of the great majority of four- and two-year colleges. In these elite liberal arts colleges, undergraduates are likely to have contact with men and women who, as we see in our data, are themselves carrying on research and are familiar with and teaching within the research currents of their disciplines. These academics, by virtue of their continuing research activity, are raising the same kinds of questions, reading the same research and scholarly literature, as are those in the leading graduate departments.[38]

If there is a division of labor between "teaching" and "research" institutions, there is also another kind that is found among the institutions where research is done. Here we find a difference between the higher-quality universities and the weaker universities and leading four-year colleges. In the former, nearly all regular faculty members are engaged in research activity of some kind and intensity. Where 70 and 80 percent of all staff are currently publishing, the division of labor between research and other functions of higher education is a division of the time and energy of individual academic men and women. The conflicts generated by that division of labor are resolved within the men and women who teach, do research and consulting, and also administer those institutions. We find then, in broad terms, that there is no marked subordination of one function to another: those who are most active in research also teach nearly as much as those less active in research, and they do a good deal more departmental and university administration.

[38] In further analysis, we shall look more closely at the training and recruitment of the teachers who remain actively engaged in research in these undergraduate colleges. Conversely, we shall also look at the large number of undergraduate colleges where little research is done, to examine the educational and career patterns of their faculty, and to see whether their conceptions of higher education in their own disciplines are similar to or markedly different from those that dominate the research-oriented universities. We suspect the latter, and if that is so, then we can begin to talk about a major "fault line" within American higher education, below which what is taught, and how, may more closely resemble "postsecondary education" than it does the higher education of the universities and elite liberal arts colleges.

Some do more than others, but it is more of everything, and the principle obtains, "the more, the more." By contrast, in the weaker universities and in the better colleges there is a division of labor within the faculty, between those who do research and those who do not. Our guess is that the former set the norms and values for all and thus influence the climate of teaching as well as of learning throughout those institutions. Nevertheless, it is possible in those colleges and universities to have an honorable and dignified place—that is to gain tenure and become a full professor—without actively carrying on research.

We are suggesting that in the leading (and doubtless some medium-quality) universities, the academic role includes the expectation of continuing research activity; in weaker universities and strong colleges there is the expectation (and acceptance) that the role may or may not include active research work; while in the middle-level and other colleges, research is not a normal expectation of the academic role.

But we can qualify that general statement, especially for the higher-quality universities, by pointing to certain kinds of teachers and certain parts of the institutions where the expectation of continuing research activity is not so strong. One exception to the general expectation of research activity can be found in certain creative and performing arts departments—for example, music, drama, painting and sculpture, and creative writing. These are ordinarily included under the broad subject area of "fine arts." In the universities (as we saw in Table 2-8), the proportion in that category who are publishing is distinctly lower than in the central academic departments. Similarly, in education and in the new and semiprofessional fields such as social welfare, a proportion of regular teaching faculty are primarily practitioners, for whom there are not the same expectations of publication.

Those marginal teachers who hold nonprofessorial appointments—instructors, lecturers, and "other" ranks—are another, and certainly more significant exception to the norm of research activity in the leading and middle-level universities. (The most important body of university teachers who are not part of the core academic staff—the teaching assistants—are not included in our sample, since they are for the most part graduate students.) Nevertheless, here is clear evidence of a division of labor *within* the leading universities: there is a group of men and women comprising about 20 percent of all academic personnel in quality I institutions, leaving TAs aside, who are nearly twice as likely as those with professorial ranks to be orientated primarily or exclusively to teaching (section A, Table 2-10) and whose rates of research activity are also much lower than those of career-grade academics in the same institutions (see section A, Table 2-9).

In the leading universities, with their strong research orientations, there are certain strains created even by the performers and practitioners whose creative work clearly has to be assessed by other than the "normal" criteria of research or scholarly productivity. "How does one judge them?" is a common plaintive question—and the difficulty of answering that question accounts in part for the long and continuing resistance in the leading universities to appointing any large number of performers and practitioners to regular academic ranks.[39]

But the strains and problems associated with the nonacademic ranks in all departments are surely greater. These men and women (and they are disproportionately women)[40] are, in the leading universities, truly marginal, with all the difficulties of those whose membership in a group or institution is partial and insecure. We shall in due course look more closely at some of the characteristics of those who occupy these "noncareer" grades in the leading and middle-level universities, and we shall show that their difficulties are the greater where the norm of continuing research activity is strongest and most encompassing. For the moment, however, it is clear that they (along with the marginal subjects) do in fact provide for a division of labor among academic functions within the leading universities, where the norm of the comprehensive academic role is strongest.

This essay has opened up a number of issues for further analysis. It will be enough here to mention three by way of illustration.

First, we shall want to see how the academic division of labor

---

[39] Our data show that these marginal departments also employ much higher proportions of marginal ranks.

[40] In all levels of universities, the proportion of women in nonprofessorial ranks (instructor, lecturer, etc.) is more than twice as high as their representation in the professorial ranks (indeed, at the leading universities it is three times as high); while in four- and two-year colleges it is roughly one-and-a-half times as high. In all institutions in our sample, 15 percent of those in professorial ranks are women, compared with 31 percent in nonprofessorial ranks. (See Chapter 6.)

within and between institutions is linked to patterns of social and academic recruitment to different parts of the academic system. What kinds of people are more likely to pursue a continuing research career, and how do their undergraduate and graduate careers equip them for and steer them into parts of the system where their research orientations are rewarded, tolerated, or discouraged? What links are there between social origins, formal education, and academic careers, and do these links shed further light on the broad functional connections between higher education and the larger society?

Second, we shall look further at the relation between research orientations and research activity, and especially at the large number of academic men and women whose attitudes and behaviors are apparently in contradiction. Are there substantial numbers of "reluctant researchers" who are required by the nature of their appointments and the reward structures of their institutions to do research when they would rather be doing less or none (and presumably more of something else, especially teaching)? What evidence is there for a widespread doctrine of "publish or perish" that, it is charged, coerces so many reluctant researchers into doing bad research, neglecting their teaching, and resenting their jobs and institutions? Conversely, are there large numbers of "frustrated researchers," strongly interested in research but unable, in their circumstances—in marginal or subordinate statuses, or in institutions that provide no time, resources, or rewards for research—to do the research work they want to do? (For example, the youngest age groups in Tables 2-11 and 2-12, who show strong research orientations but relatively low rates of publication, may fall into this category.) These are questions that may have implications for educational policy as well as for organizational role theory.

Third, and this is almost implied in the foregoing, we shall explore in much greater depth the differences in attitudes and perspectives between academics who do and do not carry on research. As we have suggested, we may find marked differences in their conceptions of higher education, of teaching and learning, of academic freedom, of innovation, and of college and university governance. Indeed, we may find that they differ in their attitude toward issues apparently far removed from academic life—for example, broad social and political issues. In our efforts to map the terrain and explore the dynamics of American higher education, the study of the division of academic labor, in the first instance through a detailed analysis of the people and institutions who perform the research function, will take us much further down these and related analytical paths.

References

Ashby, Eric: *Any Person, Any Study,* McGraw-Hill Book Company, New York, 1971.

Ben-David, Joseph: *American Higher Education: Directions Old and New,* McGraw-Hill Book Company, New York, 1971.

Fulton, Oliver, and Martin Trow: "Research Activity in American Higher Education," Center for Research in the Educational Sciences, University of Edinburgh, Edinburgh, Scotland, April 1972. (Mimeographed.)

Cartter, Allan M.: *An Assessment of Quality in Graduate Education,* American Council on Education, Washington, 1966.

Cartter, Allan M.: "Scientific Manpower for 1970–1985," *Science,* vol. 172, Apr. 9, 1971, pp. 132–140.

Hagstrom, Warren O.: "Inputs, Outputs, and the Prestige of University Science Departments," *Sociology of Education,* vol. 44, no. 4, 1971, pp. 375–397.

Halsey, A. H., and Martin Trow: *The British Academics,* Faber & Faber, Ltd., London, 1971.

Jacobson, Robert L.: "Inadequate Share of Science Research Funds Found Going to Junior Faculty Members," *Chronicle of Higher Education,* vol. 6, no. 16, Jan. 24, 1972, p. 3.

Parsons, Talcott, and Gerald Platt: "Considerations on the American Academic System," *Minerva,* vol. 6, Summer 1968a, pp. 497–523.

Parsons, Talcott, and Gerald Platt: *The American Academic Profession: A Pilot Study,* National Science Foundation, Washington, 1968b.

"Public Funds for Private Colleges Voted by More States in 1971," *Chronicle of Higher Education,* vol. 6, no. 13, Jan. 3, 1972, pp. 1, 4.

3. Religious Involvement and Scholarly Productivity among American Academics

by Stephen Steinberg

INTRODUCTION Two different views of the relation between religion and science have been prominent in the sociological tradition. The first stresses areas of compatibility between the ethos of certain religious groups and the requirements of science. The second argues that there is an essential incompatibility between religious and scientific perspectives. That both views are grounded in solid empirical evidence should indicate that the contradictions are more apparent than real. Indeed, a closer examination of these two views will suggest a basis for their reconciliation.

In his essay "Puritanism, Pietism, and Science," Robert Merton (1963) examines elements of early Protestantism that were favorable to the development of science. Like Weber, Merton focuses on value orientations embodied in seventeenth-century Puritanism in England and America, and Pietism in Germany. Unlike traditional Catholicism, these sects exalted reason, chiefly as a means for controlling the passions, and encouraged participation in worldly affairs. These orientations were compatible with basic attributes of science, especially its rational empiricism and its utilitarianism. In fact, the link between religious ideology and science was frequently direct. Early Puritans specifically sanctioned the empirical study of nature. Instead of fearing that science would undermine faith, they viewed it as a means for understanding the wonders of God's creation and for exercising control over a corrupt world. In

NOTE: Adapted from *The Academic Melting Pot: Catholics and Jews in American Higher Education*, McGraw-Hill Book Company, New York, 1974.

addition, Protestant injunctions concerning the virtue of discipline, methodic labor, and constant diligence in one's calling produced in individuals a temperament and disposition that encouraged the pursuit of science.

Like Weber, Merton is careful not to make unlimited claims about the historical significance of the Protestant ethic. Although this ethic was a radical departure from traditional Catholicism and became a historical force in its own right, it was also a product of social trends and ideological currents of the seventeenth century. At best, the Protestant ethic was only one element in the evolution of science. Its main contribution, according to Merton, was that it canonized the essential elements of the scientific spirit. In doing so, it "made an empirically-founded science commendable rather than, as in the medieval period, reprehensible or at best acceptable on sufferance" (Merton, 1963, p. 579).

Merton bolsters his thesis with evidence showing that Protestants in late nineteenth-century Germany and Austria were far more likely than Catholics to pursue scientific and technical studies. From a historical standpoint, there was an essential compatibility between ascetic Protestantism and science.

A second tradition in sociology regards religion and science as fundamentally in conflict. In the spirit of the Enlightenment, Auguste Comte regarded Christianity as an outmoded system of beliefs that was destined to be replaced by Positivism, a kind of secular religion that would be faithful to the rational tenets of science. Freud advanced the positivist tradition one step further. In his view (1962) religion resembled an infantile neurosis by creating the comforting illusion of an all-powerful and benevolent father. Just as the reality principle was the psychological ideal for the individual, Freud believed that a sophisticated civilization would reject all religious conceptions that evolved from man's individual and collective infancy. The hallmark of the positivist view is that it sees religion as essentially a relic from the past ultimately to be replaced by the secular ideologies of a scientific age.

Emile Durkheim (1958) was less confident of the outcome of the historic struggle between religion and science. He believed that the integrative functions of religion, both as symbol and as ritual, were too essential to the social fabric to be so easily negated. Durkheim would not deny that the individualism and free thought characteristic of Protestantism served the needs of science or any rational discipline. But he argued that such attributes were destructive of the social bond, and he found proof of this in the high rate of egoistic suicide among Protestants. Implicit in this analysis is a subtle view of the relation between religion and science: Protestantism may have given rise to science, but in the end science would turn its back on all religion.

Evidence supporting the incompatibility thesis is found in empirical studies of religious patterns in higher education. Prominent among these is Charles Y. Glock and Rodney Stark's analysis of data based on a 1963 sample of the nation's graduate students (1965, chap. 14). Their findings showed that the rate of apostasy in the student population far exceeded the rate for the population at large. Whereas surveys report that only 3 to 5 percent of American adults claim no religious affiliation, the figure for graduate students was 26 percent. Apostasy was even more common in the higher-ranking colleges and universities. Finally, the data showed that students with more developed scholarly interests were far less likely to have strong religious commitments. Glock and Stark's conclusion was that "religion and scholarship tend to be mutually exclusive perspectives" (1965, p. 283). Another investigator analyzing the same data suggested that in the intellectual community the canons of science and rational inquiry became a functional alternative for religion (Zelan, 1968).

One obvious difference between these two views of the relation between religion and science is that one is historical, the other contemporary. It is possible that in the seventeenth century Protestantism was conducive to science but is no longer so today. Writers frequently fail to distinguish between factors that account for the origin of a phenomenon and those that account for its perpetuation at a later point in time. Even if the scientific spirit originally sprung from certain religious values, clearly in modern society science has been removed from a religious context. As Weber wrote with respect to the religious foundations of capitalism, "Today the spirit of religious asceticism. . .has escaped from the cage. But victorious capitalism, since it rests on mechanical foundations, needs its support no longer" (Weber, 1955, pp. 181–182).

There is a still more important difference between the two views discussed above. Merton's observations concern an affinity between the religious *ethos* and certain aspects of science, whereas the contemporary studies demonstrating an incompatibility between religion and science are based on *individual* data. For this reason the two sets of findings are not necessarily in contradiction. Even if the Protestant ethic was (or is) conducive to science, it does not necessarily follow that those Protestants with deepest religious commitments will be the ones most apt to act out their secular implications. On the contrary, one suspects that even in the seventeenth century it was not the most deeply involved Puritans but their less pious coreligionists who entered the ranks of science.

There is nothing in Merton's study to either confirm or disconfirm such an interpretation. Merton at one point weighs the difference between group data and individual data, "Of course, the mere fact that an individual is nominally a Catholic or a Protestant has no bearing upon his attitude toward science. It is only as he adopts the tenets and implications of the teachings that his religious affiliation becomes significant" (Merton, 1963, p. 587). Merton, however, has no data on the religious beliefs of early scientists. His conclusions are based on data showing that Protestants were more likely than Catholics to enter programs in science. But there is nothing to indicate that it was the more religiously involved Protestants who did so.

In their study of the *Origins of American Scientists,* R. H. Knapp and H. B. Goodrich (1952, p. 275) speculate that what was significant about the Protestant ethic was not its religious qualities but rather its secularism. They write:

Protestantism has been more prone to secularization than Catholicism, and secularization of values permits the development of science. According to this view, Protestant groups and Protestant institutions have produced more scientists because Protestants have more readily abandoned their fundamentalist religious outlook and thus have been freer to accept the tenets of scientific philosophy. But it does not necessarily follow that the doctrines of Protestantism as such are more compatible with science than the doctrines of Catholicism.

If this assumption is correct, and it is the secular tendencies within Protestantism that are the basis of its compatibility with science, then one would expect the scientific spirit to be more often found among Protestants who were marginally religious than among their more devout coreligionists.

In short, the two theories of the relation between religion and science are not in fundamental conflict. The compatibility thesis may be correct in stressing an affinity between certain religious values and the scientific spirit, and the role that these values played in the historical development of science. And the incompatibility thesis may be correct in its claim that on an individual level religious involvement tends to be inimical to science and other scholarly concerns.

This paper is primarily concerned with testing the second of these theoretical positions. The focus is on the individual, particularly the relation between his religious commitments and scholarly orientations. The data are drawn from the faculty survey of the 1969 Carnegie Commission Survey of Faculty and Student Opinion, and the analysis is divided into two parts. The first assesses the nature and extent of religious commitment among faculty, taking into account institutional quality and academic discipline. The second part analyzes the consequences of religious commitment for scholarly orientations and research productivity.

THE RELIGIOUS COMMITMENTS OF AMERICAN SCHOLARS
Table 3-1 reports the distribution of responses to four questions in the faculty survey pertaining to religious commitment. The first was worded as follows: "I think of myself as (1) deeply religious, (2) moderately religious, (3) indifferent to religion, (4) opposed to religion." In the sample as a whole only 8 percent placed themselves in the extreme category of being opposed to religion; another 28 percent said they were indifferent to religion. On the other hand, 48 percent indicated they were moderately religious, and 16 percent said deeply religious. Depending upon the standard of comparison used, one could either emphasize that two-thirds of all faculty appear to have conventional religious attachments, or that one-third lack even minimal religious ties. The more important point, however, is that these proportions vary systematically with such factors as institutional quality, academic discipline, and age, as will presently be seen.

The responses of Protestants and Catholics are notably similar. The proportion saying they are indifferent or opposed to religion is 32 percent for Protestants and 25 percent for Catholics. In sharp contrast, the figure for Jewish faculty is twice as great—67 percent. This is a large difference that could have far-reaching implications if the incompatibility theory of the

TABLE 3-1
Religious
commitment by
religious
background

Questions on religious commitment	Religious background			
	Protestants	*Catholics*	*Jews*	*Total**
I consider myself:				
Deeply religious	16%	23%	5%	16%
Moderately religious	52	52	28	48
Indifferent to religion	26	19	50	28
Opposed to religion	6	6	17	8
Would you describe yourself as conservative in your religious beliefs?				
Yes	43	42	19	40
Church attendance:				
Once a week	33	62	5	25
Once a month	49	67	10	48
Present affiliation:				
None	20	19	26	22

*Includes those whose religious background was "other" or "none."

SOURCE: 1969 Carnegie Commission Survey of Faculty and Student Opinion. Unless otherwise noted, this is the source for all the tables and figures in this chapter.

relation between religious commitment and scholarship should prove correct.

Even a person who characterizes himself as "deeply religious" does not necessarily adhere to traditional tenets of faith. Thus, a second question asked respondents whether or not they were conservative in their religious beliefs. Again, Protestants and Catholics responded similarly: 43 percent of the former and 42 percent of the latter said their religious beliefs were generally conservative. The figure for Jews is just 19 percent.

A third question inquired into the frequency of church attendance. On this item Protestants and Catholics were quite different. Among Catholic faculty, 62 percent attend church once a week, compared with 33 percent of Protestants and just 5 percent of Jews. The comparatively high rate of church attendance among Catholics is customarily taken as a sign of Catholic piety. However, as we have just seen, Catholic faculty are only slightly more likely than Protestants to see themselves as deeply or moderately religious, or as conservative in their religious beliefs. In other words, the greater church attendance of Catholic faculty may not involve greater religious conviction.

After being queried about the religion in which they were raised, respondents were asked about their present religious affiliation. Twenty-two percent of all faculty indicated "none." This, of course, far exceeds the level of nonaffiliation in the general population. Most national surveys report that the proportion claiming no religion is approximately 5 percent.

The proportion of faculty claiming no current affiliation is virtually the same for Catholics (19 percent) as for Protestants (20 percent), and is only slightly higher for Jews (26 percent). Thus, although 67 percent of Jewish faculty indicate they are indifferent or opposed to religion, only 26 percent go so far as to deny any current religious identification. Put another way, among Jewish faculty who said they were indifferent or opposed to religion, only 39 percent do not still identify as Jews. Clearly this reflects the ethnic character of Judaism, and the tendency of Jews to identify as a people as well as a religion.

In contrast, among Protestants and Catholics, loss of faith more often involves a total rejection of religious labels. Thus, among Protestants who said they were indifferent or opposed to religion, 59 percent reported no current affiliation; the comparable figure for Catholics is 63 percent.

The above four measures tap different dimensions of religious commitment and form the basis for constructing a typology that will facilitate more intensive analysis. The pivotal distinction is between those who are deeply or moderately religious and those who are indifferent or opposed to religion. Among the first group we can further distinguish between those whose religious beliefs are conservative and those whose religious beliefs are more liberal. The second group—those indifferent or opposed to religion—can also be divided between those who retain a nominal religious affiliation and those who renounce all religious ties. Cross-classifying these three items produces eight types, as shown in Figure 3-1.

Because of a high consistency of responses, 94 percent of the sample are located in just four cells, each of which represents a conceptually distinct type:

- *Traditionalists* Those who have a current religious affiliation and indicate that they are both deeply or moderately religious and conservative

FIGURE 3-1
Faculty religious affiliation

Current religious affiliation?

		Yes	No
Deeply or moderately religious	*Conservative*	Traditionalists	Near-zero cell
	Not conservative	Modernists	Near-zero cell
Indifferent or opposed to religion	*Conservative*	Near-zero cell	Near-zero cell
	Not conservative	Ethnics	Dropouts

in their religious beliefs. As Table 3-2 shows, 42 percent of both Protestants and Catholics meet all three criteria of religious involvement. In contrast, only 15 percent of Jews do so.

- *Modernists* Like the traditionalists, modernists hold a nominal affiliation and are intensely or moderately religious, but they do not describe their religious beliefs as conservative. This combination of responses is characteristic of 29 percent of Protestants, 36 percent of Catholics, and 18 percent of Jews.

- *Ethnics* Those who say they are indifferent or opposed to religion, and unconservative in their religious beliefs, but who retain a nominal religious identity. This response pattern is practically unique to Jews. Among Jewish faculty, 40 percent score as ethnics, compared with just 11 percent of Protestants and 6 percent of Catholics.

- *Dropouts* Those who give nonreligious responses to all three questions. Unlike the ethnics, they renounce even nominal religious ties. Among faculty as a whole, 21 percent fall into this category. The proportion is highest among those raised as Jews—27 percent. In the case of Protestants it is 18 percent; in the case of Catholics, 16 percent.

From past research it can be expected that traditionalists and dropouts will be quite different in terms of such variables as academic achievement and political conservatism. Far less certain is how modernists and ethnics will appear. Will modernists resemble the traditionalists, since they share with them strong ties to religion? Or will the fact that their religious beliefs are not of a conservative kind mitigate or neutralize the effect of religious involvement? Similarly, will Jews classified as ethnics be closer to traditionalists or to dropouts in terms of their secular behavior? These questions are addressed presently. The analysis immediately following explores variations in religious commitment by institutional quality and academic discipline. For purposes of this analysis it is convenient to combine ethnics and

TABLE 3-2		Ranking universities			All institutions		
Religiosity	Religiosity	Protestants	Catholics	Jews	Protestants	Catholics	Jews
Traditionalists		26%	33%	13%	42%	42%	15%
Modernists		26	28	15	29	36	18
Ethnics		16	8	42	11	6	40
Dropouts		32	31	30	18	16	27
Number*		28,490	6,253	8,214	255,506	72,167	33,496

TABLE 3-2
Religiosity by religious background (ranking universities and all institutions)

*In this and subsequent tables, respondents who could not be classified on the typology of religiosity are excluded. Six percent of the sample had anomalous response patterns and seven percent did not answer all three of the component questions.

dropouts into a single group that will be referred to as *apostates.* Operationally, apostasy is defined as being indifferent or opposed to religion, whether or not this involves a rejection of nominal religious ties.

INSTITUTIONAL VARIATIONS IN RELIGIOUS COMMITMENT

Table 3-3 shows how apostasy varies with the quality rating of institutions.[1] The direction of the relationship is clear: the higher the rank of the institution, the greater is the proportion of faculty who are indifferent or opposed to religion. Among the 17 ranking universities the rate of apostasy is 54 percent. Among the lowest-ranking colleges it is 22 percent.

For Protestants, Catholics, and Jews alike, apostasy increases with institutional quality. Among Jewish faculty, however, the level of apostasy is consistently higher and shows less variation. Even among Jews in the lowest-ranking colleges the rate of apostasy is 56 percent. Indeed, the rate of apostasy for Jews in the lowest-ranking colleges is higher than the rates for Protestants and Catholics in the highest-ranking universities. This finding may provide one clue to the Jewish success in American higher education. If religious involvement is an impediment to scholarly productivity, then the lower level of religious involvement of Jewish scholars might account for some of their success relative to non-Jews.

[1] The quality rating is based upon *The Gourman Report* (Gourman, 1967). The 17 ranking universities are as follows: Brandeis University, Columbia University, Harvard University, Johns Hopkins University, Northwestern University, Princeton University, Stanford University, Tulane University, University of California at Berkeley, University of California at Los Angeles, University of Illinois, University of Michigan, University of North Carolina, University of Pennsylvania, University of Rochester, University of Washington, and Vanderbilt University.

TABLE 3-3 Apostasy* by religious background and institutional quality

Institutional quality	Religious background							
	Protestants		Catholics		Jews		Total	
	Percent	Number	Percent	Number	Percent	Number	Percent	Number
Universities								
High	48	28,490	39	6,253	72	8,214	54	47,760
Medium	37	43,926	29	10,333	71	10,369	43	70,132
Low	28	42,554	24	10,245	60	4,474	32	61,617
Colleges								
High	39	14,073	36	2,990	66	2,884	44	21,916
Medium	24	28,726	16	9,859	61	2,716	25	43,199
Low	20	58,893	15	21,190	56	2,976	22	88,458
Junior colleges	20	38,873	18	11,295	53	1,863	22	55,456
TOTAL	29	255,506	22	72,167	66	33,496	33	388,538

*Apostates are those who describe themselves as indifferent or opposed to religion.

More is involved than this, however, for even when Jews have relatively strong religious commitments, they are almost as likely to reach a ranking university. This is shown in Table 3-4 which rotates the variables in Table 3-3 so that religiosity is now an independent variable and institutional quality the dependent variable. Among Protestants and Catholics, those with stronger religious commitments are less likely to be in a ranking university. Among Protestants classified as traditionalists, only 11 percent are found in ranking institutions, whereas the figure rises to 27 percent among those classified as dropouts. In the case of Catholics, the figures are 11 and 24 percent. Among Jewish faculty, the differences are much smaller. Traditionalists are almost as likely as dropouts to be in a ranking university: the figures are 29 and 37 percent. In short, religiosity among Jewish faculty does not appear to be a handicap in climbing the academic ladder.

This analysis suggests that in matters of religion Jews have two advantages over non-Jews. First, non-Jews exhibit a pattern of greater religious involvement that is inversely related to academic success. Second, even when Jews do have strong religious commitments they do not experience the same adverse

TABLE 3-4
Institutional quality by religious background and religiosity

| Religiosity | Religious background | | | |
	Protestants	Catholics	Jews	Protestant-Jewish difference
	Percent in a ranking college or university			
Traditionalists	11	11	29	18
Modernists	15	10	28	13
Ethnics	23	16	35	12
Dropouts	27	24	37	10
TOTAL	17	13	34	17
	Numbers			
Traditionalists	106,006	30,061	5,206	
Modernists	75,394	26,173	6,084	
Ethnics	27,493	4,037	13,295	
Dropouts	46,611	11,896	8,911	
Other	31,241	8,178	4,067	
TOTAL	286,745	80,345	37,563	

effects that religiosity appears to have among non-Jews. Both these factors undoubtedly help to explain the historic over-representation of Jews in the better institutions, though they by no means constitute a complete explanation.

Table 3-4 has another implication concerning the broad historical trend. It shows that as religious commitment goes from strong to weak, there is a steady decrease in the *difference* between Jews and non-Jews in terms of representation in a ranking college or university (see last column of Table 3-4). For example, among traditionalists there is an 18 percentage point difference between Protestants and Jews, but among dropouts it is reduced to 10 percentage points. In other words, if the religious commitments of non-Jews are, over time, becoming more like those of Jews, then this may help close the gap between Jews and non-Jews in terms of representation in ranking institutions.

TRENDS IN RELIGIOUS COMMITMENT Two questions arise with respect to trends in religious commitment. Are younger faculty less bound to religion than their older colleagues? And if so, are differences between Jews and non-Jews gradually diminishing or are they as pronounced among the young as among the old?

As Table 3-5 shows, Protestants, Catholics, and Jews all have experienced a decline in religiosity. In each case the proportion of traditionalists steadily decreases with younger age. The decline has been sharpest among Catholics, where the proportion of traditionalists is 64 percent among the oldest age cohort, and then drops off to 52, 39, and 31 percent. Catholics start out having more traditionalists than Protestants, but they end up in the youngest age cohort with slightly fewer.

Although the proportion of traditionalists has dropped off among all religious groups, the shift has taken different forms. In the case of Catholics there has been a sharp increase in the number of modernists (those who say they are deeply or moderately religious but whose beliefs are not of a conservative kind). In addition, there is a sharp increase in the proportion of dropouts—from 8 to 22 percent.

Among Protestants, the decline of traditionalists has only produced an incidental rise in the proportion of modernists. Most of the change is accounted for by a sharp increase in the proportion of dropouts—from 11 to 25 percent. In contrast, the proportion of dropouts has barely increased among Jews. Most

TABLE 3-5 *Religiosity by religious background and age*	Religious background	Age			
		55+	*45–54*	*35–44*	*34–*
	Protestants				
	Traditionalists	54%	49%	38%	33%
	Modernists	27	28	31	30
	Ethnics	8	9	12	12
	Dropouts	11	14	19	25
	Number	41,452	58,522	77,198	77,789
	Catholics				
	Traditionalists	64%	52%	39%	31%
	Modernists	25	32	39	40
	Ethnics	3	4	6	7
	Dropouts	8	12	16	22
	Number	8,302	14,726	23,378	25,582
	Jews				
	Traditionalists	23%	17%	16%	13%
	Modernists	18	19	18	17
	Ethnics	35	38	39	43
	Dropouts	24	26	27	27
	Number	2,876	7,092	11,487	11,962

of the decrease in traditionalists is offset by an increase in the proportion of ethnics—from 35 to 43 percent.

If one examined only the figures on religious dropouts, they would suggest a pattern of diminishing religious differences in religiosity. Among the oldest group of faculty, the proportion of religious dropouts is much higher for Jews (24 percent) than for Protestants (11 percent) or for Catholics (8 percent). But among the youngest faculty this 16 percentage point difference is reduced to just 5. In other words, at the present time each religious group appears to be producing an almost equal number of religious dropouts. However, this is offset by the fact that Jews have always produced a higher proportion of ethnics—those whose religious ties are purely secular—and this proportion has increased over time. Thus, if one combines dropouts with ethnics, the differences between Jews and non-Jews are almost as great among the young as among the old.

In general, the data indicate that Catholic faculty have become more like Protestants in their religious commitments, but both groups continue to exhibit much higher rates of religious involvement than Jews. These differences, however, are not quite as large among the young as among the old, and they will probably decrease at an even faster rate in the future. Among Jews, the proportion of dropouts has leveled off, and since 67 percent presently are either ethnics or dropouts, Jews are bound to reach a threshold where further erosion of religious commitment will be difficult. On the other hand, religiosity is rapidly declining among Protestants and Catholics, a trend that is likely to continue into the future.

It could be argued that Table 3-5 does not indicate generational change, but only the effect of increasing age. According to this interpretation, as younger faculty grow older, many will return to the religious fold and eventually exhibit a pattern of religious commitment similar to that of today's older faculty. Without panel data this possibility cannot be discounted. But given what is known about the trend toward secularization in contemporary society, and particularly in institutions of higher learning, it is more plausible that younger faculty are simply less steeped in religious values, and are likely to remain so as they grow older.

RELIGIOSITY AND ACADEMIC DISCIPLINE Table 3-6 shows the rates of apostasy among faculty in 11 academic fields. The left half of the table refers to the 17 ranking universities, the right half to all institutions combined. Although many of the details of Table 3-6 warrant closer inspection, three general patterns emerge:

- In every field except medicine, the rates of apostasy are substantially higher in the ranking universities than in higher education as a whole.

- The applied fields generally exhibit significantly lower rates of apostasy than do the more theoretical and intellectual disciplines. Thus, apostasy is lowest among faculties in education, the semiprofessions, business, and engineering. It is highest in the social sciences, the humanities, the biological sciences, and the physical sciences. Apostasy is also generally high among faculties of medicine and law. These patterns are basically the same for Protestants, Catholics, and Jews alike.

- The differences in apostasy among Protestants, Catholics, and Jews generally stand up within academic disciplines. In every instance, the rate of apostasy for Jews far exceeds that of Protestants or Catholics, and in most cases Protestants continue to have a higher rate of apostasy than Catholics. This is true both in ranking universities and institutions of lower quality. One notable exception is the humanities: in the ranking universities the level of apostasy for Catholics is just as great as for Protestants. Although the humanities is the most Catholic of all disciplines, the more devout Catholics are not likely to achieve a position in a ranking university.

In short, each of the factors analyzed in Table 3-6—religion, academic discipline, and institutional quality—influence the rate of apostasy and do so fairly independently of each other. Thus, the high rate of Jewish apostasy cannot be explained simply by the fact that Jews are concentrated in the better institutions or in academic disciplines that are generally high in apostasy. Nor can the low rate of apostasy in certain disciplines or in lower-quality institutions be explained by the relative absence of Jews. Because religion, institutional quality, and discipline each has an independent effect on apostasy, the rate of apostasy ranges from 7 percent among Catholic faculty in education in the lowest-ranking colleges to 77 percent among Jewish social scientists in the ranking universities.

Earlier we observed a general decline in religiosity between older and younger faculty. Not all academic fields, however, are part of this overall trend. Among those that do not show a decline in religiosity are business, the semiprofessions, engineering, and medicine. These fields have traditionally attracted people with strong religious inclinations, and this is just as true now as in previous generations. On the other hand, the proportion of apostates has steadily increased in education, the fine arts, the humanities, and the physical and social sciences. Inasmuch as apostasy correlates highly with such factors as scholarly productivity and political liberalism, it is likely that the decline of religiosity is indicative of a broader transformation in the intellectual and political climate within these disciplines.

RELIGION AND SCHOLARSHIP Indirectly, the findings reported above already suggest a connection between religiosity and low scholarly productivity. We observed that the rates of apostasy vary with institutional quality, reaching their highest levels in the more intellectual disciplines. Institutional quality and academic discipline, however, are contextual variables, and as such fall short of demonstrating a direct link between an individual's religious commitments and his achievements as a scholar. With this in mind, let us now introduce measures of individual scholarship into the analysis.

TABLE 3-6 *Apostasy* by religious background and academic discipline (ranking universities and all institutions)*

Academic disciplines	Ranking universities							
	Protestants		Catholics		Jews		Total	
	Percentage	Number	Percentage	Number	Percentage	Number	Percentage	Number
Education	36	1,885	21	344	60	272	38	2,642
Semiprofessions	36	3,770	30	928	65	897	41	6,030
Business	47	1,699	29	283	62	348	47	2,494
Engineering	39	2,610	28	541	73	549	45	4,028
Fine arts	45	1,504	32	358	67	223	48	2,299
Physical sciences	61	3,174	43	642	81	996	65	5,508
Biological sciences	56	2,572	55	491	80	692	62	4,219
Medicine	33	3,098	24	782	63	1,247	42	5,510
Humanities	53	4,330	51	1,182	75	1,075	58	7,607
Law	71	409	†	†	83	376	68	939
Social sciences	66	3,206	66	498	79	1,550	72	5,926

* Apostates are those who describe themselves as indifferent or opposed to religion.

† Too few cases for stable percentages.

Three such measures are used. The first deals with the individual's self-concept, as measured by responses to the statement: "I consider myself an intellectual." The second measures his orientation toward research. Respondents were asked whether their interests lie primarily in teaching or research and were offered four response categories designating varying degrees of commitment to one or the other. A third measure deals with research activity, as indicated by the number of publications during the two years preceding the survey. These three items are not simply repetitive, but tap different dimensions of scholarship—self-concept, general orientation, and actual behavior.

Table 3-7 shows the breakdown of responses, controlling for the religion in which faculty were raised. Once again, there is no evidence of a special aversion to scholarship among Catholic faculty, at least as compared with Protestants. The responses to all three items are virtually identical for both groups. In each instance, however, Jewish faculty are far more likely than either Protestants or Catholics to respond in ways that indicate a strong commitment to scholarship. The measure of research activity—

All institutions							
Protestants		Catholics		Jews		Total	
Percentage	*Number*	*Percentage*	*Number*	*Percentage*	*Number*	*Percentage*	*Number*
16	33,206	12	8,033	58	2,109	18	45,269
18	30,441	15	7,303	58	2,569	21	43,159
20	15,182	13	4,206	44	1,656	21	22,294
23	15,499	19	4,208	61	2,237	29	24,201
28	21,125	28	4,227	63	2,230	33	29,371
32	33,800	25	8,664	69	4,217	37	51,204
38	16,823	24	3,683	75	2,651	41	25,389
36	7,249	24	1,795	68	2,897	43	12,713
36	46,085	24	19,899	65	5,687	46	76,807
43	1,359	20	532	70	779	48	2,853
44	29,643	35	7,751	77	6,243	49	47,399

which is perhaps the most trustworthy of the three measures since it deals with actual behavior—also shows the largest difference. Only 30 percent of Jewish faculty report that they did not have any professional publications in the previous two-year period. In contrast, the figure for Protestants is 55 percent; for Catholics it is 59 percent.

Given the Jewish concentration in the high-ranking, research-oriented universities, it is not surprising that they publish with greater regularity. On the other hand, the fact that Jews are more often oriented to research and more productive as scholars helps to account for their representation in quality universities in the first place. Without panel data it is not possible to unravel the causal sequence between these variables. But it *is* possible to control for institutional quality in order to find out whether Jews continue to exhibit strong orientations toward research even after this factor is taken into account.

This is done in Table 3-8. Each of the three dimensions of scholarly orientation is strongly a function of institutional quality. For example, among Jewish faculty in the ranking universi-

	Religious background		
Scholarly orientations	Protestants	Catholics	Jews
I consider myself an intellectual:			
Strongly agree	16%	18%	36%
Agree with reservations	52	50	46
Disagree with reservations	24	24	14
Strongly disagree	8	8	4
Research orientation:			
Very heavily in research	3	3	8
In both, but leaning toward research	18	17	35
In both, but leaning toward teaching	34	33	33
Very heavily in teaching	45	47	24
Publications in last two years:			
None	55	59	30
1–2	24	23	27
3–4	12	10	21
5–10	7	6	17
More than 10	2	2	5

TABLE 3-7
Scholarly orientations by religious background

ties, 62 percent report three or more publications in the last two years. This declines to 54 and 38 percent in lower-ranking universities, and to 15 percent in the lowest-ranking colleges.

To some extent, the better publishing record of Jewish scholars simply reflects their greater concentration in the higher-quality institutions. Within any single category of institutional quality, religious differences are not as great as in the sample as a whole (last column). Nevertheless, religion continues to have a pronounced effect. The publishing record of Jews in medium-ranking universities is as great as that of non-Jews in high-ranking universities; similarly, the Jewish rate in low-ranking universities matches that of non-Jews in medium-ranking universities. Thus, in terms of the sheer number of publications, Jewish scholars surpass the record of their non-Jewish colleagues in the same institutions, and do as well as non-Jews in institutions of the next highest rank.

Of course, the number of publications is only a superficial measure of scholarship. It says nothing about their quality or about the other criteria that enter into the selection of faculty for the higher-ranking institutions. At least there is nothing in Table 3-8 to suggest that there are more Jews with active publishing records in lower-ranking institutions because of religious discrimination. On the contrary, when the number of publications is controlled, Jews are more likely to have teaching positions in high-ranking institutions than non-Jews with the same number of publications.

It could be argued that Jews are concentrated in academic disciplines that typically place greater emphasis on research or where publication occurs more frequently, thereby explaining their greater tendency to publish. It is true that the fields in which Jews are least concentrated, such as education and the fine arts, are generally less oriented toward research. Even when this factor is controlled, however, the differences in Table 3-8 stand up. As an illustration, Table 3-9 repeats the analysis in Table 3-8 but does so only for social scientists. As before, Jews consistently exhibit a slightly higher rate of scholarly productivity and match the productivity level of Protestants and Catholics in the next higher institutional rank.

TABLE 3-8
Scholarly orientations by religious background and institutional quality*

Religious background	Universities			Colleges			Junior colleges	Total
	High	*Medium*	*Low*	*High*	*Medium*	*Low*		
	Percentage of self-identified intellectuals							
Protestants	25%	20%	15%	22%	15%	14%	10%	16%
Catholics	29	22	19	27	20	16	8	18
Jews	42	36	30	38	36	32	25	36
	Percentage who prefer research							
Protestants	46	37	25	22	11	9	4	21
Catholics	48	36	27	24	13	10	6	20
Jews	58	52	38	40	17	21	17	43
	Percentage with 3 or more publications							
Protestants	49	39	26	21	11	7	2	21
Catholics	46	37	24	19	11	7	4	18
Jews	62	54	38	34	17	15	12	44

*The raw numbers can be found in Table 3-3.

TABLE 3-9 *Research activity by religious background and institutional quality (social scientists only)*

Religious background	Universities			Colleges			Junior colleges	Total
	High	Medium	Low	High	Medium	Low		
				Three or more publications				
Protestants								
Percentage	58	45	30	24	16	8	5	24
Number	3,487	5,278	4,879	2,004	3,888	7,543	4,967	32,048
Catholics								
Percentage	57	48	32	14	9	7	6	20
Number	595	1,022	1,051	362	1,331	2,549	1,211	8,121
Jews								
Percentage	69	59	48	36	18	17	6	47
Number	1,628	910	977	640	305	422	422	5,304

Having established the existence of genuine religious differences in research orientation between Jews and non-Jews, the next step is to inquire into what role, if any, personal religious involvement plays in this relationship. Are persons with more traditional religious commitments less apt to have strong research orientations? And if so, does this fact help to explain differences between Jews and non-Jews with respect to research orientation and scholarly productivity?

Table 3-10 shows the relationship between religious commitment and the three measures of scholarship. Among all three religious groups, there is a tendency for greater religiosity to be associated with lower research orientation. Once again, the figures for Catholics are virtually identical to those for Protestants. In other words, there is nothing to indicate that religiosity among Catholics is any more inimical to the scholarly ethos than religiosity among Protestants.

Among Jewish faculty, the impact of religiosity is greatest on the measure of self-concept: only 24 percent of traditionalists see themselves as intellectuals, whereas 47 percent of dropouts do so. But the difference is small with respect to scholarly activity: traditionalists are almost as likely as dropouts to publish regularly. This is consistent with the earlier finding that Jews who scored as traditionalists were almost as likely as less religious Jews to achieve a teaching position in a ranking university.

From a statistical point of view, the difference between Jews and non-Jews in scholarly orientation is a product of two trends: (1) more Protestants and Catholics than Jews have traditional religious commitments, and (2) among Jews, religious involvement seems to be less incompatible with scholarship than it does among Protestants and Catholics.[2]

Earlier the question was raised of whether the scholarly orientations of modernists and ethnics would more closely resemble those of traditionalists or those of dropouts. In other words, if religion tends to be incompatible with scholarship, does it require deep religious involvement before the effects become manifest or is a moderate degree of involvement sufficient? In general, the data indicate a linear progression between lower religiosity and greater scholarship. In the case of Protestants and Catholics, however, those classified as modernists more closely

[2] Similar findings based on a student sample are reported in Caplovitz (forthcoming, chap. 4).

TABLE 3-10 **Scholarly orientations by religious background and religiosity***	Scholarly orientations	Religious background		
		Protestants	Catholics	Jews
		Percentage of self-identified intellectuals		
	Traditionalists	10%	14%	24%
	Modernists	17	17	36
	Ethnics	17	25	34
	Dropouts	28	28	47
		Percentage who prefer research		
	Traditionalists	13	14	37
	Modernists	18	17	35
	Ethnics	30	32	44
	Dropouts	37	33	51
		Percentage with three or more publications		
	Traditionalists	15	15	41
	Modernists	19	16	40
	Ethnics	29	30	44
	Dropouts	30	26	47

*The raw numbers can be found in Table 3-4.

resemble traditionalists than either ethnics or dropouts. The fact that modernists are deeply or moderately religious is enough to produce a relatively low rate of scholarly productivity; whether or not they are conservative in their religious beliefs is of relatively little consequence. Similarly, those classified as ethnics among Protestants and Catholics resemble dropouts in their scholarly orientations. That they are indifferent or opposed to religion is enough to produce a high rate of scholarly productivity; whether or not they renounce all religious ties appears to be of relatively little consequence.

Although the data point to a general incompatibility between religious involvement and scholarly orientation, one question remains. Earlier it was observed that religiosity is at lower levels in the higher-quality institutions and in the more intellectual disciplines where demands for research are great. Does religiosity simply prevent individuals from reaching high-quality institutions, or does it continue to have an effect even among those who teach in these institutions?

Table 3-11 shows that religiosity has only a modest relation to scholarly productivity once institutional quality is controlled. For example, among Protestants in ranking universities, 44 percent of traditionalists, as compared with 52 percent of dropouts, report three or more publications in the last two years. This pattern of small differences occurs at every institutional rank for both Protestants and Catholics. (As reported earlier, religiosity generally is unrelated to scholarly productivity for Jews). In other words, within a particular institution Protestants and Catholics with stronger religious ties are not appreciably less likely to publish regularly than their less religious colleagues.

If religion impedes scholarship, its chief consequence is to channel more religious individuals into lower-ranking institutions. It appears to be of only minimal significance thereafter. Those scholars with traditional religious commitments who do teach at high-quality institutions show few signs of being less productive on this account. But such individuals are less likely to reach quality institutions in the first place.

RELIGION AND PERSONAL VALUES   To say that religion is incompatible with scholarship is not to imply that religion somehow blunts the mind. It is not altogether clear from past studies exactly what it is about religion that is the source of its incompatibility with scholarship. The interpretation

TABLE 3-11 Research activity by religious background, religiosity, and institutional quality

| | Universities | | | | | | All institutions | |
| | High | | Medium | | Low | | | |
Religious background	Percentage	Number	Percentage	Number	Percentage	Number	Percentage	Number
			Three or more publications					
Protestants								
Traditionalists	44	7,253	36	14,707	23	16,935	15	103,012
Modernists	47	7,238	36	12,166	25	12,792	19	73,303
Ethnics	57	4,428	44	5,531	28	4,760	29	22,885
Dropouts	52	8,952	46	10,449	31	7,051	30	45,563
Catholics								
Traditionalists	47	2,024	34	3,759	20	4,019	14	29,116
Modernists	38	1,723	34	3,360	24	3,480	16	25,245
Ethnics	53	467	52	806	37	652	30	3,958
Dropouts	49	1,910	43	2,132	28	1,754	26	11,397
Jews								
Traditionalists	62	1,030	48	1,344	38	657	41	5,036
Modernists	59	1,180	54	1,606	38	1,081	41	5,967
Ethnics	65	3,418	52	4,315	39	1,612	44	12,862
Dropouts	62	2,432	60	2,849	38	996	47	8,810

advanced here is that religious commitment embraces other related values that influence the individual's priorities in his work and his profession. As observed earlier, faculty with strong religious commitments not only publish less often, but also are less likely to think of themselves as intellectuals, and more likely to emphasize teaching over research. This invites speculation that persons with strong religious commitments may not place highest priority on intellectual achievement and on research, precisely those qualities that define success and earn rewards within the academic enterprise. In other words, it may not be that the more religious scholars are unable to live up to prevailing values with respect to achievement and success, but rather that they subscribe to a different set of values and priorities.

There is a good deal of historical evidence to support this interpretation. American colleges under religious control have often resisted academic trends within secular universities. For example, Catholic educators traditionally have viewed science and research with skepticism. Their educational philosophy emphasized mastery of the ancient verities rather than the pursuit of specialized knowledge. In their educational program they placed higher value on the cultivation of spiritual values than on the accumulation of technical information or the development of vocational skills. This was not an educational philosophy incompatible with scholarship, but it was clearly at odds with the norms of scholarship that prevail within modern secular universities.

There is also evidence in the data that faculty with stronger religious commitments tend to hold values that conflict with the ones that govern contemporary higher education and its system of rewards. Respondents were asked to agree or disagree with the statement: "This institution should be as concerned about students' personal values as it is with their intellectual development." As Table 3-12 shows, agreement directly corresponds with religious commitment: the greater the religious commitment, the higher the proportion who place as much importance on students' values as on their intellectual development. This is true in the 17 ranking universities as well as in the sample as a whole.

In addition, Table 3-13 shows that faculty who express concern for the personal values of students are less likely to score high on all three measures of scholarly orientation. This is true for

TABLE 3-12
Concern for
student values by
religious
background and
religiosity*

	Religious background		
Religiosity	Protestants	Catholics	Jews

Percentage who agree with the statement: This institution should be as concerned about students' personal values as it is with their intellectual development.

Traditionalists	86	85	74
Modernists	80	82	75
Ethnics	68	69	65
Dropouts	58	62	63
TOTAL	77	79	70

*The raw numbers are shown in Table 3-4.

Protestants, Catholics, and Jews alike. The relationship is especially strong with respect to the question that asked respondents whether they generally preferred teaching or research. Among Protestant faculty who strongly agreed that their institution should be as concerned about students' values as with their intellectual development, only 13 percent expressed a preference for research over teaching. With less emphasis on students' values, the proportion preferring research sharply increases, from 13 to 20 to 33 to 41 percent. Similar trends can be observed for Catholics and Jews.

In short, the data indicate that faculty with stronger religious convictions tend to place higher priority on the teaching functions of the university than on its research activities.[3] This, in turn, is related to a belief that education should attend to the cultivation of spiritual values and not merely the cultivation of the mind. Such an outlook may not be conducive to scholarly productivity or to academic success. It is cast, however, in a somewhat different perspective by the reaction during the 1960s against the high degree of specialization in academic disciplines, the obsession with research, and the separation of moral values from the educational process. Just as Weber ended his essay on *The Protestant Ethic and the Spirit of Capitalism* with an admonition against the dangers of uncontrolled rationalism, perhaps it is

[3] Somewhat similar findings emerged from Earl Babbie's 1970 study of medical school faculty. Babbie found that medical faculty with stronger religious convictions were more likely to emphasize the humanistic as opposed to the scientific purposes of the medical profession (Babbie, 1970, pp. 87–97).

TABLE 3-13
Scholarly
orientations by
religious
background and
concern for
student values

	Religious background		
	Protestants	Catholics	Jews

Response to the statement: *This institution should be as concerned about students'*
personal values as it is with their intellectual development.

	Percentage of self-identified intellectuals		
Strongly agree	14	18	34
Agree with reservations	15	15	32
Disagree with reservations	19	23	38
Strongly disagree	30	29	50

	Percentage who prefer research to teaching		
Strongly agree	13	13	30
Agree with reservations	20	20	43
Disagree with reservations	33	31	54
Strongly disagree	41	36	63

	Percentage with three or more publications		
Strongly agree	16	13	36
Agree with reservations	21	19	44
Disagree with reservations	29	25	50
Strongly disagree	32	26	48

	Numbers		
Strongly agreee	108,891	34,069	12,117
Agree with reservations	106,846	28,148	12,934
Disagree with reservations	50,352	11,709	8,060
Strongly disagree	14,884	4,457	3,678

proper to acknowledge the validity of an educational philosophy
that emphasizes the spiritual aspects and purposes of education.
The alternative, as Weber warns, is to produce "specialists
without spirit" and "sensualists without heart" (Weber, 1958, p.
182).

CONCLUSION   The findings reported in this paper generally confirm the incompatibility thesis of the relation between religion and scholarship.
To say, however, that religion and scholarship are incompatible is
not to assert a simple cause-and-effect relationship. There is no
evidence that persons with strong religious commitments fail to

develop scholarly orientations on this account alone. Nor can it be assumed that in a person's life history he first disavows religious belief and then develops scholarly orientations; indeed, the reverse process is more plausible. But the data do indicate that religion and scholarship tend to be incompatible, in the limited sense that they vary inversely and that stronger degrees of one tend to be accompanied by weaker degrees of the other.

Although religiosity had little effect on Jews, Protestants and Catholics with strong religious attachments were considerably less likely to achieve a position in a ranking university, and they were also less often found in the more intellectual disciplines. Still more direct evidence supporting the incompatibility thesis is that Protestant and Catholic faculty with stronger religious commitments were less likely to have scholarly orientations or to publish regularly.

While these findings point to a basic conflict between religion and scholarship, they must be balanced against certain other findings in this paper. In the first place, the overall level of religious involvement among the nation's scholars is not nearly as low as the incompatibility thesis would suggest. In the faculty sample as a whole, 78 percent continue to have at least a nominal religious identity, 64 percent say they are deeply or moderately religious, 40 percent characterize their religious beliefs as conservative, and 25 percent attend church weekly.

Also, it must be remembered that the findings supporting the incompatibility thesis, like all such findings in the social sciences, are of a probabilistic nature. Thus, although more successful and productive scholars are generally not as tied to religion as their less successful colleagues, many nevertheless retain strong religious commitments. Even in the ranking universities nearly a majority of faculty say they are deeply or moderately religious. And even among social scientists in ranking universities—the least religious of any academic group—a substantial minority of about one-quarter say they are deeply or moderately religious. Thus, despite the general incompatibility between religion and scholarship, many individuals do manage to combine both perspectives.

Perhaps the most important qualification of the incompatibility thesis stems from the finding that faculty with strong religious commitments have a special view of the purposes and functions of education. They are committed to the spiritual as well as to the intellectual cultivation of students, and they place greater emphasis on teaching than on research. This suggests that the incompatibility between religion and scholarship does not take the form of a crude anti-intellectualism but is grounded in values that are legitimate and valuable in academic institutions.

References

Babbie, Earl R.: *Science and Morality in Medicine,* University of California Press, Berkeley, 1970.

Caplovitz, David, and Fred Sherrow: *The Religious Dropouts: A Study of Apostates among College Graduates,* forthcoming.

Durkheim, Emile: *Suicide,* The Free Press of Glencoe, Inc., New York, 1958.

Feuer, Lewis S.: *The Scientific Intellectual,* Basic Books, Inc., Publishers, New York, 1963.

Freud, Sigmund: *Future of an Illusion,* Schocken Books, Inc., New York, 1962.

Glock, Charles Y., and Rodney Stark: *Religion and Science in Tension,* Rand McNally & Company, Chicago, 1965.

Gourman, Jack: *The Gourman Report,* The Continuing Education Institute, Phoenix, Ariz., 1967.

Greeley, Andrew M.: *Religion and Career,* Sheed & Ward, Inc., New York, 1963.

Knapp, Robert H., and H. B. Goodrich: *Origins of American Scientists,* University of Chicago Press, Chicago, 1952.

Lipset, Seymour Martin, and Everett Carll Ladd, Jr.: "Jewish Academics in the United States: Their Achievements, Culture, and Politics," *American Jewish Yearbook,* vol. 72, American Jewish Committee, New York, 1971.

Merton, Robert: "Puritanism, Pietism, and Science," in *Social Theory and Social Structure,* The Free Press, New York, 1963.

Weber, Max: *The Protestant Ethic and the Spirit of Capitalism,* Charles Scribner's Sons, New York, 1955.

Zelan, Joseph: "Religious Apostasy, Higher Education, and Occupational Choice," *Sociology of Education,* vol. 41, no. 4, pp. 370–379, Fall 1968.

4. Black Students in Higher Education

by Judy Roizen

The equitable distribution of educational resources is of fundamental importance in a democratic society. Graduates of the institutions of higher learning will, for the most part, control the economy, the polity, and the academy. As long as educational attainment is of fundamental importance in determining life chances, it is essential that access to colleges and universities be free of bias based on social origin. Something is askew in a democratic society in which one or a number of groups is unrepresented, or vastly underrepresented, in the institutions of higher learning. What is askew? How much it is askew? What policies would bring about reform? These are delicate and extraordinarily difficult questions. The 1969 Carnegie Commission Survey of Faculty and Student Opinion, however, has generated some interesting and sometimes surprising data on black college students.

The discussion of open access and equity in higher education raises several difficult methodological and measurement problems.[1] Implicit in the discussion of equity is the notion that some configuration of college populations, with regard to ethnic minority representation, would indeed be fair or equitable. For the most part, this "goal" has been equated with equal or proportional representation: the proportion of college students from any "minority" should be roughly equal to the proportion of that minority in the general population. If such a situation actually existed, we could expect that little energy would be spent on reforming higher education in this regard. Several minority

NOTE: I am very grateful to Judy Weston and Frank Martucci for considerable help in gathering secondary sources and in data processing.

[1] We do not attempt to explore the policy implications of open enrollment—admitting to a college all who seek to attend. Rather, we are using "openness" to denote equality or inequality of opportunity, that is, the extent to which an individual's achieved status is influenced or determined by his ascribed status.

groups, however, are very much underrepresented in the college population. The magnitude of this underrepresentation is sufficiently great to suggest that squaring up representation is the first order of business. But it is well to recognize that proportional representation is not the only meaningful policy objective. The singular pursuit of proportionality, indeed, poses a number of problems.

First, the pursuit of proportionality does not account for the fact that all colleges are not equally good; we would not argue that equity had been achieved if a minority population—although proportionally represented—were concentrated in low-quality institutions.

Second, proportionality is susceptible to a number of different measures. We would have different equity evaluations of the system of higher education were we to measure proportional representation by proportion of admissions rather than by proportion of graduates, or were we to use as a base the minority representation in the general population as compared to the minority representation among school applicants.

Third, demands for proportionality bring with them questions as to the ability, the social origins, and the motivation of the minority students being admitted. By increasing the proportional representation of black graduates and undergraduates are we drawing only the most educationally advantaged? What access does a lower-class black, white, or Chicano have to higher learning in the United States?

We will not explore here competing standards of equity or models of compensatory justice. Our concern is rather to demonstrate the inadequacy of simple measures of proportionality in assessing whether resources are distributed in an equitable manner. We also do not attempt any analysis at the institutional level of the impact of the changing characteristics of the student body. The decade of the sixties, while bringing great changes in the character of the student body, was also a decade of institutional turmoil. The relationship between these two factors is the subject for another essay.

THE PROBLEM OF ACCESS Here we will focus on three areas central to the measurement of the educational access of black Americans to higher learning:[2]

[2] We have chosen to look at blacks because at the time the surveys were undertaken the proportions of Chicanos and Native Americans in colleges and universities were small.

the kinds of institutions that blacks have access to; within those institutions, the departments and programs that black students enter; and the characteristics, especially with respect to the social-class background, of the black students who ultimately gain access to these institutions. Let us look in some detail at each of these concerns.

First, we must recognize that equal opportunity for some postsecondary education does not mean equal educational opportunity. Access to some institutions of higher learning has been and will continue to be a fundamental tenet of American higher education. This commitment has been reiterated for minority students. The Carnegie Commission "action agenda for equal opportunity in higher education" asserts that "The American system of higher education has always been an 'open' system. There has been a place at some college for everyone who wanted to go and could afford to go. This report accepts and endorses the concept of an 'open' system. . ." (Carnegie Commission, 1970*a*, p. 1). But equal access to only some institutions does not mean equal access to certification for valued social roles: it does not mean access to a quality institution, an academic major, a degree, or a graduate career.

Blacks and other minority students want both academic experience and necessary certification. The quality of both vary with the institution selected. Access to the highly selective institutions must be considered apart from access to some institutions of higher learning. The selective institutions are both the training ground for bureaucratic and professional elites and the academic standard-bearers for all institutions. Blacks must attend selective institutions in something more than token numbers. But by definition these institutions are accessible only to the comparatively few students qualified or fortunate enough to be admitted.[3]

Discussions of minority access, such as the Crossland report, *Minority Access to College* (1971), have measured the degree of access of minority students by estimating the number of minority students and the number of white students and comparing these figures to the minority distribution in the population. This has been done, however, only on gross distributions by race. Thus, such conclusions are drawn as "the estimated black

---

[3] Twelve percent of white undergraduates and seven percent of black undergraduates attend high-quality institutions. The relationship between minority access and quality of institution is discussed in greater detail in the following sections.

enrollment in 1970 would have to be increased by 543,000—an increase of 116 percent—in order to achieve proportional representation" (ibid., p. 20). Underlying this is the assumption that undergraduate or graduate students are "of a kind" and that the same is true for educational institutions. Little has been done in the direction of measuring the representation of particular subgroups of the minority population. As we shall see, however, until we have disaggregated the black student population by age, sex, and social origin, we know little about the access of black students to higher learning. The access of *young* black men, for example, to graduate school, cannot be measured by looking at the proportion of blacks, or even black men, in the graduate student population.

Social Class and Minority Access

The question of the social-class background of minority students brings with it a host of serious sociological and legal problems. "The pressure for expansion of minority enrollment collides with the rising academic aspirations and expectations of many lower class whites for whom college has for the first time in generations become a serious prospect" (O'Neil, 1971, p. 700). Are blacks now being admitted to colleges and universities at the expense of lower-class whites? Or do lower-class students, independent of race, stand only a small chance of gaining entrance to and graduating from college? What are the effects of race and social class, taken together, in this complicated recruitment and self-recruitment process?

If black entrants to high-quality graduate and undergraduate institutions or certain academic fields come predominantly from middle-class families, it raises several questions. First, it speaks directly to the question of the openness of access to higher learning, especially social-class access. Second, it may have serious consequences for the black class structure.

The proportion of young lower-class students who graduate from college and attend graduate school will affect, in important ways, the black class structure of the future. Abram J. Jaffe, Walter Adams, and Sandra G. Meyers in their book, *Negro Higher Education in the 1960's,* reported: "The absolute number of higher class Negroes in the United States has increased during the last couple of decades . . . and is related to increased college attendance. What is not clear is whether the number of Negroes in the socioeconomically higher classes has increased more or less rapidly than the number of the lower class" (1968 p. 90). If the class structure is to change, the proportion as well as the number of upper-class blacks must increase. Barring great changes in the birthrate, in all probability the proportion will increase only if black undergraduates and graduates are disproportionately recruited from the lower classes. While, "equality of opportunity" may be great for an individual within a relatively rigid class structure, we are less concerned in this paper with the "exceptional individual" than we are with overall patterns of recruitment and self-recruitment as they exist for blacks, especially young blacks.

Third, the social origins of black students may raise serious sociolegal questions. Much of the increase in black enrollment was brought about by instituting complex formulas of preferential treatment. It has been argued that "a state university should be able to demonstrate that the primary goal and probable effect of preferential policies is the equalization of access for disadvantaged minority groups" (O'Neil, 1971, p. 717). If it were the case that blacks being admitted to graduate and undergraduate programs were predominantly advantaged blacks, the use of preferential treatment for admissions would be seriously questioned.

Before turning to the data we must consider two issues: the limitations of the present sample and the rationale for *not* perpetuating the common distinction between predominantly black and predominantly white institutions.

The samples used in this study included 7 undergraduate and 14 graduate institutions with a predominantly black student population, 182 integrated undergraduate institutions, and 153 integrated graduate institutions. The undergraduate sample was made up of students who had *entered* college six months to three years prior to the survey and were enrolled at the time the survey was conducted. The graduate sample was made up of currently enrolled graduate students. Both samples were weighted. An extensive analysis of nonresponse bias was carried out on the graduate sample and on no major dimension was there any significant response bias (see p. 314 for further details). Although the number of black graduates is small, we do not believe that these students are unrepresentative of the population of black graduates in the spring of 1969.

The response rate for undergraduates, overall, was considerably lower than the graduates. For this reason supporting data from the U.S. Office of Education (OE), American Council on

Education (ACE), and other sources have also been reported wherever available.

Although the story we will tell here is similar for both undergraduates and graduates, the analysis of each sample is carried out separately. This was done for two reasons. First, where supporting data were available for either sample they were used; this complicated the presentation of the data. And second, we felt that the data would be clearer to the reader if a similar story were told twice.

Much of the previous descriptive work on black students in higher education has focused on the black in "predominantly Negro colleges." Until recently these institutions were responsible for the education of the majority of blacks who went to college; blacks outside these institutions were widely dispersed throughout hundreds of institutions. By the late sixties predominantly black institutions enrolled slightly over a third of all black students. Although it is obvious that the predominantly black institutions differ in some important ways from integrated institutions, the distinction was not maintained for this study (see McGrath, 1965, chaps. 1 and 2). We are particularly concerned here with the relationships among race, institutional quality, academic career, and social class and, as we shall see, the relationships found in this study are consistent with those found by Jaffe, Adams, and Meyers in their work on predominantly Negro colleges.

Jaffe, Adams, and Meyers pointed out the differences in the social-class background of students in various kinds of institutions in the early 1960s. "Of great significance," they wrote, "for the future Negro class structure are the differences in the students at different types and qualities of Negro and other colleges. The student body at the elite colleges has far more upper- and middle-class students than does the student body at the 'poor colleges' " (1968, p. 90). Further, "these class differences are not new and are also found among white students, and were found in the past as well" (ibid., p. 92). Predominantly Negro institutions vary almost as much in quality and prestige, social-class access, and type of program as do predominantly white institutions. Since we are interested in access to particular *kinds* of institutions and since by kind we mean quality, we have assigned the predominantly black institutions to quality categories in the same manner as predominantly white institutions.

In this century the educational attainment of the population as a whole has increased dramatically (Figure 4-1). Nonetheless, although cohorts of 20- to 24-year-olds are increasingly better educated, whites today still receive considerably more education than nonwhites (Figure 4-2).

Between 1940 and 1970, the proportion of white men graduating from high school increased from 50 percent to 83 percent, while that for blacks increased from less than 15 percent to 63 percent. In 1940, 45 percent of white women graduated from high school compared with 83 percent in 1968. Comparable

FIGURE 4-1 *Percentage of total population 25 years old and over completing none or less than five years of schooling (Series G2), four years of high school or more (Series G3), four years of college or more (Series G4), 1910–1968*

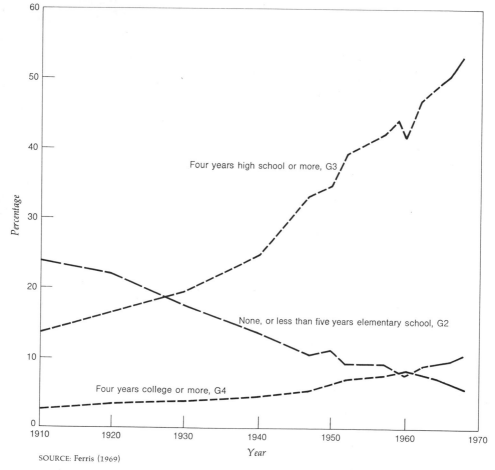

SOURCE: Ferris (1969)

FIGURE 4-2 *Percentage of the 20 to 24-year-old population completing four years of high school or more by color and sex, 1940–1968 (Series G18-G20, G42-G44, G66-G68, G90-G92).*

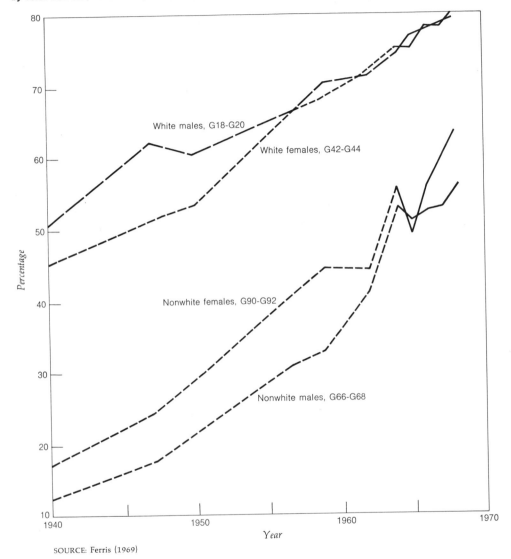

SOURCE: Ferris (1969)

figures for black women are 18 percent and 70 percent (Ferris, 1969, p. 207).

For whites as well as blacks, American colleges and universities have always been selective institutions. Except for a period during the Depression and during World War II, less than half of all high school graduates went on to college. About half of these students ultimately graduated. "Thus in the 1920s about 40 percent of (white men) finished high school and just under 20 percent entered college" (Jencks et al., 1972, pp. 19–20). In 1968, 83 percent of white men graduated from high school and of these students about 60 percent entered some kind of college.

Time-series data on black college students are only now becoming a possibility. Several different measures are necessary to adequately assess minority access to higher education: the proportion of entering freshmen who are nonwhite; the proportion of nonwhite college graduates, or conversely, nonwhite dropouts; and the proportion of currently enrolled nonwhite undergraduates. Little of this data is yet available for trend analysis. The American Council on Education has attempted to provide baseline information on black entering freshmen both in the national norms and in their 1969 and 1972 descriptive reports on black students. Table 4-1 indicates the dramatic increase in the proportions of black entering freshmen since 1966.

Both the Office of Education and the census provide statistics on currently enrolled undergraduates. In 1965, 3 percent of the currently enrolled undergraduates were black (Harris, 1972, p. 84); by 1969 this figure had reached 6.6 percent (Janssen, 1972, p. 1). It is estimated that in 1970 one-third of all black students were enrolled in black colleges, one-third in public two-year colleges, and one-third in four-year, predominantly white institutions. The dramatic increases in black enrollment are in the predominantly white institutions. Increases have been especially great in the more selective institutions; the changes reported in Table 4-2 represent a considerable increase over the proportion of blacks at selective institutions even at the time the Carnegie Commission surveys were carried out. Still, in few institutions do the proportions of black undergraduates approximate the proportion of blacks in the population.

Data collected in 1961 indicate that only 3 percent of college *graduates* were black (see Harris, 1972, p. 98). Recent census data suggest that this proportion has risen. Of the age cohort of

TABLE 4-1
Race of entering freshmen, ACE national norms, 1966–1972 (in percentages)

	1966	1967	1968	1969	1972
White	90.9	90.1	88.3	90.9	87.3
Black	4.5	3.9	4.7	6.0	8.7
Native American	0.5	0.6	0.7	0.3	1.1
Oriental	0.8	0.9	1.2	1.7	1.1
Other	3.3	4.5	5.1	1.7	3.9

SOURCE: American Council on Education, 1966–1972.

	Fall '68	Fall '70
University of Alabama	1.2	2.3
American University	2.8	4.1
Amherst College	2.9	6.4
Antioch College	7.7	8.9
University of Arizona	1.0	1.4
University of Arkansas	1.1	1.1
Auburn University	0.2	0.6
Bowdoin College	3.2	6.5
Brandeis University	3.0	5.9
Brigham Young University	.03	.03
Brown University	2.3	7.2
University of California, Berkeley	2.3	4.5
University of California, LA	2.3	3.8
Carleton College	3.5	5.4
University of Chicago	3.8	6.7
City College of New York	5.2	15.5
University of Colorado	0.5	2.0
Columbia University	3.7	5.6
University of Connecticut	1.7	3.8
Cornell University	2.8	2.9
Dartmouth College	2.5	6.4
University of Delaware	0.7	2.6
University of Denver	1.7	1.3
Duke University	1.7	2.5
Emory University	1.7	2.4
University of Florida	0.5	1.5
Georgetown University	1.3	1.7
George Washington University	1.7	3.6
Georgia Institute of Technology	0.6	0.7
University of Georgia	0.5	0.9
Harvard University	3.2	5.8
Haverford College	5.6	9.1
University of Illinois	3.1	3.9
Indiana University	2.4	3.6
Iowa State University	0.5	0.8
University of Iowa	0.6	1.2

TABLE 4-2
Two-year change in black enrollment in 100 colleges and universities (in percentages)

TABLE 4-2
(continued)

	Fall '68	Fall '70
Johns Hopkins University	1.6	3.3
Kansas State University	1.5	1.3
University of Kansas	2.3	2.5
University of Kentucky	0.9	1.0
Louisiana State University	2.0	2.9
University of Maine	0.2	0.2
University of Maryland	2.0	3.4
Massachusetts Institute of Technology	0.7	3.1
University of Massachusetts	1.3	3.9
University of Miami	1.0	2.3
Miami-Dade Junior College	7.4	10.1
Michigan State University	2.9	4.8
University of Michigan	2.5	3.8
University of Minnesota	3.5	2.0
Mississippi State University	0.9	2.5
University of Mississippi	1.4	2.6
University of Missouri	1.4	2.3
University of Nevada	0.7	0.8
University of New Mexico	1.0	1.3
New York University	6.5	7.7
University of North Carolina	0.9	2.1
University of North Dakota	0.2	0.2
Northeastern University	2.6	3.8
Northwestern University	2.3	4.3
University of Notre Dame	1.1	1.6
Oberlin College	5.4	6.1
Ohio State University	2.6	2.8
Oklahoma State University	1.5	1.9
University of Oregon	1.5	1.6
Pennsylvania State University	1.8	3.0
University of Pennsylvania	1.9	4.2
Princeton University	2.9	6.1
Purdue University	1.5	1.7
Radcliffe College	3.3	8.3
Reed College	2.8	2.7
Rhode Island College	0.6	2.2

TABLE 4-2 (continued)	Fall '68	Fall '70
University of Rhode Island	0.8	0.9
St. Louis University	1.3	6.2
Sarah Lawrence	4.9	8.0
Seton Hall University	2.6	5.2
University of South Carolina	1.9	2.6
University of South Dakota	0.2	0.2
Southern Methodist University	0.5	2.3
Stanford University	2.8	4.0
State University New York, Buffalo	3.5	5.4
Swarthmore College	4.4	8.0
Syracuse University	2.7	1.9
University of Tennessee	1.4	1.9
University of Texas	0.9	0.8
Tulane University	1.9	2.5
University of Utah	0.4	0.6
Vanderbilt University	1.5	1.9
University of Vermont	0.1	0.4
University of Virginia	0.4	1.8
Washington State University	0.8	4.6
University of Washington	2.0	2.6
Washington University	2.1	4.1
Wayne State University	10.8	16.0
Wellesley College	1.5	5.3
Wesleyan University	7.9	10.8
West Virginia University	0.9	1.0
University of Wisconsin	2.1	2.9
University of Wyoming	0.5	0.8
Yale University	2.8	5.6

SOURCE: "Undergraduate Enrollments . . . ," 1971, p. 1. These figures are based on institution reports to the U.S. Office for Civil Rights.

blacks 25 to 29 years of age in 1970, 5 percent had completed four years of college. In 1960 only 3 percent of the cohort, between the ages of 25 and 29, had completed college (U.S. Bureau of the Census, 1970a).

Although these data show considerable gains in the enrollment of black undergraduates, the gains were not as great for black graduate students. Data collected in the middle sixties indicate that approximately 3 percent of the graduate students were black. The Carnegie Commission survey estimates a slightly smaller porportion: 2.4 percent in 1968. But it was estimated in 1971 that 4.4 percent of all currently enrolled graduate students were black. This, however, masks considerable variation by state (Table 4-3); in few states did the proportion of black students equal the proportion of blacks in the population. Blacks make up 28 percent of the population of Alabama and 14 percent of the graduate students. The vast majority of these students were attending predominantly black institutions. In California in 1969, blacks made up 3 percent of graduate students, but 7 percent of the population. Almost all the black graduate students were in predominantly white institutions.

This demonstrates the complexities inherent in explicating standards of proportionality. Should admission policies be aimed

	Number of blacks enrolled in graduate school	Percentage of black graduate student body	Percentage of blacks in state
Alabama	936	14	26
Arizona	56	1	3
Arkansas	43	2	18
California	2,031	3	7
Colorado	173	3	3
Connecticut	352	5	6
Delaware	21	2	14
Washington, D.C.	2,230	20	71
Florida	329	3	15
Georgia	1,249	10	26
Idaho	6	1	0
Illinois	1,361	6	13
Indiana	462	3	7
Iowa	92	1	1
Kansas	203	3	5
Kentucky	16	0	7
Louisiana	241	3	30

TABLE 4-3
Graduate school enrollments of blacks, by state

	Number of blacks enrolled in graduate school	Percentage of black graduate student body	Percentage of blacks in state
Maine	3	0	0
Maryland	545	6	18
Massachusetts	945	4	3
Michigan	1,681	7	11
Minnesota	230	2	1
Mississippi	460	12	37
Missouri	414	3	10
Montana	0	0	0
Nebraska	21	1	3
Nevada	12	1	6
New Hampshire	8	1	0
New Jersey	153	2	11
New Mexico	27	1	2
New York	1,635	4	12
North Carolina	422	4	22
North Dakota	8	0	0
Ohio	1,024	4	9
Oklahoma	149	4	7
Oregon	96	1	1
Pennsylvania	373	2	9
Rhode Island	60	2	3
South Carolina	50	1	31
South Dakota	3	0	0
Tennessee	1,533	28	16
Texas	501	2	13
Utah	17	0	1
Vermont	12	1	0
Virginia	336	4	19
Washington	98	2	2
West Virginia	35	1	4
Wisconsin	308	3	3
Wyoming	5	1	1

TABLE 4-3 (continued)

SOURCE: "Graduate School Enrollments . . ." (1971, p. 4); compiled by author.

at bringing the proportion of black undergraduates and graduates up to parity with the minority population in the state or with the minority population in the nation as a whole? This is further complicated by the fact that large numbers of students attend school outside their home states.

BLACK UNDER-GRADUATES Access to higher learning is a complicated matter involving individual and social-class differences in motivation, finances, and ability. In order to fully measure access, we would need to consider dimensions of access for which there are currently no adequate data: detailed information on applicants to institutions of higher learning to compare with entrants; descriptions of differential drop-out patterns; detailed measures of ability and motivation. Given the scope of the problem, what can be learned about minority access from single-time, cross-sectional data and from panel data on entrants?

We can begin to disaggregate the population of black undergraduates to see what kinds of students are going where to college. We can describe the characteristics of students entering college, the kinds of institutions they enter, and the nature of their academic careers. Minority access to higher learning is bound up with a complicated educational decision-making process. For the student it involves whether to go to college, what kind of college to attend, what to study, and for how long. For the institution it involves questions of preferential treatment, quotas, financial aid, and maintaining academic standards. This process works to determine who is in college at a given point in time and the kinds of educational decisions college students make. As we have said, previous studies of minority access have defined access at a single point in time, as access to *any* college. Here we are concerned with access to different kinds of colleges and fields of study. The choices of college, field, and degree program are all related to the measurement of minority access.

The question of ability looms over any discussion of minority access. Are lower-class and minority students underrepresented in the student population because they are less able? Jencks et al. suggest that this question cannot easily be separated from consideration of social class. "It is not clear to what extent cognitive skills really cause differences in educational attainment and to what extent they are simply associated with coming from the right family" (1972, p. 144). A comparison of two groups of students—born during the early forties—whose IQ scores in elementary school differed by 15 points indicates that the clever students ended up with 1.6 years more schooling than the slower students. But individuals from similar economic backgrounds who differ by 15 points differ by 1.25 years in their estimated educational attainment. If we compare pairs of men raised in the same home whose scores differ by 15 points, our best guess is that their educational attainment will differ by less than a year.[4]

Controlling for socioeconomic background, Table 4-4 indicates that a young man of low ability in the highest quarter of the population socioeconomically is *four* times as likely to enter college as a young man of comparable ability in the lowest quarter socioeconomically. A young man in the lowest socioeconomic quarter but of high ability is eight times as likely to enter college as is his peer of low ability. More recent data suggest that the same pattern holds. Sewell reports (Sewell, 1971, p. 795) that:

Among students in the lowest fourth of the ability distribution, those in the highest SES category have a 2.5 times advantage over those in the lowest SES category in their chances to go on to *some form* of post-high school education. For students in the highest ability fourth, the chances

[4] Ibid., p. 144; see also ibid., pp. 114–145 and footnote 29, p. 167 for method of approximation used above.

	Socioeconomic quartile			
Ability quartile	Low 1	2	3	High 4
	Males			
Low 1	.06	.12	.13	.26
2	.13	.15	.29	.36
3	.25	.34	.45	.65
High 4	.48	.70	.73	.87
	Females			
Low 1	.07	.07	.05	.20
2	.08	.09	.20	.33
3	.18	.23	.36	.55
High 4	.34	.67	.67	.82

TABLE 4-4
Probability of entering college, by ability and socioeconomic status

SOURCE: Flanagan et al. (1966).

of continuing their schooling are 1.5 times greater if they are from the highest rather than the lowest SES category. Similarly, in the lowest ability fourth the rate of college attendance is 4 times greater for the highest SES group than for the lowest SES group.

We must keep in mind that data based on the general population weight heavily for white students and that these data may not be accurately generalizable to blacks.[5] Although we will have occasions to look again at ability in conjunction with social class, we will focus here on social class as a major determinant of college going and of differences in academic careers.

Because the rate of recruitment of black undergraduates has increased so dramatically in the last half of the decade, it is important to consider two kinds of data: data on entering freshmen, which, because of the high drop-out rate, cannot be generalized to the population of undergraduates; and data from the United States census that attempt to measure characteristics of the entire undergraduate population.

In 1970, black Americans made up 11.2 percent of the population of the United States and 13.5 percent of the population between 20 and 30 years of age. Although blacks accounted for 10 percent of the population of entering freshmen, they made up only 6 percent of the population of currently enrolled students at the time the study was undertaken (American Council on Education, 1970).

The majority of black entering freshmen are women (Table 4-5A) as are the majority of all currently enrolled black students (Table 4-5B).

[5] These data are not available on blacks only. However, the National Advisory Commission on Civil Disorders noted that "in the nation approximately eight percent of disadvantaged high school graduates, many of whom are Negro, attend college; the comparable figure for all high school graduates is more than fifty percent" (Kerner, 1968, p. 452). O'Neil suggests that "the prospect of matriculation for the ghetto-black ninth or tenth grader may be something like one-eighteenth the prospect for the white middle-class suburban youth" (1971, p. 724).

TABLE 4-5A
Sex of entering freshmen (in percentages)

	Blacks	Whites
Male	46	57
Female	54	43
	100	100

SOURCE: American Council on Education (1966–1972).

TABLE 4-5B Sex of undergraduates (in percentages)	Blacks	Whites
Male	48	61
Female	52	39
	100	100

SOURCE: U.S. Bureau of the Census (1969*a*).

Looking only at entering freshmen, we find that black first-time students are older than nonblack students. Table 4-6 indicates that 29 percent of the black students and 19 percent of the nonblack students are 19 years of age or older.

If we look at all currently enrolled undergraduates, we find considerable variation within age-sex cohorts in college attendance. Although census data underrepresent black men in the college-age population, it is still useful to compare black and white age cohorts since this is the best estimate of the upper limit of the proportion of young black men in college. Table 4-7 indicates that in 1970 white men between the ages of 18 and 24 were twice as likely as black men to be enrolled in college; white women in that age group were one-and-a-half times as likely as black women to be enrolled in college. Again, we must reiterate that these figures underrepresent black men. The difference may, in fact, be considerably greater for men than we are indicating here. From these initial data, it is clear that blacks in the late sixties were considerably less likely than whites to attend college; young black men were much less likely than

TABLE 4-6 Age of first-time entering freshmen (in percentages) — Age in years, as of Dec. 31, 1968	Blacks	Whites
17	7	4
18	63	76
19	19 ⎫	13 ⎫
20	4 ⎬ 29	2 ⎬ 19
21	1 ⎪	1 ⎪
Older than 21	5 ⎭	3 ⎭
	99	99

SOURCE: American Council on Education (1966–1972).

TABLE 4-7 Proportion of age cohort in college, by race and sex		Black	White
Men			
	16–17 years	2	3
	18–19 years	22	47
	20–21 years	25	47
	22–24 years	9	24
	25–29 years	2	12
Women			
	16–17 years	2	4
	18–19 years	24	36
	20–21 years	17	25
	22–24 years	5	9
	25–29 years	3	4

SOURCE: U.S. Bureau of the Census (1969*a*).

young white men to attend college; and black men were even less likely to attend college than black women (Table 4-5B). The interrelationship of causes of the underrepresentation of blacks, especially black men, is difficult to discover. Of major importance is the fact that black men are less likely than black women or whites of either sex to finish high school. Table 4-8 reports the proportion of each age cohort having completed high school. If we focus on the cohort of 18- to 19-year-olds, we see that 40 percent of the white men have *not* completed high school (from Table 4-8) compared with over 60 percent of the black men. Of

TABLE 4-8 Proportion of age cohorts having completed high school, by race and sex (1970)		Black	White
Men			
	18–19 years	35	60
	20–21 years	47	82
Women			
	18–19 years	45	56
	20–21 years	68	83

SOURCE: U.S. Bureau of the Census (1970*c*).

the white men who graduated from high school, over two-thirds entered college; of the comparable blacks, slightly over one-half entered college. (These are estimates for the single cohort based on Tables 4-7 and 4-8.) Thus, although the rate of college going among black men who graduated from high school is somewhat less than that for whites, the major differentiating factor is that proportionately many more black men do not finish high school. The fact that a majority of the black entering freshmen and currently enrolled undergraduates are women is less surprising when this is accounted for. A study done by the National Scholarship Service and Fund for Negro Students in 1971 suggests that male attrition is especially heavy among students from poor families (Table 4-9).

SOCIAL CLASS BACKGROUND Data on entering freshmen and currently enrolled undergraduates suggest that both black and white undergraduates come disproportionately from middle- and upper-middle-class homes. Over a third of the black undergraduates come from poverty-level homes. What is not clear from the available data is whether recruitment patterns are changing, whether increasing numbers of low-income blacks are being admitted to college. The evidence is ambiguous, at best.

The late sixties clearly brought educational gains for black Americans. Black enrollment nearly doubled between 1964 and 1970. Although special attempts were made to recruit "authentic ghetto youth," census data suggest that proportionately the trend was in the opposite direction. Table 4-10 shows that 74 percent of the black families with students in college had annual incomes of less than $7,500 in 1967; in 1969, 56 percent of the families had incomes this low. In 1967, 27 percent of the families of white students had an annual income of $7,500 or less; in 1969 the figure was 21 percent. Although some of this is accounted for by changes in income distribution (see Table 4-11), this accounts

TABLE 4-9 *Sex ratios* within categories of gross family income (black high school students, 1971)*				
Total	*Under $3,000*	*$3,000–$5,999*	*$6,000–$8,999*	*Over $9,000*
69.9	57.2	66.4	72.9	73.7

*Number of men per 100 women students. A ratio of 100.0 implies no differential attrition by sex.

SOURCE: National Scholarship Service and Fund for Negro Students (1972, p. 1).

TABLE 4-10 Primary families with one or more dependent members attending college full time, by income and race (in percentages)	Income	Whites			Blacks		
		1969	*1968*	*1967*	*1969*	*1968*	*1967*
	$3,000 or less	3	3	2	13	17	24
	$3,000–$4,999	5 } 21	6	7 } 27	21 } 56	25	28 } 74
	$5,000–$7,499	13	16	18	21	22	22
	$7,500–$9,999	17	20	22	21	12	9
	$10,000–$14,999	33	30	29	17	17	11
	$15,000 and over	29	25	21	6	6	5
		100	100	99	99	99	99

SOURCE: U.S. Bureau of the Census (1969c, table 13).

for only a small part of the drop in the representation of lower-income families among those of currently enrolled undergraduates. Looking at all black families, 8 percent fewer black families reported an income of less than $7,500 in 1969 as compared with 1967. Looking at comparable black families with one child in college, we see that the proportion of low-income (under $7,500) families with one child in college is 18 percent smaller in 1969 than it was in 1967, two years earlier. This suggests that the attrition of black undergraduates from low-income families may have increased at the same time that access generally increased.

Census data on educational attainment of the head of the household support data using only income as a measure of

TABLE 4-11 Income of primary families, by race (in percentages)	Income	Whites			Blacks		
		1969	*1968*	*1967*	*1969*	*1968*	*1967*
	$3,000 or less	10	11	12	27	31	37
	$3,000–$4,999	14 } 46	15	16 } 54	26 } 76	27	27 } 84
	$5,000–$7,499	22	24	26	23	22	21
	$7,500–$9,999	20	20	20	12	9	8
	$10,000–$14,999	23	21	18	10	8	6
	$15,000 and over	12	10	8	3	2	1
		101	101	100	101	99	100

SOURCE: U.S. Bureau of the Census (1969c, table 13).

TABLE 4-12A
Educational attainment of heads of household with dependent child in college full time—1969 (in percentages)

Schooling	White	Black
0–4 years	1	7
5–7 years	3	17
8 years	8	8
1–3 years high school	12	17
4 years high school	37	22
1–3 years college	15	10
4 or more years college	25	18
	101	99

SOURCE: U.S. Bureau of the Census (1969c, table 12).

socioeconomic status. Both black and white undergraduates come disproportionately from homes where the head of the household is better educated than the probable cohort in the general population.[6] Five percent of the black men and women in the general population have at least a college degree (see Tables 4-12B and 4-12C). Table 4-12A indicates that 18 percent of the heads of households of black undergraduates have reached at least this level of education. The data on whites indicate that 14 percent of the white men and 8 percent of the white women in the general population are college graduates (Tables 4-12B and 4-12C). Twenty-five percent of the household heads of white undergraduates are college graduates or hold advanced degrees.

The social-class background data on entering freshmen generally support the data on currently enrolled undergraduates (Table

[6] We will use as the "probable age cohort" black men in the general population who in 1970 were between the ages of 45 and 74.

TABLE 4-12B
Educational attainment for men 45 to 74 years of age (1970), by race (in percentages)

	Black			White		
	45–54	*55–64*	*65–74*	*45–54*	*55–64*	*65–74*
Eighth grade or less	49 ⎱71	66 ⎱82	87 ⎱93	23 ⎱40	38 ⎱56	55 ⎱70
Some high school	22 ⎰	16 ⎰	5 ⎰	17 ⎰	18 ⎰	15 ⎰
High school graduate	20	10	4	34	25	15
Some college	6 ⎱9	3 ⎱8	3 ⎱4	12 ⎱26	9 ⎱19	6 ⎱16
College graduate	3 ⎰	5 ⎰	1 ⎰	14 ⎰	10 ⎰	10 ⎰
TOTAL	100	100	100	100	100	101

SOURCE: U.S. Bureau of the Census (1970b, table 1).

	Black			White		
TABLE 4-12C *Educational attainment for women 45 to 74 years of age (1970), by race (in percentages)*	*45–54*	*55–64*	*65–74*	*45–54*	*55–64*	*65–74*
Eighth grade or less	46	66	76	19	34	50
Some high school	24	18	12	18	18	15
High school graduate	20	11	5	46	31	21
Some college	6	2	4	10	10	7
College graduate	5	3	3	8	8	6
TOTAL	101	100	100	101	101	99

SOURCE: U.S. Bureau of the Census (1970*b*, table 1).

4-13). These data, however, indicate that black entrants, compared to currently enrolled black undergraduates, more nearly reflect the social-class characteristics of the general population. This suggests that the drop-out rates among lower-class blacks are considerably higher than among upper-class blacks, or that recruitment patterns are changing, or that both factors are operating simultaneously. In 1969, 76 percent of all black families reported incomes of less than $7,499 (Table 4-11); approximately 70 percent of black entrants reported this level of family income (section A of Table 4-13); but in 1968, 64 percent of the currently enrolled black students reported this level of family income (Table 4-10). This same pattern is reflected in education of fathers. Five percent of black men and women between the ages of 45 and 65 had at least a college degree (Tables 4-12B and 4-12C); 10 percent of the black entrants had fathers with at least a college degree (section B of Table 4-13); but 18 percent of the currently enrolled black undergraduates had heads of households with this level of education (Table 4-12A).

The most significant differences in socioeconomic level between the fathers of black students and the probable cohort of black men in the population is found in the data on occupation. Four times as many fathers of black entering freshmen are professionals as are black men in the general population (Table 4-13). Twice as many white entering freshmen had professional fathers compared with white men in the general population.

The increased recruitment of lower-class blacks has the effect of raising the average socioeconomic status of currently enrolled black undergraduates. Selective attrition has the opposite effect. Operating together any change over time may not be apparent in

TABLE 4-13 *Weighted national norms for entering college freshmen by type of institution and race: all freshmen, fall 1968 (in percentages)*

	All institutions		
	Black	*White*	
A. Estimated parental income			
Less than $4,000	31 ⎤	5 ⎤	
$4,000–$5,999	25 ⎬73	9 ⎬29	
$6,000–$7,999	17 ⎦	15 ⎦	80 percent of *all* black families report incomes of less than $7,499
$8,000–$9,999	11	17	
$10,000–$14,999	11	28	46 percent of *all* white families report incomes of less than $7,499
$15,000–$19,999	4	12	(See Table 4-11)
$20,000–$24,999	1	6	
$25,000–$29,999	1	3	
$30,000 or more	1	5	
B. Father's education			
Grammar school or less	25 ⎤56	10 ⎤26	71 percent of the black men between the ages of 45 and 54 have not completed high school
Some high school	31 ⎦	16 ⎦	
High school graduate	24	30	40 percent of the white men between the ages of 45 and 54 have not completed high school
Some college	11	18	
College degree	6	17	
Postgraduate degree	4	9	(See Table 4-12B)
C. Father's occupation			
Professional	17	24	
Business	6	32	3 percent of all black men were professionals in 1960
Skilled workers	13	13	
Semiskilled workers	19	8	13 percent of all white men were professionals in 1960
Unskilled workers	17	4	
Unemployed	4	1	(See Table 4-39)
Other	24	18	

NOTE: In making the comparison of the incomes of families of undergraduate students with the distribution of incomes in the general population (Tables 4-11 and 4-13) it must be noted that the bases for the two tables differ slightly. The census and the ACE use different reporting categories for income. The reader will note that 76 percent of all black families have an income under $7,499 while 73 percent of the families of black undergraduates have an income under $7,999.

SOURCE: American Council on Education (1968).

the characteristics of currently enrolled students, even though proportionately many more students from lower-class backgrounds are spending some time in college. Thus, over-time measures of the characteristics of both entrants and currently enrolled students are necessary to measure access patterns.

Partialing out the relative effects of social class and race on college attendance is a complicated task. Table 4-14 reports income of families with one or more dependents of college age who report no dependents attending college. For both blacks and whites, total family income is strongly related to having a dependent child in college. However, net of income, race appears to have an independent effect. Black families with annual incomes comparable to whites are less likely to report a child in college. Surprisingly this holds even among families with considerable family income ($10,000 or more).

There are obviously many factors we have not considered here: number of siblings, intact family, and geographical location of family. However, what these data indicate is that the relationship between social origins and college attendance is a strong one; that the relationship has remained remarkably constant over time; and that, over and above the effects of social class, race has an independent negative effect on college attendance.

INSTITUTIONAL QUALITY

The life chances of most black students are bound up with the quality of the institutions they attend. Faculty, curriculum, academic background of fellow students, and educational aspirations all vary by institutional quality. Eighty-five percent of the undergraduates in high-quality institutions plan to obtain some graduate education as compared with 50 percent at low-quality

---

[7] The estimates below are based on the number of primary families with dependent children in college. Less than 10 percent of the families have more than one dependent child in college.

TABLE 4-14 *Families with one or more dependents 18 to 24 years old reporting none attending college, by family annual income and race (in percentages)*

1969	$3,000 or less	$3,000– $4,999	$5,000– $7,499	$7,500– $9,999	$10,000– $14,999	$15,000 and over
White families reporting no dependent attending college	81	75	67	58	50	34
Black families reporting no dependent attending college	88	80	77	60	69	*

*Too few cases to report.

SOURCE: U.S. Bureau of the Census (1969c, table 13).

institutions. The quality of these institutions also affects career opportunities. In particular, the research-minded student's chances of ultimately obtaining a faculty or research position at a major university will depend, in large part, on the quality of his or her undergraduate and graduate institutions.

The evidence suggests that in 1971 blacks were concentrated in low-quality colleges and junior colleges and that relatively few attended high-quality undergraduate institutions. Commenting on this in *Social Policy*, Thomas Propos and Stephen Stearns suggest that "what passes for minimal standards of literacy among college juniors and seniors who have gone through two full years of community college would probably shake any serious high school teacher" (1971, p. 17). Jaffe, Adams, and Meyers, in an earlier work on predominantly Negro colleges, question "whether higher education at a 'poor' college is of any great value" unless accompanied by intensive remedial work (1968, p. 39).

The Coleman report was one of the first national efforts which attempted to assess whether significant characteristics of colleges varied by the racial composition of the student body. Or more specifically, the authors attempted to determine whether black "students attend colleges that are different with respect to characteristics presumably related to the quality of education" (Coleman et al., 1966, p. 368).

The data presented are confusing, however, and sometimes contradictory. On some reported dimensions (e.g., library resources) institutions with a significant proportion of black students were above the median level of all institutions, while on other dimensions (e.g., percentage of students pursuing degrees) black students were concentrated in institutions far below the institutional median (ibid., pp. 379–380). The analysis suffers generally from the lack of a composite index of institutional quality, which would weight for those institutional characteristics of greater or lesser relevance to student achievement. The findings are suggestive, however, of the importance of controlling for institutional quality. In 1965, nearly 7 in 10 black students attended institutions below the median in the percentage of students pursuing degrees, "a measure that should reflect the success the institution has in moving its students through to graduation" (ibid., p. 324). Nearly half of all black students were enrolled in institutions in the bottom quarter. Further, black students attended colleges in which small percentages of the faculty held a doctorate (ibid., p. 393).

The sample of colleges and universities used in the Carnegie Commission survey was classified at the time of the survey into seven quality groups: three quality groupings of universities, three of four-year colleges, and one of all junior colleges.[8] The classifications systems are based on information on selectivity from the American Council on Education, the Office of Education, and *The Gourman Report*.[9] The Gourman quality ratings are highly correlated with other less complete rating systems.[10] The *College-Rater* system was used to classify four-year colleges along with Gourman (*College-Rater*, 1967). The major criteria for *College-Rater* are: SAT-ACT scores of recently enrolled freshmen, proportion of faculty with doctorate, faculty salaries, and library collection. The two systems have roughly similar rankings, but both are necessary to cover all institutions in the universe.

The most complete recent information on the distribution of black undergraduates is found in a survey of institutions done by the *Chronicle of Higher Education* and reported in detail in the issue of March 29, 1971.[11] For our purpose, we assigned each institution in that report a quality category using the system described above. Table 4-15 indicates the distribution of black undergraduates by institutional quality. In 1970, 70 percent of the black undergraduates were attending the lowest-quality four-year colleges and junior colleges, as compared with only 52

8 For a detailed account of the sampling procedures and the institutional quality rankings, see Appendix A of this volume.

9 See Creager, 1968; U.S. Office of Education, 1969; and Gourman, 1967. Gourman provides three composite ratings for each institution: a rating of the academic departments in terms of such things as accreditation and the proportion of students receiving scholarships and fellowships; a rating of nondepartmental aspects of the institution, such as the administration's "commitment to excellence," the level of financial aid available to students, the board of trustees, and faculty morale (e.g., rank, tenure, salary scale, research facilities); and a total institutional rating that is simply the arithmetic mean of the departmental and nondepartmental ratings. The correlation between the departmental and nondepartmental ratings is very high ($r = +.956$). We decided, therefore, to use the institutional rating (which correlates $+.99$ with the departmental rating.)

10 The correlation between the rating system of Edward Gross and Paul Grambsch, using information supplied by Allan Cartter, is .83.

11 This issue was devoted to black enrollment in American colleges and universities and includes the number of full-time black students enrolled in 2,300 schools.

	Black undergraduates	White undergraduates
High-quality university	3	6
Medium-quality university	6	12
Low-quality university	9	14
High-quality college	4	6
Medium-quality college	8	11
Low-quality college	43 ⎫ 70	29 ⎫ 52
Junior college	27 ⎭	23 ⎭
Total percentage	100	101
Total number	311,662*	4,762,339*

TABLE 4-15
Quality of institution: distribution of black and white undergraduates (in percentages)

*In the survey by the Office for Civil Rights of the U.S. Department of Health, Education, and Welfare, institutions were asked to report only on full-time students. These estimates then do not include part-time students, nor do they include first-professional students. The numbers of students reported here are somewhat lower than that reported in the Office of Education, *Opening Fall Enrollment, 1971*. Differences are due to discrepancies in reporting standards.

SOURCE: *Chronicle of Higher Education* (1971).

percent of the white undergraduates. As we shall see, the characteristics of students and their academic plans vary considerably by institutional quality.

SOCIAL-CLASS BACKGROUND AND INSTITU-TIONAL QUALITY For both black and white undergraduates the social-class background of the student varies by the quality of the institution he attends. Even using gross measures of quality—two-year and four-year, predominantly white and predominantly black institutions—Table 4-16 indicates considerable variation in the social-class backgrounds of students at different types of institutions. Using these gross measures, however, there appears to be as much variation in the characteristics of white students at different types of institutions as exists between blacks and whites. If we use a more refined measure, we find an even stronger relationship between the social-class background of a student and the quality of the institution he attends; this is especially pronounced for blacks. Using two measures of SES and using a refined quality measure, we find that middle- and upper-middle-class students, both black and white, are more likely to attend

TABLE 4-16 Weighted national norms for entering college freshmen by type of institution and race: all freshmen, fall 1968

Item	All institutions		Predominantly white 2-year colleges		Predominantly white 4-year colleges		Predominantly Negro 4-year colleges		Predominantly white universities	
	Black	Nonblack	Black	Nonblack	Black	Nonblack	Black	Nonblack	Black	Nonblack
Father's occupation										
Professional	17	24	13	20	14	26	20	25	14	28
Business	6	32	6	26	7	33	5	17	8	36
Skilled workers	13	13	13	16	15	12	12	18	14	11
Semiskilled workers	19	8	19	11	19	8	18	14	21	6
Unskilled workers	17	4	18	5	15	3	17	4	17	2
Unemployed	4	1	5	1	5	1	5	2	3	1
Other	24	18	26	21	25	17	23	20	23	16
Estimated parental income										
Less than $4,000	31	5	27	7	27	4	38	17	21	3
$4,000–$5,999	25	9	29	13	22	9	25	20	23	7
$6,000–$7,999	17	15	19	19	19	15	14	17	21	12
$8,000–$9,999	11	17	10	19	11	17	9	16	13	16
$10,000–$14,999	11	28	10	26	14	29	9	20	14	30
$15,000–$19,999	4	12	3	9	4	12	3	7	5	14
$20,000–$24,999	1	6	1	4	1	6	2	2	1	7
$25,000–$29,999	1	3	0	2	1	3	1	0	1	4
$30,000 or more	1	5	0	2	1	5	1	1	1	7

TABLE 4-16 *(continued)*

Item	All institutions		Predominantly white 2-year colleges		Predominantly white 4-year colleges		Predominantly Negro 4-year colleges		Predominantly white universities	
	Black	*Nonblack*	*Black*	*Nonblack*	*Black*	*Nonblack*	*Black*	*Nonblack*	*Black*	*Nonblack*
Father's education										
Grammar school or less	25	10	27	14	21	8	27	17	20	7
Some high school	31	16	32	23	26	15	32	26	30	11
High school graduate	24	30	26	34	27	30	22	31	25	27
Some college	11	18	9	16	14	19	9	11	13	20
College degree	6	17	5	10	7	17	6	10	7	22
Postgraduate degree	4	9	1	3	5	10	4	6	5	13

SOURCE: American Council on Education (1966–1972).

TABLE 4-17A ***Family income,*** ***by institutional*** ***quality (entering*** ***freshmen, 1969)***	

Institutional quality: *colleges and universities*	*Percentage of families reporting* *income over $7,999 per year*
Black undergraduates	
High quality	62
Medium quality	38
Low quality	22
White undergraduates	
High quality	90
Medium quality	84
Low quality	77

SOURCE: 1969 Carnegie Commission Survey of Faculty and Student Opinion: all black undergraduates; random sample of 20,000 white undergraduates.

high-quality institutions (Tables 4-17A and 4-17B).[12] Of the black undergraduates at high-quality colleges and universities, 62 percent come from families reporting an income over $7,999; only 22 percent of the students in low-quality colleges and universities report this income. For white undergraduates the comparable figures are 90 percent and 77 percent. Of the black undergraduates at high-quality colleges and universities, 39 percent come from families in which the father has at least a college degree; only 9 percent of the fathers of black students at low-quality schools have a college degree. The same pattern holds for white undergraduates. The evidence, then, suggests that blacks are concentrated in low-quality colleges and junior colleges and that the majority of students not in low-quality institutions are from middle- and upper-middle-class homes. What is important to note is that the difference between whites and blacks in the high-quality institutions is smaller than in

[12] Because of an undersampling of junior colleges by ACE in 1966 and the withdrawal of several institutions before the first mailing, junior colleges are very much underrepresented in the Carnegie undergraduate sample. Therefore in some parts of the analysis supplementary data have been included; in others, junior colleges have been excluded, and in still others junior college students have been analyzed in combination with students from low-quality colleges. Almost none of the black students in the Carnegie sample are in junior colleges. However, from other sources we know that the social-class characteristics of black junior college students, overall, are very similar to those of blacks in low-quality colleges. See especially Bayer (1972). Therefore, where we have wanted to look at all students in low-quality colleges, we felt justified in combining these with the few junior college respondents.

TABLE 4-17B **Father's** **education, by** **institutional** **quality (entering** **freshmen, 1969)**	

Institutional quality colleges and universities	Percentage of fathers with at least a college degree
Black undergraduates	
High quality	39
Medium quality	6
Low quality	9
White undergraduates	
High quality	49
Medium quality	33
Low quality	27

SOURCE: 1969 Carnegie Commission Survey of Faculty and Student Opinion: all black undergraduates; random sample of 20,000 white undergraduates.

low-quality institutions: educated blacks are more *concentrated* in the more selective institutions.

If we look at these matters in another way, we can ask a different question. It is clear that, by and large, blacks are concentrated in low-quality institutions. Is this primarily because blacks are more likely to be poor? Table 4-18 addresses this question and examines how social origins and race together influence the likelihood of attending low-quality institutions. And what we find is that even when we control for father's education and occupation (seeing them as indicators of class origins), blacks are far more likely to be at more modest kinds of institutions than whites from similar class backgrounds. For example, roughly two-thirds of the black students from homes where the father is a college graduate, or alternatively, where the father is a professional, attend low-quality or two-year institutions. By contrast, only 40 percent of whites from homes where the father has a higher degree, and only a quarter of whites from professional homes, attend these low-quality institutions.

Similar access patterns exist even among very good students. Table 4-19 indicates that a large majority of the most able black students are attending low-quality colleges and junior colleges. Seventy-nine percent of black students with A, A-, and B averages in high school are in the lowest-quality schools. Eighty-three percent of the black students with a B average are in low-quality schools. Comparable figures for whites are 39 percent and 63 percent (Table 4-19).

Since social class and ability interact to affect life chances, it is necessary to consider both simultaneously (Table 4-20). Nearly half of the best students from black middle-class families attend higher-quality institutions; this is true for only 14 percent of able black students from lower-class families. While only a third of the middle-class students with a B or B- average attend higher-quality schools, 44 percent of the white students of comparable background and ability attend the better institutions (Table 4-20).

Thus, both ability and social class affect a student's chances of attending selective institutions. But there appears to be a racial component as well. Middle-class white students of only somewhat better than average ability are more likely than blacks of comparable background and ability to attend better institutions.

THE ACADEMIC CAREERS OF BLACK AND WHITE UNDER-GRADUATES There are many similarities in the educational decision-making processes of black and white undergraduates, but there are some notable differences. Black undergraduates, overall, are more pragmatic in their orientation to higher learning, but at the same

TABLE 4-18 **Institutional quality, by father's education and occupation (in percentages)**	All universities; high- and medium-quality colleges		Low-quality colleges and junior colleges	
	Blacks	Whites	Blacks	Whites
Father's education				
Postgraduate degree	36	60	64	40
College degree	26	53	74	47
Some college	22	39	78	61
High school graduate	21	36	79	63
Some high school	11	31	88	69
Grammar school or less	9	24	91	76
Father's occupation				
Professional	32	74	68	26
White collar	21	45	79	55
Farm	0	37	100	63
Skilled labor	17	33	83	67
Semiskilled labor	17	30	83	70
Military	39	40	61	60

SOURCE: 1969 Carnegie Commission survey.

TABLE 4-19
Quality of
entering
institution, by
secondary school
grade point
average (in
percentages)

	Grade point average		
	A, A−, B+	B, B−	C or below
Black undergraduates			
All universities; high- and medium-quality colleges	21	17	10
Low-quality colleges and junior colleges	79	83	90
Total	100	100	100
White undergraduates			
All universities; high- and medium-quality colleges	61	37	17
Low-quality colleges and junior colleges	39	63	83
Total	100	100	100

SOURCE: 1969 Carnegie Commission survey.

time they have very high educational aspirations. Although black undergraduates report lower grades and generally lower scores on standardized tests, they are not less likely to want to pursue advanced degrees or to rate themselves poorly when compared with their high school and college peers. This suggests that motivation is a major factor in making the choice to enter college. The American Council on Education indicates that:

1 "Black students report lower high school grades than do nonblack students. Almost 14 percent of the nonblack students and 6 percent of the black students report high schools grades of A- or better.

2 Blacks tended to rate the academic standards of their high school lower than the nonblack students."

3 'Black and nonblack students rank themselves similarly in their high school class. . . and

4 Proportionately more black students than nonblack students have postbaccalaureate degree aspirations" (Bayer, 1972, p. 16).

ACADEMIC MAJORS   Minority access can be measured by looking at these degree aspirations and the kinds of departments and educational programs in which blacks are engaged. Are blacks concentrated in particular fields? Are blacks "cooled out" to particular departments or programs or are they seemingly making the same kinds of educational decisions as are white undergraduates? Are the initial high aspirations of black undergraduates dampened by their educational experience?

If we compare the "probable" majors of undergraduates in the Carnegie sample as entering freshmen with the distribution of major fields of undergraduates who are currently enrolled, we find that the distributions of majors are quite similar

TABLE 4-20
Quality of entering institution, by income and secondary school grade point average (in percentages)

	Grade point average		
	A, A−, B+	B, B−	C or below
Lower-income families (black)			
All universities; high- and medium-quality colleges	14	13	10
Low-quality colleges and junior colleges	86	87	90
Total	100	100	100
*Lower-income families (white)**			
All universities; high- and medium-quality colleges	52	23	11
Low-quality colleges and junior colleges	48	78	89
Total	100	101	100
Middle- and high-income families (black)			
All universities; high- and medium-quality colleges	52	32	14
Low-quality colleges and junior colleges	48	68	86
Total	100	100	100
Middle- and high-income families (white)			
All universities; high- and medium-quality colleges	66	44	11
Low-quality colleges and junior colleges	35	57	89
Total	101	101	100

*Families with reported total family incomes of less than $7,999 in 1969.
SOURCE: 1969 Carnegie Commission survey.

for black and white undergraduates at entrance and over time. Table 4-21 indicates that black entering freshmen are as likely as whites to choose the sciences and the old professions. Blacks are somewhat more likely than whites to choose the social sciences and less likely to choose engineering. But, it is clear, and the graduate data support this, that blacks see the world outside the university opening up to them. Blacks are entering the sciences, the professions, and business in almost the same proportions as white undergraduates.

Importantly, there appear to be no significant shifts of individuals into so-called easy or soft fields. Table 4-22A and 4-22B compare the probable majors of two cohorts of black students at entrance and the actual major three to four years later.[13] There is no evidence of substantial shifts in major field after the time of entrance. This is not to say that individuals do not change major fields; but black students in general are not entering or being "cooled-out" to particular fields after having had some contact with academic life.

[13] The coding conventions used for the data collected on juniors and seniors varied somewhat from those used on the initial (freshman) data. The later coding scheme coded double majors as a legitimate category rather than using the ACE scheme of choosing one or another major. There is no evidence that these double majors concentrated in any particular field.

TABLE 4-21
Probable major at time of entrance, by race—black and white undergraduates; all cohorts (in percentages)

	Black undergraduates	White undergraduates
Humanities	15	17
Social sciences (including history and social work)	21	14
Biological sciences	4	4
Physical sciences	7	6
Education	12	11
Engineering	4	9
Business (including secretarial)	16	12
Other professions and fields	20	26
TOTAL	99	99

SOURCE: 1969 Carnegie Commission survey.

TABLE 4-22A Probable major field of two cohorts of black students at entrance* (in percentages)	
Arts and humanities	13
Biological sciences	6
Accounting	2
Business administration	7
Other business	5
Engineering	4
Physical sciences	13
Social sciences (including history and social work)	26
Education	7
Other professions and fields	18
	101

*Cohorts who were freshmen in 1966 and 1967.

SOURCE: 1969 Carnegie Commission survey.

There is a somewhat more pessimistic side, however. Field choice varies considerably by institutional quality, and although the patterns of field choice are similar for blacks and whites within quality categories, the fact is that few blacks attend

TABLE 4-22B Major field in junior or senior year* (in percentages)	
Arts and humanities	12
Biological sciences	6
Accounting	2
Business administration	7
Other business	3
Engineering	1
Physical sciences	10
Social sciences (including history and social work)	27
Education	9
Other professions and fields	5
Double majors	18
	100

*Cohorts who were freshmen in 1966 and 1967.

SOURCE: 1969 Carnegie Commission survey.

high-quality colleges and universities. In high-quality colleges and universities 7 percent of the blacks are in engineering; only 2 percent of the blacks in low-quality institutions are in engineering (Table 4-23). Blacks in low-quality colleges and universities are considerably more likely to enter business-related fields when compared with those in other institutions. Many of the students are secretarial students. Although more blacks than whites at high-quality institutions are planning careers in the old professions (law and medicine), these black undergraduates are a very small proportion of the black student population.

Degree aspirations as well as major field vary with the quality of the institution. Significantly more students in high- and medium-quality institutions plan to obtain advanced degrees. This is especially true among blacks (Table 4-24).

It is important to note, too, that the aspirations of blacks do not change significantly over time. Comparing the level of aspiration of entering freshmen for a higher degree with that of black juniors and seniors indicates that aspirations are as high or higher three or four years after entering college as they are at the outset (Table 4-25A and 4-25B).

Another measure of aspiration or possible "cooling-out" is

TABLE 4-23 *Major or intended major of black and white undergraduates by quality of institution*

	High-quality college and universities		Medium-quality college and universities		Low-quality college and universities	
	Black	*White*	*Black*	*White*	*Black*	*White*
Humanities	19	22	10	22	15	21
Social sciences	39	31	30	29	28	23
Biological sciences	8	7	5	7	6	6
Physical sciences	9	13	11	11	12	9
Education	5	3	18	10	10	15
Engineering	7	14	5	7	2	4
Business	4	3	7	6	19	12
Other professions (including home economics, nursing, agriculture)	8	7	14	7	9	10
TOTAL	99	100	100	99	101	100

SOURCE: 1969 Carnegie Commission survey, all cohorts.

	A.A.	B.A.	M.A. or other first professional	Ph.D. or Ed.D.	Total
Black undergraduates					
High-quality	1	14	46	39	100
Medium-quality	1	22	42	35	100
Low-quality	3	30	49	18	100
Junior colleges	15	34	49	2	100
White undergraduates					
High-quality	1	17	54	28	100
Medium-quality	3	31	50	28	101
Low-quality	4	39	46	12	101
Junior colleges	16	39	36	9	100

TABLE 4-24
Highest degree intend to obtain, by quality of the institution, black and white undergraduates, (in percentages)

SOURCE: 1969 Carnegie Commission survey, all cohorts.

probable career choice. Here there are some aggregate changes, but distributions of the career choices of entering freshmen and upper-class students are still quite similar. Comparing career choices of black freshmen with those of the same students three or four years later, we find that fewer blacks as juniors and seniors intend a career in the old professions, but a larger proportion hope to become college teachers. Similarly, many fewer blacks, by the time they are juniors or seniors, plan with certainty to be social workers and teachers (Table 4-26).

We have seen from these data that race, social class, and ability all affect the chances that a student will finish high school and attend college, particularly a selective college or university.

TABLE 4-25A
Highest degree black undergraduates expect to obtain (asked at entrance) (in percentages)

	High-quality colleges and universities	Medium-quality colleges and universities	Low-quality colleges and universities
Associate in arts	2	2	4
Bachelor's	7	19	24
Master's	51	52	49
Ph.D. or Ed.D.	40	27	22
TOTAL	100	100	99

SOURCE: 1969 Carnegie Commission survey, 1966 and 1967 cohorts.

TABLE 4-25B *Highest degree* *black* *undergraduates* *expect to obtain*		*High-quality* *colleges and* *universities*	*Medium-quality* *colleges and* *universities*	*Low-quality* *colleges and* *universities*
(asked in junior *or senior year)* *(in percentages)*	*Associate in arts*	0	0	1
	Bachelor's	4	8	15
	Master's	46	66	61
	Ph.D. or Ed. D.	50	26	23
	TOTAL	100	100	100

SOURCE: 1969 Carnegie Commission survey, 1966 and 1967 cohorts.

In summary, the data here suggest that:

1   Blacks are concentrated in the lowest-quality colleges. This is true even for black undergraduates of considerable ability.

2   Social-class access patterns of blacks are similar to those of white undergraduates: students from lower-class families, both black and white, are less likely than others in their age cohort to be enrolled in college; and if enrolled, they are more likely to be in unselective institutions.

3   The data suggest, however, that the whole story does not depend on social class. There is a racial component as well. Census data suggest

TABLE 4-26 *Career choice* *(selected*		*At entrance*	*As juniors* *and seniors*
professions)— *black students at* *entrance and as* *juniors and*	*Business executive* *and accountant*	8	14
seniors (in *percentages)*	*Social welfare,* *counseling, psychology*	16	11
	Teacher:		
	Elementary	8	3
	Secondary	16	5
	College	2	11
	Medicine (doctor, *dentist)*	7	5
	Law	6	5
	Engineer	3	4
	Scientist, researcher	4	4

SOURCE: 1969 Carnegie Commission survey.

that blacks are less likely than whites from comparable homes to attend college. Further, able blacks are more likely than whites of comparable ability to attend lower-quality institutions.

4   Black students currently enrolled in college have very high academic aspirations that do not appear to change significantly over time. There is little evidence that blacks are "cooled-out" to particular departments or fields. Blacks are somewhat more likely than whites to be in the social sciences (which may include ethnic studies), a phenomenon that may mask some self-recruitment or "cooling-out." But there is no direct evidence of this.

5   It must be stressed that lower-class blacks, especially young men, are very much underrepresented in institutions of higher learning and are especially underrepresented in the best institutions.

6   The careful measurement of minority access to higher learning demands a close look at the characteristics of entrants, currently enrolled students, and graduates—especially with respect to sex, age, and social-class background. This must be looked at in the context of the kinds of institutions minority students attend, the fields they enter, and the level of aspiration that they have.

THE DIS-
TRIBUTION
OF BLACK
GRADUATE
STUDENTS

Before turning to the relationship among social class, race, and access at the graduate level, we will look at some of the institutional and demographic characteristics significant for the analysis of this larger question.

In 1969, blacks made up between 2.5 and 3.0 percent of the total graduate student population.[14] The fact that this proportion is as small as it is is partly due, of course, to the fact that increased minority enrollment among undergraduates was not yet reflected in graduate student enrollment. The distribution of graduate students by quality of institutions is given in Table 4-27.

There were proportionately twice as many black graduate students at low-quality universities as at high-quality universities; white graduate students, too, were concentrated in low-quality institutions (Table 4-28). From Tables 4-27 and 4-28 we can see that blacks are vastly underrepresented in the general population of graduate students but that the distribution of blacks in the sample institutions by quality does not differ greatly from that of white graduates. The majority of *all* graduate students are

[14]   The weighted estimate from the present study is 2.5 percent. Other sources have estimated between 2 and 3 percent. This difference is a function of different institutional samples and weighting schemes. See "Graduate-School Enrollments . . . ," (1971).

TABLE 4-27
Representation of black graduate students by quality of institutions (percentage of graduate students who are black for each quality cell)

Universities	
High quality	1.7
Medium quality	2.0
Low quality	3.4
Four-year colleges	2.5

SOURCE: 1969 Carnegie Commission survey.

in low-quality universities and four-year colleges. (The latter are master's candidates, and largely in education.)

Table 4-29 indicates that black graduate students in the Carnegie sample are as likely as whites to be in private institutions. This may reflect the increased recruitment efforts in recent years on the part of specific institutions. Preliminary institutional analysis supports this. Forty-three percent of the black graduates at predominantly white schools are located in 10 (all high- and medium-quality universities) of the 165 sample institutions, but only a quarter of the white graduates are in these same 10 institutions.

These initial tables suggest that blacks and whites are *similarly* distributed in the graduate institutions, but the pool of blacks is very small. Again, however, gross figures such as these mask the considerable differences that exist between the populations of black and white students. There are, even at the graduate level, proportionately more women among black graduate students than among white graduate students, and overall, the black graduate students are older than the whites. We must take both factors into consideration in order to assess, in a meaningful way, the access of black students to graduate school.

TABLE 4-28
Quality of current institution (in percentages)

	Black graduate students	White graduate students
Universities		
High quality	12	16
Medium quality	22	26
Low quality	29	22
Four-year colleges	37	37
TOTAL	100	101

SOURCE: 1969 Carnegie Commission survey.

TABLE 4-29
Control of present institution (in percentages)

		Black graduate students		White graduate students	
		All graduate colleges and universities	High-quality universities	All graduate colleges and universities	High-quality universities
Public		63	46	66	46
Private		37	54	35	54
	TOTAL	100	100	100	100

SOURCE: 1969 Carnegie Commission survey.

As we have said, central to any discussion of minority access is the necessity of disaggregating the population into more or less homogeneous subsets whose relative representation can be measured. Age is a significant variable in this regard. The graduate students range in age from 20 to 40 and over. Different generations pursuing quite different objectives are all included in the designation "graduate student."

AGE   The black students, overall, are considerably older than the white students (Table 4-30). Of the black graduates, 56 percent are 30 and older as compared with 38 percent of the white graduate students. The median age of black and white students varies by type of institution. Typically, younger graduate students are found in universities, and older graduates are found in four-year colleges. But even at high-quality universities, where we would expect a higher proportion of younger students, we find that only 56 percent of the black graduates are under 30, compared with nearly 80 percent of the white graduate students.

TABLE 4-30   *Age: black and white graduate students (in percentages)*

	Total		High-quality universities		Medium- and low-quality universities		Four-year colleges	
	Blacks	Whites	Blacks	Whites	Blacks	Whites	Blacks	Whites
Under 30	44	62	56	78	54	65	27	48
30–39	28	24	31	16	27	24	27	28
40 and over	28	14	13	6	18	11	45	23
TOTAL	100	100	100	100	99	100	99	99

SOURCE: 1969 Carnegie Commission survey.

At the four-year colleges nearly half of the black graduate students, but only a quarter of the white graduate students are over 40. Thus, we find that although the same proportion of black and white graduate students are in four-year colleges (37 percent), the blacks are, overall, much older than the white students.

We saw in Table 4-29 that the distribution of students in public and private institutions is much the same for both blacks and whites. If we introduce age, we again find differences in the distributions by race. Table 4-31 indicates that young blacks are more likely than young whites to attend private institutions. This is, no doubt, further evidence of the selective recruitment taking place at many integrated private institutions. It also reflects the fact that many of the black graduates are attending predominantly black private colleges. For older blacks, however, the public institutions clearly afford the greatest access. Eighty-one percent of the black graduate students 40 and over were in public institutions.

SEX Sex is also important in measuring minority access to graduate education. As Table 4-32 indicates, nearly half of the black graduate students are women, compared with only a third of the white graduate students. The largest differences in the sex distribution exist in the four-year colleges and the low- and medium-quality universities. Sixty percent of black students at four-year institutions are women, and nearly half of the students at low- and medium-quality universities are women. Only at the high-quality universities is the ratio of men to women similar for blacks and whites. Of the white graduates, 72 percent are men; of the black graduates, 67 percent are men.

TABLE 4-31 Control of institution by age and race (in percentages)

Control	Black graduates			White graduates		
	Under 30	30–39	40 and over	Under 30	30–39	40 and over
Public	52	64	81	65	61	65
Private	48	36	19	35	39	35
TOTAL	100	100	100	100	100	100

SOURCE: 1969 Carnegie Commission survey.

TABLE 4-32 *Sex: black and white graduate students (in percentages)*

		Total		High-quality universities		Medium- and low-quality universities		Four-year colleges	
		Blacks	Whites	Blacks	Whites	Blacks	Whites	Blacks	Whites
Women		48	32	32	28	45	26	60	36
Men		52	69	67	72	55	74	40	64
	TOTAL	100	101	99	100	100	100	100	100

SOURCE: 1969 Carnegie Commission survey.

In terms of evaluating minority access we are interested particularly in the representation of *young* black men and women relative to *young* whites. As we shall see later, the older black students are quite unlike the younger students in both academic and career plans. Table 4-33 indicates that there are proportionately fewer young black men among graduate students than there are young white men. We can pursue this further by asking what percentage of all black graduates are young men relative to the percentage of young men among whites. Table 4-34 indicates that of the blacks only 26 percent are men under 30; this compares with 45 percent for whites. Of *all* graduate students 42 percent are young white men and 0.5 percent are young black men (Table 4-35). This is a ratio of over 80 to 1. In the general population the ratio of young white men to young black men is 8 to 1.

GEOGRAPHICAL MOBILITY A word must also be said about physical access to institutions of higher learning. How close a student lives to a college or

TABLE 4-33 *Sex, by age, for black and white graduate students (in percentages)*

		Black graduate students			White graduate students		
		Under 30	30–39	40 and older	Under 30	30–39	40 and older
Men		56	58	39	72	75	42
Women		44	42	61	28	24	57
	TOTAL	100	100	100	100	99	99

SOURCE: 1969 Carnegie Commission survey.

TABLE 4-34 *Proportions of* *graduate* *students, by age* *and sex, for* *blacks and for* *whites*		*Black graduate* *students*	*White graduate* *students*
Men			
	Under 30	26	45
	30 and older	28	24
Women			
	Under 30	20	19
	30 and older	26	13
		100	101

SOURCE: 1969 Carnegie Commission survey.

university plays a part in college going, although probably a less important part for graduate students than for undergraduates. From Table 4-36 we can see that only a third to a half of all graduate students in our sample attend graduate school in their home state. The reasons for this, however, may be different for black students and for white students. Many blacks, especially Southern blacks, may be forced to look outside their home state for a school of their choice. Clearly, much more must be known about geographical mobility and its effect on patterns of access.

TABLE 4-35 *Proportions of* *black and white* *graduate* *students in total* *graduate* *population, by* *age and sex*		*Total graduate sample*
Men		
	White under 30	41.5
	White 30 and older	21.1
	Black under 30	.6
	Black 30 and older	.6
Women		
	White under 30	16.9
	White 30 and older	11.8
	Black under 30	.4
	Black 30 and older	.5
	Other minority students	5.7
		99.1

SOURCE: 1969 Carnegie Commission survey.

	Black graduate students			White graduate students		
	Under 30	*30–39*	*40 and over*	*Under 30*	*30–39*	*40 and over*
Grew up in state	41	35	36	49	43	53

TABLE 4-36 Percentages of graduate students who grew up in state attending school, by age (for black and white students)

SOURCE: 1969 Carnegie Commission survey.

SOCIAL ORIGINS

As we have seen, social-class origins of black students are of particular significance in determining both the degree of opportunity and the mobility that exists in American society. For all races taken together, the simple correlation between father's educational attainment and son's educational attainment is .45; the simple correlation between father's occupation and son's education is .43.[15] These correlations can be taken as crude indicators of the relative chances of sons of lower-class parents attaining considerably more education than their parents and attaining jobs of higher status. Thus, a perfect correlation would offer no hope to the child of lower-class parents, a zero correlation much hope. As it stands, the moderate correlation indicates that a lower-status child is not wholly excluded from an occupational status or a level of educational attainment higher than his father's. For blacks from lower-class homes, however, the avenues are not as open as these correlations might suggest. For most lower-class youth the path toward upward mobility leads to college. But as Table 4-37 indicates, the child of a blue-collar worker has only one-third as great a chance of entering college as the child of a professional or semiprofessional. For children from blue-collar black families the chances are smaller still. Yet nearly three-quarters of all black children come from blue-collar homes. Thus, blacks are less likely to be in graduate school simply because a smaller proportion of blacks become undergraduates. This is especially true, as we have seen, for young black men.

EDUCATION OF FATHER AND MOTHER

Although parents' educational attainment is only one indicator of social class, it is useful here because we know it is positively associated with favorable attitudes toward the value of academic

[15] From Christopher Jencks (1968, p. 280); for a detailed argument on the effects of education on occupational status, see Blau and Duncan (1967, p. 170).

TABLE 4-37
Relation
between father's
occupation and
probability that a
high school
graduate will
enter college
and graduate

Father's occupation	Percentage of high school graduates who enter college	Percentage of college entrants who graduate from college	Percentage of high school graduates who also graduate from college
Professional and semiprofessional	67	60	40
Managerial	50	55	28
White collar (clerical, sales, service)	48	57	27
Farmer	24	44	11
Factory, craftsmen, unskilled, etc.	26	58	15

SOURCE: Harris (1972, p. 61); see also Jencks et al. (1972, pp. 19–20).

training. Several significant factors emerge from data on parents' educational attainment. The parents of black graduate students have considerably less education than the parents of white graduate students, but they have considerably more education than their (probable) cohorts in the general population.

Over 40 percent of all the fathers of black graduate students have less than an eighth-grade education; 19 percent of the fathers of white graduate students have less than eight years of education (Table 4-38). If, however, we look only at young graduate students (under 30) we see that, overall, fathers' educational attainment is quite *similar* for both black and white students, differing significantly only in the proportions having less than an eighth-grade education. For young blacks the proportion of fathers having at least a college degree is close to the proportion for whites. This similarity in father's educational attainment does not hold true for older graduate students. Over three-quarters of the fathers of black graduate students who are 30 and over have less than a high school education as compared with less than half of the fathers of older white graduate students. (It is important, here, not to lose sight of absolute numbers. There are proportionately many more older black graduate students than white; so, overall, many more of the black graduate students have fathers with less than a high school diploma.)

Although the fathers of black graduate students are less well educated than fathers of white graduate students, they are considerably better educated than their peers in the black population. This is especially true for younger blacks. Black men between the ages of 45 and 74 make up the probable age cohort of men comparable to the fathers of graduate students. The distribution of education by race and age in the general population is given in Table 4-39. If we look only at black men between 45 and 54, so as not to give undue weight to the older and, therefore, less-educated, we find that 71 percent have had less than a high school education. Among the fathers of young black graduate students, only 41 percent have had less than a high school education (Table 4-38).

If we compare the proportions having some college, we find that 40 percent of the fathers of young black graduate students have had some college; but only 9 percent of the black men between 45 and 54 have had some college. Among the older blacks the distributions of fathers' education more nearly approximates that in the general population of black men, although educational attainment of the fathers of graduate students is still somewhat higher.

TABLE 4-38 *Father's education, for black and white graduate students, by age (in percentages)*

	Black graduate students			White graduate students		
	Under 30	*30–39*	*40 and older*	*Under 30*	*30–39*	*40 and older*
Eighth grade or less	27 ⎫ 41	39 ⎫ 79	54 ⎫ 78	14 ⎫ 28	32 ⎫ 49	41 ⎫ 57
Some high school	14 ⎭	40 ⎭	24 ⎭	14 ⎭	16 ⎭	16 ⎭
Completed high school	20	12	3	23	19	16
Some college	12 ⎫	4 ⎫	7 ⎫	16 ⎫	14 ⎫	10 ⎫
Graduated from college	10	2	5	15	9	8
Attended graduate or professional school	6 ⎬ 40	2 ⎬ 10	2 ⎬ 18	6 ⎬ 50	4 ⎬ 34	3 ⎬ 26
Attained advanced degree	12 ⎭	2 ⎭	4 ⎭	13 ⎭	7 ⎭	5 ⎭
TOTAL	101	101	99	101	101	99

SOURCE: 1969 Carnegie Commission survey.

**TABLE 4-39
Educational attainment for men, ages 45 to 74, by race (in percentages)**

	Black			White		
	45–54	*55–64*	*65–74*	*45–54*	*55–64*	*65–74*
Eighth grade or less	49	66	87	23	38	55
Some high school	22	16	5	17	18	15
(subtotal)	71	82	92	40	56	70
High school graduate	20	10	4	34	25	15
Some college	6	3	3	12	9	6
College graduate	3	5	1	14	10	10
(subtotal)	9	8	4	26	19	16
TOTAL	100	100	100	100	100	101

SOURCE: U.S. Bureau of the Census (1970*a*, table 1).

To summarize, for all graduate students the level of father's educational attainment is higher than the level of attainment for the probable cohort in the general population. Young black graduate students are especially likely to come from homes where the father's educational attainment is significantly higher than the mean attainment in the probable cohort.

MOTHER'S EDUCATION Although the mothers of black graduate students have less education than the mothers of white graduate students, there are several noteworthy observations to be made. First, the mothers of *young* black graduate students are as likely to have graduated from college or attended graduate school as are the mothers of white graduate students. Over a quarter of both groups have at least a bachelor's degree. Still, even among young black students a considerable proportion of mothers have less than a high school diploma.

Young black and *young* white graduate students have mothers with a considerably higher level of educational attainment than is true in the general population. Of all black women 45 to 54 years of age, 70 percent have less than a high school education (Table 4-41); this is true of only 37 percent of the mothers of the young black graduate students (Table 4-40). *Older* black graduates are also disproportionately from homes with well-educated mothers, although a much higher proportion of the mothers of older students do not have a high school diploma.

FATHER'S
OCCUPATION The occupation of the graduate student's father is important in determining both level of aspiration and financial ability to continue with graduate training. The data on occupations suggest that black graduate students come disproportionately from homes where the father has a high-status occupation. This is especially true for young black graduate students. Further, it is apparent from these data that children of blue-collar workers, both black and white, are vastly underrepresented in the graduate student population. Among young black and white graduate students, only a fifth of the fathers have blue-collar jobs.

If we compare the occupational distribution of the fathers of black graduate students with the distributions in the general population, we find a much larger proportion of blue-collar workers in the general population than in the sample of student fathers.

Table 4-42 indicates that only about 3 percent of the employed black men in the general population are professional or technical workers. Table 4-43 indicates that among the fathers of *young* black graduate students 25 percent are professionals. Looking again at Table 4-42, we find that fewer than 15 percent of black

TABLE 4-40 *Mother's education, for black and white graduate students, by age (in percentages)*

	Black students			White students		
	Under 30	30–39	40 and older	Under 30	30–39	40 and older
Eighth grade or less	18 ⎫ 37	29	46	9 ⎫ 20	24	31
Some high school	19 ⎭	33	20	11 ⎭	15	18
Completed high school	26	26	8	38	30	24
Some college	11	5	21	18	14	16
Graduated from college	12 ⎫	3 ⎫	5 ⎫	15 ⎫	10 ⎫	8 ⎫
Attended graduate or professional school	7 ⎬ 27	3 ⎬ 8	1 ⎬ 6	5 ⎬ 25	2 ⎬ 16	3 ⎬ 12
Attained advanced degree	8 ⎭	2 ⎭	— ⎭	5 ⎭	4 ⎭	1 ⎭
TOTAL	101	101	101	101	99	101

SOURCE: 1969 Carnegie Commission survey.

TABLE 4-41
Educational
attainment of
women 45 to 74
(1970), by race
(in percentages)

	Black women			White women		
	45–54	*55–64*	*65–74*	*45–54*	*55–64*	*65–74*
Eighth grade or less	46	66	76	19	34	50
Some high school	24	18	12	18	18	15
High school graduate	20	11	5	46	31	21
Some college	6	2	4	10	10	7
College graduate	5	3	3	8	8	6
TOTAL	101	100	100	101	101	99

SOURCE: U.S. Bureau of the Census (1970*a*, table 1).

men between the ages of 45 and 65 are white-collar workers, while this is true for 44 percent of the fathers of *young* black graduate students. The discrepancy between the proportion of professionals in the general population compared with graduate students' fathers is even greater when we consider that the base used in Table 4-42 is the base of employed men. This, of course, underrepresents older black men, who have relatively higher rates of unemployment and disability.

The older black graduate students are less likely than younger blacks to come from professional and white-collar families but are still more likely to come from professional and white-collar families than members of their cohort outside the student community.

If we compare the distribution of fathers' occupation for black graduate students with that for white graduate students, we find that white graduate students are also more likely to come from professional homes. In the general population, 11 percent of the white men between the ages of 45 and 65 are professionals, whereas 23 percent of the fathers of white graduate students are professionals. Comparing the statuses of fathers of young white and young black graduate students with the comparable cohort in the general population, we find that while there are twice as many professional fathers as professionals in the general population for whites, there are six times as many professional fathers as exist in the black population as a whole.

It is important to note that the overrepresentation of young blacks from white-collar families is not a function of a change in the distribution of occupations of the cohorts of men from ages

35 to 44, 45 to 64, and 65 and over. The changes in black occupation structure have not matched the changes in educational attainment that have occurred in this century. There are remarkable differences in the educational attainment of black men now in their sixties compared with that of young black men. Table 4-39 indicates educational attainment by age for men in the general population. Looking at Table 4-39, we see that 46 percent of the black men 45 to 54 years of age reached, at most, the eighth grade; this is true for 89 percent of the black men age 65 to 74. These changes are not reflected in the occupational "attainment" of black men, as Table 4-42 suggests.

The most dramatic finding in the data on occupation is the proportion of black graduate students reporting fathers in the military. Nearly a third of all black graduate students in 1969 had military fathers (see Table 4-43). This accounted for the majority

TABLE 4-42 *Occupation of employed black men, by age (civilian labor force) (in percentages)*

Occupation	40–44	45–49	50–54	55–59	60–62	63–64	65–69
Professional, technical, and kindred workers	6	5	4	3	3	3	4
Farmers and farm managers	1	1	1	2	2	2	4
Managers and officials, except farmers	4	4	3	3	3	3	3
Clerical and kindred workers	8	7	7	5	5	5	4
Sales workers	2	1	1	1	1	1	1
Craftsmen and kindred workers	18	18	16	14	13	14	11
Operators and kindred workers, including transportation	31	30	28	26	24	22	18
Private household workers	1	1	1	1	1	1	2
Service workers, except private household	14	15	17	20	23	25	27
Farm laborers and farm foreman	3	3	4	4	5	6	8
Laborers, except farm	15	16	18	20	19	18	18
TOTAL	103	101	100	99	99	100	100

SOURCE: U.S. Bureau of the Census (1970*b*, table 41).

TABLE 4-43 *Occupation of fathers of graduate students, by age and race (in percentages)*

Father's occupation	Whites			Blacks		
	Under 30	*30–39*	*40 and older*	*Under 30*	*30–39*	*40 and older*
College or university teaching	3 ⎤	2 ⎤	2 ⎤	5 ⎤	1 ⎤	1 ⎤
Elementary or secondary teaching	3 ⎟	2 ⎟	2 ⎟	11 ⎟	3 ⎟	3 ⎟
Physician	3 ⎬ 22	2 ⎬ 15	1 ⎬ 14	3 ⎬ 24	— ⎬ 6	— ⎬ 10
Lawyer	2 ⎟	1 ⎟	2 ⎟	1 ⎟	— ⎟	— ⎟
Other professional	11 ⎦	8 ⎦	7 ⎦	4 ⎦	2 ⎦	6 ⎦
Managerial	19	13	14	6	4	5
Owner, large business	2	1	1	0	—	—
Owner, small business	15	17	20	9	11	6
Other white-collar	6	10	12	4	5	15
Skilled wage worker	7	7	5	5	2	3
Semiskilled wage worker	16	23	16	19	26	11
Armed forces	6	10	11	21	35	32
Farm owner	2	1	2	3	0	0
Other	5	4	5	8	12	18
	100	100	100	99	100	100

SOURCE: 1969 Carnegie Commission survey.

of students who had fathers who were not white-collar workers. Even among young black graduate students, 21 percent had military fathers. If we look at the proportions of black men in the military in 1960 (focusing on the probable cohort of graduate student fathers), we find that for no age group was the proportion in the military greater than the proportion of blacks in the total population (or over 10 percent) (Table 4-44). For older black men, the proportion was about 6 percent. Thus, the data suggest that black graduate students in the late sixties were five times as likely to have fathers in the military as were black nonstudents. Older black graduate students were more likely to have fathers in the military than younger black graduate students. Thirty-eight percent of black students over 30 have military fathers.

These findings, of course, must be tested on a larger population of graduate students. But there are several possible explanations. Blacks are more likely to reenlist in the military than whites, indicating that for many blacks the military is an avenue of upward mobility and a source of security not elsewhere available in the occupational structure (Glick, 1971, p. 18). Further, the military offers many advantages to black men, encouraging them to continue their education, and especially to obtain a high school diploma. It also contributes to keeping the family intact and provides a steady income. The children of blacks in the military are more likely to have attended integrated schools than blacks in the general population and are thus likely to have an educational advantage. It may also be the case that black children of military parents receive more educational support from teachers and administrators than lower-class black children. It may be significant, too, that school districts are reimbursed for military children attending school within the district and thus we may find that these children are encouraged to remain in school and not become early academic casualties. Military children may, then, find themselves under the same pressure to avoid downward mobility as children of the upper social strata.

In summary, we have found that social origins appear to have a strong effect on the likelihood of attending graduate school for both black and white students. Graduate students, both black and white, are relatively unlikely to come from working-class

TABLE 4-44 Of total men in the armed forces, percentage that are black, by age	
Age in years	*Percentage black of total*
14–24	7
25–29	11
30–34	10
35–39	7
40–44	5
45–49	6
50–54	6
55–59	8
60–64	6

SOURCE: U.S. Bureau of the Census (1960c, table 37).

families. This is especially true for young black graduate students.

Given the very large proportion of lower-class blacks in the general population, the "opening up" of institutions of higher learning to blacks will depend on finding ways to change this pattern. It is important to note, again, that many forces act to select out black students before they reach college or graduate school. What these data indicate is that much of this selection is due to social class rather than simply to race. We have found that, independent of race, the children of blue-collar workers have a much smaller chance of reaching graduate school than the children of professionals. However, race and social class are independent and cumulative in their effects on educational achievement. Their joint effects operate at each level of education—on the proportion who graduate from high school, who go on to college, who graduate from college, and who enter graduate school—so that these effects are cumulative over time. It is this continuation of racial and class forces, operating over time, that constitutes the problem of the underrepresentation of blacks in those professions that require some kind of postgraduate education.

FIELD OF STUDY AND DEGREE ASPIRATIONS The academic department that the graduate student enters is perhaps even more important than his institution. Departments vary in the kinds of degree programs offered, research orientations, and political and social attitudes. Two of every five black graduate students (compared with one in five whites) are in departments of education. Entering the education profession has long been seen as a path of upward mobility for the lower classes. This is true both in this country and in England (Halsey and Scott, 1961). It is worth questioning, however, whether this recruitment to education works as an avenue of upward mobility or as a process of channeling or "cooling out" that discourages black students from competing for places in other professions.

We have focused here on several questions related to field choice: First, are *young* blacks entering education disproportionately, or is the predominance of blacks in education due to the large number of older students returning to pursue higher degrees and amass unit credits? Second, are students from lower-class families more likely to enter departments of education for graduate study? And, is this equally true among younger and older black graduate students? Third, what departments other than education have substantial numbers of black students?

As we noted above, nearly half of all black graduate students are in departments of education, twice the proportion of white graduate students (Table 4-45). By contrast, white graduate students are almost twice as likely as blacks to be in academic departments. Overall, blacks are heavily concentrated in schools and departments leading to service professions.

If, however, we control for age, a rather different picture emerges. Although only 28 percent of all blacks are in academic departments, 44 percent of the blacks *under the age of 30* have chosen academic fields (Table 4-46). And if we look only at young students in academic majors (Table 4-47), we find that the distributions by field are similar for both black and white graduate students. Black graduate students are as likely as white graduate students to be in the physical and biological and social sciences, but they are somewhat less likely to be in humanities and fine arts.

Students enter graduate school with vastly different objectives and interests. In the same institution we can find older teachers returning every four or five years to take refresher courses and young students preparing for careers in the pure sciences. We might expect minority students to be particularly interested in areas that are directly concerned with their social conditions. This would support other findings on black college students.

TABLE 4-45 Fields for black and white graduates (in percentages)	Black graduates	White graduates
Education	42	23
Engineering	7	9
Old professions (medicine and law)	9	9
New professions (including social work)	10	7
Business	3	9
Academic fields	28	42
Other	2	1
TOTAL	101	100

SOURCE: 1969 Carnegie Commission survey.

TABLE 4-46   *Fields for black and white graduate students, by age (in percentages)*

	Black			White		
	Under 30	*30–39*	*40 and older*	*Under 30*	*30–39*	*40 and older*
Education	18	43	76	16	32	44
Engineering	3	16	0	9	11	4
Old professions (medicine and law)	16	5	0	13	3	1
New professions (including social work)	11	9	6	7	7	8
Business	4	3	0	8	12	9
Academic fields	44	21	14	47	35	32
Other	3	0	3	1	1	1
TOTAL	99	99	99	101	101	101

SOURCE: 1969 Carnegie Commission survey.

Clearly, education and the service professions are areas in which blacks, especially older blacks, have found the greatest opportunity. Of the older blacks, 76 percent are in education; this compares with 39 percent of the older whites. Although older whites are also more likely than younger white graduates to be in education, over a third are in academic fields (see Table 4-46).

We have among the blacks two quite distinct populations— young graduate students, the majority of whom are in academic fields and the old professions; and older graduate students, the vast majority of whom are in education. The latter are concentrated in four-year colleges. Only a quarter of the black students at high-quality universities are in education. This is a much smaller porportion than exists in all other institutions. Among

TABLE 4-47
Graduate students in academic majors, by race and age (in percentages)

	Blacks under 30	Whites under 30
Physical sciences (including mathematics)	23	23
Biological sciences	17	13
Social sciences	38	24
Humanities	21	39
TOTAL	99	99

SOURCE: 1969 Carnegie Commission survey.

TABLE 4-48 *Black students in the field of education, by age and institutional quality*

	High-quality universities		Other universities		Four-year colleges	
	Under 30	*30 and over*	*Under 30*	*30 and over*	*Under 30*	*30 and over*
Percentage of black students in education	12	28	19	50	36	69

SOURCE: 1969 Carnegie Commission survey.

young blacks in high-quality institutions only 12 percent are in education. In the four-year colleges over a third of even the young black graduate students are in education.

These findings are important in several ways. First, it is clear that given the already small proportion of black graduate students and the disproportionate number in education, the number of young black students training for academic or professional careers outside of education is very small. Although the numbers are small, they reflect the image particular fields present outside the university. The "old professions" appear to be opening up for blacks; proportionately more young blacks than whites are in medicine and law. Interestingly, however, few blacks in this sample are preparing for careers in business.

RECRUITMENT OF FIELD OF STUDY: THE EFFECT OF SOCIAL ORIGINS

Writing on "Recruitment to College Teaching," Martin Trow notes that:

Among the complex forces that shape career lines are the manifold influences of social origin. The social and economic class into which one is reared, and the values and orientations of one's family and its subculture heavily affect the kinds of talents a person develops. The effects of social origins on the nature of intellectual development and academic career can be observed all along a life line. . . . Students do not recruit themselves to different fields of study in random ways (Trow, 1961, pp. 605–606).

The evidence, here, suggests that although social origins have some effect on academic career, the effect is smaller than has been noted in the past. Given the small number of black graduate students, we can only analyze these data in an exploratory way.

The relationship between social class and recruitment to field

TABLE 4-49 *Father's occupation of black graduate students under 30, by field (in percentages)*

	Education	Engineering	Old professions	New professions	Natural sciences	Social science and humanities
Professional	7	9	28	21	28	44
Other white collar	29	1	20	25	27	19
Blue collar	42	45	34	36	33	25
Military	20	44	17	17	11	11
TOTAL	98	99	99	99	99	99

SOURCE: 1969 Carnegie Commission survey.

of study is clearest if we look at graduate students under 30. Table 4-49 indicates that few young black graduate students in education are from professional families, compared with nearly half of the students in the social sciences and humanities. As Table 4-49 suggests, differential social class recruitment to field of study is most apparent in education and engineering. In these fields proportionately many more students are from blue-collar and military families. Although black students in the professions are disproportionately recruited from professional families, it is worth noting that nearly a third of the black students in the old professions are from blue-collar families.

There is also some variation by field in the social-class background of white graduate students (Table 4-50), but less than might be expected. Among young white graduate students

TABLE 4-50 *Father's occupation of white graduate students under 30, by field (in percentages)*

	Education	Engineering	Old professions	New professions	Natural sciences	Social science and humanities
Professional	14	21	31	16	27	25
Other white collar	46	42	46	55	35	38
Blue collar	33	32	21	26	33	31
Military	6	5	2	2	5	5
TOTAL	99	100	100	99	100	99

SOURCE: 1969 Carnegie Commission survey.

we find that students in the old professions are twice as likely to come from professional families as students in education. Outside of the professions, however, there is little variation in the class composition of various field areas. Nearly a third of the students in all other fields come from blue-collar families.

Looking in more detail at the data on black graduate students, we find that what appears as blue-collar recruitment to some fields is due primarily to the large number of older students in these fields. Thus, what looks at first glance to be simply the effect of social class is, in fact, a function of the recruitment of disproportionate numbers of *older* black graduates from blue-collar families. Table 4-51 reports the proportion of graduate students in education by age and social class. From this table we see that three-quarters of the older black graduate students from blue-collar families but only one-quarter of the younger blacks are in education. Older students, on the whole, come from a less well educated cohort of parents. Thus, what first appears to be differential social class recruitment to education is explained by the interaction of social class and age. Although most older black graduate students from white-collar families are also in education, they are few in number. The great majority of the older black students come from blue-collar families.

It is reasonable to conjecture that we are seeing the effect of several different forces. Older returning black students had few career choices open to them when originally entering graduate school. Older first-time black students still face many of these same blocks in career opportunities and are disproportionately entering the education profession. Although education is still a path of upward mobility for young black graduates from blue-collar families, there appear to be many other available oppor-

TABLE 4-51 *Proportion of black and white graduate students in education, by social class and age (in percentages)*

	Age—black graduates			Age—white graduates		
Father's occupation	Under 30	30–39	40 and older	Under 30	30–39	40 and older
White collar	16	34	73	11	37	35
Blue collar	28	37	78	14	33	40

SOURCE: 1969 Carnegie Commission survey.

tunities. For white graduates there are only small differences in the social-class background of students in education compared with other fields when we account for age.

EDUCATIONAL
ASPIRATIONS—
AGE AND
SOCIAL
CLASS

The degree aspirations of black and white graduate students are quite similar, overall. This is somewhat surprising given the large proportion of older students among the black graduate students. Slightly over 40 percent are seeking a Ph.D. (See Table 4-52.) Clearly the relatively few blacks who have made it to graduate school have had to set their sights high early on. Nearly half of the students under 30, black and white, are in graduate school with the expectation of receiving a Ph.D. As would be expected, given the disproportionate number of blacks in education, black graduate students are more likely to expect to obtain a doctorate in education than their white counterparts (see Table 4-53). This is especially true for *older* black graduate students.

Social-class background, as measured by father's occupations, has some effect on degree aspirations, but by and large, this is a reflection of differential recruitment to field of study, which in turn affects degree aspirations. Black graduate students from

TABLE 4-52 *Highest degree goal (in percentages)*	Black graduates	White graduates
Ph.D.	42	43
First-professional medical degree	3	3
First-professional law degree	3	3
Doctorate of education	17	7
Other doctorate	3	2
Doctorate of arts	4	4
Other first-professional degree	3	2
Master of arts in teaching	0	2
M.A.	24	30
Other	2	3
TOTAL	101	99

SOURCE: 1969 Carnegie Commission survey.

TABLE 4-53 *Highest degree goal of graduate students, by age (in percentages)*

	Black graduate students			White graduate students		
	Under 30	30–39	40 and older	Under 30	30–39	40 and older
Ph.D.	48	57	14	49	36	28
First professional degree in law and medicine	10	3	0	9	1	1
Doctorate of education	13	12	30	5	12	12
Other doctorate	7	6	6	5	6	11
Master's degree	16	14	48	25	37	41
Other	6	8	2	7	8	7
TOTAL	100	100	100	100	100	100

SOURCE: 1969 Carnegie Commission survey.

blue-collar families are less likely to expect to obtain a Ph.D. but are considerably more likely to seek an Ed.D. than are students from white-collar or professional families.

We have to keep in mind the small number of graduate students that we are looking at. What these data suggest is that differential recruitment to fields of study, as between blacks and whites, is largely a function of age with a smaller added effect of social class. This, in turn, is reflected in expected ways in differences in degree aspirations.

SUMMARY These data indicate that institutions of higher learning are opening up for black students. Degree aspirations and field choices suggest also that black students' perceptions of life chances outside the universities are changing. On the other hand, there is considerable evidence that blacks are still underrepresented in institutions of higher learning. Young black men and lower-class blacks, both men and women, are especially underrepresented. And although black undergraduates are reaching proportional representation with respect to their numbers in the general population in high-quality institutions, the absolute number of black students in high-quality institutions is small, though growing.

It further appears that the increases in enrollment are not increases taking place throughout the system. Much increased

TABLE 4-54 *Degree goal, by father's occupation (in percentages)**

	Black graduate students				White graduate students			
	Profes- sional	White collar	Blue collar	Military	Profes- sional	White collar	Blue collar	Military
Ph.D.	52	55	33	43	43	39	41	39
Ed.D.	17	15	34	7	7	8	11	13
First-professional degree in law or medicine	5	5	4	5	11	5	4	3
Other doctorate	4	7	6	2	5	9	6	6
Other master's and professional	5	3	4	3	7	4	4	8
Master's in teaching	17	16	19	39	26	34	33	30
	100	101	100	99	99	99	99	99

*Excludes students with fathers who owned large businesses or farms or were business executives.

SOURCE: 1969 Carnegie Commission survey.

enrollment appears to be taking place primarily in two-year and low-quality four-year institutions. For able blacks this may represent an educational graveyard. The curricula and the faculty in many of these institutions differ little from the high schools from which the blacks have come. It is apparent that many of the black freshmen never enter a four-year institution at all. The City University of New York offers a case in point:

A disproportionate component of the enrollment gains is the rapid expansion of two-year junior and community colleges located in or near the ghetto and barrio. The experience of City University of New York just before the advent of open admissions provides an illustration. Minority enrollments throughout the system increased steadily during the 1960s to about fifteen percent at the close of the decade. But the comprehensive data were misleading. Black and Puerto Rican students were highly concentrated in several two-year units, probably Bronx and New York City Community Colleges. And far more non-whites than whites were not in regular degree programs even at the four-year campuses. Thus the minority shares of the full-time enrollments at the senior units of the system were not radically different from major public universities elsewhere—three percent Black and Puerto Rican at Brooklyn and Queens Colleges; 6.1 percent at City College (Uptown); Hunter-Park and Hunter-Bronx. The one exception was making the painful but effective transition from a business college to a liberal arts and university center; minority enrollment there was fourteen percent even before open admissions. Other recent studies confirm the CUNY pattern by finding pyramidal distribution of minority students in large city and state systems (O'Neil, 1971, p. 722).

Burton Clark, in *The Open Door College* (1960), suggests that nearly half of the students in community colleges never transfer to a four-year institution. Propos and Stearns are even more pessimistic: "For the California community college system: 70 percent of those entering two-year colleges complete one year of study; only 30 percent complete the two years" (1971, p. 16).

Before we have a complete picture of minority access, much more must be known about these drop-out patterns, especially the effects of sex and social class on attrition. Although there is no question that access for blacks to higher learning increased dramatically in a single decade, the evidence suggests that much of this increase was due to the increased enrollment of middle-class students. Proportionately, many fewer lower-class than middle-class men and women, black or white, are attending college and graduate school, a pattern that appears to be persistent. As we have noted, this is most pronounced in the selective institutions.

What emerges from the data on black students is the inadequacy of simple measures of proportionality, alone, for determining standards of equity. Summary statistics such as these mask relationships relevant to the assessment of minority access. Without analysis of the kinds of institutions students of different backgrounds attend, as well as analysis of patterns of recruitment to field of study and degree programs, we know little about the nature of access patterns.

The effect of race and socioeconomic background on educational decision making is a complicated matter. The patterns are changing, as is obvious from enrollment data over time, yet even in a period of intense change certain patterns of social-class access have persisted. Whether these persist into the future is the question for subsequent research.

References

American Council on Education: *National Norms for Entering College Freshmen* (title varies slightly), Washington, D.C., annual, 1966 to 1972.

Bayer, Alan E.: "The Black College Freshmen: Characteristics and Recent Trends," *ACE Research Reports,* vol. 7, no. 3, 1972.

Bayer, Alan E.: "The New Student in Black Colleges," *School Review—University of Chicago,* vol. 81, no. 3, 1973.

Berg, Ivar: *Education and Jobs: The Great Training Robbery,* Frederick A. Praeger Inc., New York, 1970.

Blau, Peter M., and Otis Dudley Duncan: *The American Occupational Structure,* John Wiley & Sons, Inc., New York, 1967.

Bureau of Social Science Research, Inc.: *Two Years after the College Degree,* U.S. Government Printing Office, Washington, D.C., 1963.

Carnegie Commission on Higher Education: *Quality and Equality: New Levels of Federal Responsibility for Higher Education,* McGraw-Hill Book Company, New York, 1968.

Carnegie Commission on Higher Education: *A Chance to Learn: An Action Agenda for Equal Opportunity in Higher Education,* McGraw-Hill Book Company, New York, 1970a.

Carnegie Commission on Higher Education: *Quality and Equality: Revised Recommendations, New Levels of Federal Responsibility for Higher Education,* McGraw-Hill Book Company, New York, 1970b.

Carnegie Commission on Higher Education: *Recent Alumni and Higher Education,* McGraw-Hill Book Company, New York, 1970c.

Carnegie Commission on Higher Education: *Breaking the Access Barriers,* McGraw-Hill Book Company, New York, 1971a.

Carnegie Commission on Higher Education: *Less Time, More Options: Education beyond the High School,* McGraw-Hill Book Company, New York, 1971b.

Centra, John A.: "Black Students at Predominantly White Colleges: A Research Description," *Sociology of Education,* vol. 43, no. 3, 1970.

Clark, Burton: *The Open Door College,* McGraw-Hill Book Company, New York, 1960.

Coleman, J. S.: "The Concept of Equality of Educational Opportunity," *Harvard Educational Review,* vol. 38, pp. 7–22, winter 1968.

Coleman, J. S.: "Equality of Educational Opportunity: Reply to Cain and Watts," *American Sociological Review,* vol. 35, pp. 242–249, April 1970.

Coleman, J. S., Ernest Q. Campbell, Carl F. Hobson, et al.: *Equality of Educational Opportunity,* U.S. Office of Education, Washington, D.C., 1966.

College-Rater, College Rater, Inc., Allentown, Pa., 1967.

Crain, Robert L.: "School Integration and the Academic Achievement of Negroes," *Sociology of Education,* vol. 44, no. 1, 1971.

Creager, John A.: *General Purpose Sampling in the Domain of Higher Education,* American Council on Education, Washington, D.C., 1968.

Crossland, Fred E.: *Minority Access to College,* Schocken Books Inc., New York, 1971.

Crowley, Anne, and Hayden Nicholson: "Negro Enrollment in Medical Schools," *Journal of the American Medical Association,* vol. 214, 1970.

Ferris, Abbot L.: *Indicators of Trends in American Education,* Russell Sage Foundation, New York, 1969.

Flanagan, J. C., W. W. Cooley, P. R. Lohnes, et al.: *Project Talent One-Year Follow-up Studies,* final report to the U.S. Office of Education, Cooperative Research Project No. 2333, Project Talent Office, University of Pittsburgh, Pittsburgh, Pa., 1966.

Flanagan, J. C., J. T. Dailey, Marion F. Shaycoft, et al.: *The Talents of American Youth,* Houghton Mifflin Company, Boston, 1962.

Folger, John K., and Charles B. Nam: *Education of the American Population,* U.S. Government Printing Office, Washington, D.C., 1967.

Gellhorn, Ernest: "The Law School and the Negro," *Duke University Law Journal,* Durham, N. C., 1968.

Glick, E. B.: *Soldiers, Scholars and Society,* Goodyear Publishing Company, Pacific Palisades, Calif., 1971.

Gourman, J.: *The Gourman Report,* The Continuing Education Institute, Phoenix, Ariz., 1967.

"Graduate-School Enrollments of Negroes, Other Minorities," *Chronicle of Higher Education,* vol. 5, no. 27, p. 4, Apr. 12, 1971.

Gurin, Patricia, and Daniel Katz: *Motivation and Aspiration in the Negro College,* University of Michigan, Ann Arbor, 1966.

Halsey, Jean, and W. Scott: "Recruitment to Teaching in England and Wales," in Halsey, Floud, and Anderson (eds.), *Education, Economy and Society,* The Free Press of Glencoe, Inc., New York, 1961.

Harris, S. E.: *A Statistical Portrait of Higher Education,* McGraw-Hill Book Company, New York, 1972.

Hartness, Rodney T.: "Differences in Selected Attitudes and College Orientation between Black Students Attending Traditionally Negro and Traditionally White Institutions," *Sociology of Education,* vol. 43, no. 4, 1970.

Hunter, J. S.: *The Academic and Financial Studies of Graduate Students,* U.S. Office of Education, Washington, D.C., 1967.

Jaffe, Abram J., Walter Adams, and Sandra G. Meyers: *Negro Higher Education in the 1960's,* Frederick A. Praeger, Inc., New York, 1968.

Janssen, Peter A.: "Higher Education and the Black American," *Chronicle of Higher Education,* vol. 6, no. 34, May 30, 1972.

Jencks, Christopher: "Social Stratification in Higher Education," *Harvard Education Review,* vol. 38, no. 2, Spring 1968.

Jencks, Christopher, et al.: *Inequality: A Reassessment of the Effect of Family and Schooling in America,* Basic Books, Inc., Publishers, New York, 1972.

Kerner, Otto (Chairman): *Report of the National Advisory Commission on Civil Disorders,* E. P. Dutton, Co., Inc., New York, 1968.

McGrath, Earl J.: *The Predominately Negro Colleges and Universities in Transition,* Teachers College, Columbia University, New York, 1965.

Miller, S. M., and F. Reissman: "The Credentials Trap," in S. M. Miller and F. Reissman (eds.), *Social Class and Social Policy,* Basic Books, Inc., Publishers, New York, 1969, pp. 69–78.

National Scholarship Service and Fund for Negro Students: *A National Profile of Black Youth: The Class of 1971,* New York, 1972.

O'Neil, Robert: "Preferential Admissions: Equalizing the Access of Minority Groups to Higher Education," *The Yale University Law Journal,* vol. 80, March 1971.

Propos, Thomas, and Stephen Stearn: "Educational Wastelands: The Upper Division Colleges," *Social Policy,* vol. 2, no. 1, 1971.

Sewell, William H.: "Inequality of Educational Opportunity," *American Sociological Review,* vol. 36, October 1971.

Trow, Martin: "Recruitment to College Teaching," in Halsey, Floud and Anderson (eds.), *Education, Economy and Society,* The Free Press of Glencoe, Inc., New York, 1961.

"Undergraduate Enrollments of Negroes and Other Minorities," *The Chronicle of Higher Education,* vol. 5, no. 25, p. 1, Mar. 29, 1971.

U.S. Bureau of Labor Statistics: *The Social and Economic Status of Negroes in the United States,* Report 384, 1970.

U.S. Bureau of the Census: *Census of Population 1960,* vol. 1, Characteristics of the Population, part I, U.S. Summary, table 173, 1960*a*.

U.S. Bureau of the Census: *Current Population Reports,* Population Characteristics, Series P-20, no. 207, table 1, 1960*b*.

U.S. Bureau of the Census: *Economic Characteristics of the Negro Population 14 Years and Over by Age,* Report PC (2), 1960*c*.

U.S. Bureau of the Census: "School Enrollment, and Education of

Young Adults and Their Fathers: October 1960," *Current Population Reports,* Series P-20, no. 110, July 1961.

U.S. Bureau of the Census: *Enrollment Status of the Population by Age, Race, and Sex for the U.S., October 1969,* 1969*a.*

U.S. Bureau of the Census: "Factors Related to High School Graduation and College Attendance: 1967," *Current Population Reports,* Series P-20, 185, July 1969*b.*

U.S. Bureau of the Census: *Population Characteristics: School Enrollment, October 1969,* Series P-20, no. 206, 1969*c.*

U.S. Bureau of the Census: "Educational Attainment: March 1970," *Current Population Reports,* Series P-20, 207, November 1970*a.*

U.S. Bureau of the Census: *Occupational Characteristics,* Subject Report PC (2)-7A, 1970*b.*

U.S. Bureau of the Census: *Years of School Completed by Persons 14 Years Old and Over by Age, Race and Sex for the United States, March, 1970,* 1970*c.*

U.S. Bureau of the Census: "School Enrollment: October 1970," *Current Population Reports,* Series P-20, 222, June 1971.

U.S. Office of Education: *Opening Fall Enrollment in Higher Education: Part A—Summary Data,* 1969.

5. Undergraduates in Sociology

by Joseph Zelan

Those of us who teach undergraduate sociology courses are well aware that students come to us with a myriad of goals that they see as appropriately served by concentration in sociology. A recent survey of undergraduate course offerings in sociology and of the educational goals of sociology faculty members concluded that there is some inherent tension between the three goals of undergraduate sociology education: general education, preprofessional training for sociologists, and preprofessional training for social workers and persons in other professions (Reid & Bates, 1971). In this paper we shall describe the distribution of these educational goals among various categories of students and types of institutions and compare the goals of students with the goals of teachers of sociology. We shall then look at the levels of interest and satisfaction that sociology undergraduates manifest toward their courses and toward their colleges. To conclude, we shall assess the extent to which the diverse objectives of undergraduate sociology instruction can be met without tension.

As part of its research program, the American Council on Education (ACE) has, since 1965, conducted questionnaire surveys of all entering freshmen in United States colleges and

NOTE: The data for this analysis are drawn from a survey conducted at the Survey Research Center, University of California, Berkeley, with the collaboration of the American Council on Education. The survey of undergraduates was part of a larger endeavor—the Carnegie Commission Survey of Faculty and Student Opinion—that included surveys of faculty members and graduate students and was conducted under the auspices of the Carnegie Commission on Higher Education during 1969 and 1970. The survey was funded in part by the U.S. Office of Education. The author's interpretations do not necessarily reflect the position of the Office of Education, and no official endorsement by the Office of Education should be inferred.

This article is a revised version of a paper presented at the Sixty-sixth Annual Meeting of the American Sociological Association, Denver, Colorado, August 30, 1971. This article also appeared in *The American Sociologist*, February 1974, vol. 9, pp. 9–17. I thank Leonard Broom for his many helpful suggestions.

universities, using a sample of several hundred institutions. As part of the survey, it acquires names and addresses from the respondents, and these facilitate follow-up studies. In 1966, approximately 300 institutions were included in the annual survey.

Our study drew data from 186 institutions that (1) had participated in the 1966, 1967, 1968, and 1969 ACE surveys; (2) had attained high response rates (85 percent or better) in the years 1966 through 1968 (the 1969 results were not available when our sample was designed); and (3) had names and addresses for most respondents. We sampled individuals from the ACE roster of entering freshmen for each of the four years 1966 through 1969, and we sent a lengthy questionnaire to those individuals in December 1969. The response rate was about 40 percent, or approximately 70,000 individuals, a result that caused us much initial concern. We were in the fortunate position, however, of knowing a great deal about our nonrespondents because we had access to the data from the freshmen questionnaires.

An analysis of response bias indicated that the low rate of response was not serious. The largest discrepancies between our sample and a perfect response were in a slight underrepresentation of men (less than 6 percentage points) and nonwhites (less than 3 percentage points). Other correlates of nonresponse led us to infer (although we do not have the data to confirm this) that those who dropped out of college were less likely to respond. The latter bias was irrelevant to the present paper because we were concerned only with students enrolled in a college at the time of the survey.

All discussion of the respondent's college or university is in terms of the institution the student entered, not the one attended at the time of the survey. This was necessary because our sampling and weighting were done with reference to college entrants. Our principal institutional characteristic was quality, and the correlation between the quality of the institution entered and the quality of the institution currently being attended is $r = .986$. This resulted from two facts: that 83 percent of the respondents attended only one institution and that respondents infrequently transferred to a different quality institution.

For institutions defined by the U.S. Office of Education (1965–66) as "universities," our measure of quality is based on the composite index in J. Gourman (1967). For institutions defined by the U.S. Office of Education as "four-year colleges," the quality measure is based on Gourman (1967) or College-Rater (1967), whichever was available, or the higher of the two measures if both were available. These indexes gave results comparable to results obtained from other methods of assessing quality. Comparisons of the indexes, procedures for constructing the quality index, and details of study designs, sampling, and response bias are to be found in Appendix A.

Respondents were weighted to compensate for differential sampling rates among institutions of different quality and control as well as for varying rates of response from institutions. In the present analysis, only students who entered four-year colleges and universities and only students who entered with the 1966 and 1967 cohorts were included. This means that students who pursued a normal four-year course of study were juniors and seniors at the time of our survey and students who lagged behind had also had sufficient time to make a realistic assessment of their major field.

Our analysis makes two comparisons: a comparison of sociology majors with majors in other fields and a comparison of categories of sociology majors. Sociology is compared with other social science fields, with the humanities, with the physical sciences, with the biological sciences, and with miscellaneous other fields. The categories have been constructed so as to encompass primarily fields with an academic content; fields that are primarily applied have been placed in the "other" category (for example, drama is included not in the humanities but in "other").

Table 5-1 presents selected characteristics for comparison. For our purposes, the two most important characteristics are sex and the quality of the institution. The first entry in Table 5-1 shows that sociology is strikingly female at the undergraduate level, with only 27 percent of the students male. (As previously stated, since there is a slight underrepresentation of men among respondents, 27 percent is an estimate subject to error; however, the margin of error is small.) "Quality of institution" in Table 5-1 shows that sociology is underrepresented as a major field at the highest-quality institutions.

Sex and institutional quality, furthermore, are not in-

TABLE 5-1 *Undergraduate student characteristics, by major field of study (in percentages)*

	Major field*					
	Sociology	Other social sciences	Humanities	Physical sciences	Biological sciences	Other
Weighted N	(62,396)	(36,345)	(47,567)	(53,895)	(39,608)	(77,503)
Sex						
Male	27	63	42	70	65	46
Female	73	37	58	30	35	54
Father's education						
College graduate	32	38	36	32	38	32
Some college	18	23	16	19	21	16
High school graduate	24	27	28	28	26	31
Less than high school graduate	26	12	20	21	15	21
Parent's annual income						
$15,000 or more	24	29	31	21	25	22
$10,000–14,999	23	32	26	25	31	27
$8,000–9,999	16	13	16	18	19	18
Less than $8,000	37	25	26	35	25	32
Religion reared in						
Protestant	55	48	57	58	58	65
Catholic	32	28	29	29	26	24
Jewish	8	20	10	7	10	7
Other	3	2	2	3	3	3
None	1	2	1	2	3	1
Present religion						
Protestant	44	31	40	47	46	55
Catholic	23	20	23	24	20	19
Jewish	6	17	7	5	7	6
Other	9	5	4	8	6	5
None	18	26	26	16	20	15
Race						
White/Caucasian	92	94	95	93	94	94
Black/Negro/Afro-American	7	4	3	5	5	3
Other	2	2	2	2	2	3
Quality of institution						
High	9	19	17	19	15	10

TABLE 5-1 *(continued)*

	Sociology	Other social sciences	Humanities	Physical sciences	Biological sciences	Other
			*Major field**			
Medium	25	35	33	32	29	30
Low	66	46	50	49	56	61
Highest degree planned by students at all institutions						
Ph.D. or Ed.D.	14	26	21	38	27	9
Master's or professional	59	56	63	50	60	63
Bachelor's or less	27	18	16	12	13	28
Highest degree planned by males at high-quality institutions						
Ph.D. or Ed.D.	53	34	36	49	17	11
Master's or professional	40	55	53	46	78	73
Bachelor's or less	7	11	12	5	5	16

*These fields were sampled from the entire body of respondents at different rates. Thus the fields cannot be combined unless each weighted N is adjusted by the appropriate factor to give a population estimate. The sampling rates for each field and the respective unweighted N's are: sociology: 100 percent ($N = 1,327$); other social sciences: 20 percent ($N = 944$); humanities: 20 percent ($N = 1,251$); physical sciences: 50 percent ($N = 1,384$); biological sciences: 50 percent ($N = 972$); other fields: 10 percent ($N = 1,112$).

SOURCE: Carnegie Commission Survey of Faculty and Student Opinion. Unless otherwise noted, this is the source for all tables in this chapter. Total percentages may add up to 99 or 101 percent due to rounding error.

dependent, as seen in Table 5-2. At the least-distinguished institutions, 78 percent of sociology majors are female, 22 percent are male; at medium-quality institutions, 67 percent are female and 33 percent are male; at high-quality institutions, 56 percent are female and 44 percent are male—but only 9 percent of all sociology majors attend these high-ranking institutions. Nor are other factors independent of institutional quality, as, for example, religion, also shown in Table 5-2.

Some notable differences between sociology and other fields can be attributed to this distribution by sex and institutional quality. As seen in Table 5-1, only 14 percent of the sociology majors at all institutions indicate that they are planning to acquire a doctorate—a lower proportion than in all other fields except "other"—but among male students at high-quality insti-

TABLE 5-2 *Sex and religion of sociology majors, by quality of institution (in percentages)*

	Quality of institution		
	High	*Medium*	*Low*
Weighted N	(5,645)	(15,622)	(41,102)
Sex of student			
Male	44	33	22
Female	56	67	78
Religion reared in			
Protestant	56	54	55
Catholic	18	28	36
Jewish	21	11	5
Other	3	3	3
None	3	3	0

tutions, the proportion aiming at a doctorate is highest in sociology.

In addition to focusing upon students' sex and the quality of the institution they attend, we should examine the career goals of sociology majors in order to understand their educational orientations. As many of us are aware, the bulk of sociology students are aiming for careers as social workers (though changes in the market for social work personnel may force them to alter these goals). This phenomenon is due primarily to the number of women in sociology. Men, disproportionately located at the higher-quality institutions, are more likely to opt for academic careers. This pattern is also reflected in the choice of field of graduate study among students who are planning to obtain advanced degrees (Table 5-3).

Table 5-4 shows some of the goals students have in college. We shall not consider the last three items on Table 5-4, the "life adjustment" goals of college students, because they show no striking differences between fields other than the lower people-orientation of natural scientists. The first three goals in Table 5-4 concern major manifest functions of a college and show differences of some magnitude between fields. The first goal, "detailed grasp of a special field," taps both vocational and scholarly pursuits. In order to sort out the scholarly from the vocational dimensions, we have cross-tabulated "grasp of a special field" with "training and skills for an occupation," producing the typology shown below:

		Detailed Grasp of a Special Field	
		Not essential	*Essential*
Training and skills for an occupation	*Not essential*	Generalists	Academic specialists
	Essential	Vocational opportunists	Vocational specialists

TABLE 5-3
Anticipated field of graduate study and anticipated career of sociology majors, by sex (in percentages)

	Sex		
	Male	*Female*	*Total*
Weighted N	(8,083)	(23,989)	(32,072)
*Graduate field**			
Social welfare	13	45	37
Sociology	42	32	35
Education	6	7	7
Psychology	5	3	4
Library science	0	3	2
Theology	5	0	1
Other fields	29	10	14
Weighted N	(14,796)	(41,596)	(56,392)
Anticipated career			
Social/group worker	14	33	28
College professor, researcher	30	11	16
Public/social service, other	9	16	14
Housewife	0	18	13
Counselor, psychologist	4	8	7
Teacher, primary/secondary	4	6	5
Business	12	4	5
Lawyer	9	0	2
Clergy	4	0	1
Other	14	4	9

*Students who are not planning graduate study are excluded.

TABLE 5-4 *Percentages of students who deem specific goals essential**

Goal	Sociology	Other social sciences	Humanities	Physical sciences	Biological sciences	Other
Detailed grasp of a special field	47	35	45	56	55	63
Well-rounded general education	60	68	63	56	61	50
Training and skills for an occupation	44	26	35	42	43	64
Learning to get along with people	78	80	77	69	72	79
Preparation for marriage	13	7	9	11	11	15
Formulating the values and goals of my life	72	71	69	69	73	68

*The query was "How important is it to you to get each of the following at college?" Possible replies were "essential," "fairly important," or "not important."

The designation for each of the four types derives from its correlates. Generalists are undergraduates who are low on "special field" and on "skills for an occupation," while endorsing general education. Academic specialists are students who have a scholarly interest in an academic discipline, disproportionately concentrated in the sciences. Vocational specialists see college as a place that will prepare them to pursue a particular occupation, resulting, they hope, in material rewards. Vocational opportunists, like vocational specialists, seek material rewards from their college training, but they have little commitment to a particular vocation through which to realize their goals; they tend to value general education more than do the vocational specialists; they are after a degree, which they hope will better their occupational life chances.

Table 5-5 shows students categorized into the above four types, and it is apparent that sociology majors, especially women, are more vocational in their aims than are students in other social sciences. Women in sociology are less oriented than women in other social sciences to general education; the percentage differences between men in these fields is smaller. Since men in sociology are more likely to be in higher-quality institutions (where general education is a goal more often than is vocational education), we ought to look at the relations between sex, orientation, and institutional quality.

Looking at Table 5-6, we see that even with institutional quality controlled, men are more likely than women to be generalists; in fact, the proportion of generalists among men does not fall below 50 percent regardless of the quality of their institution. Women, on the other hand, are more vocational than men, irrespective of institutional quality. The distribution of

TABLE 5-5
Orientation of students to college, by major field (in percentages)

Sex	Sociology	Other social sciences	Humanities	Physical sciences	Biological sciences	Other
			Major field			
Male						
Generalists	54	60	59	31	34	34
Academic specialists	17	20	21	29	24	13
Vocational specialists	22	10	14	32	31	41
Vocational opportunists	6	10	7	8	12	12
Female						
Generalists	33	47	37	32	32	18
Academic specialists	17	18	18	21	24	9
Vocational specialists	32	25	34	26	31	62
Vocational opportunists	17	9	11	21	13	12
Both sexes						
Generalists	39	55	46	31	33	25
Academic specialists	17	19	19	26	24	11
Vocational specialists	30	15	26	30	31	52
Vocational opportunists	14	11	9	12	12	12

**TABLE 5-6
Orientation of
sociology majors
to college, by
sex and quality
of institution (in
percentages)**

Sex	Institutional quality		
	High	Medium	Low
Male			
Generalists	81	52	50
Academic specialists	12	22	15
Vocational specialists	5	14	32
Vocational opportunists	3	12	4
Female			
Generalists	66	39	28
Academic specialists	16	19	17
Vocational specialists	4	26	38
Vocational opportunists	14	16	18

academic specialists is less regular and warrants separate analysis.[1]

Sociology majors are thus predominantly women with vocational goals; men in sociology have predominantly general-education goals. Since men *and* general-education goals are more frequent at high-quality institutions and women *and* vocational goals are more frequent at low-quality institutions, there should be little conflict in institutional goals.

There is, however, another important element that figures in the goals of students, namely, the faculty. The fact that students in a given institution want pretty much the same things from their education does not mean that their desires will be fulfilled; they must also have the agreement of the faculty.

S. T. Reid and A. P. Bates (1971) report that sociology faculty members are overwhelmingly committed to general-education goals. Data from our survey of faculty are consistent with that finding as well as the finding that sociology faculty members perceive institutional goals as placing greater emphasis upon

[1] The lower proportion of academic specialists at the highest-quality institutions does not indicate that these institutions are sending a smaller proportion of students into academic careers in sociology. On the contrary, they are sending the highest proportion. What it reflects is students' reasons for pursuing academic careers. In the highest-quality institutions, the students' motivations seem to arise less often from scholarly aims than from a general attraction to academic careers or, possibly, from a repugnance to other careers.

preprofessional training in applied fields (Table 5-7).[2] Because our faculty survey did not include the Reid and Bates option of "preprofessional training leading to graduate work in sociology," what we have in the "liberal education" response of faculty is an index of orientation toward undergraduate teaching. (Hardly any professor sees the primary activity of college to be to prepare undergraduates for their chosen occupation.) Since the bulk of sociology faculty members can hardly be unaware of the vocational goals of most of their students, this implies that they see general education in sociology as appropriate preparation for vocational activities in social welfare, education, etc. (We assume, of course, that sociology professors are not out to subvert the educational goals of their students.)

Table 5-7 also shows that at the highest-quality institutions

[2] Our survey of faculty comprised a six-sevenths sample of faculty members (it excluded teaching assistants and research assistants) in 303 institutions, including all institutions in the undergraduate survey in the spring of 1969. Response rate for the survey was 60 percent. Sociology faculty are those whose teaching appointment is in a department of sociology. Details on sampling, weighting, and response bias will be found in Appendix A.

TABLE 5-7 *Importance to sociology faculty and perceived importance to institutions of four academic activities* (in percentages)

	Importance to faculty				Importance to institution			
	Institutional quality				Institutional quality			
Activity	High	Medium	Low	Total	High	Medium	Low	Total
Provide undergraduates with a broad liberal education	45	58	71	62	39	49	56	50
Prepare undergraduates for their chosen occupation	1	6	4	4	6	22	32	24
Train graduate or professional students	8	10	5	7	12	10	2	7
Engage in research	46	26	20	27	43	20	9	19

*The query was "Given the following four possible activities of academic men, please mark the first three in order: (1) according to their importance to you personally; (2) according to your understanding of what your institution expects of you." The percentages are for persons who ranked each of the four activities as of first importance. Only sociology faculty members who teach undergraduates are included in this table. The weighted and unweighted N's, by institutional quality, are: High: weighted $N = 998$ (unweighted $N = 221$); Medium: weighted $N = 1,974$ (unweighted $N = 301$); Low: weighted $N = 5,549$ (unweighted $N = 783$).

more than half the faculty list research and graduate teaching combined as their most important activities. At these institutions sociology undergraduates tend to be general education oriented, whereas a sizable portion of the faculty tends to be discipline oriented.

We shall focus next on two consequences of the foregoing findings for students: interest in course work and general satisfaction with the college attended. With respect to the former, we shall look at student responses to the statement, "I am not interested in most of my courses." Is this related to institutional quality or to student goals? Looking at Table 5-8, in the Total row under "interested in courses," we see that interest in courses increases very slightly as we go from high-quality to low-quality institutions. If we look at the column of totals on the right, we see that vocational specialists are most interested in their courses and vocational opportunists are least interested; but again, the overall differences are not overwhelming.

When we look across the rows, however, we see some intriguing differences. Among generalists there is a small drop in interest as we move from high-quality institutions to low-quality institutions. Among academic specialists there is also a small decline in interest. Among the two types of vocational students, on the other hand, there is a marked increase in interest as institutional quality declines. To what do we attribute this finding? Certainly not to any general preference among vocational students for lower-quality institutions, because when we ask them "What is your overall evaluation of your college?" (Table 5-8), they, like the nonvocational students, are more likely to be satisfied at an institution of high quality than at an institution of low quality. Interest in courses seems tied to some other factor that is related to institutional quality.

A possible explanation is that vocational students get more vocational education and less general education at low-quality institutions, indicating, perhaps, that sociology professors at such institutions are inclined to follow the institutions' desires rather than their own preferences (Table 5-7). Partly from the data and partly from my experience as a teacher of sociology, I doubt that this is so. Insofar as the data are concerned, it seems to me that if professors at the low-quality institutions really did subvert the goals of general education in favor of vocational training to the degree they think their colleges want them to, it

TABLE 5-8 Interest of sociology majors in courses and satisfaction of sociology majors with college, by student orientation to college and quality of institution

| | Institutional quality | | | | | | | |
| | High | | Medium | | Low | | Total | |
Student orientation	Percent	Weighted N	Percent	Weighted N	Percent	Weighted N	Percent	Weighted N
*Interested in courses**								
Generalists	77	4,095	76	6,647	72	13,284	74	24,026
Academic specialists	81	785	70	3,079	75	6,762	74	10,626
Vocational specialists	52	240	80	3,434	82	14,838	81	18,512
Vocational opportunists	47	513	59	2,279	77	6,010	70	8,802
Total†	73	5,639	73	15,558	79	41,039	76	62,236
Very satisfied with college‡								
Generalists	27	4,042	18	6,572	14	13,207	17	23,821
Academic specialists	26	785	9	2,991	6	6,634	9	10,410
Vocational specialists	11	240	17	3,386	6	14,585	8	18,211
Vocational opportunists	13	513	7	1,922	5	6,098	6	8,533
Total†	25	5,586	14	15,032	9	40,670	12	61,288

*The student was instructed to answer "true" or "false" to the statement, "I am not interested in most of my courses."

† Includes students not classified by college orientation.

‡ The query was "What is your overall evaluation of your college?" Possible replies were "very satisfied," "satisfied," "on the fence," "dissatisfied," or "very dissatisfied."

would show up among generalist students as a much more marked drop in interest than we see in Table 5-8, a drop comparable to the increase in interest among vocational students.

More important, my experience leads me not only to doubt that professors will follow the wishes of their institution rather than their own wisdom, but to doubt that there is anything that can be considered particularly vocational in the undergraduate sociology curriculum that does not at the same time serve general-education functions. By providing general education in sociology, teachers are also providing vocational education, and this is reflected in the interest that vocational students express in their courses.

In this view, I am taking issue with Reid and Bates's contention that there is some inherent incompatibility between sociology's function to preprofessionally train students destined for social work and to communicate to undergraduates the sociological perspective that is part of sociology's general-education function. I do not disagree with their view that we can do better in teaching sociology to undergraduates, but I do not think that improvement will come from tinkering with the curriculum to separate "real" sociology from "service" courses. A sociology course in the sociology of social welfare or the sociology of education can introduce future social workers or future teachers to their field of special interest and at the same time introduce all students to the institutional and structural perspectives of the discipline called sociology.

Returning to Table 5-8, we can understand the high interest of academic-specialist students who want to do precisely the kind of work their professors are doing, but why are the generalists so interested in their courses, even at high-quality institutions, where so many of the professors claim to be interested primarily in research? My guess is that the generalists are interested because when the professors actually are teaching undergraduates they are engaged in general education, not in training future sociologists or preparing social workers. As Table 5-7 shows, the lower endorsement given to "liberal education" by professors at high-quality institutions, as compared with professors at medium- and low-quality institutions, stems primarily from the high endorsement they give to research as their most important activity. In fact, there is some evidence from the faculty survey that sociology faculty members who teach undergraduates in high-quality institutions are more favorable to general education than are their counterparts in low-quality institutions: 34 percent of the faculty at high-quality institutions, 25 percent of the faculty at medium-quality institutions, and 27 percent of the faculty at low-quality institutions strongly agreed that "undergraduate education in America would be improved if there were less emphasis on specialized training and more on broad liberal education." In other words, when sociologists are teaching undergraduates, they see their function to be to provide liberal education.

We should not overlook the fact that in our elite institutions the generalists share with the academic specialists a favored trait: they are nonvocational. Their orientation is to knowledge rather than to vocational skills, resulting in "identification with the intellectual concerns of the serious faculty members" (Clark & Trow, 1966, p. 22).[3] From this perspective, vocational students are the deviants.[4] Furthermore, as we noted above, there is a tie between the generalist students and professors at high-quality institutions because the generalists are frequently headed for academic careers, even though they seem not to share the discipline orientation of their professors.

Thus far I have maintained that general education in sociology and preprofessional training for vocational students majoring in sociology are identical. I would go even further and say that general education in sociology and undergraduate education for future sociologists should be identical. What future sociologists ought to receive at the undergraduate level is the kind of education that assures their being well-educated persons. The graduate departments can see to it that they become technically competent sociologists. I would suggest, in fact, that in order to become well-educated sociologists, undergraduates should major

[3] An alternative forumlation is found in Christopher Jencks and David Riesman (1962, pp. 735–736). These authors draw a distinction between questions of general interest to intelligent people everywhere, which they call *intellectual,* and discipline-centered questions, which they call *academic.*

[4] A similar interpretation is offered by David Riesman, in a personal communication. He suggests that perhaps the low interest shown by vocational students in high-quality institutions reflects the scorn shown them by their fellow students and faculty. From this perspective, the phenomenon is not so much one of increase in interest among vocational students in low-quality institutions as it is depression of interest among those in high-quality institutions.

in something other than sociology. Their capacity to function as sociologists would be greatly enhanced if they came to graduate work with a background in history, or mathematics, or philosophy of science, or comparative literature.

In sum, students want a number of different things from their undergraduate work in sociology—some want preprofessional education, some want general education, and some want an introduction to a future academic specialty. There is only one way to serve all these goals, and that way is general education in sociology, education that conveys the unique view sociology brings to the understanding of social institutions and the individuals implicated in the institutions.

References

Clark, Burton, and Martin A. Trow: "The Organizational Context," in T. H. Newcomb and E. K. Wilson (eds.), *College Peer Groups*, Aldine Publishing Company, Chicago, 1966, pp. 17–70.

The College-Rater, College-Rater, Inc., Allentown, Pa., 1967.

Gourman, J.: *The Gourman Report*, The Continuing Education Institute, Phoenix, Ariz., 1967.

Jencks, Christopher S., and David Riesman: "Patterns of Residential Education: A Case Study of Harvard," in Nevitt Sanford (ed.), *The American College*, John Wiley & Sons, Inc., New York, 1962, pp. 731–773.

Reid, S. T., and A. P. Bates: "Undergraduate Sociology Programs in Accredited Colleges and Universities," *American Sociologist*, vol. 6, pp. 165–175, May 1971.

U.S. Office of Education: *Education Directory, Part 3, Higher Education*, 1965–66.

6. Rewards and Fairness: Academic Women in the United States

by Oliver Fulton

MEMBERSHIP OF THE ACADEMIC PROFESSION For several years now in the United States, interest and concern have been growing about the position of women in academic life. This concern has become more visible and better articulated since the rise of the women's liberation movement, paralleling other "minority-group" movements; in the last year or so, in particular, "equal employment" legislation has been used more extensively in cases of sex discrimination—and has been used against academic institutions.[1] The Carnegie Commission Survey of Faculty and Student Opinion, conducted in the spring of 1969, provides, in its wide range and large numbers, unrivaled data on many aspects of academic life (see Appendix A). This paper is a brief report on the data bearing on women in academia—providing a statistical portrait of the position of women faculty members in the 1968–69 academic year.[2] The first section shows the subjects and the kinds of institutions in which

NOTE: This article was published in June 1973 as Occasional Paper 15 by the Center for Research in the Educational Sciences, University of Edinburgh, Scotland. It is based in part on data gathered by the 1969 Carnegie Commission Survey of Faculty and Student Opinion, sponsored by the Carnegie Commission on Higher Education and supported in part as a cooperative research project by funds from the U.S. Office of Education. The interpretations put forward in this publication do not necessarily reflect the position of the Office of Education, and no official endorsement by the Office of Education should be inferred.

   I should like to thank Lynne Alexander, Liam Hudson, Carolyn Miller, Malcolm Parlett, Peter Sheldrake, and Martin Trow for their comments on an earlier draft. They are not responsible for errors of fact or interpretation; nor should it be supposed that they share my opinions and prejudices.

[1] Shulman (1972) discusses the current state of the law and its enforcement on campus.

[2] After four years, the world has somewhat changed: but there is reason to think that the data are still highly relevant (see below p. 247).

women are concentrated, and their age and status in relation to their male colleagues; the second section shows their career prospects in the light of the criteria normally used for promotion (previous studies have not provided this in detail).

This report covers only those women who are, however marginally, already members of the academic profession. As far as the author is aware, most discussion—and most demands for action—still center on possible inequality or discrimination in recruitment, that is, at the time of first appointment. The data do not bear directly on this subject; and in discussing discrimination, I shall concentrate on promotion and on salary levels, since the survey was restricted to those who have passed the first obstacle.

I have deliberately forsworn here the use of elaborate multivariate statistical techniques, such as multiple regression analysis, which is often used in similar work. Even in the most sophisticated hands, multiple regression is neither foolproof nor always convincing. Percentage cross-tabulations, which I do use, combine almost universal intelligibility with easy handling of nominal and ordinal variables; and they make the "specification" of relationships within subsets of the population an aim of analysis, instead of a "contaminating factor" to be detected.

The Societal Context

Before discussing the survey findings, it is worth reminding the reader of the wider setting in which they should be examined. Discrimination usually starts at the earliest moment the relevant characteristics can be detected—for women, in other words, in the cradle. Society at large, as well as its institutions—the family, religion, the schools, and later, marriage and employment—differentiates, and thus, it is argued, both handicaps and discriminates against women and reinforces women's own internalized sense of difference and inferiority. By adolescence at latest, most girls have a self-image and a set of values and ambitions sharply different from those of boys, setting their sights, in career terms, both lower and within narrower limits. Long before they become undergraduate students (and certainly before they enter the academic job market, if they do) women as a whole have been so affected by the cultural expectations of their society—as well as its frequently outright rejection of their ambitions—that they have been subjected to a kind of selective attrition. In the educational context, a few figures sum up the problem: in 1965, women constituted 51 percent of high school graduates (that is, at the highest point where education is nearly universal), they were 41 percent of college graduates, 32 percent of those earnings master's degrees, and 11 percent of those earning doctorates (Epstein, 1970, p. 58, table 6). Although universities and colleges no doubt deserve their share of blame for this decline, they do so along with all the other major institutions of society; and even if they apply universalistic, "objective" criteria when they make faculty appointments,[3] there should be no surprise (given, for example, the low number of women Ph.D.'s available) if the proportion of women on academic staffs is far below the proportion of women in the population as a whole—as of course it is. In higher education as a whole, according to our figures, women were in 1968–69 only 20 percent of all faculty members. (The figure is 13 percent for universities, with which the second section of this report is concerned.)

The underrepresentation of women gives rise to a whole series of questions and problems, ranging from fundamental questions of causation and moral responsibility to the more easily approachable theme of possible remedies. The latter, in turn, raises the now classic problem of "strong" and "weak" conceptions of equal opportunity. Should particular institutions compensate for society's misdeeds (by admitting or employing underqualified members of groups that have been collectively underprivileged) or merely ensure equality using "objective" criteria? In this particular case, as we shall see, even the latter course would be a considerable advance.

Women Academics: Current Trends and Marriage Patterns

The next section gives the broad statistics on women's total membership in the profession. Although it is certainly true, as will be seen, that women *are* discriminated against by universities and colleges, the tables that follow here should be read with appropriate caution: when looking at descriptive statistics such as these, it is not possible to effectively separate out the specific consequences of discrimination by institutions from those of the

---

[3] This is the chief aim of guidelines issued by the Office for Civil Rights in the U.S. Department of Health, Education, and Welfare: affirmative action programs will be judged on the basis of "availability data"—the proportion of women and minorities earning doctoral degrees, either nationally or (in the case of elite universities with highly selective recruitment policies) at the graduate schools from which these universities normally recruit ("U.S. Announces . . .," 1972, pp. 1–2).

broader cultural phenomenon, which affects the women members of every profession[4] and which prevents so many potentially able women from ever attempting to join the professions.

At the present time, women are 20 percent of the teaching staff in higher education. This proportion, however, has not risen steadily; indeed, according to U.S. Department of Labor and Census Bureau statistics (Epstein, 1970, p. 6, Table 1), it reached a peak of 32 percent in 1930, but by 1960 had dropped back to 19 percent—the level it had first reached in 1910. This pattern is found generally in the professions and in higher managerial posts. It is also true that in net terms there has been a huge increase in women's participation in these areas. The increase, however, has not matched the total growth in these employment sectors, so that the proportion of women relative to men has declined (Epstein, 1970, pp. 6–7).[5] Indeed, when we look at the sex ratio of faculty members in different age groups, we can see the same pattern in the Carnegie data (Table 6-1).

Table 6-1 has several different aspects: first of all, there is a gentle but persistent decline in the proportion of female faculty from around one-quarter among those over 55, to under one-seventh (14 percent) in their early thirties. The oldest two groups were born before the end of the First World War; these are the women who took advantage of the new social climate and new opportunities for their sex in the 1920s and early 1930s; their successors, however, stayed at home in increasingly large numbers.[6] Adding to the historical trend, no doubt, would be an extra decline among women in their thirties, who often retire when their first child is born, and in some cases take up their jobs again a few years later.[7] But perhaps the most striking part of Table 6-1

---

[4] Indeed academic women may be comparatively well shielded from it.

[5] Jessie Bernard (1968) and others have examined this trend. From the 1930s until the early or mid-1960s, women's age at marriage declined, and the birthrate increased, while the proportion of women gaining first and higher degrees, as well as entering the professions, declined. At the same time, the proportion of women in the labor force rose steadily (excluding the war years). In other words, the "motherhood mania" (to use Bernard's term) has not been incompatible with working, except for a few years; but it has discouraged women from developing long-term, especially professional, careers.

[6] Bernard (1963, pp. 30–37) sees even the 1920s as a period of decline—probably a correct view of morale at women's colleges, but clearly wrong in numerical terms, as her tables show.

[7] If this is the case, the survey data should show more women in their thirties to be single, or married but childless, than those either older or younger; this will be examined in a moment.

TABLE 6-1 Sex distribution of faculty in higher education, by age (base totals in parentheses)

Age	Date of birth	Men, percent	Women, percent	Total	
61 and over	1908 or earlier	77	23	100%	(32,483)
56–60	1909–1913	75	25	100%	(28,402)
51–55	1914–1918	78	22	100%	(40,178)
46–50	1919–1923	79	21	100%	(56,201)
41–45	1924–1928	80	20	100%	(65,556)
36–40	1929–1933	84	16	100%	(71,614)
31–35	1934–1938	86	14	100%	(73,143)
26–30	1939–1943	78	22	100%	(57,631)
25 and under	1944 or later	63	37	100%	(9,078)
All ages		80	20	100%	(435,409)

NOTE: See App. A for a description of the survey, of weighting procedures, and of conventions used in the tables. Nonrespondents are omitted from percentages in all tables. To allow the reader to recompute tables, the base totals also exclude nonrespondents, and therefore vary slightly from one question to another. Base totals are omitted from some tables to improve legibility, but wherever these become critically small, the smallest unweighted N is given in a footnote to the table.

SOURCE: 27,000-case sample of the faculty from the 1969 Carnegie Commission Survey of Faculty and Student Opinion. This sample includes all respondents from two- and four-year colleges and a 1:4 systematic sample from universities.

shows that under the age of 30 the proportion of women is far higher, rising to over one-third of the very youngest group.[8] It would be easy to greet these women under 30 as the first wave of a new revolution, inspired by the new feminist revolution in the world at large. But there are good reasons for skepticism. Chief among these is the rather powerful evidence that not even young academics have reached total equality in their own married lives. Saul Feldman (see Chapter 7), in his analysis of graduate students (from the Carnegie Commission survey), has shown very clearly that while unmarried female graduate students seem to do as well as their male contemporaries in terms of grades and of the time taken to finish their courses, married women tend to delay their own graduate careers for the sake of their husbands'. Looking at faculty members (Table 6-2), we find that 87 percent

[8] This is not an artifact of subject differences—caused, for example, by the possibility that the subjects that contain more women recruit earlier than the more male-dominated fields. All fields in which women are significantly represented show a similar increase relative to their base. The actual numbers involved, however, are small; only 2 percent of all academics in our sample are under 25; even among women, the proportion is 4 percent.

Marital status	Men	Women
Single (never married)	10	42
Married (once only)	80 ⎱ 87	40 ⎱ 45
Married (remarried)	7 ⎰	5 ⎰
Separated	1 ⎱	1 ⎱
Divorced	2 ⎬ 4	7 ⎬ 12
Widowed	1 ⎰	4 ⎰
	101%	99%
	(349,509)	(86,000)

TABLE 6-2 Marital status, by sex (in percentages; base totals in parentheses)

SOURCE: 27,000-case sample.

of the men (of all ages) are currently married; 3 percent have been but are not now married (that is, they are divorced, separated, or widowed); and only 10 percent are single. In the case of women, however, 42 percent are single; 12 percent have been but are not now married; and less than half (46 percent) are currently married. In a society where marriage is almost overwhelmingly the norm, the fact that more than half of all female academics are unmarried—and that four times as many women as men are divorced—demonstrates all too clearly the difficulty for women of combining marriage with an academic career. On the other hand, if almost half of all female academics *are* married, there is little excuse for discriminating against women on the grounds that marriage will interfere with their careers.

If we now look at the marriage rates of men and women within age categories (Table 6-3), we see that, once over 30, the men are almost all married, whatever their age. But women vary in their marriage rates: except for the very youngest group (and except for a slight unevenness around 40), there are more married women in each age group than in the next older group. As before, the question is whether this is a generational effect or one of age. On one hand, the oldest women come from a generation where marriage was seen as demanding a more total commitment, and a firmer choice between it and a career, so that more women will have chosen, or will have been compelled, to remain single. If those days are past, we might extrapolate the steady linear trend from the oldest women down to those in their early forties (the increase continues during the thirties at a level about 10 percent lower, which could well be due to temporary withdrawal for child rearing) and suggest that another 20 years will see equal marriage rates among academic men and women when they reach 40. But part of the trend may also be due to women's age—that is, to their stage in the life cycle and not in history. For example, there is no question that women's chances of marriage, and especially remarriage, drop much more sharply than men's with increasing age. And the fact that even in the youngest age groups (under 30) 20 percent more men than women are married, combined with Feldman's evidence, suggests that equality is still some way off, even though the proportion of women in the profession does seem to be rising.

But Table 6-4 shows that the increase under 30 comes entirely from women who are childless:[9] whatever change may be taking place, it has not extended, so far as I can tell, to women with children. There is no clear evidence, obviously, about whether these youngest female academics (many of whom are not yet married) will continue childless, will have children but continue to work (the increasing recognition by universities of the special needs of mothers of small children can only help here), or will have children and drop out of the profession, as many earlier generations of women did. Since, as we shall be seeing, many of them occupy nontenured, and often highly marginal, positions

[9] Readers who are led by Table 6-4 to suspect older male academics of strikingly low fertility or of losing their children in excessive numbers should be reassured that respondents were asked only for the number of their "dependent" children, a definition that is convenient for our present purpose.

TABLE 6-3 Marital status (percent who are currently married), by sex and age (base totals omitted)		
Age	*Men*	*Women*
61 and over	88	26
56–60	87	30
51–55	91	39
46–50	90	47
41–45	88	51
36–40	89	48
31–35	89	55
26–30	77	56
25 and under	64	43
All ages	87	46

SOURCE: 27,000-case sample.

TABLE 6-4 **Sex and dependent children combined, by age** *(in percentages)*

Sex, children						Age					
	61 and over	56–60	51–55	46–50	41–45	36–40	31–35	26–30	25 and under	All ages
Men, no children	54	37	19	12	12	14	19	40	49	23
Men, with children	24	40	59	68	69	71	67	38	14	57
Women, no children	20	20	15	11	9	8	8	17	36	13
Women, with children	2	3	7	9	10	8	7	5	1	7
	100%	100%	100%	100%	100%	101%	101%	100%	100%	100%
	(31,281)	(27,399)	(39,459)	(55,433)	(64,928)	(71,016)	(72,713)	(57,314)	(8,992)	(429,605)

NOTE: Sex percentages differ slightly from Table 6-1 owing to nonresponse variations.

SOURCE: 27,000-case sample.

in the academic hierarchy, it seems likely that even this fairly high proportion will drop quite substantially as the women grow older.[10]

The Uneven Distribution of the Sexes within Academia

Tables 6-5, 6-6, and 6-7 show where women are concentrated in the academic world at present. Section A of Table 6-5 probably contains little to surprise anyone familiar with this world.[11] The category of "new and semiprofessions" contains just those areas in which women's participation is well known to be strongest,

[10] Recent figures from the National Center for Educational Statistics confirm that universities are finding it easier to increase the proportion of women at "instructor" level than in the "ladder faculty" positions. Further, more intensive research is needed on what happens to young and untenured female appointees.

[11] The question of "sex typing" of academic fields and of occupations is a subtle and interesting study in itself, which I cannot do justice to here. As well as their own experience, readers are referred to Feldman (1974), who discusses the "masculinity" and "femininity" of subject fields, as revealed not only in recruitment of female students and faculty, but also in the status and prestige of the field, and in the stereotyped perceptions of outsiders—all of which he found to be closely linked.

TABLE 6-5
(A) Sex distributions, by subject taught (in percentages) (B) subject fields, by sex (in percentages)

Subject field	(A)				(B)	
	Men	Women	Total		Men	Women
New and semiprofessions*	65	35	100%	(48,265)	9	20
Education	71	29	100%	(49,462)	10	17
Humanities	74	26	100%	(86,095)	18	27
Fine arts	77	23	100%	(33,681)	8	9
Business and commerce	84	16	100%	(25,221)	6	5
Biological sciences	86	14	100%	(29,742)	7	5
Social sciences	86	14	100%	(52,069)	13	9
Physical sciences	90	10	100%	(58,490)	15	7
Old professions†	92	8	100%	(17,541)	5	2
Engineering	100	≠	100%	(26,934)	8	≠
All subjects	80	20	100%	(436,799)	99%	101%
					(343,228)	(84,273)

*Agriculture, architecture, design, forestry, health sciences other than medicine, home economics, journalism, library science, nursing, social work, social welfare, and all other fields not specified above.

† Medicine and law.

‡ Less than 0.5 percent.

SOURCE: 27,000-case sample.

TABLE 6-6
(A) Sex distributions, by type and quality of institution (in percentages)
(B) type and quality of institution, by sex (in percentages)

Quality level and type		(A) Men	(A) Women	(A) Total		(B) Men	(B) Women
Universities							
High	I	90 ⎤	10 ⎤	100%	(55,100)	14 ⎤	7 ⎤
Medium	II	87 ⎬87	13 ⎬13	100%	(79,120)	20 ⎬50	12 ⎬31
Low	III	84 ⎦	16 ⎦	100%	(68,979)	16 ⎦	13 ⎦
Four-year colleges							
High	IV	84 ⎤	16 ⎤	100%	(24,907)	6 ⎤	4 ⎤
Medium	V	78	22	100%	(47,876)	11	12
Low	VI	71 ⎬74	29 ⎬26	100%	(97,757)	20 ⎬50	33 ⎬69
Junior colleges							
All	VII	74 ⎦	26 ⎦	100%	(63,060)	13 ⎦	19 ⎦
All institutions		80	20	100%	(436,799)	100%	100%
						(350,154)	(86,645)

SOURCE: 27,000-case sample.

less so perhaps as academic teachers than as full-time professionals: social work, nursing, home economics, library science, etc. (The presence of some predominantly male fields such as agriculture and forestry may partly account for the proportion of women here being so much lower than in the professions themselves.) The newer professional schools, including education, not only have the highest proportion of women, but also, whether coincidentally or not, have the lowest status in the university community. It has been pointed out recently (Eble, 1972, p. 5) that not only are the female faculty members in these departments paid lower salaries individually, but the male faculty members are as well.[12] Following these professional fields, there is an intermediate group of subjects—fine arts and humanities—in which women have traditionally had a "legitimate" interest, originating in their compatibility with Victorian notions of subjects fit for lady amateurs; and here women constitute about

12 This observation is confirmed by the present data. For each of the 69 subject groups identified in the survey, the proportion of female faculty, and the average rates of pay for men, women, and both sexes combined, were computed. The following are the rank correlations (Spearman *rho*) with the proportion of women faculty ($N = 58$, excluding 11 subjects where women are insignificantly

one-quarter of all faculty members. In business and the biological and social sciences, women are around one-sixth of the staff; in physical sciences, medicine, and law, they are less than one-tenth, and there is a negligible proportion of women (less than half of 1 percent) in engineering.

Section B of Table 6-5, however, which gives the same figures repercentaged to compare the distribution of men and women across subjects, may be a less familiar way of thinking about the situation. Compared with 19 percent of men, no less than 37 percent of all female faculty are concentrated in the two groups of education and the newer professions; over one-third of all women, therefore, not only suffer from the lower pay and lower status to which both their sex and their association with these fields contribute, but also spend their working lives in specialized professional schools, isolated—sometimes physically and usually intellectually—from the core campus. If we move one step further and add in the proportions in the humanities, we find that 64 percent (that is, almost two-thirds) of all women are in these three areas alone, compared with 37 percent of the men. Men, as a glance down the table will show, are fairly evenly distributed over the whole breadth of subject fields, but women are highly concentrated in a few areas.[13]

Section A of Table 6-6 shows the proportion of women in different types and quality levels[14] of universities and colleges. The proportion of women rises fairly steadily as the quality of institution declines, and more sharply among four-year colleges

---

represented): men's average salary $-.40$ ($p<.001$); women's average salary $-.17$ ($p<.10$); average salary (both sexes combined)$-.57$ ($p<.001$); differential between men's and women's pay $-.35$ ($p<.005$). The proportion of women, in other words, is a better predictor of men's than of women's salaries. In fields where women are few, women's salaries are somewhat higher, but men's are much higher: pay differentials increase. Men derive some of their status from the "nonfemininity" of their field, but women's status as women overrides the status of their field and depresses their salaries. We shall be looking much more closely at salaries in the second section of this paper.

[13] It is fair to add, however, that if one leaves out the professional schools—which happen to be the two extreme groups at each end of the table—62 percent of the women and 67 percent of the men teach subjects in the "letters and science" core of the university or college.

[14] See App. A for a description of type and quality classifications.

TABLE 6-7 Sex distribution (percentage of women), by subject field and type and quality of institution

| | Quality level and type | | | | | | | | | |
| | Universities | | | Four-year colleges | | | Junior colleges | All universities | All colleges | All institutions |
	High (I)	Medium (II)	Low (III)	High (IV)	Medium (V)	Low (VI)	All (VII)	(I–III)	(IV–VII)	(I–VII)
New and semiprofessions	22	26	34	30	49	50	50	28	52	35
Education	18	26	26	34	27	36	27	24	32	29
Humanities	14	17	19	20	28	34	34	17	31	26
Fine arts	18	9	22	26	27	28	21	16	26	23
Business and commerce	0	3	10	8	14	20	33	5	24	16
Biological sciences	9	9	10	24	19	19	26	9	21	14
Social sciences	7	10	8	13	15	25	15	8	19	14
Physical sciences	4	4	8	6	11	16	13	6	13	10
Old professions	8	8	7	n.a.*	n.a.*	n.a.*	n.a.*	8	n.a.*	8
Engineering	—	1	0	1	—	1	0	—	1	—
All subjects	10	13	16	16	22	29	26	13	26	20

*Not applicable.

SOURCE: 27,000-case sample.

than among universities. As the author has pointed out earlier in this chapter, the high-quality universities are in very many ways the pattern for the rest of the system: their manifest superiority in research output (and in attracting research funds) and in other visible indicators of academic excellence provides a structural model—and with it a set of norms and values—at which other lower-quality institutions will tend to aim, however inappropriately for their purposes. The fact that these institutions have the lowest proportion of women on their staffs can only reinforce the association of women with lower status: on the other hand, any success in changing the balance here might have considerable influence on the rest of the system.[15]

How much the imbalance is due to institutional discrimination, and how much to the broader cultural climate that leads women either not to choose to compete at the highest levels or to be unable to do so, is a central concern of this research. Since, as a group, female academics are less well qualified than their male counterparts, as I shall be showing shortly, one might therefore expect women to be found in larger numbers in lower-quality institutions whose requirement of a doctorate is less rigid. But the facts are clear enough. In section B of Table 6-6 we see that more than two-thirds of all female academics are currently teaching in four- or two-year colleges (and less than one-third in universities), while men are equally divided between universities and other institutions.

Table 6-7 combines the two preceding tables into one, showing the percentage of women by subject for each level of institution. In general, the patterns of Tables 6-5 and 6-6 persist, though with notable exceptions. For example, business and commerce turns out to be one of the most exclusively male-dominated areas in universities, and elsewhere more female than most, especially in junior colleges. Education, at the other extreme, is fairly consistently female and is less affected by quality level than other fields.

WOMEN AND THE REWARD STRUCTURE OF THE PROFESSION The main focus of this paper is women's prospects for promotion, tenure, and high salary—their position, in other words, in the status and reward structure of the profession. I referred

---

[15] Granting that events at these leading universities are always more visible, it does appear that they are receiving more attention from federal agencies and from militant women.

earlier to "strong" and "weak" conceptions of equality of opportunity: this was, perhaps, something of a simplification. It is possible to imagine a whole range of criteria against which to measure whether equality has been achieved. The simplest is to set a target figure for the proportion of the supposedly discriminated-against group, nonachievement of which would be *prima facie* evidence of discrimination. There could of course be argument about the appropriate figure. A radical viewpoint would take the proportion of the relevant group in the adult, employment-age population: 50 percent or near enough, in the case of women. This radical definition of equality has been endorsed in principle by some highly respectable authorities. For example, a recent report on educational opportunity from a UNESCO commission states that equal educational opportunity must be defined not as equal access, but as "equal chance of success" ("Text of UNESCO . . .," 1972, p. 9). Others might be content, for example, with a proportion equal to that in the working population, or, least ambitiously, in the segment of the working population holding all the qualifications normally judged necessary for performing the job (e.g., Bernard, 1963, p. 52).[16] This last would correspond to the weak conception of equality of access using "objective" criteria. The reader has doubtless had some such figure in mind (perhaps not a very precise one, if he or she does not accept a radical conception of equality) when looking at the tables of sex distributions that we have shown so far.

Tables 6-8 and 6-9 are of this type: they show to what extent women are represented among the different academic ranks of the profession, both taken as a whole and divided by type and quality of institution. In no rank anywhere does the proportion of women come near 50 percent (39 percent among lecturers at colleges is the closest), but aside from this, there is a remarkable degree of variation. Women's representation is especially small in the regular career grades of professorship (the "ladder faculty") and among those having tenure; it is largest among the ad hoc grades of instructor and lecturer, and among those with "acting" (that is, temporary) appointments. This is the case in all types of institutions, although the overall proportion of women

---

[16] The new federal guidelines appear to rely on the proportion qualified, but not necessarily working.

TABLE 6-8 *Sex distribution (percentage of women), by academic rank and quality/type of institution*

| | Universities | | | All | Four- and two- | All |
Rank	High	Medium	Low	universities	year colleges	institutions
Professor	4	5	6	5	14	9
Associate professor	7	10	10	10	21	15
Assistant professor	11	15	18	15	26	21
Instructor	20	31	36	31	35	34
Lecturer	26	32	21	27	39	32
All others	26	20	24	23	24	23
All ranks	10	13	16	13	26	20

SOURCE: 27,000-case sample.

varies considerably among institutions. In the universities, notably, the proportion of female assistant professors is three times as high as the proportion of female full professors; and the proportion of female instructors is twice as high as the proportion of female assistant professors.

The scale of these differences suggests that something is badly wrong, but however suggestive such descriptive figures are, they do not tell us very much about the extent or nature of discrimination. Whether or not we are outraged by the discovery that (only) 4 percent of full professors at the country's leading universities are women will probably depend on our choice of a desirable bench mark percentage. Those to whom 50 percent is the only acceptable figure might well choose to stop reading here: one final piece of information—that according to our respondents the average (mean) salary of academic men is

TABLE 6-9 *Sex distribution (percentage of women) by tenure and type of institution*

Type of appointment	Universities	Four- and two- year colleges	All institutions
Regular with tenure	9	23	16
Regular untenured	18	27	23
Acting	26	38	33
Visiting	13	21	17
All respondents	13	26	20

SOURCE: 27,000-case sample.

$13,000, while for women it is $9,800—completes the indictment. But the most interesting questions remain to be asked; namely, given a fairly wide acceptance of the principle of nondiscrimination—and most academic institutions have cheerfully endorsed the principle for a long time—is it the case that weak nondiscrimination exists in universities and colleges, so that these massive differences can be accounted for by measurable differences in qualifications, motivation, etc.? Or if not—that is, if not even weak equality exists—what are the mechanisms that allow arguably well-meaning men to ignore or to discount the effects of prejudice?

The second of these questions is partly a matter for speculation; but the former is susceptible to empirical test. In the rest of this paper, I shall try to answer it. Rephrased in the language of survey research, it reads: can one discover criteria—qualifications, achievements, motivation, etc.—that are so strongly related to access to rewards (rank, tenure, and high salary) that the relation of these rewards to sex disappears? (The form of table that would indicate this would show the rewards as "dependent" variables, sex as the "independent" variable, and our other criteria as "control" variables: within categories of these control variables, the percentage of men and women in each category of the dependent variable would be the same.) If no such criteria can be found, separately or in combination—that is, if it turns out that discrimination does exist, even measured against the weakest standards of equality of access—we should be in a better position to answer the second question: How can women be systematically discriminated against in a nominally egalitarian institution?

The Overall Distribution of Rewards Tables 6-10 and 6-11 follow the pattern just described, by showing the distribution of rank and tenure for men and women, both in academia as a whole, and separately for universities and colleges. At this level,[17] there is a very substantial degree of apparent inequality. In the universities, where it is most marked,

---

[17] One important control variable has already been introduced: membership of the profession. It is worth reemphasizing what was said at the beginning of this chapter—that this report does not deal with discrimination at first recruitment. It is possible to imagine a system that had severely discriminatory entry criteria but that dealt fairly with successful entrants thereafter. Tables such as these would not reveal such discrimination.

TABLE 6-10 *Academic rank, by sex and type of institution (in percentages)*

	Universities		Four- and two-year colleges		All institutions	
	Men	Women	Men	Women	Men	Women
Professor	32	10	20	10	26	10
Associate professor	25	17	20	16	22	16
Assistant professor	28	31	26	27	27	29
Instructor	9	29	22	35	16	32
Lecturer	3	7	2	3	2	5
Other designations	—	—	8	5	4	4
No ranks designated	2	5	2	3	2	4
	99%	99%	100%	99%	99%	100%
	(175,803)	(27,549)	(173,541)	(59,308)	(349,344)	(86,337)

SOURCE: 27,000-case sample.

one-third of men are full professors, and another quarter are associates. Only just over a quarter of all women hold either of these ranks. Similarly, more than half of all men in universities are tenured (Table 6-11), but just over a third of women. In the colleges, women's chances of high rank are no better than at universities—indeed even more of them are instructors; but men's chances are worse—the rank structure for men is nearer to that of women. In terms of tenure, both sexes converge from the more extreme inequality in universities.

TABLE 6-11 *Tenure, by sex and type of institution (in percentages)*

	Universities		Four- and two-year colleges		All institutions	
Type of appointment	Men	Women	Men	Women	Men	Women
Regular with tenure	54	34	50	44	52	41
Regular untenured	41	60	46	51	44	53
Acting	2	3	2	3	2	3
Visiting	3	3	2	2	3	2
	100%	100%	100%	100%	101%	99%
	(175,161)	(27,248)	(172,743)	(58,548)	(347,904)	(85,277)

SOURCE: 27,000-case sample.

	Men	Women
Below $7,000	6	17
$7,000–$9,999	23	45
$10,000–$11,999	21	18
$12,000–$13,999	17	10
$14,000–$16,999	16	7
$17,000–$19,999	8	2
$20,000–$24,999	6	1
$25,000–$29,999	2	—
$30,000 and over	1	0
	100%	100%
	(346,934)	(85,365)
Mean salary	$13,100	$9,800
Median salary	$12,000	$9,200

TABLE 6-12
Salary, by sex (all institutions) (in percentages)

SOURCE: 27,000-case sample.

In levels of pay (Table 6-12), we find marked inequality once again. On average, women are paid $3,000 less than men; practically none of them, compared with 3 percent of men (and that is an estimated 10,000 people) earn over $25,000; only 10 percent—compared with one-third of men—earn over $14,000. This inequality is not confined to the top end of the scale; there is a difference of $2,800 in median salaries. Bernard (1963, p. 180) reported a survey of 1959–60 that found a difference of $1,200. On the grounds that the difference was smaller in the lowest ranks, she suggested that pay inequality was decreasing. Rita J. Simon, Shirley M. Clark, and Kathleen Galway (1967) offered rather cautious agreement. Clearly, it has in fact worsened substantially.

Table 6-13 shows average salaries (though not distributions) for each quality level and type of institution: differentials, as in the case of rank, are far sharper at the top of the quality scale. (They are shown both as net differences in thousands of dollars and in standardized form.) Again, one can only speculate about the reasons why women are so much more disadvantaged at the very best universities; but any theory must take into account the fact that in the best four-year colleges women's salaries not only come closer to men's than anywhere else, but are higher on average than they are even at elite universities. There is certainly no question, however, of women dominating these colleges and so dictating their terms or filling the more desirable jobs by default: there are proportionately fewer women here than in colleges lower in quality (Table 6-6).

We have already introduced two criteria that might "explain away" apparent discrimination. The first is simply membership of the academic profession: if men and women first entered the profession at different rates (whether because of discrimination on first appointment or, more likely, because of factors not directly attributable to universities and colleges) but were equally treated once inside, we should find that average salaries and the proportions holding high ranks were equal for the two sexes. We have not found that to be so, nor have we been able to account for the inequality by finding different rates of entry to colleges and universities—which might have different rank and salary structures. Another obvious source of confusion might be the age distributions of men and women, which we know to be different. When we look at Tables 6-14, 6-15, and 6-16, however, we find that, if examined age for age, the inequality turns out much worse. In universities as a whole, for example, 21 percent more men are full professors than are women (Table 6-14); however, among those aged 51 to 55 the difference is no less than 53 percent. The majority of men in universities are already profes-

TABLE 6-13
Average salary (in thousands of dollars), by sex and type/quality of institution

Quality level and type		Men	(Δ)	Women	Index*
Universities					
High	I	16.0 ⎫	(4.8) ⎫	11.2 ⎫	.31 ⎫
Medium	II	15.2 ⎬14.8	(3.9) ⎬(4.2)	11.3 ⎬10.6	.27 ⎬.29
Low	III	13.5 ⎭	(3.5) ⎭	10.0 ⎭	.26 ⎭
Four-year colleges					
High	IV	13.8 ⎫	(1.2) ⎫	12.6 ⎫	.08 ⎫
Medium	V	11.6	(1.9)	9.7	.18
Low	VI	10.7 ⎬11.3	(1.9) ⎬(1.9)	8.8 ⎬9.4	.18 ⎬.17
Junior colleges					
All	VII	10.9 ⎭	(1.3) ⎭	9.6 ⎭	.12 ⎭
All institutions		13.1	(3.3)	9.8	.26

*$(Mq - Wq)/Tq$ where Mq = men's, Wq = women's, Tq = all respondents' mean salary for type/quality of institution.
SOURCE: 27,000-case sample.

TABLE 6-14 *Rank (percent who are full professors), by sex, age, and type of institution*

Age	Universities		Four- and two-year colleges		All institutions	
	Men	Women	Men	Women	Men	Women
61 and over	77	38	56	31	67	33
56–60	71	31	44	22	58	25
51–55	66	13	40	19	53	17
46–50	54	14	30	11	43	12
41–45	37	10	25	8	31	9
36–40	15	3	11	2	13	2
31–35	3	0	2	1	2	1
30 and under	—	0	—	0		0
All ages	32	11	20	10	26	10

SOURCE: 27,000-case sample.

sors by their late forties; at the same age, only 13 percent of women are full professors. The difference is less large in the colleges. As before, however, this is only a relative improvement; women's promotion prospects are no better than in

TABLE 6-15 *Tenure (percent who have tenured appointments), by sex, age, and type of institution*

Age	Universities		Four- and two-year colleges		All institutions	
	Men	Women	Men	Women	Men	Women
61 and over	86	77	76	66	81	69
56–60	85	75	78	66	82	69
51–55	83	50	76	71	79	64
46–50	78	50	70	53	74	52
41–45	69	37	61	47	65	44
36–40	51	27	48	43	50	38
31–35	22	11	30	22	26	19
26–30	6	3	11	11	9	8
25 and under	7	9	11	9	10	9
All ages	54	35	50	44	52	41

SOURCE: 27,000-case sample.

TABLE 6-16 *Average salary (in thousands of dollars), by age, sex, and type of institution*

	Universities			Four- and two-year colleges			All institutions		
	Men	*[Δ]*	*Women*	*Men*	*[Δ]*	*Women*	*Men*	*[Δ]*	*Women*
61 and over	17.4	[5.0]	12.4	12.9	[1.9]	11.0	15.3	[3.9]	11.4
56–60	18.2	[6.0]	12.2	13.4	[3.0]	10.4	15.8	[4.8]	11.0
51–55	18.1	[6.2]	11.9	13.0	[2.4]	10.6	15.5	[4.5]	11.0
46–50	17.4	[5.1]	12.3	12.8	[2.9]	9.9	15.2	[4.5]	10.7
41–45	16.0	[4.8]	11.2	12.3	[2.8]	9.5	14.2	[4.2]	10.0
36–40	14.3	[3.3]	11.0	11.2	[2.1]	9.1	12.8	[3.2]	9.6
31–35	12.2	[2.7]	9.5	10.0	[1.5]	8.5	11.1	[2.3]	8.8
26–30	10.0	[1.7]	8.3	8.9	[0.6]	8.3	9.4	[1.1]	8.3
25 and under	7.4	[0.5]	6.9	7.8	[0.7]	7.1	7.7	[0.6]	7.1
All ages	14.8	[4.2]	10.6	11.3	[1.9]	9.4	13.1	[3.3]	9.8

SOURCE: 27,000-case sample.

universities (in fact they are slightly worse), but men's prospects are also worse. Tables 6-15 (tenure) and 6-16 (salary) show the same pattern of inequality. For example (Table 6-16), in the universities men in their fifties may be earning more than half as much again as women. There is not much difference in salaries between the sexes among those under 30; but this surely has more to do with the marginal position of most young academics of either sex than with a new breakthrough in universities' treatment of the youngest generation.

One might wonder, finally, whether the inequality is confined to access to promotion. Women are less likely to reach high ranks; but are those that do so then paid as well as their male counterparts? This seems unlikely. We already know,[18] for example, that both men and women in subject areas with more women tend to be lower paid; and Table 6-17 (which looks separately at universities and colleges and gives average salary by rank within 10-year groups) shows that there is no combination of rank and age in which women on average earn as much as men. Indeed, in universities there is always a difference of at

[18] See footnote 11.

TABLE 6-17		Universities		Four- and two-year colleges		All institutions	
Average salary (in thousands of dollars) by sex and type of institution, within rank and age categories. Rank and age		Men	Women	Men	Women	Men	Women
Professor							
51 and over		19.8	15.9	15.1	13.3	18.0	14.1
41–50		20.0	16.8	15.4	12.6	18.3	13.9
31–40		18.9	15.1	14.1	9.1	16.9	11.1
All ages		19.8	16.1	15.1	13.0	18.0	13.9
Associate professor							
51 and over		13.8	12.6	11.8	11.0	12.7	11.5
41–50		15.1	13.5	12.3	11.0	13.9	12.0
31–40		14.8	12.9	12.1	10.6	13.7	11.5
All ages		14.8	13.0	12.1	10.9	13.6	11.7
Assistant professor							
51 and over		11.8	10.2	9.9	9.1	10.5	9.6
41–50		12.8	10.8	10.2	9.3	11.4	9.9
31–40		12.2	10.4	10.0	9.1	11.2	9.6
Under 30		11.0	9.7	9.6	8.9	10.4	9.3
All ages		12.0	10.4	9.9	9.1	11.0	9.6
Instructor							
51 and over		9.5	8.3	10.8	9.0	10.6	8.9
41–50		9.5	8.5	10.1	8.4	10.0	8.4
31–40		9.4	8.6	9.0	8.0	9.1	8.2
Under 30		8.4	7.9	8.2	8.0	8.3	8.0
All ages		9.0	8.2	9.0	8.2	9.0	8.2
All ranks		14.8	10.8	11.3	9.4	13.1	9.8

SOURCE: 27,000-case sample (but for women in universities, all respondents). For the multivariate analysis that follows, a special sample was created, containing, for universities only, all female respondents (N = 5,777) and a 1:4 systematic sample of male respondents (N = 9,308): a sample hereafter referred to as "special sex-weighted sample."

least $1,000 above the level of instructor.[19] Women's disadvantages, it seems, go very deep.

19 Within certain subjects, however, there are occasional exceptions to this—but only at ranks below full professor. Female associate professors in the natural sciences, to take the one clear example, are paid almost as much as their male counterparts at the same ranks—slightly more, if they are over 50. It is to be hoped that this compensates for their smaller chance of promotion to full

Research and the Reward Structure of Universities

Elsewhere in this volume (see Chapter 2) the author and a colleague demonstrated the extent of the truth underlying the "publish or perish" maxim. Although "perish" may well be an exaggeration,[20] since there seem to be fairly long-term roles for nonresearchers to perform, "publish and flourish" is a very accurate description of the reward structure of universities. At all ages, activity in research, and especially publication—the more frequent the better—has an enormous impact on academics' chances of promotion and high salary; other activities seem at best to be necessary but not sufficient conditions for success. So it is only natural to wonder if this may be the key to women's low promotion rate—in the universities at least. If women publish less, for whatever reason, it is inevitable, given the present structure of rewards, that women's promotion rates will be lower. Their publication rates, therefore, were examined (Table 6-18); they are shown separately for each of the subject areas in which women take much part.

At this point, we must restrict our attention to the universities only. The other criteria for promotion—devotion to teaching, administration, public service, the good of the institution, etc.—are so unspecific and (in the case of teaching) so private that they are exceptionally hard to measure. (This difficulty, of course, constrains not only survey researchers but also university administrators—and it is one important reason why research, when available, is so heavily weighted.) In the colleges, where research is not part of the normal expectation,[21] the survey data cannot reveal how well women and men fulfill their more diffuse role obligations. Regretfully, then, the colleges must be excluded from further tables.[22]

In fact, women do turn out on average to be markedly less productive of published research than men, both over their lifetimes (section A, Table 6-18) and within a recent period

---

professor—and for the fact that in every subject female full professors' salaries are at least $2,000 lower than males'.

[20] Using a one-time cross-sectional survey, it was not possible to find out who "perishes" from the academic profession.

[21] This is not entirely true of some subjects at the highest-quality colleges (see Chap. 2, this volume), but the university/college distinction is the simplest and clearest available.

[22] The possibility of generalizing from these findings to cover the colleges is discussed briefly on p. 242.

TABLE 6-18
Average number
of articles
published;
average number
of publications in
the last two
years; and
research activity
(in percentages),
by sex and
subject taught
(universities only)

		Subject						
	Physical science		Social science		New professions		Education	
	Men	Women	Men	Women	Men	Women	Men	Women
A. Number of articles (ever)	13.3	6.8	8.5	4.6	9.4	2.8	7.0	3.6
B. Number of publications (last two years)	3.9	2.0	3.2	1.8	3.0	0.9	2.6	1.3
C. Research activity								
Inactive, no recent publications	7	27	6	15	17	47	19	38
Active, no recent publications	11	14	16	20	14	18	14	18
Few recent publications	52	49	56	57	49	32	49	38
Many recent publications	30	10	22	8	21	3	18	6
	100%	100%	100%	100%	101%	100%	100%	100%

NOTE: Smallest unweighted N is 422 (Fine arts, female).

SOURCE: Special (universities) sex-weighted sample.

(section B).[23] In general, men seem to have published about 2½ times as much, though in some areas—notably natural science, social science, and education—the ratio is 2 or less. (It is possible that the category "new professions" conceals much internal variation, between, say, productive men in agriculture, and nonpublishing women in social work.) Section C of Table 6-18 shows distributions on a measure of research activity that combines two questions: publication in the last two years, as before, and—for those who have not published—whether or not they are "active in research." And it brings out the full extent of the difference between men and women. Women not only

[23] The survey was inevitably focused on quantity, rather than quality—or visibili-ty—of publication (see Chap. 2, this volume).

field								
	Humanities		Fine arts		All others		All respondents	
	Men	Women	Men	Women	Men	Women	Men	Women
	6.5	1.9	3.7	2.0	9.7	5.7	9.3	3.4
	2.4	1.0	1.5	0.8	3.0	1.7	3.0	1.2
	8	36	31	43	12	33	12	38
	26	29	23	26	14	14	16	20
	51	31	38	28	53	43	51	37
	14	4	8	3	21	10	21	5
	99%	100%	100%	100%	100%	100%	100%	100%

publish less frequently, but over one-third of them describe themselves as "not active in research"—compared with 12 percent of men. This proportion is smaller in natural science—in line, perhaps, with the even higher emphasis there on research —and, interestingly, much the smallest in social science. In all other areas, however, there is a very substantial number of women, who, it seems, simply do not accept for themselves the role of active researcher that the vast majority of men (except in the fine arts) claim to perform.

But further reflection suggests this may be a mistaken interpretation. We have already seen how women are concentrated in the junior ranks, and especially in the noncareer grades such as instructor. They may, in fact, be disproportionately the victims of the vicious circle to which many young faculty members are

	Full professor		Associate professor		Assistant professor		Instructor	
Research activity	Men	Women	Men	Women	Men	Women	Men	Women
	Natural science							
Inactive, no recent publications	5	5	8	13	4	14	25	52
Active, no recent publications	6	8	10	12	13	13	26	15
Few recent publications	44	47	55	57	64	66	44	33
Many recent publications	46	39	28	18	18	7	4	0
	101%	99%	101%	100%	101%	100%	99%	100%
	Humanities							
Inactive, no recent publications	4	9	7	11	4	19	24	54
Active, no recent publications	14	4	16	17	34	30	50	33
Few recent publications	58	68	61	63	53	46	26	13
Many recent publications	25	20	17	9	8	4	1	0
	101%	101%	101%	100%	99%	99%	101%	100%

TABLE 6-19
Research activity, by sex and academic rank, within four subject areas (universities only) (in percentages)

NOTE: Smallest unweighted *N* is 55 (female, social science, full professor).

SOURCE: Special sex-weighted sample.

subject: the high teaching loads that are required of their position prevent them from doing enough research to earn promotion out of it.[24] In fact, if we look at research activity rank by rank (which we show in Table 6-19 for four subject areas), the differences between men and women are substantially re-

[24] Not only this, but at every level, women's teaching loads are higher. We looked at the average hours taught by men and women, rank by rank, in six broad subject areas. There was a consistent tendency, with only a few exceptions, for women to be teaching more hours than their male counterparts. (The difference was generally about one hour per week, but it would be larger if we could

Full professor		Associate professor		Assistant professor		Instructor	
Men	Women	Men	Women	Men	Women	Men	Women
Social science							
6	6	4	7	1	8	20	37
7	15	10	15	22	20	46	20
55	57	64	66	59	64	30	43
32	22	22	12	17	8	4	0
100%	100%	100%	100%	99%	100%	100%	100%
Education							
11	17	16	31	16	32	37	53
5	12	11	7	18	22	25	26
60	54	51	50	48	41	31	21
24	17	22	12	18	5	6	0
101%	100%	100%	100%	100%	100%	99%	100%

accurately exclude part-time staff, who are disproportionately women.) And long teaching hours are not rewarded by promotion or higher salaries. We compared men and women teaching equal numbers of hours, within age groups; not only were men always better rewarded than women, but for both sexes there was an inverse relationship between the length of time spent teaching and access to rewards. It is fair to add that women do tend to express more interest in teaching than men. It is an interesting question how much this is a genuine preference, and how much a way of "opting-out" of an unequal race. On this topic see, for example, Tessa Blackstone (1973, pp. 10–14, 30–31). The whole question of constraint and conflict in research and teaching roles will be explored in another paper by the author and Martin Trow.

duced.[25] Men of equal rank are still somewhat more likely to have published "many" articles, but there are no longer very large differences in the proportions who have published at all. There may well be sex differences not just in the constraints on faculty members, but also in their own personal preferences and interests. We shall return to this question later; for the moment, however, we must rely (as committees concerned with promotion seem to do) on actual achievement in research, regardless of possible difficulties, and ask how well it predicts the rewards of promotion, tenure, and salary.

Before answering this question we should be clear about the possible implications of what we find. By introducing activity in research as a control variable, we are accepting the influence that it has on access to academic rewards and acknowledging that, however inescapable the pressures may be that lead to women's lower rates of activity, the chances are that those who decide on promotion in universities are unaware of these pressures, or choose to ignore them, not feeling it their business to compensate for any handicaps. There are, as has already been said, many people who would not accept this as legitimate. But given that this has been the way in which promotion is distributed, what can we expect to find? In a purely meritocratic system (and assuming that all relevant types of merit are being measured—which, especially for those less active in research, is unlikely) we ought to find that, within each level of research activity, women and men are equally rewarded by their employing institutions. As was pointed out, measurement of merit at the low end of research is inadequate; moreover, observation suggests, and knowledge about discrimination would predict, that the more diffuse nature of criteria at this end would make discrimination easier.[26] It would not be surprising, therefore, if

---

25 This finding is in line with most earlier research (see Bernard 1963, pp. 146–163; and Epstein, 1970, pp. 172–173, 178–180), but it partly conflicts with Simon et al.'s study (1967, pp. 230–231) of female doctoral degree holders (although they did not take age or rank into account).

26 Bernard (1963, pp. 41–53, especially p. 49) and Astin (1969, pp. 84, 106–110) argue that it is the elite among women who will be most discriminated against, on the grounds that it is they who are stepping outside socially approved female roles and intruding on traditionally male territory. To some extent this may be true; certainly, as Astin points out, they will be most conscious of being discriminated against. But unequal treatment is unjust whether its victims know it or not; and I believe (although the evidence is hard to find) that less ambitious women are especially open to exploitation.

there are differences in access to rewards between men and women with little or no involvement in research. But it is clear that there is a number of women (however few compared with men) who, so far as can be judged, score as high on the crucial criterion of productivity as anyone in the universities. These women, at least, ought to be as well rewarded as their male counterparts, age for age, with high rank, high salary, and early tenure.

Table 6-20 shows the depressing, indeed the damning, reality.

TABLE 6-20 *Access to rewards, by sex, age, and research activity (universities only)*

	Research activity									
	Inactive, no recent publications		Active, no recent publications		Few recent publications		Many recent publications		All	
Age	Men	Women	Men	Women	Men	Women	Men	Women	Men	Women
	A. Percentage who are full professors									
61 and over	53	20	77	30	84	59	93	74	77	39
56–60	39	16	58	24	74	37	93	66	71	29
51–55	46	10	51	10	70	23	80	47	66	18
46–50	19	4	32	4	57	21	74	41	54	13
41–45	13	3	10	6	38	7	60	27	37	7
36–40	2	0	4	0	15	5	27	9	15	3
31–35	0	0	1	0	2	0	6	7	3	—
26–30	0	0	0	0	—	0	1	0	—	0
Under 26	0	0	0	0	0	0	*	*	0	0
All ages	20	5	16	5	33	16	49	33	32	10
	B. Percentage who are tenured									
61 and over	79	76	88	70	90	86	89	85	86	80
56–60	76	66	85	64	87	73	91	87	85	70
51–55	74	47	76	44	86	54	88	73	83	51
46–50	69	35	71	31	76	56	88	55	78	44
41–55	56	25	47	31	72	40	79	57	69	35
36–40	30	20	30	16	53	27	64	32	51	23
31–35	14	12	10	7	23	13	32	29	22	12
26–30	9	4	4	6	5	4	15	2	6	4
Under 26	8	6	13	4	0	4	*	*	7	5
All ages	49	28	36	24	56	41	67	53	54	34

TABLE 6-20 *(continued)*

				Research activity						
	Inactive, no recent publications		Active, no recent publications		Few recent publications		Many recent publications		All	
Age	Men	Women	Men	Women	Men	Women	Men	Women	Men	Women
				C. Average salary (in thousands of dollars)						
61 and over	14.1	11.2	16.1	12.3	18.1	14.3	21.3	17.0	17.4	12.8
56–60	14.1	10.8	15.5	11.7	18.8	13.7	21.2	17.2	18.2	12.4
51–55	15.7	10.2	14.9	11.4	17.8	12.7	21.5	15.6	18.1	11.8
46–50	13.4	10.3	14.3	10.5	17.5	13.1	20.7	15.4	17.4	11.9
41–45	12.9	9.5	12.8	9.8	16.0	12.3	19.2	15.8	16.0	11.2
36–40	10.6	9.0	11.7	9.8	14.2	11.5	17.5	13.6	14.3	10.5
31–35	9.7	8.4	10.6	9.2	12.4	10.2	14.3	12.5	12.2	9.4
26–30	8.2	7.8	9.2	8.2	10.6	9.1	11.7	11.2	10.0	8.3
Under 26	6.8	7.0	7.1	7.2	8.2	7.0	*	*	7.4	7.1
All ages	12.0	9.2	11.9	9.7	15.0	11.9	18.2	15.0	14.8	10.6

*N (unweighted) is less than 20.

NOTE: Smallest unweighted N is 21 (male, under 26, few recent publications, and female, 26–30, many recent publications).

SOURCE: Special sex-weighted sample.

Apart from a few cells containing men and women under 30, there is no category in which men are not considerably better off than women (leaving aside the natural ceiling reached in tenure). Not only in the low-activity categories, where one might expect it, but even among men and women whose publication rates are very high, differences of 30 percent and more in the proportion holding full professorships, and of $4,000, $5,000, or even $6,000 in salary, can be found in the forties and fifties. In the very productive group, men's salaries almost double between their late twenties and their early fifties; women's salaries increase by half—by their late fifties. At their highest salary level (the late fifties), female researchers earn less than men 20 years their junior: and as many men achieve a full professorship in their late forties as do women, finally, in their sixties. Perhaps one of the most remarkable things about this table is that these remarks about the most prolific researchers apply, almost word for word, to the other three groups, even though their access to rewards is so much lower. The influence of research on promotion is enormous, certainly; but so is the influence of sex.

Before the case is complete, there are one or two other variables that should be examined. Women earn comparatively few of the Ph.D.'s awarded by universities (11 percent of all doctoral degrees in 1965). This could account for their low membership in the academic profession, and may help to explain their lack of promotion: in most universities, a Ph.D. is a formal prerequisite for tenure. Indeed (Table 6-21), women are less well qualified than men, especially at the lower-quality universities; but Table 6-22 duplicates Table 6-20, for Ph.D. holders only (necessarily in 10-year age groups)—with little effect. The differentials, in full professorships, tenure, and salary, are largely unchanged. The most productive respondents look much the same as before: for those who are less active in research, a Ph.D. leads to somewhat higher pay prospects—but no more so for women than for men.

In view of such massive differences, there seems little reason to doubt that women are penalized for their sex. Achievements that to the best of our knowledge are equivalent seem to be rewarded very unevenly. But the kind of evidence produced so far does leave important questions unanswered. The problem for anyone concerned with change is that of the mechanisms of discrimination. In American universities, promotion procedures are, within broad limits, largely nonbureaucratic:[27] the figures

---

[27] In Bernard's terms (1963, p. 45) competition is judgmental, not autonomous.

TABLE 6-21 Percentage who hold Ph.D. degree, by sex and type/quality of institution	Quality level and type	Men	Women
	Universities		
	High I	62 ⎫	40 ⎫
	Medium II	64 ⎬ 62	36 ⎬ 34
	Low III	61 ⎭	27 ⎭
	Two- and four-year colleges		
	All IV–VII	38	20
	All institutions	49	24

SOURCE: 27,000-case sample.

TABLE 6-22 **Access to rewards, by sex and research activity (universities only, Ph.D. holders only)**

Age	Inactive, no recent publications		Active, no recent publications		Few recent publications		Many recent publications		All	
	Men	Women	Men	Women	Men	Women	Men	Women	Men	Women
A. Percentage of respondents who are full professors										
51 and over	69	28	74	27	84	53	93	77	84	48
41–50	31	20	29	12	54	20	73	39	56	21
31–40	3	0	4	0	9	2	20	10	11	2
B. Percentage who have tenure										
51 and over	90	73	90	56	90	81	93	83	90	76
41–50	84	50	74	44	80	57	88	54	82	54
31–40	27	7	27	9	42	18	54	31	43	18
C. Average salaries (in thousands of dollars)										
51 and over	16.5	13.1	16.5	12.7	18.5	14.9	21.0	16.6	18.7	14.3
41–50	15.5	11.5	14.5	11.6	16.8	13.5	19.5	15.8	17.2	13.4
31–40	12.3	9.9	11.8	10.3	13.2	11.1	15.2	12.2	13.6	11.0

NOTE: Smallest unweighted *N* is 25 (female, 31–40, inactive, no recent publication).

SOURCE: Special sex-weighted sample.

we have found are the outcome of thousands of individual decisions, weighing up academics' past contributions and future promise in a range of job requirements, with no clear and explicit criteria for weighting or measuring even the more specific achievements such as research publication. In such situations, intermittent, mild, and frequently unconscious prejudice could easily account for the massive aggregate differences now revealed.[28]

But the defenders of the status quo (whose broad outlines, in terms of women's overall representation, have been known for a

[28] Theodore Caplow and Reese McGee (1958) have documented the range of "nonobjective" considerations that enter into academic appointments. Many of these, as they point out, are to women's disadvantage, especially the requirement that one's colleagues should be generally "compatible" or congenial. Because of their sex, this is automatically problematic for women. There is also the likelihood that women's publications may be undervalued, or even "invisible" (Epstein, 1970, pp. 180–182).

long time) offer a type of explanation that ought to be taken seriously—both for purposes of understanding and because it could affect policy. It has to do, in one way or another, with notions of dedication and commitment. Men and women are seen as having different degrees of competitiveness, seriousness, or single-mindedness about their jobs. These may be personality differences, or they may be less intrinsic, stemming from women's social situation and from divided loyalties to work and to their families. (Such theories are, primarily, accounts of women's lower overall achievement; to expect them to explain away findings such as Table 6-20 is a little insulting to dedicated and productive women.) Once again, even if it could be shown that women and men with equal degrees of commitment to their work had equal chances of promotion and high salary, it would not satisfy everyone. Those who see differences in commitment as innate would presumably be content—as would those who see them as generated by society, but necessary for society's efficient functioning. Then there are those who hold a "moderate" point of view, which sees society as responsible but regards the differences as modifiable, though there is a wide range of opinion about the moral consequences of this perception. Finally, at the other extreme are the radicals, who deny any "real" differences and regard them as the inventions of a prejudiced imagination. Bearing in mind that to become an academic already demonstrates a rather higher level of ambition than that shown by the average American woman, we shall investigate some of the ways in which women may be less dedicated than men, and whether this can help to explain their lower achievement.

Marriage—or its avoidance—is a key factor in most women's careers. We know (Table 6-2) that academic women are far less likely to be married than their male colleagues. Those that are married will perhaps have divided loyalties and almost certainly will experience conflicting demands on their time—and may be the chief object of discrimination, since they are more easily defined as lacking commitment. An examination of the influence of marriage on careers reveals some of the most interesting results in this study (Table 6-23). Single women are promoted far more often than married women; at every age they are more than twice as likely to be full professors (formerly married women fall somewhere in between). In fact, single women do

TABLE 6-23
Access to
rewards, by sex,
marital status,
and age
(universities only)

	Marital status							
	Married		Divorced, separated, widowed		Single		All	
Age	Men	Women	Men	Women	Men	Women	Men	Women
A. Percentage who are full professors								
51 and over	73	16	52	24	44	38	71	28
41–50	46	7	48	8	21	15	45	10
31–40	9	1	10	2	5	2	9	1
B. Percentage who have tenure								
51 and over	85	50	78	58	85	80	85	66
41–50	74	32	64	38	62	51	73	40
31–40	37	13	26	18	30	24	36	17
C. Average salaries (in thousands of dollars)								
51 and over	18.1	11.3	16.7	12.5	14.9	13.0	17.9	12.3
41–50	16.9	10.8	16.2	11.3	13.8	12.7	16.7	11.6
31–40	13.5	9.8	12.8	10.2	11.7	10.0	13.3	9.9

NOTE: Smallest unweighted N is 139 (female, divorced/separated/widowed, 31–40).
SOURCE: All respondents ($N = 60,028$).

nearly, but not quite, as well as single men—but the latter do markedly less well than their married counterparts.

Table 6-23 is a rather different table from earlier ones concerned with research productivity. Research is a recognized criterion for promotion; marital status, as such, is not.[29] Single men are only 10 percent of the male academic population; to show that single women do nearly as well as them is in no way to justify their treatment, as it would have been in the case of highly productive men and women. There is no reason not to compare the two modal categories, unmarried women and married men, in which case the women are still unfairly treated. But the discovery that single men also do badly is a fascinating key to the whole

[29] Apart, that is, from the negative effect of nepotism rules, which are now crumbling fast. The new federal guidelines from the Office for Civil Rights in the Department of Health, Education, and Welfare outlaw such "policies and practices" if they "have an adverse impact upon one sex or the other" ("U.S. Announces . . .," 1972, pp. 1–2).

complex process of discrimination and differential access to rewards. There are, however, several possible ways of interpreting it. Traditionalists might couch their explanation in psychological terms, and argue that the "failure" to marry in a man is a sign of emotional immaturity (which could also express itself in lack of academic success)—just as one might, on rather similar grounds, argue that "career women" (married or not) are refusing to accept the domestic destinies for which their female personality is best suited. A sociological explanation would look rather different. Since neither women nor single men conform to the conventional role of the worker as a male breadwinning head of a family, they will appear, however mildly, as deviant to the majority of their colleagues who are married males. This may or may not be a sufficient cause for prejudice; but normal expectations of commitment or stability or of congeniality become problematic, and this may be enough in some cases to reject an applicant. And the problem arises not only in promotion committees. People who deviate in some way from normal role expectations have to defend themselves against such unspoken, and often unconscious, doubts, and may well internalize some of the uncertainties which others feel about them. In addition, of course, married women who attempt both to work and to fill the traditional role of wife and mother may suffer very real conflicts that reduce the time and energy they can devote to their job, whereas married men may rely on their wives to smooth their paths and protect their working lives.[30] Finally, given conventional norms, whereby husbands are normally seen as supporting their wives out of their own salaries, married men may be more aggressive, and married women correspondingly inhibited, in introducing a "need element" into their bargaining for pay.[31] But this should not affect their chances of promotion to higher rank.

Table 6-24 combines marital status with research activity as joint predictors of career success. Once again, nothing changes. Research productivity is as important as before; but so is marital status, for men as well as for women. Compared with married

---

[30] For a discussion of the effect of marriage and divorce on male and female graduate students, see Chap. 7, this volume.

[31] I owe this point to Martin Trow. For a brief discussion of academics' own assessment of their salaries, see below, footnote 36.

TABLE 6-24 *Access to rewards, by research activity, marital status, sex, and age (universities only)*

	Inactive, no recent publications						Active, no recent publications					
	Married		D.S.W.*		Single		Married		D.S.W.*		Single	
	Men	Women	Men	Women	Men	Women	Men	Women	Men	Women	Men	Women
A. Percentage who are full professors												
51 and over	50	7	38	9	36	25	59	8	54	20	47	26
41–50	19	2	18	1	14	6	23	1	38	7	12	8
31–40	3	0	0	0	0	0	2	0	0	0	0	0
B. Percentage who have tenure												
51 and over	76	49	74	51	78	80	80	35	78	52	81	76
41–50	57	19	25	19	52	51	60	19	61	39	58	44
31–40	21	9	13	8	24	26	19	6	19	14	21	16
C. Average salary (in thousands of dollars)												
51 and over	14.8	9.5	15.0	10.7	13.3	11.7	15.8	10.9	15.7	11.8	13.6	12.2
41–50	13.4	9.0	11.7	10.2	11.7	10.9	13.8	9.6	15.6	10.3	12.2	10.8
31–40	10.6	8.2	9.7	8.6	10.0	9.3	11.3	9.3	11.0	10.0	10.3	9.6

*Divorced, separated or widowed.

NOTE: Smallest unweighted N (female) is 31 (many publications, not married, 31–40); (male) is 31 (inactive/no publications, divorced/separated/widowed, 41–50).

SOURCE: All-respondents sample (N = 60,028).

men, single men are always underrewarded—though never as heavily as single women, who in their turn have more success than married women. It is astonishing how consistently marital status counterbalances achievement as a predictor of success.

In the questionnaire an attempt was made to discover the degree of commitment respondents themselves felt to their jobs, by offering them the statement, "I tend to subordinate all aspects of my life to my work." Table 6-25 shows how men and women of different marital statuses answered. Compared with stereotyped views of marriage, of sex differences, and especially of the all-embracing nature of higher professional careers like the academic's, the results may be surprising. Taken as a whole, less than half the population agreed. Moreover, the proportions of men and women are very similar, although women are slightly more likely to disagree. The difference between married and

Few recent publications						Many recent publications			
Married		D.S.W.*		Single		Married		Unmarried	
Men	Women	Men	Women	Men	Women	Men	Women	Men	Women
77	20	64	36	52	48	88	54	84	67
48	11	48	9	28	19	70	29	55	42
8	1	11	3	7	4	17	0	12	23
88	52	79	63	87	80	91	72	75	88
77	43	73	48	66	52	84	55	76	57
36	15	33	30	26	24	51	28	38	38
18.5	12.2	16.8	14.4	15.9	13.9	21.3	16.3	18.4	16.7
16.9	11.8	16.3	12.3	14.4	13.8	19.9	15.3	17.4	15.7
13.6	10.8	13.7	11.6	12.2	10.5	15.6	13.3	13.8	13.3

single men is fairly small (less than 10 percent), with married men, predictably, less single-minded about their jobs. Among women, the difference is larger: one-third of married women agree, compared with almost half of the unmarried.[32] But none of the differences are very large; that between single women and single men is negligible. Clearly, to be less than totally dedicated

[32] There is a similar difference between married and single women in their publication rates, providing an interesting cultural contrast. Blackstone (1973), in a study of British university teachers, found that married women were substantially *more* likely to publish than single women—indeed, they published as much as their male colleagues. She suggests that in pursuing full-time careers, married university teachers in Britain are defying convention to such an extent that they must have "exceptional drive and confidence," or need to justify their unusual behavior by exceptional achievement. In the United States, I suspect, prejudice against working mothers is much less strong, but that against women overshadowing men is, if anything, stronger.

TABLE 6-25 "I tend to subordinate all aspects of my life to my work" (dedication), by sex and marital status (universities only; in percentages)

"Subordinate life to work"	Men				Women			
	Married	Divorced, separated, widowed	Single	All	Married	Divorced, separated, widowed	Single	All
Strongly agree	10 ⎫44	15 ⎫52	16 ⎫53	11 ⎫45	8 ⎫32	15 ⎫47	15 ⎫49	12 ⎫41
Agree with reservations	34 ⎭	37 ⎭	37 ⎭	34 ⎭	24 ⎭	32 ⎭	34 ⎭	29 ⎭
Disagree with reservations	36	31	31	36	41	34	32	36
Strongly disagree	20	17	16	20	26	20	19	22
	100%	100%	100%	101%	99%	101%	100%	99%
	(154,655)	(4,585)	(14,667)	(174,115)	(12,570)	(3,393)	(11,173)	(27,273)

SOURCE: Special sex-weighted sample.

to one's work, as most married women are, is not in itself a grossly deviant position. What consequences does this sense of dedication have for promotion and salary prospects?

Tables 6-26 and 6-27, which show the effect of dedication, first alone and then combined with research activity, make it clear that this again is not the variable to account for all differences. Taken alone, it makes some difference to prospects of success; but in combination with research activity it becomes insignificant. It is not entirely clear, on reflection, exactly what attitude this question taps. Although enthusiasts for academic life describe it as an intellectual commitment that informs and inspires all other activities, the majority of American academics evidently have reservations about describing their lives as dominated by their jobs. If we take it literally, all this question tells us is that many academics compartmentalize their lives. We cannot be sure that those who separate their work from the rest of their lives are less ambitious, and there is no special reason to think that they

TABLE 6-26 **Access to rewards, by dedication and sex, within age categories (universities only)**

| | "Subordinate life to work" | | | | | | | | | |
| | Agree strongly | | Agree with reservations | | Disagree with reservations | | Disagree strongly | | All | |
Age	Men	Women	Men	Women	Men	Women	Men	Women	Men	Women
	A. Percentage who are full professors									
51 and over	73	38	74	28	71	23	63	24	71	28
41–50	53	17	49	13	44	6	35	7	45	10
31–40	10	2	9	1	9	1	8	2	9	1
	B. Percentage who are tenured									
51 and over	89	68	82	69	87	65	82	61	85	66
41–50	75	48	73	44	73	40	71	30	73	40
31–40	37	17	38	17	36	19	33	15	36	17
	C. Average salaries (in thousands of dollars)									
51 and over	18.4	12.9	18.3	12.5	17.8	11.8	16.9	12.2	17.9	12.3
41–50	17.4	12.3	17.0	12.1	16.5	11.4	16.1	10.7	16.6	11.6
31–40	13.2	9.8	13.7	10.1	13.0	9.9	13.0	9.8	13.3	9.9

NOTE: Smallest unweighted N is 146 (female, "strongly agree," 31–40).
SOURCE: Special sex-weighted sample.

TABLE 6-27 Access to rewards, by research activity, dedication, sex, and age (universities only)

	Research activity															
	Inactive, no recent publications				Active, no recent publications				Few recent publications				Many recent publications			
	Agree		Disagree		Agree		Disagree		Agree		Disagree		Agree		Disagree	
"Subordinate life to work": Age	Men	Women	Men	Women	Men	Women	Men	Women	Men	Women	Men	Women	Men	Women	Men	Women
	A. Percentage who are full professors															
51 and over	45	17	50	13	71	26	55	12	76	39	75	34	91	56	83	68
41–50	22	6	12	2	22	3	18	6	50	20	45	8	72	36	62	26
31–40	0	0	2	0	1	0	3	0	8	2	9	3	18	9	16	8
	B. Percentage who have tenure															
51 and over	74	67	78	59	81	64	85	50	86	69	89	69	88	81	89	80
41–50	71	39	57	26	52	29	61	33	73	53	76	44	84	68	82	50
31–40	25	16	18	15	17	11	20	11	39	19	38	20	52	31	46	32
	C. Average salaries (in thousands of dollars)															
51 and over	14.9	10.9	14.4	10.5	15.6	11.8	15.4	11.7	18.4	13.6	18.0	13.1	21.5	17.0	21.2	16.0
41–50	13.7	10.2	12.8	9.7	13.6	9.9	13.3	10.3	17.1	13.5	16.4	12.1	19.9	15.5	20.1	15.4
31–40	10.2	8.5	10.1	8.7	11.2	9.3	10.9	9.6	13.3	10.9	13.3	10.7	16.6	12.6	15.3	13.7

NOTE: Smallest unweighted N is 35 (female, "agree," many publications, 31–40).

SOURCE: Special sex-weighted sample.

are less competent. But this is really another topic: the fact remains that the accusation that women differ from men in seeing their jobs as peripheral to their lives is untrue for single women; moreover, women who see their jobs as central do not escape discrimination.

Of the many other suggested explanations for women's lower success, some, such as their visibility to the profession as a whole, or their exclusion from membership in the informal "invisible college" of their discipline, are not directly verifiable with available data. But it is often said that women may suffer from their inability or unwillingness to make strategic geographical moves. It was possible to compare the length of time women and men of similar ages had spent in their present institution, within marriage categories—and there were differences. Single women, after their mid-thirties, stay longer than married or divorced women, whereas married men, on the whole, stay longer than single men; and certainly men stay longer than women, although there is a slight tendency for younger women (under 40) to stay longer than men of the same age. The differences are larger among older academics: men in their early and late fifties have stayed at the same institution up to 75 percent longer than women. But the implications of these crude figures are obscure. Married women who allow their husbands' jobs to determine their own location are liable both to be prevented from moving when they might do so with advantage (which would increase their average stay at an institution) and to be forced to move—and wait for a suitable job in their new location—when they should not (which would reduce their average stay). It looks as if the second phenomenon is more common; but since single women also stay less long than men, the unequal pressures of marriage do not entirely account for the difference. If one combines, as predictors of success, respondents' length of stay in their present institution with their research activity, the difference between men and women is not significantly reduced, either in access to full professorships or in salary differentials. The most that can be said is that women who have stayed in their present institution for more than 20 years finally all[33] earn tenure (men do so after 15 years).[34]

---

[33] To be accurate, over 90 percent. The remaining 10 percent of both sexes are visiting, semiretired, or part-time staff, or otherwise disqualified from securing tenure.

[34] The whole subject of the recruitment and mobility of academic men and women

The first section of this paper looked at the fate of women in specific subject areas and in different types of institution. After our attempt to account for sex differences by allowing for publication rates, we should look again at the institutional context, since this is strongly related to the emphasis on publication. We found before that the largest differences between the sexes were at the top of the institutional quality scale. Table 6-28 shows that this is still true when we hold constant age and research activity.[35] In all three cases, the sharpest differences are at the leading universities. Here, on average, 27 percent fewer women are full professors than are men of similar age and research involvement, while at the lowest-quality universities the difference is 16 percent. In salary women are nearly $3,000 worse off at low-quality institutions, but $4,000 worse off at those of high quality. Quality fails to exacerbate differences only in the case of tenure. (This appears to be equally true of the most and the least productive men and women.)

In her study of law firms, Cynthia Epstein (1970, p. 195) found that elite firms were least likely to discriminate against women. Their secure status allowed them to take, without too much

(including their social origins and educational careers) will be given separate attention in a forthcoming book on the American academic profession by the author and Martin Trow.

[35] Instead of several massive tables on the pattern of Table 6-20, Tables 6-28 and 6-29 show the average of the differences between men and women in each of 12 possible categories of age and activity. The full table from which this summary is derived was examined closely. The patterns that we saw before persist: after their fiftieth birthday, women "catch up" with men in tenure, though not in rank; salary differences, too, are sharpest in the forties.

TABLE 6-28
Average sex differences in proportions holding full professorships and tenure, and in average salaries, controlling for age and research activity, by institutional quality (universities only)

University quality	Percentage full professors (Δ)	Percentage tenured (Δ)	Average salary (in thousands of dollars) (Δ)
High (I)	27	21	3.9
Medium (II)	20	19	3.4
Low (III)	16	18	2.8

SOURCE: Special sex-weighted sample.

concern, risks of which more marginal organizations were afraid. Why does the hierarchy of universities not operate in the same way? One difference is the nature of the perceived risk. Organizations like law firms are liable to excuse their preference for men by pointing to their dealings with the public, which might be upset by the status inconsistency of women lawyers. Universities cannot externalize their problem so easily: if anyone is to be upset by women, it is their own colleagues—who are responsible for their appointment and promotion. Students, who are the only other "public," do not appear to have similar problems, except at the stage when they need an academic "sponsor," when marginal members of the profession, such as women, may be a liability. At earlier stages, as David Riesman, Joseph Gusfield, and Zelda Gamson (1970, p. 76) point out, women tend to make especially good teachers—though because of their marginality, which encourages a closer and more equal relationship with students, and not, as Bernard (1963, pp. 127–145) goes to some lengths to argue, because of their sex. Caplow and McGee argue, brutally, that women are "of no use to a department" because they are outside the prestige system (1958, p. 111), but this should at least be less true of the most active researchers. The answer, I think, lies more in the different status structure of lower-quality universities. I have argued elsewhere (see Chapter 2, this volume) that the leading universities are distinctive in that in them research is virtually the only road to prestige and influence; lesser institutions permit other contributions to weigh as alternatives, but the elite schools permit them only in addition to research. It will require more analysis to discover the varieties of interaction between teaching and research on one hand, and promotion on the other, at different kinds of institution. Riesman et al. (1970, p. 6) suggest that in lower-quality, upwardly mobile institutions, research contributions tend to be weighted much more quantitatively, while the "top 36" schools differentiate research much more by quality. It is clear by now that women are liable to lose whenever more subjective criteria are legitimate. Another explanation would involve subject differences. Many of the largest universities are found in quality levels I and II. Women in these institutions often tend to be isolated in professional schools and "female subject" departments, where rates of pay and promotion can be lower without the possibility of direct comparison; in smaller and better-integrated universities, women's reference groups are larger and it is harder to justify apparent discrimination.[36]

Most of these points also apply to the four- and two-year colleges. Overall, differentials are lower in them than in the universities (Tables 6-14, 6-15, and 6-16)—but they still exist. Doubtless, the higher numbers of women, and the colleges' more local quality and teaching orientation, all tend to help women; but the diffuseness of promotion criteria will lend legitimacy to differences. It seems unlikely, given what we now know, that all such differences are justifiable.

When we look directly at subject differences (Table 6-29), we find that, indeed, the professional schools (including education), where women are a larger proportion of the staff, have lower differentials than the academic "letters and science" subjects.[37] As in the case of quality, the standards of comparison available to women are obviously important; but the fact that these are more "teaching-oriented" subjects (see Chapter 2, this volume) permits (as in lower-quality universities) promotion on other criteria than research. None of the differences between subjects, however, should disguise the fact that inequality exists in every field, and especially in salaries: the difference between $2,800 (education) and $3,500 (humanities) is probably not much comfort to the women concerned.

FEMALE ACADEMICS: SOME ALTERNATIVE PERSPECTIVES

Inequality, then, is documented. It exists, it appears to have worsened in the 1960s, and it cannot be excused on the basis of unequal achievement by men and women. Its broad outlines have been known for some time—and, until recently, discounted. The author, like many people familiar with the academ-

36 This again is a matter for further research. On investigating women's and men's satisfaction with their salaries, however, it was found that at every salary level women tend to rate their present salaries higher than do men of equivalent rank or age. Men may be greedier (to be fair, they may also think they need more; working wives, at least, often define their salary as a bonus, rather than a living wage); but in many cases, men and women will be comparing themselves against different standards. This topic—the relation of "objective" to "subjective" deprivation—needs further investigation.

37 We have already seen this for the population as a whole (see footnote 12), but it is still true when research activity is taken into account. Fine arts is something of an oddity, having the highest inequality in the proportion of professorships, and the lowest salary differences. Controlling for research productivity in this subject is an awkward procedure, where the definition and relevance of research are so ambiguous.

	Percentage full professors (Δ)	*Percentage tenured* (Δ)	*Average salary (in thousands of dollars)* (Δ)
Education	10	7	2.8
New and semi-professions	20	11	2.9
Social sciences	21	25	2.9
Humanities	26	23	3.5
Natural sciences	27	27	3.2
Fine arts	28	23	2.7

SOURCE: All-respondents sample.

ic scene, was aware that women on the whole seemed to be "underachieving," and had noticed certain rather overnumerous, slightly stereotyped figures, for whom there were no male counterparts. For example, there are the "lady associate professor" (who for lack of a certain something—undefined—goes no further),[38] the "research center wife" (whose field is the same as her husband's, but who has been kept out of a career job by nepotism rules),[39] and perhaps a few "superwomen," for whom the barriers finally gave way before efforts of which many successful men would be incapable. (Sometimes such women had to go to extraordinary lengths to deny their female status; in less self-conscious times, their male colleagues might even tell you that they never noticed they were not men.) Like any self-respecting social scientist, I knew that if women are under-achievers this might be due to broad social and cultural factors and not to any (sex-determined) intellectual difference or inferiority. I had also realized that an emphasis on research rather than teaching was liable to work to the detriment of women. But—perhaps naively—I had supposed, minimally, that those women who fully adopt the norm of research, and choose to compete on equal terms with men, would be treated fairly. It should be clearly understood that this is not the case.

[38] She may eventually achieve a special status as a respected elder stateswoman: indeed, in some subjects, (see above, footnote 19) she may, by her fiftieth birthday or so, be given a slightly higher salary than her male counterparts, who are more likely to be defined as failures.

[39] See footnote 29.

It may be useful to return to one of the popular stereotypes of women: namely that most women choose not to compete with men on equal terms. It is true that they tend to do less research and to concentrate more on teaching; they are content with lower salaries; married women, at least, are more likely to work part-time; and, so it is said, they tend to see themselves as having jobs, not careers. Is this not a legitimate exercise of free choice? Women are quite properly rewarded less if they choose not to compete for rewards. Leaving aside the fact that such stereotypes are often self-fulfilling—that is, some women may accept them as valid self-descriptions or believe that it is not worth fighting them—it is clear that this view somehow gets attached to more women than deserve it. And (see Table 6-25) the notion that men dedicate themselves primarily to their work, while women put it in second or lower place, does justice to neither sex.

I would also suggest that whether or not these supposed preferences of women are genuine, they are not to be despised. The fact that universities reward research highly does not necessarily make its exclusive pursuit the highest virtue, as a wide alliance of forces is now beginning to insist. Those academics (predominantly women) who are content with $10,000 rather than $20,000 or $30,000 salaries look from some perspectives not so much hopelessly self-denying as reasonably well-off. And the choice of part-time work over full-time, too, is distinctly double-edged. Everett Hughes has pointed out how full of nonproductive moments an academic's workday can be. Others have suggested, more forcefully, that nominal part-time workers often are forced to compress into four hours as much work as nominal full-time staff do in eight; they are simply paid at half the rate.[40] If, in the future, married couples manage to share their household and other obligations more equally, women will be able to work longer hours; men, on the other hand, will probably have to work shorter hours, and as a result, the hours required of full-time workers will probably decrease. (Although the academic profession regards a very long workweek as legitimate, it is noticeable that average hours worked have decreased in line with national trends.) In this respect, I cannot do better than to quote Erik Erikson (1964, p. 604): "It is as yet unpredictable what the [consequences] will be once women are not merely adapted to

---

[40] They may also lose out in other ways: they are likely to miss the academic socializing and gossip from which many new research ideas come.

male jobs but when they learn to adapt jobs to themselves. Such a revolutionary reappraisal may even lead to the insight that jobs now called masculine force men, too, to inhuman adjustments."

To return, however, to the question of choice: the fact that women behave differently, and that many appear to lead moderately well-satisfied lives doing so, is no guarantee that their choice is free. Indeed, one can list a whole range of constraints that limit women's freedom in ways that do not affect men. At the most universal level, there are the different cultural expectations (page 200 above) that date from early childhood: these discourage women from working at all, from working seriously, and from being ambitious or competitive (especially from competing with men); and certainly they communicate the role of teacher as one of the few acceptable identities for women. Second, for those who are married, marriage and child-rearing place unequal burdens on women. Third (and this is the central lesson of this paper), if they do become researchers, women are scarcely rewarded by increased status. Men can improve their status by publishing; but women's most salient status is their sex, and publishing research does nothing to change this.[41] Because of this, and because of their generally marginal position, they are excluded, and often exclude themselves, from the informal communications network of the "invisible college" of their subject, which makes effective research doubly difficult for them. And finally, male academics, who share society's stereotypes, tend to expect and approve women's devotion to teaching and to discourage any competition in research.

THE FUTURE   Until very recently, writers on women were able to point to the shortage of skilled manpower as a compelling reason for improving the status of women in academia. Now that the shortage has passed,[42] we must fall back on more fundamental principles. The practice of discrimination on the basis of sex is indefensible in educational institutions. That it should bear hardest on those women who most thoroughly assimilate the paramount values of their institutions is both ironic and cruel. The question of remedies, however, is hard to tackle. The last few years have seen an increasing awareness of the problem—to which this

---

[41] Age, on the other hand, does reduce the salience of female status, explaining perhaps why women seem to "catch up" a little on men in their fifties and later.

[42] The shortage of qualified skilled manpower has passed, but that is no reason for failing to use large reserves of potential talent.

article will hopefully contribute—and this has already stimulated intervention by federal agencies as well as action by more militant women. This can only help to counteract the cruder forms of discrimination. I have suggested that the marginal status of women offers advantages to universities. Like other marginal members of the institution—notably graduate teaching assistants and the most junior faculty of either sex—women are vulnerable to exploitation. If, until recently, the costs of exploiting them have been small, and the consequences insignificant, universities have been lucky.

It seems likely that universities will continue to take advantage of women until such discrimination becomes too costly. Federal intervention is a high price indeed: its first effect is to limit universities' (and still more, departments') treasured autonomy in setting their own standards for judging research and scholarship. Considering the subtlety both of selection procedures and of forms of discrimination, the new federal guidelines are crude weapons. But even they depend on the supply of qualified and ambitious women. Currently, only 13 percent of doctorates are awarded to women (up from 11 percent in 1965). We know that a very high percentage of female Ph.D.'s continue to work (Astin, 1969), so there is not a large qualified pool of potential professors who might be tempted back. Since the proportion of women among assistant professors at universities is 15 percent, it does not seem likely that, on the "availability" criteria required by the Office for Civil Rights, many universities will be found seriously wanting in recruitment—though what happens later, as we have seen, is another matter. Battles for higher status are not often won without the support of the deprived. I am inclined to agree with Alice Rossi (Mattfeld & van Aken, 1965)—and with most polemicists of women's liberation—that women themselves are unlikely to raise their expectations without fairly substantial social and cultural changes, not only in job opportunities, but in childhood socialization and in the structure of marriage. Universities and colleges can, and should, ease many of the strains for willing women and demonstrate to the more hesitant that their efforts will not be penalized; they can, and should, practice positive discrimination, both in employing faculty, and especially in encouraging women students to persevere. And in both cases they can be rewarded for doing so. Through their example, and of course through their teaching and research, they can educate society to demand further change. In conclusion, Rossi's "socially androgynous conception of the roles of men and women"

(Graubard, 1964, p. 608) seems to me both possible and just. Universities are now hindering its realization. I believe they should help it.

POSTSCRIPT Since this paper was drafted, the National Center for Educational Statistics has released preliminary figures for the year 1972–73. In the first press reports (Jacobson, 1973, pp. 1, 6), final accuracy was not guaranteed; and in any case it is not entirely clear how, for example, part-time employees were handled, or whether the university/college break is identical to the one adopted by the Carnegie Commission survey. Moreover, unlike the Carnegie study, the report appears to cover only academics on 9- or 10-month contracts. Rigorous comparison, in other words, may be unreasonable; but, with a certain amount of caution, one can get an idea of changes over $3^{1}/_{2}$ years. Taking salaries first, there has clearly been some improvement. Women's average salaries have moved up faster than men's—from 25 percent worse in 1969 to 17 percent worse now. The gap, however, is still widest at the top—in the universities; and there are still differences even among men and women of equal rank. The differentials between men and women at universities, compared with the 1969 figures (see Table 6-17), are now: full professors, $2,800 ($3,700—1969); associate professors, $700 ($1,800—1969); assistant professors, $700 ($1,600—1969); instructors, $600 ($800—1969). But differentials at ranks below the top are not an adequate test if access to higher rank is blocked (see above, page 220, footnote 19); and the fact that the overall differential at universities has dropped from $4,000 only to $3,400 is not very encouraging. Turning to access, the changes, again, are less than impressive. Given that in the past universities have, if anything, been overrecruiting women in relation to the supply of Ph.D.'s, it is not surprising that most of the increase (from 13 to 16 percent at universities, from 20 to 22 percent overall) is at the level of instructors (in universities the proportion who are women has risen from 31 to 43 percent, while in junior colleges more than half of all instructors are now women). But the fact that the proportion of female full professors has only increased by 1 percent suggests that there is still plenty of room for improvement.

References

Astin, Helen S.: *The Woman Doctorate in America*, Russell Sage Foundation, New York, 1969.

Bernard, Jessie: *Academic Women,* The Pennsylvania State University Press, University Park, 1963.

Bernard, Jessie: "The Status of Women in Modern Patterns of Culture," *Annals of the American Academy of Social and Political Science,* vol. 375, 1968, pp. 3–14.

Blackstone, Tessa: "Women Academics," in Gareth Williams, David Metcalf, and Tessa Blackstone (eds.), *The Academic Labour Market in Britain,* Elsevier Publishing Company, Amsterdam, Holland, 1974.

Caplow, Theodore, and Reese McGee: *The Academic Marketplace,* Basic Books, Inc., Publishers, New York, 1958.

Eble, Kenneth: "A 3-Point Program for Strengthening the Position of Women Faculty Members," *Chronicle of Higher Education,* vol. 6, no. 30, May 1, 1972, p. 5.

Epstein, Cynthia F.: *Woman's Place: Options and Limits in Professional Careers,* University of California Press, Berkeley, 1970.

Erikson, Erik: "Inner and Outer Space: Reflections on Womanhood," in Stephen R. Graubard (ed.), "The Woman in America," *Daedalus,* vol. 93, no. 2, Spring 1964, pp. 581–606.

Feldman, Saul D.: *Escape from the Doll's House: Women in Graduate and Professional Education,* New York, McGraw-Hill Book Company, 1974.

Jacobson, Robert L.: "Faculty Women Earning 17 Percent Less than Men," *Chronicle of Higher Education,* vol. 7, no. 23, Mar. 12, 1973, pp. 1, 6.

Mattfeld, Jacquelyn A., and Carol G. Van Aken (eds.): *Women and the Scientific Professions,* The M.I.T. Press, Cambridge, Mass., 1965.

Riesman, David, Joseph Gusfield, and Zelda Gamson: *Academic Values and Mass Education: The Early Years of Oakland and Monteith,* Doubleday & Co. Inc., New York, 1970.

Shulman, Carol H.: *Affirmative Action: Women's Rights on Campus,* ERIC Clearinghouse on Higher Education, Washington, 1972.

Simon, Rita James, Shirley Merritt Clark, and Kathleen Galway: "The Woman Ph.D.: A Recent Profile," *Social Problems,* vol. 15, no. 2, 1967, pp. 221–236.

"Text of UNESCO Panel's Recommendations on Education in the World's Developed and Developing Nations," *Chronicle of Higher Education,* vol. 7, no. 2, Oct. 2, 1972, p. 9.

"U.S. Announces Job-Bias Rules for Colleges," *Chronicle of Higher Education,* vol. 7, no. 3, Oct. 10, 1972, pp. 1–2.

7. External Constraints: Marital Status and Graduate Education

by Saul D. Feldman

Higher education in the United States began in 1636 with the founding of Harvard College; yet it was not until 1837, when Oberlin College admitted women, that higher education became a reality for American women. Both before and after the founding of Oberlin, controversy raged over how much (if any) education women should receive, what subjects they should be taught, and whether they should be educated along with men. Some worried about the effects of female education upon women, some were concerned about the effects of female education upon men, and still others wondered what the education of women would do to society. Would educating women price them out of the marriage market? Would educated women simply get married and waste their education?

A traditional rallying point against female education has been that it would be a major force for defeminization. Typical is Erasmus Darwin's (1797, p. 10) argument: "The female character should possess the mild and retiring virtues rather than the

NOTE: This article is based on data gathered by the 1969 Carnegie Commission Survey of Faculty and Student Opinion, a project sponsored by the Carnegie Commission on Higher Education and supported in part as a cooperative research project by funds from the U.S. Office of Education. The data consist of approximately 33,000 completed mail questionnaires—a 65 percent response rate from a spring 1969 sample of graduate and professional school students in 158 colleges and universities in the United States.

The data were weighted to represent the universe of over 1 million students in American graduate and professional education in the 1968-69 academic year (full details on sampling and weighting may be found in Appendix A).

The interpretations put forward in this article do not necessarily reflect the position of the Office of Education, and no official endorsement of the Office of Education should be inferred. I would like to thank Marie R. Haug and Sandra Acker Husbands for their helpful comments in the revision of this article.

bold and dazzling ones; great eminence in almost anything is injurious to a young lady; whose temper and disposition should appear to be pliant rather than robust; to be ready to take impressions rather than to be decidedly mark'd; as great apparent strength of character, however excellent is liable to alarm both her own and the other sex; and to create admiration rather than affection."

As more and more women became educated, a series of studies reported a lower marriage rate among college-educated women. To many, especially those who believed in eugenics, this lower marriage rate was a cause for alarm that could signal the end of the human race. A sociologist (Wells, 1909, p. 737) wrote: "To speak plainly, children have become to many women, a nuisance, or at least unwelcome beings of an alien domestic world which years of intellectual training have unfitted the college women to like and understand." If college women were less likely to marry and have children, those of a weaker biological strain would predominate, bringing about in due course, "race suicide."[1]

At the turn of the century, in fact, some feminists questioned the utility of marriage for educated women either because of the increased effort it took to maintain both a marriage and a career—"She should be sure that the man is of such a disposition as to be worth her effort" (Miller, 1899, p. 29)—or because they felt that educated women had the ability and the obligation to be self-supporting—". . . a woman must not ask a man to support her. It is economic beggary" (Stetson, 1898, p. 89).

A contrary view is that the educated woman can make her greatest contribution by accepting what Philip Slater (1970, p. 62) has called the Spockian Challenge. This challenge posits that child rearing is the most important task for any woman.[2] A guide on college life for women advises potential coeds that "the educated woman may make a profound contribution in the direction of home and family living, and *in addition* [emphasis mine] extend her influence outside the home into the community" (Muller & Muller, 1960, p. 198). Many college undergradu-

---

[1] For a review of this controversy, see Goodsell (1923, p. 34–61).

[2] Also illustrative is Bruno Bettelheim's (1965, p. 15) statement, "We must start with the realization that as much as women want to be good scientists or engineers, they want first and foremost to be womanly companions of men."

ates traditionally accepted this Spockian Challenge. Of college women in a 1968 national study 55 percent (Cross, 1968, p. 10) stated that they expected their lifelong satisfactions to come from marriage and the family, while only 18 percent stated their major satisfactions would come from a career. In another study of over 1,400 female Los Angeles high school seniors, 4 percent opted for a lifetime career, 48 percent stated that they planned only to be homemakers, and another 48 percent stated that they would try to combine both a career and homemaking (Turner, 1964, p. 280).

Attempting to combine a career and homemaking appears to be a considerable source of strain for many women (Coser & Rokoff, 1971). Marriage may (depending upon the woman's viewpoint) enable or force a woman to drop out of a career (Ginzberg, 1966, p. 82). Married women who do remain employed may feel what one writer described as "self-conscious gratitude toward their husbands for helping them to maintain a career" (Lopate, 1968, p. 148) and for giving them the emotional support needed for maintaining two diverse and potentially conflicting roles. A consistent finding, in studies of married professional women, is that women view their careers as second to their husbands and children, and their own careers as subordinate to their husbands' (see Arreger, 1966; Hubback, 1957; Lopate, 1968; Poloma & Garland, 1970; Sommerkorn, 1966).

Clearly today's discussions of women in higher education primarily center not on race suicide or defeminization, but on the conflict between the spouse role and the student role. This paper examines how the spouse role affects both men and women in graduate education. We will be concerned especially with the effects of divorce, for if there are conflicts between the two roles, abandonment of the spouse role may alleviate or lessen the conflict.

DEMOGRAPHIC CHARACTERISTICS Women in graduate education are less likely to be married than their male counterparts (Table 7-1), thus avoiding a potential conflict situation by remaining single. Our data, however, were gathered at one period of time and we are not able to ascertain motivations for remaining single or obtaining a divorce. We are only able to control for marital status and infer the possible effects of marriage and divorce from differential behavior.

TABLE 7-1
Marital status by sex* (in percentages; weighted numbers in parentheses)

	Marital status				Weighted
	Single	Married	Divorced or separated	Total	N →
Males	29	69	2	100	(687,387)
Females	39	56	6	101	(312,305)

*Based on entire sample (32,963).

SOURCE: 1969 *Carnegie Commission Survey of Faculty and Student Opinion.* Unless otherwise noted, this is the source for all the tables in this chapter. Totals may add up to 99 or 101 percent owing to rounding error.

As Table 7-2 illustrates, if graduate women do marry, they are much more likely than men to have a spouse with graduate education. Traditionally, it has been deemed unacceptable in our society for a woman to dominate her husband in any way—from height (Feldman, 1975) to education. Married women are thus

TABLE 7-2
Percentages of married graduate students whose spouses have attended graduate school, by age and sex (weighted totals in parentheses)

	Males	Females	Ratio— percentage female/ percentage male
22 or younger	13.7 (13,707)	63.0 (9,396)	4.60
23	20.1 (25,432)	53.8 (12,431)	2.68
24	21.5 (39,484)	68.7 (13,224)	3.20
25	32.6 (43,573)	62.8 (12,517)	1.93
26–27	27.3 (83,078)	64.0 (19,693)	2.34
28–29	28.9 (57,300)	69.9 (12,734)	2.42
30–34	22.0 (98,340)	57.7 (20,185)	2.62
35–39	19.8 (46,640)	64.0 (20,977)	3.23
40 or older	23.7 (56,969)	41.1 (52,633)	1.73
TOTAL	24.2 (467,765)	55.4 (174,507)	2.29

freer to pursue postgraduate education if their spouses have also done so. No such limitations exist for married men. Less than a quarter of married male students have spouses with graduate education compared with over half the married graduate women. This marked difference obtains for all age groups. Even women who return to graduate school after the age of 40 are more likely to have spouses with graduate education than men of a similar age.

One of the major limitations brought about by marriage is enrollment status. Whatever the marital status, women are less likely to be enrolled full time than men (Table 7-3). Although marriage affects the full-time enrollment status of both men and women, it is more likely to affect women than men. About half the married men are enrolled full time compared with less than one-third of the married women. Divorce, too, affects enrollment status, but not as severely as marriage.

Since nationality may have a strong effect upon attitudes toward the role of spouse and since part-time student status may have strong effects upon orientation toward graduate education, a special subsample was selected of only full-time students who were United States citizens.[3] Subsequent analysis will be from this subsample.

Marital status varies significantly by the age of graduate students (Table 7-4). As we might expect, single graduate

---

[3] This subsample of full-time students who are United States citizens consists of a 1-in-3 sample of single men ($N=1,704$); a 1-in-4 sample of married men ($N=1,821$); all single ($N=2,301$) and married women ($N=1,382$); and all divorced or separated men ($N=161$) and women ($N=227$).

	Full time	Part time	Weighted total
Single males	75.5	24.5	206,832
Single females	62.0	38.0	118,201
Married males	50.9	49.1	467,765
Married females	29.0	71.0	174,507
Divorced or separated males	63.6	36.4	9,627
Divorced or separated females	52.0	48.0	12,880

TABLE 7-3 *Enrollment status of graduate students, by sex and marital status (in percentages)*

	22 or younger	23–25	26–29	30–34	35 or older	Total
Single males	24.4	52.8	18.4	3.4	1.1	100.1
Single females	29.8	46.2	13.4	5.4	5.3	100.1
Married males	5.9	38.5	32.6	13.6	9.5	100.1
Married females	11.6	29.9	20.2	10.1	28.3	100.1
Divorced or separated males	1.9	13.8	28.6	38.0	17.7	100.0
Divorced or separated females	1.3	15.1	29.8	20.0	33.8	100.0

TABLE 7-4 Age distribution of graduate students, by sex and marital status (in percentages)

students tend to be younger than married or divorced students, and married students tend to be younger than divorced students. Married or divorced female students tend to be older than male students of the same marital status. Of the married women 28 percent are over 35, as compared with 10 percent of the married men; similarly, 34 percent of the divorced or separated women are over 35 as compared with 18 percent of the men. The tendency of married or divorced women to be older than men of the same status reflects the fact that women are more constrained by the role of spouse. Unlike women, men do not have to wait until their children are grown or until their spouse has an established career in order to continue in graduate school.

FINDINGS Table 7-5 examines students' motivations for attending graduate school by two measurements of intellectual motivation and one measurement of financial motivation. Intellectual and financial motivations appear to be independent. There is little relationship between agreement with "I am in graduate school in order to continue my intellectual growth," and "I am in graduate school to increase my earning power" (among men, the gamma = $-.093$, while among women the gamma = $+.073$).

At all levels of marital status, women are more likely than men to express intellectual motivations for attending graduate school. Since the traditional role of women has not been one of principal provider, it would seem that they would be freer to attend graduate school for intellectual reasons. Our data indicate that this is true for married women, who may be partially supported by their spouses and who reveal less financial motivation than married men. In their less dependent single and divorced states, however, women are just as likely as male students to express pragmatic financial motivations for attending graduate school. Financial motivations are most frequently expressed by divorced students. Men may be under pressure to pay child support or alimony, and some women may be striving for a more independent financial state.

Marital status has an effect upon the intellectual motivations of women but not of men. At all levels of marital status, men show similar percentages in their motivations of continuing their intellectual growth or of studying a field for its intrinsic interest; among women, however, these motivations are lowest among single students and noticeably higher among married and divorced or separated students. We interpret these differences as reactions against some of the constraints of the marital role. Few of the duties of the housewife require intellectual prowess. Boredom and restlessness may enhance a desire for more intellectual stimulation, especially among college-educated housewives.[4]

Just as sex and marital status influence motivations for entering graduate school, they give rise to similar differences in pressures and attitudes toward dropping out of graduate school. Section A of Table 7-6 shows that among those who are single or married, men are more likely than women to state that they have never considered quitting graduate school for good; among

[4] The problem of the bored college graduate housewife is amplified by Friedan (1963).

TABLE 7-5 *Motivations for attending graduate school, by sex and marital status (in percentages)*

	A Continue intellectual growth*			B Study field for intrinsic interest[†]			C Increase earning power[†]		
	Males	*Females*	*Gamma*	*Males*	*Females*	*Gamma*	*Males*	*Females*	*Gamma*
Single	56.0	69.6	.285	28.6	39.3	.235	32.2	33.0	.017
Married	60.5	81.2	.475	32.5	47.6	.307	43.1	37.0	.127
Divorced or separated	61.6	78.4	.388	27.8	58.5	.570	48.2	49.5	.025

*Percentage who "strongly agree."

[†] Percentage who "strongly agree" or "agree with reservations."

TABLE 7-6 *Pressures and attitudes toward dropping out of graduate school, by sex and marital status*

	A			B			C		
	Percentage who never considered (in the past year) quitting graduate school for good			Percentage who strongly disagree that they would be happier if they had not entered graduate school			Percentage who state that emotional strain will or may force them to drop out of graduate school		
	Males	*Females*	*Gamma*	*Males*	*Females*	*Gamma*	*Males*	*Females*	*Gamma*
Single	61.0	43.4	.250	60.2	57.4	.046	24.4	33.5	.221
Married	65.3	53.9	.191	66.6	65.9	.022	18.8	29.0	.275
Divorced or separated	37.7	57.3	.378	43.6	72.9	.472	56.9	41.9	.295

divorced graduate students, however, women are much more likely than men to express a commitment to remain in school. We see in section B of Table 7-6 that among single or married graduate students, no sex differences appear on agreement with "I think I would have been happier if I had not entered graduate school." Among divorced students, women are much more likely than men to disagree with this item. Divorced men are less committed to remaining in graduate school and they are unhappier with the graduate student role than single or married men; divorced women are more highly committed to remaining in school and seem happiest with the graduate student role.

In our sample of graduate students, sex or marital status has no bearing on the belief that such things as a job offer or inability to do the work will cause them to drop out. Among married students, however, 21 percent of the women compared with 9 percent of the men (gamma of sex differences = +.444) state that pressure from their spouse may cause them to drop out of school. Observe in section C of Table 7-6 that single and married women are more likely than single or married men to feel that emotional strain may be a force causing them to quit their graduate education. As we might expect, emotional strain is highest among divorced students, but a reversal in the pattern occurs, as women are less likely than men to state that this strain may cause them to drop out. In all three sections of Table 7-6, divorced women show a higher degree of commitment to remaining in graduate school than do divorced men, while the situation is reversed among single and married students.

**EFFECTS OF
MARRIAGE ON
PROFESSIONAL
ATTAINMENT**

A large proportion of our sample of full-time graduate students plan a career in college or university teaching, which, for many, will involve publishing articles or presenting papers at professional meetings. Table 7-7 looks at these activities among graduate students who plan university or college teaching careers. The greatest difference between men and women in publication rates are among married students. Married men seem most productive, while productivity for married women is much lower. The time needed to prepare a manuscript probably cannot be budgeted as easily by married as by divorced or single women. Married men have somebody to cook and care for them and an easily available sexual partner. For married women, who have in addition to their academic responsibilities those of caring for a husband and family, the student role may become secondary; hence, the lower publication rate.[5]

Socialization in graduate school takes place outside as well as inside formal settings such as classrooms or laboratories. Much of the development of commitment and professionalization takes place in informal interaction with fellow students (see Becker, Geer, Hughes & Strauss 1961; Becker & Carper 1956; Fox 1957; Kadushin 1969). To a large extent, married women are denied this type of interaction (section A of Table 7-8). Although women of all three marital statuses are less likely than men to see their fellow students socially, the greatest differences are found between married men and women. Presumably, for many

---

[5] Students in higher-quality institutions are more likely to publish than those in low-quality institutions. Women constitute about a quarter of the total enrollment in high-quality, medium-quality, and low-quality universities.

TABLE 7-7
Percentages of graduate students who have presented a paper before a professional meeting or have published a journal article, by sex and marital status: future college or university faculty only (weighted totals in parentheses)

	A *Presented paper*			*B* *Published article*		
	Males	*Females*	*Gamma*	*Males*	*Females*	*Gamma*
Single	12.0	11.6	.021	16.0 (11,401)	11.8 (17,592)	.175
Married	19.4	9.5	.395	23.1 (17,745)	12.8 (14,095)	.343
Divorced or separated	14.3	13.3	.040	20.3 (2,634)	18.1 (2,265)	.069

TABLE 7-8
Career primacy
and informal
peer interaction
among graduate
students, by sex
and marital
status **(in**
percentages)

		Males	Females	Gamma
(A)	*About how many of the people you see socially are fellow graduate students in your department?*			
	"Almost none"			
	Single	17.8	25.3	.194
	Married	22.8	43.8	.402
	Divorced or separated	18.7	32.8	.283
(B)	*I tend to subordinate all aspects of my life to my work.*			
	"Strongly agree" or "agree with reservations"			
	Single	27.9	25.4	.136
	Married	29.2	23.7	.173
	Divorced or separated	22.7	37.6	.344
(C)	*My career will take second place behind my family obligations.*			
	"Strongly disagree" or "disagree with reservations"			
	Single	32.5	27.4	.253
	Married	29.9	17.5	.247
	Divorced or separated	34.2	34.3	.013

couples, most of their socializing is done with friends of the husband's or mutual friends—not the wife's fellow students. This arrangement usually works well for the male graduate student, but the married woman is placed at a considerable disadvantage.

Total commitment to the student role involves subordinating all other roles. As we see in section B of Table 7-8, the majority of all graduate students do not make the student role the prime role. Although the differences between single and married men and women are minimal, men are slightly more likely than women to subordinate all to their graduate work. Among divorced or separated individuals, sex-based differences are much greater. Whereas divorced men are the least likely of all students to state that they tend to subordinate all to their work, divorced women are the most likely. We cannot establish causality, but the trend of the data indicates that divorced men are burdened with more responsibilities than their single or married male counterparts and thus must pay attention to other roles. Divorced women have shed some responsibilities and thus are freer to pursue the student role.

Komarovsky (1953, pp. 53–59) maintained that women are socialized to be family-oriented. Less than a third of graduate students place career ahead of family (Table 7-8, section C); but among both single and married graduate students, women are more family-oriented than men. Both single and married women are less likely than men to place career ahead of family but these differences do not obtain between divorced or separated students. Divorced or separated women are also more likely than their single or married female counterparts to place career ahead of family. This pattern leads us to speculate that in some instances the forced primacy of family over career was a factor that led to divorce.

MARITAL STATUS AND FUTURE PLANS Marital status also has an effect on the future plans of graduate students, by affecting spatial mobility. Constraints on mobility may severely limit the range of job alternatives. Local students are much more likely than out-of-state students to plan to remain in the state after they complete their graduate education (Table 7-9). Among single graduate students, 60 percent of the local men and women plan to remain in the state compared with 20 percent of out-of-state men and 27 percent of the out-of-state women. Among out-of-state students, married men feel that they are just as free as single men to leave, but married women feel constrained to remain in the state of their graduate school. We see marriage having no effect on the plans of spatial mobility of men but having a strong effect on women. Among divorced students, however, the male "locals" are more likely to plan to remain than the female "locals." We previously noted a high degree of emotional strain and a questioning of commitment among divorced men. It may be that they are better able to find supportive relationships if they remain at home. Among out-of-state divorced students, women are much more likely to plan to remain in the state than are men. They and their children may be more constrained than men by the local attachments they have developed.

In American society, teaching has been deemed an expression of the female sex role (see Epstein, 1970, pp. 154–162). We find in section B of Table 7-9 that among single or married students who plan careers in college or university teaching, women are more

TABLE 7-9
Future plans of graduate students, by sex and marital status

(A) *Percentages intending to remain in state after completing graduate education, by "I grew up in this state"*

	Grew up in state of graduate school			Did not grow up in state of graduate school		
	Males	*Females*	*Gamma*	*Males*	*Females*	*Gamma*
Single	59.0	60.6	.033	20.0	27.3	.201
Married	59.0	78.0	.305	21.8	52.3	.594
Divorced or separated	74.1	56.7	.395	27.6	51.6	.472

(B) *Percentages leaning heavily toward teaching (rather than research): future college or university teachers only*

	Males	*Females*	*Gamma*
Single	20.2	32.7	.216
Married	18.0	34.6	.308
Divorced or separated	53.9	21.9	.489

NOTE: Smallest cell (divorced males who grew up in state) has 51 unweighted cases.

likely than men to be strongly oriented toward teaching rather than research. The pattern reverses among divorced students, however. Divorced women are the least likely to be strongly teaching-oriented, while divorced men are most likely to be so. If divorce represents an escape for graduate women from the traditional family-oriented sex role, it may also serve to break the bonds of other aspects of the traditional female role. Divorced men are in a less secure position than married or single men. Under emotional and financial strain, they indicate that teaching offers more security than research.

MARITAL STATUS AND FINANCIAL CONDITIONS

Although marriage may have deleterious effects upon the student role for women, it has certain advantages. The stereotype of men being put through graduate school by their wives is true; 60 percent of married men state that a source of income is their wife's job. But it is also true that married women are being put through graduate school by their husbands; 74 percent of married female graduate students state that one source of their income is their husband's job.

Single men and women differ little in the perception of their financial situation (section A, Table 7-10). Like single graduate students, the majority of both married men and women tend to see their current financial situation as adequate. Among divorced students, however, the men rather than the women are likely to be discontented. Only 32 percent of the divorced women compared with 58 percent of the men view their current finances as inadequate or very inadequate.

Marital status has very little relationship to the receipt of financial aid. The general pattern is that men are more likely to receive teaching or research assistantships and women are more likely to receive fellowships (sections B and C, Table 7-10). Decisions concerning financial aid may take sex into account but probably not marital status.

CONCLUSIONS A consistent pattern appears in our data. There is conflict between the role of wife and the role of full-time graduate student. Married women students are under greater pressure to drop out, and if they remain in school, they are less likely to

TABLE 7-10
Finances and
financial aid of
graduate
students, by sex
and marital
status

	Males	Females	Gamma
(A) Percentages stating their current finances are inadequate or very inadequate			
Single	26.1	30.0	.096
Married	32.4	24.5	.188
Divorced or separated	57.6	32.4	.298
(B) Receiving a fellowship during the current (1968–69) academic year			
Single	26.6	32.7	.147
Married	28.2	30.1	.047
Divorced or separated	22.6	29.1	.169
(C) Percentages receiving a teaching or research assistantship during current (1968–69) academic year			
Single	30.5	27.2	.080
Married	34.7	29.2	.125
Divorced or separated	33.4	24.2	.221

engage in the forms of anticipatory or informal socialization that are important facets of graduate-student life. Once they leave graduate school, job opportunities are limited. Married men, on the other hand, feel little conflict between the role of spouse and the role of graduate student. They appear to be quite productive and the best-adjusted of all graduate students.

In comparing single and divorced women, the most committed and active graduate students are divorced women. Once divorced or separated, it is almost as if they were making up for lost time by becoming fully immersed in the student role, despite the fact that almost 70 percent of the divorced female graduate students have at least one child. It appears that divorce becomes a force for liberation for women students, but it becomes a source of strain for men. Men lose a supportive relationship, while women lose a source of severe role conflict.

Our data imply that, for some women, the following sequence occurs: from role conflict between the spouse and student roles, to divorce, to increased commitment to the student role. Although I cannot establish causality, it does appear that marital status has an effect upon the student roles of both men and women; greatest "success"—that is, ability to adhere to a career-primacy model, obtains among married men and divorced women. Durkheim (1951) has written about the stabilizing effect of marriage upon men, and our data are consistent with his observations. But, while marriage lessens conflicts for men, it increases them for some women. Some women obviously choose divorce. Others become part-time students (indeed more women are enrolled on a part-time basis than men) and thereby reduce the conflict between their two roles. Others abandon their education.

The student and the spouse roles for women are neither independent nor constant. In some instances they conflict and in other instances they complement one another. The effect of marital status upon the student role is dependent upon adherence to traditional sex roles. Less rigidity in adhering to these sex roles should ease some of the conflict between the spouse and student roles.

References

Arreger, Constance E.: *Graduate Women at Work,* Oriel Press, Ltd., Newcastle upon Tyne, England, 1966.

Becker, Howard S., and James Carper: "The Development of Identification with an Occupation," *American Journal of Sociology,* vol. 61, pp. 289–298, January 1956.

Becker, Howard S., Blanche Geer, Everett Hughes, and Anselm Strauss: *Boys in White,* University of Chicago Press, Chicago, 1961.

Coser, Rose Laub, and Gerald Rokoff: "Women in the Occupational World: Social Disruption and Conflict," *Social Problems,* vol. 18, pp. 535–554, Spring 1971.

Cross, Patricia A.: "College Women: A Research Description," paper presented at 1968 annual meeting of National Association of Women Deans and Counselors. (Mimeographed.)

Darwin, Erasmus: *A Plan for the Conduct of Female Education in Boarding Schools,* Drewry, Derby, England, 1797.

Durkheim, Emile: *Suicide,* translated by J. A. Spaulding and G. Simpson, The Free Press, New York, 1951.

Epstein, Cynthia: *Women's Place,* University of California Press, Berkeley and Los Angeles, 1970.

Feldman, Saul D.: "The Presentation of Shortness in Everyday Life—Height and Heightism in American Society: Toward a Sociology of Stature," in Saul D. Feldman and Gerald W. Thielbar (eds.), *Lifestyles: Diversity in American Society,* 2d ed., Little, Brown, Boston, 1975, pp. 437–442.

Fox, Renée C.: "Training for Uncertainty," in *The Student Physician,* Robert K. Merton (ed.), Harvard University Press, Cambridge, Mass., 1957.

Friedan, Betty: *The Feminine Mystique,* W. W. Norton & Company, Inc., New York, 1963.

Ginzberg, Eli: *Life Styles of Educated Women,* Columbia University Press, New York and London, 1966.

Goodsell, Willystine: *The Education of Women,* The Macmillan Company, New York, 1923.

Hubback, Judith: *Wives Who Went to College,* William Heinemann, Ltd., London, 1957.

Kadushin, Charles: "The Professional Self-Concept of Music Students," *American Journal of Sociology,* vol. 75, pp. 389–405, November 1969.

Komarovsky, Mirra: *Women in the Modern World,* Little, Brown and Company, Boston, 1953.

Lopate, Carol: *Women in Medicine,* The Johns Hopkins Press, Baltimore, 1968.

Poloma, Margaret M., and T. Neal Garland: "Role Conflict and the Married Professional Woman," paper presented at 1970 annual meeting of Ohio Valley Sociological Society, Akron, Ohio. (Mimeographed.)

Slater, Philip: *The Pursuit of Loneliness*, Beacon Press, Boston, 1970.

Sommerkorn, Ingrid: "On the Position of Women in the University Teaching Profession in England," unpublished Ph.D. dissertation, University of London, 1966.

Turner, Ralph H.: "Some Aspects of Women's Ambition," *American Journal of Sociology*, vol. 70, pp. 271–285, November 1974.

Wells, D. Collin: "Some Questions Concerning the Higher Education of Women," *American Journal of Sociology*, vol. 14, pp. 731–739, 1909.

8. The Impact of Peers on Student Orientations to College: A Contextual Analysis

by Ted K. Bradshaw

The college experience exerts its impact on the extracurricular development of students in several ways. First, the college experience facilitates the development of attitudes or behavior which, being characteristic of some young people, might develop even without a college experience. In this sense, the college community may be the stage on which the drama of adolescence is played; the role of the college itself is to protect the stage from some of the disturbances of early adult responsibilities. A second type of college impact comes from the nature of the institution and its organized program of courses, faculty, and student activities. A third type of college impact comes from the association of student peers, one with another, within the social and academic setting of the college. The recruitment of students and their placement in close proximity to each other within the college context may encourage either the development of new attitudes and behavior or the persistence of the old, regardless of the faculty, facilities, and curricula. Educators, sociologists, and social psychologists have long had an interest in the impact of college on students. In the late 1950s, the "Jacob Report" (Jacob, 1957) with its conclusion that college had little impact on changing student values, touched off a flurry of research, much

NOTE: This essay is a substantial revision and elaboration of a paper read at the 1971 meetings of the American Sociological Association, Denver, Colorado. Some material is from the author's unpublished Ph.D. dissertation: "The Impact of Education on Leisure: Socialization in College," (University of California, Berkeley, 1974). I am especially grateful to Joseph Zelan and Betty Lou Bradshaw for help and encouragement on this project.

of which was compiled by Kenneth A. Feldman and Theodore M. Newcomb. Their review of hundreds of research reports led them to write:

In a sense, our conclusions are more optimistic than Jacob's. There are conditions under which colleges have had (and we assume, will continue to have) impacts on their students, and not least upon student's values. Moreover, the consequences of these impacts often persist after the college years (1969, p. 4).

I shall not deal here with the question of whether or not college exerts an impact because I cannot do the "perfect study" and compare students with adolescents who never entered college. Instead, I shall rely upon the Feldman and Newcomb evidence that changes observed in students over time are due in part to the impact of their college experiences, and focus on the more interesting question (which has not been so thoroughly studied) of the nature of the college experiences that exert whatever impact there is. It is not enough to simply say that college changes people; we must learn what it is about college that affects this change. Several theories deal with this impact of college on the persistence or change of student values and behavior.

THE NATURE OF COLLEGE IMPACT Research on the impact of higher education can be organized around the three types or sources of college impact suggested above.[1] In this section I shall articulate the theoretical basis for each type of explanation and suggest the direction that the research reported here shall take.

Although social life is fragmented, we must not assume that a person's behavior in one social institution, such as a college, is isolated either from his or her coincidental involvement in another institution, such as a family, or from past involvements of any sort. Students usually do maintain contact with family, friends, churches, and home community while at college, and even if contact is weak and infrequent, the values and behavior of these institutions are carried to college and are changed only with difficulty. Thus, there is reason to suspect that noncollege factors may play a large part in determining the behavior

---

[1] For a similar formulation, see Newcomb (1966).

changes of students in colleges. This may be called the "noncollege" theory.

The noncollege theory finds several expressions. First, the student's social status (as transferred from his parents) *predisposes* him to take advantage of certain college opportunities or to reject others. Associated with social status for both adults and their children are values, patterns of social behavior, and expectations about the behavior of persons of similar and different status. It is well known, for instance, that participation in student demonstrations—a new type of activity for most youth—has been more frequent among students with a higher socioeconomic status than among their lower-status colleagues, who, in their pursuit of a degree, have no extra time for campus politics. Similarly, the decisions to attend graduate school, to change career plans, to get married, to drop out of school, to cheat, or to reduce the importance placed on getting good grades are all related to one's social background and the aspirations, values, and abilities associated with that background.[2]

Secondly, the noncollege theory examines the impact of continuing contact between the student and his family and noncollege friends. These contacts have been found to have a conservative effect on political attitudes and behavior and to reduce the extent of intellectual and social development at college.

Third, the noncollege theory examines the impact of specific precollege experiences and attitudes on behavior change in college. For example, patterns of child rearing (e.g., "My parents kept after me to do well in school") have their impact on performance, careers, and activism. The type of high school attended, whether the community was rural or urban, the religion in which one was raised, and the political interest of one's parents—all have their continuing impact on the student's adaptation to college life.

A second theory about the nature of the impact of college is based directly on the nature of the institution itself. This might well be called an "institutional" theory. It focuses on such things as the quality of the college and its students, the various fields and the students majoring in them, the faculty in these fields,

---

[2] Findings are from unpublished results of the 1969 Carnegie Commission Survey of Faculty and Student Opinion (undergraduate section).

and finally the facilities, location, and organization of the college.

While the quality of a school reflects the recruitment of students to it (and much more), quality is also indicative of a certain potential it possesses to create a lasting impact on students. The studies of Harvard, Bennington, Vassar, Reed, Antioch, and Swarthmore point this out clearly (see Clark, 1970; Clark et al., 1972; Jencks & Riesman, 1962; Newcomb et al., 1967; Sanford, 1962). Christopher Jencks and David Riesman, in the *Academic Revolution* (1968), describe the varying impact of women's colleges, Protestant colleges, Catholic colleges, Negro colleges, community colleges, and universities. Everywhere the difference between colleges is clearly seen, but we must be careful, for it is not clear that the differences mean that the colleges will have differing impacts on students of similar ability and background. For instance, Alexander W. Astin and Robert J. Panos (1969) argue that

Contrary to popular belief, the student's scholastic achievement does not seem to be enhanced by his attending an institution with relatively high concentrations of able students and abundant financial resources. . . . The implication here is not that his choice of college is an unimportant factor in his development, but rather that the college environment is of relatively little importance in comparison to his initial characteristics upon entering college (p. 149).

Thus, the debate goes on about whether any particular college has a significant impact or not, but Astin and Panos still have to convince most researchers, who still maintain that the college makes a difference.[3]

Within any institution there is tremendous diversity between students in different major fields. In fact, the variation between students in the various majors at most colleges is as great as the variation between the student bodies at institutions of widely differing reputations. Thus, the student's choice of major field foretells very different channels of socialization and exposure to different types of people, ideas, and values. R. S. Vreeland and Charles Bidwell (1966) show that different majors had different

---

[3] See Clark et al. (1972) and Stern (1963) for data that illustrate the differential impact of college on change.

orientations and goals. The most impressive data on this issue are presented by Feldman and Newcomb from data supplied by C. W. Huntley's 1,027 subjects at Union College. The experience of majoring in different fields had different effects on the change or persistence of values from the time of entrance to graduation. For instance, 48 percent of the students majoring in science increased their Allport-Vernon-Lindzey "theoretical-value" score, as compared with only 25 percent of students in other majors. Students majoring in humanities increased in aesthetic values; majors in engineering and industrial (business) administration increased in economic and political values (Feldman & Newcomb, 1969, pp. 178–179). These data suggest one reason why Astin and Panos or the studies reported by Jacob found little or no change, taking colleges as the unit. A school taken as a whole may demonstrate few meaningful patterns of change, but within the school considerable change may occur. And the researcher who neglects to consider major field may be led to false conclusions about the impact of college.

The evidence is much weaker about the impact of faculty members on student attitudes and values. There is little evidence that they account for much change at all, partly because of their usual role insulation from questions of values; instead they tend to deal almost exclusively with curricular questions. Furthermore, it is probable—since the faculty are diverse themselves—that for every change of student values or behavior made in one direction by one professor, a change is made in the opposite direction by another professor. Thus, we are not yet able to understand the role of the faculty in the college's impact.

Finally, the institutional theory suggests that the material resources of the school will have an impact—its facilities, location, size, complexity, and patterns of residence. While the evidence is sketchy, it seems that rural schools provide different opportunities from urban; small schools have greater solidarity and cohesion, large schools have more student activism; schools with complex bureaucratic and administrative structures have different problems than schools organized more simply; resident schools have greater impact on their students than commuter schools, and in all schools the type of residence the student chooses is crucial in determining his college behavior (see Corwin, 1965; Feldman & Newcomb, 1969; and Selvin & Hagstrom, 1960).

The third theory of the impact of college emphasizes the interpersonal relationships between students, regardless of the direct impact of their background or the direct impact of the institution. The influence that students have on each other may be as great as the impact of the other two explanations combined. This theory suggests that the qualities of students put in close proximity to each other are more consequential to a college's impact than the qualities of the college itself. We may call this the "peer" theory. The purpose of this paper is to discover empirically how much merit this theory has, for although it is neither a new idea nor an unfamiliar one, according to Newcomb "the empirical grounds for concluding that substantial peer group effects do in fact occur in contemporary American colleges are not as solid as many of us would like to believe" (1966, p. 5).

The theoretical basis for the study of peer-group effects is relatively straightforward and generally has to do with the power of a group over its individual members: The peer group provides the context in which individuals agree upon common expectations, similar definitions of social reality, and appropriate patterns of behavior, with reference to salient parts of their group life. These agreements are group norms, and the group has rewards and sanctions to enforce compliance with these norms. Compliance with the norms of a peer group means changes in the attitudes and behavior of some members and the persistence (or lack of change) in the attitudes and behavior of other members. Further, the group may enforce its norms by using the ultimate sanction, termination of membership, and by selective recruitment of only potentially compliant members. In this paper we assume these dynamics of peer-group operation, and are concerned with the relative strength of peer-group impacts compared with other sources of college impact.

The analysis of interpersonal relations, especially peer-group effects, has had a long tradition in educational research. Woodrow Wilson wrote that "the real intellectual life of a body of undergraduates, if there be any, manifests itself not in the classroom, but in what they do and talk of and set before themselves as their favorite objects between classes and lectures" (Clark & Trow, 1966, p. 17). Newcomb (1943), in his famous study of Bennington College students during the late 1930s, documented the existence of strong liberal pro-New Deal norms,

norms that were especially strong at this particular college. As part of the college culture rather than something brought to the college by incoming students, these norms were very effective in changing the values of a large proportion of the Bennington students. But perhaps Willard Waller is the most sensitive to the social processes among students:

The indigenous tradition of the school is found in its purest form among students. This tradition, when it has been originated on the spot, is passed on, largely by word of mouth, from one student to another. Some of the indigenous tradition has been originated by the faculty, and then imposed upon the students; once it has been accepted by students, however, it may be passed on by student groups. . . . Besides, there exists in the culture of any community a set of traditional attitudes toward school and school life, varying from one social class to another, and from family to family; these attitudes influence profoundly the attitudes which students have toward school life. Nevertheless the tradition of students is largely indigenous within the particular school (Waller, 1932, p. 109).

The more recent study of student culture in high school has provided considerable development of many of the ideas hinted at by Waller. James Coleman, in *The Adolescent Society* (1961), advances the thesis that students, through their student-peer culture, form norms that favor achievement in sports and social popularity, and give little status to students who excel academically, thus undermining the academic values of the faculty. But equally important is Coleman's interest in the definition and articulation of the value climates of schools. As Coleman sees it, climate is based on the feelings of individual students, and has much to do with the popularity or status of individual students. C. Wayne Gordon, in *The Social System of the High School* (1957), also explores the impact that social status in the school has upon orientation to grades, participation in a variety of extracurricular activities, indeed a whole way of life. Student organizations played a key role in Gordon's analysis in that they differentiated students into a prestige hierarchy, ranging from athlete and yearbook queen to knitting and riding clubs. In sum, these studies have shown that peer-status hierarchies have a substantial impact on the behavior of students.

Several researchers have made valuable contributions to the understanding of the impact that interpersonal relations have on student behavior by analyzing the conditions under which high school students aspire to attain higher education. The most valuable is by Ernest Q. Campbell and C. Norman Alexander, who attempted to integrate interpersonal and structural variations. Several studies have shown that an individual's friends influence his educational and vocational aspirations (Simpson, 1962; Alexander & Campbell, 1964). These studies have also shown that academic aspirations are substantially improved or hindered for any individual (regardless of his own status) depending upon the status level of his friends. Interpersonal relations are thus shown to have a strong impact. Structural influences are illustrated by a study showing that, with background held constant, the higher the average social status of a high school, the greater the proportion of students aspiring to college (Wilson, 1959). Campbell and Alexander (1965) point out that both interpersonal relations and structural variation are part of a two-step process whereby the structural effect creates conditions conducive to a particular type of interpersonal effect. In particular, Campbell and Alexander suggest that the effect of attending a high-status school is to increase the probability of high-status friends; the school does not directly influence the individual's educational aspirations but does this only through the mediation of friendship groups. Despite these studies and others (e.g., Becker et al., 1968), there is much to learn about the way peers influence each other.

CONTEXTUAL ANALYSIS   The study of the effect of peers on each other is not a simple methodological task. Since there has been considerable debate in the literature about the proper methodology for this type of analysis, some comments are called for in this paper. I shall first describe the methods used to determine the effect of peers on each other and then describe the major issues raised in the literature about these methods.

Since the theory of peer groups suggests that group norms change behavior, three questions must be explored. First, what constitutes a relevant group for an individual student? Second, what norms are relevant for that group? And third, what methodology is appropriate to demonstrate this effect?

The context or peer-group influence on the development of student norms may be detected on several levels. The largest possible relevant group for a contextual analysis is the entire institution or college in which the student is enrolled. At this level, the composite character of the student body and the "ethos" of the institution have an impact on the behavior and values of any individual student in the institution. Newcomb's analysis of Bennington (Newcomb, 1943; Newcomb et al., 1967) focused on this level, as did Burton Clark's study of Reed, Antioch, and Swarthmore (1970). However, there is considerable doubt that the total institution is the most relevant context for most students at institutions more diversified and larger than these small liberal arts colleges. This leads to the next level of analysis. An intermediate-level contextual group would be some subdivision within the institution, such as major field or place of residence. At this level the possibility of distinctive group norms exists, yet the interpersonal relations among the members of the group must be inferred. Finally, at the individual level of analysis, the friends and acquaintances of a student may actually be identified and questioned about their behavior and values. By focusing on the people who individually most influence the behavior of others, the dynamics of behavior and the place of peers is learned. Campbell and Alexander's (1965) work on the effect of peers on college aspirations and attainment, for example, indicates the powerful research that can be done at this level of analysis. It probably can be said that the closer we come to identifying the individual people who are in contact with a student, the more accurate will be the description of peer-group effects.

In this study, unfortunately, data are not available at the individual level, but information is available on substantially large samples of people from an individual's institution who have chosen the same major field. Although this is not the ideal way to assign individuals to peer groups, it is not unreasonable. It is known, for instance, that 80 percent of the students in the Carnegie Commission survey indicate that some or most of their best friends are in their major field. Thus, we shall proceed on the premise that students in related majors at a single institution will reflect a conservative estimate of the peer effect as long as other variables are controlled. If the peer effect at this level of analysis is significant, it would be even more so if we could identify the particular peers of each individual student.

The norms of a group of students who have never known each other upon entering college can be established mainly by knowing and measuring the existence of particular attitudes and behavior brought to college by these students. Although this ignores the dynamics of norm formation, it is a workable approximation for our purposes as long as we realize that we are assuming that the group norm reflects only the background input of the students. It does not take into consideration the impact of the institution and of the upperclassmen. The effect of this assumption is conservative, and the relations found would be stronger if more accurate methods were available for the calculation of group norms.

For this analysis, the percentage of respondents having each value and behavior at entrance to college was based on those individual students who said they would probably major in one of six major field areas (social science–humanities, physical and biological science, business, engineering, education, and other). This was done separately for each institution included in the sample. Thus, these contextual scores describe the proportion of students in each "context" or "peer group" who were active in an activity at entrance. Presumably, the contextual scores reflect the strength of the group support for either adopting or persisting in the activity. Percentages were calculated for about 1,000 groups of students with similar major fields within the same institution. Those groups of students with fewer than 15 student respondents were excluded from the analysis. Although this exclusion is less than 10 percent of the sample, it does slightly bias the sample in favor of large institutions and of majors with many students.

This analysis falls into the general category of "contextual analysis" because of the use of group properties to explain the behavior of an individual (Volkonen, 1969, p. 63). We shall discuss below some of the more common methodological criticisms that have been raised about contextual analysis and show how the methodology used in this study does not violate the rules of good research.

W. S. Robinson (1950) was the first to focus attention on the problems of drawing conclusions about individuals on the basis of information about groups. His article articulated the error of the "ecological fallacy" and warned researchers that the relation between several variables within a society or other group did not necessarily imply that the same relation would be found among the individuals who make up the society or group. Robinson's warning, although accepted by most researchers today, has initiated perhaps too much concern about the fallacies of drawing conclusions from the behavior of individuals whenever a group-level variable is involved. With regard to research in higher education, however, Robinson's warning has not always been heeded. In his study of student activism, for example, Alexander Astin draws his main conclusions on the basis of observed correlations between various characteristics of the student body as a whole and the incidence of student activism at the campus.[4] In this study, however, we are explaining the behavior of an individual by observing the relation between the characteristics of his group and his own behavior, thus avoiding the ecological fallacy.

Further articles have attempted to clear up the methodological confusion about when group-level variables can validly be used in analysis. Peter Blau argues that an analysis including "structural effects" does not commit an ecological fallacy because individual scores can be combined into a measure of the nature of the social "structure" wherein the individual is located. "If it were found that the average IQ scores in fraternities are associated with the scholastic records of their members when the individual's [IQ] score is held constant, there could be no doubt, provided other relevant conditions are controlled, that the level of intelligence in a fraternity influences performance on examinations through *social* processes" (Blau, 1960, p. 191). Blau is saying that regardless of the individual's own IQ, if he happens to reside in a fraternity where there is a generally high IQ level, *social* processes *may* cause him to achieve more than a similarly talented student in a less favorable social setting. Blau goes on to warn that such a finding does not indicate whether "social stimulation of learning or collaboration on examinations" is responsible.

James Davis, Joseph Spaeth, and Carolyn Huson have further added to the understanding we have of valid possibilities for this type of analysis by discussing several preliminary methods of thinking about "group level effects" and by classifying several forms of effect. They point out that contextual effects may be due to differences in the impact of the individual's own characteristics

---

[4] Astin (n.d.); see also Astin and Panos (1969) for a similar analysis of college achievement.

(there will be variation attributed to individuals of high and low IQ within a given context, e.g., fraternity IQ level). Additional contextual effects may be due to a variation in the impact of the context—it may be weak or strong when individual-level variables are controlled. (The Blau example suggests at least some positive impact.) An interesting possibility is that group impact may be either positive or negative. Finally, group effects may interact with individual effects to form a wide variety of patterns (Davis, Spaeth, & Huson, 1961, pp. 218–221).

But even these efforts are not without criticism. Arnold Tannenbaum and Jerald Bachman (1964) argue that either Blau's or Davis, Spaeth, and Huson's methods may lead to spurious results, since individual-level variables are dichotomized in their examples although the variables are not necessarily dichotomous. (For example, the individual's IQ in the example from Blau was dichotomized for the sake of simplicity into high IQ and low IQ.) This dichotomization could produce, according to their article, spurious contextual or structural effects when none really exists. This is true, they argue, because even in dichotomously divided groups there is an underlying normal distribution of scores with reference to any one variable. For example,[5] if enough fraternities were studied, the individual IQs of fraternity members in "low-IQ groups" would produce a normal distribution around a mean of perhaps 110. In "high-IQ groups" the normal distribution would be around a mean of perhaps 120. If individuals were dichotomized as high IQ if they were over 115 and low if not, then because of the normal distribution, students with high individual IQs in high-IQ fraternities would be more likely to have *higher* IQs on average than high-IQ students in the low-IQ fraternities. (In a high-IQ group there is more probability of having a sizable number of students with IQs of more than 125, for example, while in a low-IQ group most students who are "high IQ" are more likely to be only marginally high.) This distribution of talent, assuming IQ and grades are related, will produce a relation between fraternity IQ level and grades that is the result of individual factors rather than contextual factors. In short, Tannenbaum and Bachman argue that dichotomous categories can never completely control for the individual-level variable.

---

[5] This example is mine to maintain consistency in examples.

Since categories are dichotomized in this analysis, a critique of the Tannenbaum and Bachman position is necessary. Their argument is relevant only in limiting cases, but until a replication is made some general comments must suffice. The first difficulty comes from their own methodological problems. Tannenbaum and Bachman use artificial "Monte Carlo" randomly generated data. Although nothing is wrong with using these kinds of data, they use them to *exaggerate* the finding they are considering. Their method is as follows: 150 "Monte Carlo" individuals were randomly fit into 50 groups of 3 individuals each. The group variables were computed on the average scores of the three group members. A dependent variable was computed as a perfect linear correlation of 1.0 with the individual variable, but it had nothing whatsoever to do with the group variable. The results showed that the mean of this variable was higher in the high group than the low group, controlling individual-level scores. On this basis Tannenbaum and Bachman conclude that contextual analyses using dichotomies of the individual variable are suspect and that if more categories were used the apparent relationship would vanish. But there are some problems with their case. First, as Hanan Selvin and Warren Hagstrom point out (1966, p. 175), the scores of three-member groups are very unstable in comparison with larger groups. Second, if there were more individuals in the group, all groups would have an identical group score because individuals were assigned to the group randomly. In real life, individuals are rarely randomly assigned to groups. Third, the relation between the individual and dependent variables is unnaturally strong in the Tannenbaum and Bachman example (correlated, 1.0). As this strong a correlation is rarely found in real social research, it is important to realize that the apparent relation between the dependent variable and the group variable is proportionate to the strength of the actual correlation. In research, this statistical problem would probably be minimal, though some data simulations are necessary to determine how weak it really is. Thus, since IQ and grades are only weakly related, the statistical distortion would probably be only minor. Finally, given Tannenbaum and Bachman's results and sample size, they are very likely of only marginal statistical significance, although such a significance test cannot be computed from the data they provide.

Another set of criticisms focuses on interpretation of the

observed results of Tannenbaum and Bachman. Let us assume that the groups were larger and that there was significant variation in group scores owing to some nonrandom means of distributing individuals such as, for example, selective recruitment in a real setting. The observed inability to fully control for individual-level scores with dichotomies is likely to remain. This problem is no different from any other social science research application where it is always difficult to control for anything with a dichotomous variable. For example, in a two-by-two table showing the relation between IQ and grades, high-IQ people with low grades still should have better grades on average than low-IQ people. This is a common problem in social research, but as Tannenbaum and Bachman correctly point out, it is exacerbated when combined with group variables. The warning to be alert to this type of problem is good advice in all research settings. The real problem, however, lies in estimating the strength of the distortion. In most research applications it is probably not large.[6] Thus, if the observed statistical relationship is strong enough to be interesting, it is also quite probably not due to this type of statistical problem.

A more salient criticism of contextual analysis is that it attributes to contextual causes relationships that in fact are individual. For example, it might be argued that students who are "liberal" in institutions where many others are also "liberal" hold more "liberal values" than "liberals" in "conservative" institutions. It is difficult in such a contextual analysis to satisfactorily show that the difference in values is due to structural effects rather than to different standards for calling oneself "liberal." Also, it is hard to know whether "liberalism" or "liberal values" is the appropriate contextual variable (with the other being the dependent variable), for the causes and effects in this type of analysis are most likely confounded (Selvin & Hagstrom, 1966, p. 162).

The methodology used in this paper avoids most of these criticisms. First, because I use the reported behavior and values of the same student at two points in time, the assumption is stronger (though not necessarily true) that the student is using the same standards for reporting his behavior. Second, because the dependent variable in the analysis in this paper is change or

---

6 For a similar set of estimates, see Bradshaw (1971a).

persistence in some behavior or attitude, it cannot be confounded with the contextual variable even if the contextual variable reflects the group norms with reference to the same behavior or attitude. In fact, analysis of the change or persistence of a behavior when the context is characterized by initial behavior patterns is the most theoretically sound basis for a contextual analysis, as well as being methodologically safe.

DATA AND VARIABLES The data to be presented in this analysis are from the 1969 Carnegie Commission Survey of Faculty and Student Opinion conducted at the Survey Research Center at the University of California, Berkeley. Mail questionnaires were received from over 70,000 undergraduate students in a stratified sample of 189 institutions of higher education of all kinds across the nation. The respondents are a sample of all students who entered these institutions during the fall of 1966, 1967, 1968, and 1969, and who completed a Freshman Student Information Form administered by the American Council on Education (ACE) at the time they entered college. Thus, the analysis will be of panel data on a large sample of students in a wide variety of colleges, which, when weighted, represent the diversity of American higher education.

The use of the panel data is limited, however, because the ACE did not ask many questions of the entering students that are of particular relevance to this study. Nonetheless, a few questions can be used to provide clues about the impact of college on the change in student values and behavior over time. Further, seniors had to be eliminated because neither of the dependent variables were asked of them upon their entrance to college. Respondents who indicated that they were no longer students (about 10 percent) were eliminated, as were students who entered junior colleges (because many transferred, leaving their peer groups). Most of the analysis will be on a subsample of 12,933 students. The entire data file was used to compute scores for the student peer groups (see below).

Using these data I shall focus as best I can on two variables reflecting powerful and somewhat opposed norms about the proper orientation of students to their college experience. The most well-known characterization of these orientations is found in Clark and Trow's study of student subcultures. The two types

of student that stand out as most important in their discussion
are the *academic* and the *vocational:*

Present on every college campus, although dominant on some and
marginal on others, is the subculture of serious *academic* effort. The
essence of this system of values is its identification with the intellectual
concerns of the serious faculty members. The students involved work
hard, get the best grades, talk about their course work outside of class
and let the world of ideas and knowledge reach them (Clark & Trow,
1966, p. 22).

To these students [*vocational*] . . . college is largely off-the-job training, an organization of courses and credits leading to a diploma and a
better job than they could otherwise command. These students have
little attachment to the college . . . and are resistant to the intellectual
demands on them beyond what is required to pass the course (ibid., p.
21).

These student types are also characteristic of the educational
philosophy of institutions themselves (elite versus service) and of
the types of programs within the institution (general education
versus vocational or professional).

A brief historical sketch of this relationship indicates the
pervasiveness of these orientations as they are found in American higher education, and thus serves to justify my use of them
as variables. From its roots in European, and particularly English, conceptions of higher education, the American university
was early challenged in its orientation to mental discipline and
"cultivated taste" (or high culture)—characteristic of the elite
college. Skepticism about the value of college led to declining
enrollments during the mid-nineteenth century and then to
reform movements that were largely vocational in nature. The
Morrill Act of 1862 gave federal aid to state colleges whose
curricula included agricultural and mechanical instruction. In
addition, the presidents of universities at this time found it
necessary to "campaign like politicians in seasons of crisis. With
one hand they built the university, borrowing from Europe and
improvising as they went; with the other they popularized it"
(Veysey, 1965, pp. 16–17). The popularization increasingly took
the form of relating college studies to the "world of action and
reality, the world in which men and women earn their bread and
live and die" (ibid., p. 62). Later, John Dewey articulated the

importance of education for health, vocation, and the quality of family and community life (Dewey, 1916; Cremin, 1961). Currently the responses to these efforts in terms of vocational programs are still concentrated in the newer colleges and universities rather than in the older ones with their traditions of high culture, their command of scarce resources, and their higher prestige. Furthermore, the new programs appeal variably to individual students in all schools, but these students are predominantly found in special vocational programs such as education, business, and engineering, regardless of the type of school (Trow, 1962; Gottlieb & Hodgkins, 1963).

At the historical root of American higher education, then, lies the distinction between high culture and vocationalism. The student's perspective on what is desirable and proper with regard to these educational orientations is the focus of concern in this paper. First, as an indicator of a student's orientation to academic values and high culture, I shall analyze the questionnaire item asking the frequency with which the respondent visited art galleries or museums.[7] This item is not as desirable as might be wished, but it is all that is available for panel analysis from earlier ACE surveys. Among the students responding to the Carnegie Commission survey follow-up, however, the art gallery item is positively correlated with several items indicating a strong liberal arts and cultural orientation, such as listening to classical music (.237), reading poetry (.236), attending concerts or plays (.127), and reading books not required for class (.191). Second, as an indicator of a strong vocational orientation, I shall analyze the question on agreement with the statement, "The chief benefit of a college education is that it increases one's earning power." This item is correlated with an item not available from the entering student questionnaire stating, "Getting a degree is more important to me than the content of my courses" ($r = .272$), the most essential thing to get from college is "training and skills for an occupation" ($r = .178$), and the personal importance of "being very well-off financially" ($r = .313$). The

---

[7] Visiting art galleries is only a small part of an individual's academic orientation. The availability of galleries varies by college location, and it is not clear whether a respondent answers in terms of art museums or any type of museum. Further analysis of the item since this paper was written shows that these problems are not severe (Bradshaw, 1974).

two items used in this analysis do reflect somewhat opposing points of view as is indicated by their negative correlation of $-.10$. Furthermore, a factor analysis of a large set of items reflecting student attitudes and behavior identified these two sets of items as the strongest factors in the matrix (Bradshaw, 1971*b*).

INSTITUTIONAL VARIATION IN STUDENT ORIENTATIONS

Before discussing the impact of peers on changing student orientations to college, it is necessary to set out the parameters of the variation in orientation that characterize different institutions. At the root of the peer process is selective recruitment of students into colleges where they come into contact with one another and establish norms for what is expected. How different, then, are the various institutions they choose to attend?

For our purposes, institutions will be classified according to their quality. "Quality" is a relative term that reflects the ranking of institutions according to the amount of scarce resources they command: wealth, prestige, talented students, and faculty who are highly certified and nationally well known.[8]

Since individual students have different orientations to their college education, this is reflected in the schools they choose to attend and in the impact of these schools on their future beliefs and activities. Students who have a strong orientation to culture and the liberal arts more often attend elite, high-quality institutions, whereas students with a strong orientation to vocational concerns more often attend the new, lower-quality institutions. This relationship is shown in Table 8-1. The first six items in this table present data on the orientations of students at the time they entered college and thus illustrate the type of selective recruitment that takes place. Other items illustrate the type of responses students have at the time of the follow-up; these responses reflect the combination of entering values and the values that changed after college entrance.

The first theme to be noted from this table is that there is in fact considerable variation in the selection of students to different "qualities" of university or college, and that high school scholastic achievement is probably the most important factor. Associated with this, students at higher-quality institutions have a stronger cultural or academic orientation, as is indicated by more frequent visits to art galleries and museums, more reading

---

[8] For more details, see App. A.

TABLE 8-1   *Variation in student academic orientations, by college quality and type: entrance and follow-up data*

| | Quality level | | | | | |
| | Universities | | | Four-year colleges | | |
	High	*Medium*	*Low*	*High*	*Medium*	*Low*
At entrance						
Visit art gallery or museum (responses: frequently and occasionally)	82	72	72	77	74	71
Do extra (unassigned) reading for a course (response: frequently)	20	12	15	16	14	16
Importance of being very well-off financially (response: essential)	38	45	41	42	36	36
The chief benefit of a college education is that it increases one's earning power (response: agree)	30	47	50	35	44	50
Highest degree intended (response: graduate degree)	80	67	67	78	62	55
High school grade point average (response: A−, A, or A+)	51	27	21	46	24	14
At follow-up						
Visit art gallery or museum (responses: frequently and occasionally)	61	48	44	53	49	46
Do extra (unassigned) reading for a course (response: frequently)	10	6	8	9	8	10
Importance of being very well-off financially (response: essential)	26	35	36	32	33	34
The chief benefit of a college education is that it increases one's earning power (response: agree)	24	41	42	31	40	43
Highest degree intended (response: graduate degree)	77	70	61	78	70	65
Attend concert or play (response: monthly)	26	15	16	26	24	16
Listen to classical music (response: weekly +)	36	24	20	32	24	22
Attend an "art" film (response: yearly +)	71	64	57	75	61	58
Watch TV more than one hour (response: weekly +)	40	54	56	39	51	63
Undergraduate education in America would be improved if there were less emphasis on specialized training and more on broad liberal education (response: agree)	46	41	39	51	41	39

TABLE 8-1 *(continued)*

| | Quality level | | | | | |
| | Universities | | | Four-year colleges | | |
	High	Medium	Low	High	Medium	Low
Importance of training and skills for an occupation (response: essential)	36	50	56	32	52	61
Getting a degree is more important than the content of my courses (response: true)	12	22	21	16	20	22

SOURCE: 1969 Carnegie Commission Survey of Faculty and Student Opinion, undergraduate survey marginals. Based on students enrolled at time of follow-up only.

outside of class, and more frequent aspirations for a graduate degree. In contrast, students at lower-quality institutions are more often recruited to college, agreeing that the chief benefit of college is increased earnings.

It is important to also examine the variation in student academic orientation at the time of the follow-up. There is a substantial amount of change in the raw percentages for items included in both surveys. The percentage of students visiting art galleries or museums drops substantially. In part, this is due to a change in the wording of the questionnaire. The entering-student questionnaire asked the student how often he or she did the activity "during the past year in school" (i.e., high school). For the follow-up, the wording was changed to ask the student to indicate how often he or she did the activity "during your most recent college term." This change in time reference from a whole high school year to a four-month college term produced, of course, lower rates of participation in visiting art galleries. In contrast, wording of the items about vocational orientations did not change and differences in response at the different times are due to other causes. After being in university or college for a while, students are less likely to think that it is essential to be very well-off, and they are less likely to agree that the chief benefit of college is increased earnings. There are small, but relatively unimportant, changes in the proportion of students aspiring for higher degrees. Overall, the gross impact of college suggests a reduction in academic or cultural orientations, as well as a change in vocational attitudes away from a high value on earnings.

The follow-up data suggest another important point. The differentiation of students by institutional quality persists. The lower section of Table 8-1 presents some additional data on the cultural commitment of students. These data show that there is a substantial propensity for students at higher-quality colleges to be involved in many of the forms of high-brow culture histori-cally characteristic of college graduates. In contrast, students at lower-quality colleges are more likely to spend their time watch-ing TV. With regard to academic or vocational attitudes, the college's quality has the same effect, as is shown by other items. Students at high-quality colleges emphasize the liberal arts, and students at lower-quality colleges prefer to learn skills and think that getting a degree is more important than the content of their courses.

CHANGE IN STUDENT ORIENTATIONS The growing-up process is one of continual change, and the data already reported suggest that there is considerable change to be found in students' orientations to their college. The best way to understand this change, however, is to examine the way in-dividuals change over time.

For convenience, in this discussion of individual change the variables will be dichotomized and I shall look for conditions under which individuals not doing or thinking something *change* and start doing or thinking it; also I shall look for conditions under which individuals doing or thinking something *persist* and keep on doing or thinking it. To put it another way, with regard to either academic or vocational orientation to college, my focus will be on the conditions under which individuals change and adopt the orientation, and the conditions under which they *persist* and *keep* the particular orientation. Methodologically, this means that the proportion of students *changing* is the percentage of students who do not have the particular orientation at time of entrance but who eventually adopt it; the proportion *persisting* is the percentage who have the orientation at college entrance and who still have it at the time of the follow-up.

There is considerable change in student orientations to col-lege, as is shown by the data in Table 8-2 and 8-3. Almost one in three students (29 percent) changed from never going to art galleries to going at least occasionally. Furthermore, only about half (54 percent) of those who reported visiting art galleries in high school persisted in this behavior at college; once they got to college, the remainder never had the inclination or opportunity

TABLE 8-2
Change in
frequency of
visiting art
galleries or
museums

Frequency at entrance	Frequency at time of follow-up		Total number*
	Never, %	Occasionally and frequently, %	
Never	71	29 (change)	(2,038)
Occasionally and frequently	46	54 (persistence)	(5,777)

*Number is weighted response, given in hundreds. (Variation in total weighted response is due to elimination of nonresponse.) The total *real* number of cases is a sample of 12,933 currently enrolled freshmen, sophomores, and juniors. This sample is the source for all subsequent tables in this chapter.

to go. Agreement with a vocational orientation to college also found considerable amounts of individual change. Almost 2 in 10 changed and agreed at the time of the follow-up that the chief benefit of college was increased earnings, even though these individuals did not agree at the time they entered college. Furthermore, only 6 in 10 who agreed at entrance persisted in their agreement through the time of the follow-up. Thus a considerable amount of change takes place in college, and the change strikes at some very important aspects of a student's commitment to his or her college education.

EXPLAINING Since there is a considerable amount of change among students,
CHANGE: THE we now must consider what causes this change. The first step
PEER EFFECT will be an examination of the peer effect, which turns out to be considerable. Then the other theories will be tested to see if they also have an impact or if they make the peer relationship spurious. The first alternate theory to be tested is the noncollege theory, which looks at the impact of family background. Then institutional factors such as quality and major field and particularly the impact of the faculty are considered. Finally, the chapter ends with a comparison of the impact of the peer group on

TABLE 8-3
Change in
agreement with
statement, "The
chief benefit of
college is that it
increases one's
earning power"

	At time of follow-up		
	Percent who disagree	Percent who agree	Total number
Disagreed at entrance	82	18 (change)	3,955
Agreed at entrance	41	59 (persistence)	3,698

Percentage of group visiting	Never visit at entrance (Change)	Visit some at entrance (Persistence)
0–59	25 (217)	54 (279)
60–69	24 (521)	45 (1,027)
70–79	30 (868)	51 (2,378)
80–89	35 (298)	60 (1,411)
90–100	50 (33)	72 (319)

TABLE 8-4 **Percentage of students visiting art galleries or museums occasionally or frequently at follow-up, by entering frequency and group frequency**

freshmen, sophomores, and juniors in an attempt to determine when peer-group changes take place.

The peer effect is considerable, as shown by the data with regard to both academic-cultural orientations to college and vocational orientations. In general, the greater the percentage of the group of students who held a behavior or attitude at the time of college entrance, the greater the probability that students not holding the behavior or attitude would change and adopt it, and the greater the probability that those holding the attitude would persist and continue to hold it. The data are presented in Table 8-4 and 8-5. Change rates for visiting art galleries range from 25 percent in the least favorable peer-group contexts to 50 percent in the most favorable (Table 8-4). Persistence rates vary from a low of 45 percent to a high of 72 percent, though there is one notable exception: a very high persistence rate among students in unfavorable contexts (54 percent). This exception, based on a small number of students, is not easily explained and may be due

Percentage of group agreeing	Disagreed at entrance (Change)	Agreed at entrance (Persistence)
0–29	17 (730)	40 (222)
30–39	23 (736)	52 (393)
40–49	28 (1,066)	57 (1,016)
50–59	37 (663)	60 (812)
60–100	34 (511)	10 (1,025)

TABLE 8-5 **Percentage of students at follow-up agreeing with statement, "The chief benefit of college is that it increases one's earning power," by entering agreement and group agreement**

TABLE 8-6	Percentage of group visiting	Never visit at entrance (Change)		Visit some at entrance (Persistence)	
Percentage of students visiting art galleries or museums at follow-up, by entering frequency, group frequency, and father's education		Father's education		Father's education	
		High school	College	High school	College
	0–59	33 (100)	18 (114)	57 (114)	52 (163)
	60–69	23 (342)	25 (175)	45 (540)	44 (477)
	70–79	27 (445)	34 (419)	51 (1,122)	53 (1,228)
	80–100	34 (150)	38 (177)	57 (661)	65 (1,064)

either to abnormality in the sample or possibly to concerted nonconformity by students in this type of group context.

The peer relationship is also strong with regard to changing students' orientation to the vocational aims of college (Table 8-5). Change rates for agreeing that the chief benefit of college is increased earnings range from 17 percent in the least-favorable group to 37 percent in more-favorable groups. Persistence rates vary from 40 percent in less-favorable contexts to 70 percent in the most favorable. Again, exceptions to the patterns are found—*change* being less than expected in the most-favorable context.

The existence of a strong peer relationship, as shown here, does not necessarily mean that change is ultimately due to peers. As was suggested before, change is also rooted in the family and the institution. Table 8-6 and 8-7 show the impact of group norms on change and persistence when the student's background is controlled. The educational level of the student's

TABLE 8-7	Percentage of group agreeing	Disagree at entrance (Change)		Agree at entrance (Persistence)	
Percentage of students at follow-up agreeing with statement, "The chief benefit of college is that it increases one's earning power," by entering agreement, group agreement, and father's education		Father's education		Father's education	
		High school	College	High school	College
	0–39	19 (585)	20 (891)	48 (240)	47 (372)
	40–49	31 (497)	25 (568)	55 (475)	58 (531)
	50–59	36 (294)	38 (363)	62 (385)	59 (427)
	60–100	29 (288)	40 (220)	67 (650)	72 (357)

father—high school graduation or less on the one hand and college attendance or more on the other—provides a test of the impact of social status and family background, probably the most important part of the noncollege theory. In Table 8-6 differences in rates of change and persistence are shown to be roughly similar within each level of peer group, regardless of father's educational level, though the differences are generally in favor of more change and persistence by students from more-educated families. Furthermore, this suggests that the peer effect shown in Table 8-2 is not simply due to the selective recruitment of students with similar backgrounds into similar contexts so that the effect is really one of background rather than peers. In Table 8-7 the results are roughly similar for the item on vocational orientation, yet there are fewer exceptions to the overall pattern—parents' background makes little difference within peer groups and the relation to peer group remains strong.

Other items reflecting the student's background were explored with roughly similar findings, and so the data are not reported in detail here. Even if all the possible variables reflecting background were combined into a model predicting change or persistence, preliminary analysis suggests that these background factors would not explain much of the variation that is now attributed to peers. It must also be recalled that this analysis of peer effects has been carried out with several compromises that have a conservative effect on the measurement of the actual strength of peer influences.[9]

The impact of background is more important for sorting students into different types of institutions than in directly affecting student attitudes and behavior once they get to college. The impact of the different qualities of college, controlling for peer-group effects, is shown in Tables 8-8 and 8-9. Again, the data suggest that most of the change and persistence can be explained by peer group rather than by the quality of institution the student attends. With regard to the proportion of students changing and persisting, high-quality schools have an advantage, regardless of peer group; but within each quality range, the more-favorable peer context had substantially better rates of recruitment and persistence. The same general conclusions apply with regard to vocational orientations to college. The data

---

[9] For a more detailed analysis, see Bradshaw (1974).

TABLE 8-8 Percentage of students visiting art galleries or museums at follow-up, by entering frequency, group frequency, and school quality							
	Percentage of group visiting	*Never visit at entrance (Change)*			*Visit some at entrance (Persistence)*		
		School quality			*School quality*		
		High	*Medium*	*Low*	*High*	*Medium*	*Low*
	0–59	16 (35)	25 (45)	27 (137)	41 (49)	59 (72)	57 (158)
	60–69	18 (13)	23 (99)	24 (409)	54 (21)	47 (187)	44 (819)
	70–79	43 (70)	35 (310)	35 (488)	62 (221)	53 (855)	53 (1,203)
	80–100	41 (61)	41 (91)	32 (178)	70 (398)	59 (477)	60 (854)

clearly show that students change their orientation to college more in response to other students they are likely to have contact with than to the quality or quantity of their college's resources. This is especially impressive when it is recalled that selection to college is so strongly related to institutional quality (see Table 8-1). Thus, these data suggest that the impact of college comes not so much from anything unique about the college as from the kinds of students who are put in proximity to one another. This is something that has often been discussed: students learn a considerable amount of both academic and extracurricular material from one another. The institution simply provides the reason and the place for them to interact.

What about the particular orientation of the faculty? The direct impact of faculty may be examined in the instance of attending art galleries. From the Carnegie Commission survey of faculty at the same sample of institutions used in the student studies, data

TABLE 8-9 Percentage of students at follow-up agreeing with statement, "The chief benefit of college is that it increases one's earning power," by entering agreement, group agreement, and school quality							
	Percentage of group agreeing	*Disagree at entrance (Change)*			*Agree at entrance (Persistence)*		
		School quality			*School quality*		
		High	*Medium*	*Low*	*High*	*Medium*	*Low*
	0–39	14 (448)	21 (295)	23 (737)	43 (150)	49 (139)	49 (327)
	40–49	18 (50)	29 (497)	27 (518)	52 (56)	58 (460)	58 (503)
	50–59	50 (59)	43 (202)	32 (402)	67 (83)	61 (231)	59 (499)
	60–100	*	30 (85)	34 (420)	*	67 (186)	70 (832)

*Too few cases for reliable percentage.

were collected on how often the faculty visited art galleries. For all faculty who responded, contextual data were computed by major field area within the institution in exactly the same fashion as the student contextual norms were computed. In those contexts where less than 30 percent of the faculty went to galleries monthly or more, there is a generally lower level of student change or persistence than in contexts where over 30 percent of the faculty visit art galleries this often (see Table 8-10). It is clear that the faculty have some impact, although it is hard to say from these data how much. It seems moderate in terms of change and weak in terms of persistence; but it is not known how this finding would hold up if it were tested by institutional quality or major. Such analysis is beyond the scope of this paper. In any case, faculty seem to have much less impact on the rate of change of academic orientation among students than do other students.

The final issue that needs to be explored is the impact of peer groups over time. Since the Carnegie Commission survey included only one time period for each student, an approximation of the dynamics of change may be derived from the examination of successive cohorts of students. Tables 8-11 and 8-12 present data on the impact of the peer group on change and persistence for the three cohorts included in this analysis.

The most interesting finding shown in Tables 8-11 and 8-12 is that there is an *early* change in student orientations to college, and that most of this change occurs during the student's first semester at school. After that time relatively little additional change takes place. In line with this pattern, the peer-group

TABLE 8-10 *Percentage of students visiting art galleries or museums at follow-up, by entering frequency, group frequency, and faculty frequency of visiting art galleries*	*Never visit at entrance (Change)*		*Visit some at entrance (Persistence)*	
	Faculty visit art gallery		*Faculty visit art gallery*	
Percentage of group visiting	*Low**	*High**	*Low*	*High*
0–69	22 (466)	29 (30)	47 (861)	54 (59)
70–79	26 (390)	45 (241)	51 (1,224)	57 (537)
80–100	36 (171)	40 (102)	63 (765)	65 (632)

*Low = 0 to 29 percent of faculty visiting art galleries monthly or more; high = 30 to 100 percent of faculty visiting art galleries monthly or more.

TABLE 8-11 *Percentage of students visiting art galleries or museums at follow-up, by entering frequency, group frequency, and cohort*

| Percentage of group visiting | Never visit at entrance (Change) | | | Visit at entrance (Persistence) | | |
| | Cohort | | | Cohort | | |
	Freshmen	Sophomores	Juniors	Freshmen	Sophomores	Juniors
0–59	16 (81)	27 (65)	32 (70)	50 (115)	48 (73)	65 (91)
60–69	24 (163)	27 (192)	21 (167)	40 (346)	47 (370)	47 (311)
70–79	25 (297)	34 (323)	30 (248)	47 (786)	51 (873)	51 (719)
80–100	36 (135)	40 (114)	32 (81)	58 (668)	62 (538)	67 (524)

effect is also strongest early on in a student's career—among freshmen and sophomores. By the time a student is a junior, the peer-group effect has become quite weak, probably because the students change majors or otherwise move out of their initial peer group.

Walter Wallace (1966) found the same phenomenon in his studies of the effect of the student culture in a Midwestern college on student attitudes toward the importance of grades. During the first few months of their college experience, the value freshmen placed on getting good grades rapidly diminished. Associated with this change in values was a decline in achievement. According to Wallace, this change in values occurred because the freshmen conformed to the attitudes of older stu-

TABLE 8-12 *Percentage of students at follow-up agreeing with statement, "The chief benefit of college is that it increases one's earning power," by entering agreement, group agreement, and cohort*

| Percentage of group agreeing | Disagree at entrance (Change) | | | Agree at entrance (Persistence) | | |
| | Cohort | | | Cohort | | |
	Freshmen	Sophomores	Juniors	Freshmen	Sophomores	Juniors
0–39	22 (610)	19 (460)	18 (396)	54 (206)	46 (209)	42 (200)
40–49	32 (416)	30 (346)	20 (304)	69 (405)	53 (353)	44 (261)
50–59	40 (211)	34 (237)	37 (215)	67 (248)	59 (295)	56 (270)
60–100	35 (168)	36 (166)	30 (177)	80 (269)	72 (406)	58 (349)

dents. Supporting evidence showed that the students who changed the most had more nonfreshmen friends and wanted most to be accepted and liked. In any case the data presented here suggest that there is a continuing, though diminishing, peer-group impact after an initially strong impact at college entrance.

CONCLUSION

So much for the findings. In conclusion, I want to discuss these findings in light of several questions that might be raised. I shall start by discussing several things I did *not* do in this paper.

This is an early and tentative analysis of a very complex set of data. I have not carried out an extensive search for the most relevant group, other than major field, for a particular student—especially living groups, special-interest groups, and ethnic or religious groups. Second, I have not carried out a search for behaviors and attitudes where the group impact is particularly potent or where it is particularly weak. And third, I have not explored other responses to group pressure besides persistence or change. Such responses as alienation, rebellion, or withdrawal come to mind.

I have shown, however, that students have an impact on each other regardless of noncollege background and institutional factors. I have demonstrated, in the words of Ernest Campbell and Norman Alexander (1965) that there is a "two-step model" for the analysis of structural effects on individual behavior that includes the impact of interpersonal peer-group relations. And since this impact can be demonstrated with the strength shown here *in spite of* the limitations of the data, it lends limited support to the peer-group theory about the impact of college. To sum it all up, the impact of a college comes less from a student's predispositions or from the institution he attends than from the students he is in contact with at school. Thus, for the institution, recruitment and social interaction have substantial consequences for the orientation of students to their educational experiences.

References

Alexander, C. Norman, and Ernest Q. Campbell: "Peer Influences on Adolescent Aspirations and Attainments," *American Sociological Review*, vol. 29, pp. 568–575, August 1964.

Astin, Alexander: "Personal and Environmental Determinants of Student Activism," n.d. (Mimeographed.)

Astin, Alexander W., and Robert J. Panos: *The Educational and Vocational Development of College Students*, American Council on Education, Washington, 1969.

Becker, Howard S., Blanche Geer, and Everett Hughes: *Making the Grade: The Academic Side of College Life,* John Wiley & Sons, Inc., New York, 1968.

Blalock, Herbert: *Social Statistics*, McGraw-Hill Book Company, New York, 1960.

Blau, Peter M.: "Structural Effects," *American Sociological Review*, vol. 25, pp. 178–193, April 1960.

Bradshaw, Ted K.: "The Robustness of Correlation in Survey Research: A Data Simulation," paper read at the 1971 meetings of the American Association for Public Opinion Research, Pasadena, Calif., 1971*a*.

Bradshaw, Ted K.: "Culture through Education: The Effect of Educational Experiences on Cultural Leisure Patterns," paper read at the 1971 Meetings of the Pacific Sociological Association, Honolulu, Hawaii, 1971*b*.

Bradshaw, Ted K.: *The Impact of Education on Leisure: Socialization in College*, unpublished Ph.D. dissertation, University of California, Berkeley, 1974.

Campbell, Ernest Q., and C. Norman Alexander: "Structural Effects and Interpersonal Relations," *American Journal of Sociology*, vol. 71, pp. 284–293, November 1965.

Clark, Burton: *The Distinctive College*, Aldine Publishing Company, Chicago, 1970.

Clark, Burton, and Martin Trow: "The Organizational Context," in Theodore M. Newcomb and Everett K. Wilson (eds.), *College Peer Groups*, Aldine Publishing Company, Chicago, 1966, pp. 17–70.

Clark, Burton R., Paul Heist, T. R. McConnell, Martin A. Trow, and George Yonge: *Students and Colleges: Interaction and Change*, Center for Research and Development in Higher Education, University of California Press, Berkeley, 1972.

Coleman, James: *The Adolescent Society*, The Free Press of Glencoe, Inc., New York, 1961.

Corwin, Ronald: *A Sociology of Education*, Appleton Century Crofts, New York, 1965.

Cremin, Lawrence: *The Transformation of the School*, Random House, Inc., New York, 1961.

Davis, James, Joe Spaeth, and Carolyn Huson: "A Technique for

Analyzing the Effects of Group Composition," *American Sociological Review*, vol. 26, pp. 215–225, April 1961.

Dewey, John: *Democracy and Education*, The Macmillan Company, New York, 1916.

Dogan, Mattei, and Stein Rokkan (eds): *Quantitative Ecological Analysis in the Social Sciences*, The M.I.T. Press, Cambridge, Mass., 1969.

Feldman, Kenneth A., and Theodore M. Newcomb: *The Impact of College on Students*, vol. 1, Jossey-Bass Publishers, Inc., San Francisco, 1969.

Gordon, C. Wayne: *The Social System of the High School*, The Free Press of Glencoe, Inc., New York, 1957.

Gottlieb, David, and Benjamin Hodgkins: "The College Student Subcultures: Their Structure and Characteristics in Relation to Student Attitude Change," *School Review*, vol. 71, pp. 266–289, Autumn 1963.

Jacob, Philip: *Changing Values in College*, Harper & Row, Publishers, Incorporated, New York, 1957.

Jencks, Christopher, and David Riesman: "Patterns of Residential Education: A Case Study of Harvard," in Nevitt Sanford (ed.), *The American College*, John Wiley & Sons, Inc., New York, 1962, pp. 731–773.

Jencks, Christopher, and David Riesman: *The Academic Revolution*, Doubleday & Company, Inc., Garden City, N.Y., 1968.

Newcomb, Theodore M.: *Personality and Social Change*, The Dryden Press, Inc., New York, 1943.

Newcomb, Theodore M.: "The General Nature of Peer Group Influence," in Theodore M. Newcomb and Everett K. Wilson (eds.), *College Peer Groups*, Aldine Publishing Company, Chicago, 1966, pp. 2–16.

Newcomb, Theodore M., Kathryn Koenig, Richard Flacks, and Donald Warwich: *Persistence and Change: Bennington College and Its Students after Twenty-five Years*, John Wiley & Sons, Inc., New York, 1967.

Newcomb, Theodore M., and Everett K. Wilson: *College Peer Groups*, Aldine Publishing Company, Chicago, 1966.

Robinson, W. S.: "Ecological Correlations and the Behavior of Individuals," *American Sociological Review*, vol. 15, pp. 351–357, June 1950.

Sanford, Nevitt: *The American College*, John Wiley & Sons, Inc., New York, 1962.

Selvin, Hanan, and Warren Hagstrom: "Determinants of Support for

Civil Liberties," *British Journal of Sociology*, vol. 11, pp. 51–73, March 1960.

Selvin, Hanan, and Warren Hagstrom: "The Empirical Classification of Formal Groups," in Theodore M. Newcomb and Everett K. Wilson (eds.), *College Peer Groups*, Aldine Publishing Company, Chicago, 1966, pp. 162–189.

Simpson, Richard L.: "Parental Influence, Anticipatory Socialization, and Social Mobility," *American Sociological Review*, vol. 27, pp. 517–522, August 1962.

Stern, G. G.: "Characteristics of the Intellectual Climate in College Environment," *Harvard Educational Review*, vol. 32, pp. 5–41. Winter 1963.

Tannenbaum, Arnold S., and Jerald Bachman: "Structural Versus Individual Effects" *American Journal of Sociology*, vol. 69, pp. 585–595, May 1964.

Trow, Martin: "The Second Transformation of American Secondary Education," *International Journal of Comparative Sociology*, vol. 2, pp. 144–166, September 1962.

Veysey, Laurence: *The Emergence of the American University*, University of Chicago Press, Chicago, 1965.

Volkonen, Tapani: "Individual and Structural Effects in Ecological Research," in Mattei Dogan and Stein Rokkan (eds.), *Quantitative Ecological Analysis in the Social Sciences*, The M.I.T. Press, Cambridge, Mass., 1969, pp. 53–68.

Vreeland, R. S., and Charles Bidwell: "Classifying University Departments: An Approach to the Analysis of Their Effects upon Undergraduates' Values and Attitudes," *Sociology of Education*, vol. 39, pp. 237–254, Summer 1966.

Wallace, Walter: *Student Culture*, Aldine Publishing Company, Chicago, 1966.

Waller, Willard: *The Sociology of Teaching*, John Wiley & Sons, Inc., New York, 1932.

Wilson, Alan B.: "Segregation of Social Classes and Aspirations of High School Boys," *American Sociological Review*, vol. 24, pp. 836–845, December 1959.

Appendix A: A Technical Report on the 1969 Carnegie Commission Survey of Faculty and Student Opinion

by Martin Trow and associates

This report derives from a questionnaire survey of faculty, graduate students, and undergraduates conducted by the staff of the Carnegie Commission Survey of Faculty and Student Opinion in the spring and fall of 1969. In broad outline, the study comprises three major sample surveys of the 2,300 institutions of higher learning in the United States: one of faculty members, a second of graduate students, and a third of undergraduates. A fourth study, smaller in sample size than the other three, was conducted of professional researchers in the largest universities in our sample.

The study had two general purposes: to gather information and develop ideas useful to the Carnegie Commission on Higher Education in making recommendations on public policy and to investigate and illuminate aspects of American higher education of interest to a wide audience of social scientists, faculty, and administrators.

DESIGN AND METHOD The faculty and graduate student surveys were done in cooperation with the Office of Research of the American Council on Education (ACE); the survey of undergraduates was done col-

NOTE: The following were members of the professional staff of the Carnegie Commission survey: Lynne Alexander, administrative assistant; Ted Bradshaw, postgraduate research sociologist; Glenn Edwards, administrative assistant; Saul Feldman, junior specialist; Oliver Fulton, postgraduate research sociologist; Travis Hirschi, associate research sociologist; Carlos Kruytbosch, postgraduate research sociologist; Sandra Meyers, postgraduate research sociologist; Judy Roizen, postgraduate research sociologist; Richard Scheffer, project coordinator; Stephen Steinberg, postgraduate research sociologist; DonTrummell, programmer; Joseph Zelan, associate research sociologist.

laboratively with them. Since 1966, ACE has been conducting surveys of new students in a national sample of over 300 institutions of higher education, representative of all types of American colleges and universities, two-year and four-year, public and private. The data ACE has collected and the procedures it developed for gathering and processing survey data were helpful in carrying out the present study.

The ACE sample institutions were selected by a stratified probability method. This sample was used, with some modifications, for the three major surveys. All four surveys used mail questionnaire forms. Detailed enumerations were carried out for the faculty, graduate students, and professional researchers.

SURVEY OF FACULTY MEMBERS Some 461,000 full- and part-time faculty members serve in over 2,300 American colleges and universities. In 1967, the institutions in the ACE sample employed about 115,000 faculty members. The decision to conduct a census of this population was based on several considerations:

1 Most colleges are small: to sample their faculty would produce too few cases to allow us to represent either the faculty as a whole or its major segments.

2 Relatively large numbers of responses allow much finer analyses of specific categories of faculty than would otherwise be possible.

The population to be studied was to include all people, other than graduate teaching assistants, actually carrying the burden of instruction in these institutions at the time the survey was administered.

SURVEY OF GRADUATE STUDENTS In 1967 the ACE sample institutions enrolled approximately 370,000 students beyond the baccalaureate level; the great majority attended the 90 universities in the sample. Nearly 40,000, however, were enrolled in what are predominantly four-year institutions, most of them concentrated in some 60 of the larger four-year colleges.

This survey was to include 50,000 graduate students sampled randomly from the fall lists of graduate students in the ACE institutions. The aim was to sample students in all graduate fields and professional schools in ways that allowed the preparation, through appropriate weighting, of estimates describing the population of graduate students in American colleges and universities.

SURVEY OF UNDERGRADUATES During the fall of 1969 there were an estimated 6 million (U.S. Department of Health, Education, and Welfare, 1969, p. 2) undergraduate students in accredited colleges in the United States. The institutions in the undergraduate sample enrolled about 750,000 of these students.

The undergraduate survey utilized a sample of those students who responded to the ACE ongoing research of first-time students during the fall terms from 1966 to 1969 inclusive. This sample design provided the benefit of panel data for all respondents and easy access to student names and addresses, though it failed to reach those students in sample institutions who first entered college more than four years earlier and those students who transferred into a sample institution after first enrolling in another institution. But the survey did include those who dropped out or transferred from a sample institution after entering during these four terms.

The undergraduate sample was designed to include approximately 200,000 students. These students were sampled from the respondents to the ACE freshman surveys in a manner that ensured representation from each initial cohort in each institution sufficient to provide reliable data on the student body as a whole and on its major segments, as the other surveys aimed to do. These sampling goals were achieved by eliminating from the original sample of 310 institutions those that had not participated during all the years from 1966 to 69, those with poor response rates to the ACE freshmen questionnaires, and those with inadequate student name and address files. This reduced the institutional sample to 189. Then, up to 1,000 students were selected from each institution, distributed by their entrance cohort.

SURVEY OF PROFESSIONAL RESEARCHERS The study of professional researchers was aimed at those researchers employed in the largest "federal-grant" universities. Unlike the other major surveys, the aim was not to include a representative sample of institutions. Data from various sources indicated that research personnel constituted 20 to 33 percent of the academic staffs of institutions granting graduate degrees, with the proportions rising to over 50 percent in a few major universities. But U.S.Office of Education (OE) figures (OE, 1964) indicated that 31 institutions employed 61 percent of all "nonfaculty" researchers. Of the top 31 employers of research personnel, 22 were ACE sample institutions. The aim of the survey was to do a census of researchers in these institutions, attempting to reach some 10,000 researchers.

Work on the surveys began December 1, 1967. During the first period of the study, December 1, 1967 to February 1, 1969, all the planning, determination of basic sample design, enumeration of faculty and graduate students, and development of questionnaires for all the studies except the undergraduates was completed. This stage was funded entirely by the Carnegie Commission on Higher Education.

A major effort during this period was gathering ACE individual and institutional data from prior years for preliminary analysis. Data were also obtained from the Bureau of Applied Social Research and the Office of Education for use in preliminary analysis and later in the preparation of final data.

THE SAMPLE OF INSTITUTIONS

The decision to use the ACE sample of institutions was made at this time, and preliminary letters were sent to ACE institutional representatives.

Faculty and Graduate Students

Every sample represents a compromise among different, and to some degree incompatible, research interests. For example, insofar as we wish to generalize our findings to all (or nearly all) American higher education, we want a broadly representative sample of all the kinds of institutions that make it up. Insofar as we want to write in more detail about a specific kind of institution—say, the public junior colleges—not only is a representative sample of those institutions needed, but one large enough to reveal the diversity within a category that appears homogeneous only to those who do not know it.

The ACE sample draws on the whole universe of American higher education, omitting only those institutions that were created since the *1965–66 Education Directory, Part 3* (1966) was prepared, and those that grew into "eligibility" (having a freshman class of at least 30) since that time. The sampling design provides adequate samples of students and faculty in all sizes of institutions and in most categories of institutions. The advantages of using the ACE sample rather than designing and drawing a new sample were felt to outweigh any marginal gains that a new sample might allow.

1 Use of the ACE sample afforded us access to some 300 institutions with whom the ACE has a continuing research relationship and established procedures for gathering data.

2 Using the ACE sample of institutions presented us with a very large amount of information about the sample institutions and their student bodies.

3 For the undergraduates, panel data were available for individuals who entered and continued in the sample institutions.

4 The ACE procedures provided our own survey with a means of reaching with our own questionnaire those who entered the sample institutions during given years. This would otherwise have been a serious problem, since many institutions have no records of the home addresses of their students.

5 The ACE data, in addition, allowed us to identify and study the special characteristics of dropouts, as well as those who transfer, looking also at the characteristic patterns of interinstitutional mobility and of discontinuous college careers.

In 1966, 1,968 institutions were eligible for the ACE sample. These institutions were stratified by institutional type (two-year colleges, four-year colleges, universities),[1] size of enrollment (two-year colleges only), and per-student expenditures[2] (four-year colleges and universities only). ACE deliberately oversampled universities and institutions in upper-end categories of enrollment and affluence, eventually inviting 371 institutions to participate in their research program (Astin, Panos & Creager, 1966, p. 12). The actual selection of sample institutions is described by ACE:

The institutions were initially sorted into the appropriate stratification cells, the cell members shuffled, and 371 institutions randomly chosen for the contact samples. . . . The only departure from strict randomness was the deliberate inclusion in the 371 of 61 institutions that had been

---

[1] ACE follows the definition of institutional type used by the U.S. Office of Education. This definition is discussed in the section on institutional quality ranking.

[2] This measure of affluence is the per-student expenditure for "educational and general" purposes.

selected from a similar stratification design for [a] 1965 pilot study. . . . An additional 25 institutions, not included as part of the sample, were also selected either by their own request or because they were known to have educational programs of some special interest to the research staff (ibid., p. 11–12).[3]

Of the 371 institutions selected, 307[4] agreed to participate in the research program (85 percent of the four-year and 60 percent of the two-year institutions).

The Carnegie enumeration began in the fall of 1968. The 1966 sample had changed in several ways by 1968:[5] 25 institutions dropped out of the research program; 2 institutions moved from the university to the college category, 4 colleges became universities and 2 institutions disappeared as separate entities as a result of consolidation. In 1967, 24 additional junior colleges were added to the ACE sample owing to an undersampling of junior colleges and the relatively high rate of withdrawal of junior colleges. Late in the enumeration the 24 junior colleges were added to the Carnegie sample (see Table A-1).

As Table A-1 shows, the response of the institutions in the ACE sample to the 1968 request for faculty and graduate student lists was excellent. Only 7 of the 310 institutions included in the sample at that time did not participate in the faculty survey—and this in most cases was due to circumstances beyond their control.

[3] The institutions mentioned by ACE are those that remained in the pilot-study sample of the 71 initially chosen. Of this 71, 36 institutions were selected randomly and 35 "primarily because their presidents had recently been active in various committees or commissions of the Council" (Astin & Panos, 1966, pp. 5–17). Although the rate of participation in the pilot study would presumably be higher among those selected at least partly on the basis of anticipated cooperation, ACE notes that "there was no significant difference between the samples of 36 and 35 institutions in rate of agreement to participate" (p. 12). In the final pilot-study sample, "very poor, relatively small institutions of moderate size, and relatively wealthy large institutions" are substantially overrepresented. As will be evident subsequently, these biases carried over to some extent into the final ACE sample selected in 1966.

[4] The sample used by ACE in 1968 was modified considerably over the 1966 sample. One hundred thirty-five institutions were added to the total sample and the entire sample was restratified using criteria other than those used in 1966. In order to preserve the panel, we chose to use the 1966 sample with modifications made necessary by changes in institutions from 1966 to 1968.

[5] ACE reported in 1966 that 295 institutions agreed to cooperate. Subsequent descriptions of the 1966 sample list 307 institutions. It appears in fact that 309 participated, but 2 were not included in the published 1966 National Norms.

Although the number of four-year colleges failing to participate in the graduate survey appears to be quite large, in fact only a small number of graduate students are enrolled in nonparticipating institutions (see Table A-1, footnote h).

Undergraduates Several considerations led to a reduction of the institutional sample for the undergraduate survey from 310 institutions to 189.

1 Four-year colleges and universities that had not participated in the ACE freshman studies during the years from 1966 to 1969 were eliminated. Two-year institutions that had not participated in both of the years 1966 and 1967 were eliminated. This was done to assure that for each of the sample institutions there would be panel data available for all respondents and that there would be adequate representation of students at all stages of their college careers.

2 Some institutions in the ACE freshman surveys had achieved poor response rates or had distributed questionnaires in a nonsystematic manner. Those institutions that, according to information provided by ACE, had achieved a response rate of less than 85 percent or had distributed questionnaires in a manner that was questionable (e.g., distribution at voluntary freshman orientation meetings) during the years from 1966 to 1968 were excluded. Information for the ACE 1969 freshman survey was not available at the time of sampling for this survey.

3 Steps 2 and 3 left 195 institutions available for the study. Six more institutions were eliminated when the name and address files delivered to National Computer Systems for mailing were discovered to be lacking either names or addresses or both for a majority of the students.

The above steps resulted in an institutional sample size of 189. These were accepted as the institutions from which the sample of four cohorts of entering students would be selected. The number and range of institutions was sufficient for our purpose of characterizing the entire range of American colleges and universities, and the sampling of approximately 1,000 students from each institution would keep us within our intended sample size of approximately 200,000.

Professional Like federal research dollars, researchers, whose principal source
Research of support is grants and contracts, are concentrated in relatively
Personnel few institutions of higher education in the United States. Accord-

TABLE A-1 ACE sample institutions through 1968, and responses to 1968–69 solicitation for faculty and graduate student lists

	ACE 1966 sample	Dropped out[a]	Reclassified			Added[a]	Total solicited	Faculty lists		Graduate lists	
			In[b]	Out[b]	(Out)[c]			Sent	Not sent	Sent	Not sent
Universities	91	13	2	4	0	1	92	80	0	79	1[e]
Four-year colleges with graduate students	183	9	4	2	2	3	104	103	1[f]	78	26[g]
Four-year colleges without graduate students							82	76	0	1[g]	75
Junior colleges	35	10	0	0	0	24 (1967)	59	44	6[h]	0	50
TOTAL	309[i]	25	6	6	2	28	337	303	7	158	152

[a]Thirteen universities withdrew from the ACE 1966 panel between 1966 and late fall 1968. Three of these were persuaded by the Commission to send faculty and graduate lists for the Carnegie surveys. Nine four-year colleges withdrew (one as a result of closure); three of these sent lists. Ten two-year colleges withdrew before the first mailing, of which one sent a faculty list. Another college withdrew after the first mailing (see footnote h).

[b]The current OE/ACE classification of six institutions differs from ACE's 1966 National Norms listing. Four institutions are newly classified by OE as colleges; two are now classified as universities.

[b]One institution was dropped when its lists were grouped with a neighboring and affiliated institution. The other was dropped when two institutions (a university and a college) formally merged.

[c]These additions are institutions not part of the 1966 ACE sample. Because of an undersampling of junior colleges in 1966 and because of the relatively high rate of withdrawal of junior colleges from the ACE panel (see footnote a) it was decided in early January 1969 to request faculty lists from an additional 24 junior colleges, all of which had been added to the ACE panel in 1967. Because of the limited time available, 5 of these additional 24 were unable to send faculty lists before the questionnaire mailing date. This accounts for five of the six junior college nonresponses (see footnote h). It appears that one university was accidentally asked for lists because of an error in ACE's mailing list.

[d]Owing to difficulties attendant on its consolidation, one institution (see footnote c) was unable to supply us with graduate student lists.

[e]The faculty lists from another college appear to have been lost at an early stage in processing. It is classed as "not sent," although strictly speaking the list that was sent was simply not sampled.

[f]All these four-year colleges sent faculty lists (see footnote f). According to Office of Education figures, they enroll a total of 7,219 graduate students, with three institutions accounting for 66 percent of these. The largest college in terms of graduate enrollment, which accounts for 44 percent of the missing students, agreed to send a graduate student list, which did not arrive in time for the mailing of questionnaires. Several of the schools the Office of Education shows as having a small number of graduate students informed us that in fact no graduate students were enrolled at the time of the 1968 survey. Conversely, one college listed by OE as having no graduate students sent us a short list.

[g]Five junior colleges were unable to provide faculty lists in time (see footnote d); one withdrew from the whole ACE panel after the request for lists was mailed.

[h]The ACE 1966 National Norms list is said to be based on 307 institutions. It appears, however, that two extra institutions were in fact surveyed in 1966 and included in the ACE panel from 1967 on.

SOURCE: ACE and Carnegie Commission survey files.

ing to the Office of Education survey, *Faculty and Other Professional Staff in Institutions of Higher Education, 1963-64* (1964) of 1,431 institutions, 31 employed 61 percent of all researchers. Seventeen of these had complements of more than 1,000 researchers each. The remaining 14 institutions employed between 500 and 1,000 researchers each. Comparison of the Office of Education figures with other available figures for specific fields showed quite a wide variation in the figures for each institution. On the grounds that any attempt to get at the total distribution of researchers at all institutions would be based on unreliable figures, it was decided to focus only on institutions employing large complements of researchers. A principal consideration in this decision was the cost of visiting such institutions and the relatively large number of institutions that would have had to be sampled to provide sufficient respondents.

The decision having been made to look only at institutions with large complements of researchers, the second constraint upon the sample was that it be included in the ACE sample.[6] Of the 17 institutions listed by the OE survey as having more than 1,000 researchers each, 14 were included in the ACE sample. Of the 14 institutions reported by OE as employing between 500 and 1,000 researchers each, 9 were included in the ACE sample. In all, the ACE sample included 23 of the top 31 employers of research personnel as of 1963–1964.

Of the institutions that dropped out of the ACE sample, three were major employers of research personnel. As substitutes for these, three institutions that employ between 300 and 500 researchers were selected from the ACE sample. According to Office of Education records, the combined total of researcher employment at the institutions dropped was 4,000 and the combined total of researchers at the three added institutions was approximately 1,000.

The total number of researchers reported by OE for the institutions in the researcher sample was about 21,000. By using a "narrow" definition of researcher, the number of full-fledged research personnel was cut by half.

Although this reduced research personnel considerably for most of the institutions, researchers defined in this manner

---

[6] Some of the major universities employing over 750 researchers were not included in the ACE sample.

represent the core group closest to the regular faculty in research qualifications and academic orientation.

Thus, it was estimated that the 23 institutions would yield approximately 10,000 researchers as defined in the narrow sense. In fact, the number ended up at approximately 7,300.

THE ENUMERATION Since ACE had not heretofore studied graduate students, faculty, or professional researchers, an enumeration of the relevant populations was necessary.

Faculty and Graduate Students Requests for lists of faculty members were sent first to the ACE representative on the participating campuses in the fall of 1968. In many cases someone other than the representative assisted in the preparation of the lists. The request specified that the faculty list include:

A list of the names and departmental addresses of the regular faculty of the academic departments and professional schools of your institution. This list should include any staff member who is in charge of courses: including visiting professors, visiting lecturers, and any lecturers, instructors, etc. whether "acting" or not, who are responsible for the teaching of any course during the '68–'69 academic year creditable towards a degree (associate, bachelor's, or higher). If possible, this list should not include graduate students acting as teaching assistants. If any question arises as to whether or not to include an individual, please include him.

The faculty study thus includes all people, other than graduate teaching assistants, giving regular courses. The population includes both visitors and part-time faculty. It also includes a small number of senior administrators who are ordinarily recruited from the ranks of the faculty and whose work bears directly on the academic program. Other administrators and nonteaching personnel were removed from faculty lists whenever possible. Some clinical professors of law and engineering were excluded where they did not seem to constitute "regular faculty." But when a person's position was ambiguous, the lists are inclusive rather than exclusive.

Names and local addresses of graduate students were gathered for all institutions in the ACE sample. Each sample institution was asked for:

A list of names and local, but not departmental, addresses of graduate and professional students enrolled in the departments and schools of your institution in degree programs beyond the undergraduate bachelor's degree. If the student is not in residence and does not have a local address, a home address would be appreciated. In order that we may arrive, for our own definitional purposes, at an accurate description of the kinds of students included in our sample, we would appreciate your attaching a note of the sources you have used to obtain these lists.

Computer printout and data card lists sent by sample schools were presumed to include appropriate faculty and graduate students as defined in the request letter. When faculty directories were sent, only "regular faculty not on leave" were enumerated. Professional schools were included if they did not constitute separate campuses. Branch or satellite campuses were included, although lists for these campuses were less complete than for main campuses.

The graduate student lists were treated, for the purposes of enumeration and sampling, as one continuous list. To reduce processing costs, three in every four names were eliminated from the graduate list during the enumeration. This list was then enumerated. A final one-sixth sample was obtained by removing one-third of the cases from the remaining cases. The first procedure involved a systematic sample with a random start, the second a random sample with a random start.

Although the intention was to do a census of the faculty, a sixth-sevenths sample was drawn from the final faculty lists to reduce costs.

The enumeration indicated that 116,115 faculty members were employed in the participating sample institutions and that 310,088 graduate students were enrolled in the graduate institutions (see Table A-2).

TABLE A-2 Faculty and graduate students in participating institutions	Number of participating institutions	Total faculty and graduates in participating institutions*	Enumerated faculty and graduates	Number of questionnaires sent after final sampling
Faculty	303	116,115	116,115[†]	100,290
Graduates	158	310,088	77,522[†]	51,682

*Number of names supplied to the Carnegie project by institutions.

[†]All faculty and one-fourth of the graduate students were enumerated; the final samples included six-sevenths of the listed faculty and two-thirds of the listed graduate students.

SOURCE: Carnegie Commission survey files.

Undergraduates   Instead of enumerating all the undergraduates in the 189 undergraduate sample institutions, we drew the sample of individuals from among the respondents to the ACE freshman surveys in those institutions. Respondents to the ACE surveys had been asked to give a "permanent" address at which they could be reached. ACE was instructed by us to sample these names and addresses randomly within cohorts in such a manner as to attain a maximum of 1,000 individuals per institution, distributed among the four cohorts as follows:

Freshman cohort	
1966	300
1967	275
1968	225
1969	200
	1,000 TOTAL

When a cohort for an institution totaled fewer than the assigned maximum, all the students in that cohort were to be selected.

These maximum cohort sizes were chosen so as to ensure that a sufficient absolute number of respondents would be available for each cohort, since response rates were expected to be inversely related to the time elapsed since the individual's address had been acquired. The differential sampling rates were to be adjusted by weighting.

Questionnaires were mailed just prior to Christmas 1969, with the aim of reaching the sampled individuals at their homes during the Christmas recess.

Upon receiving the complete data files for all sampled individuals, whether they had responded or not (nonrespondents were represented only by ACE freshman data), we discovered that ACE had not adhered to the sampling quotas that we had established for each cohort. As far as we were able to determine, these quotas had been exceeded in all institutions that had more students than the maximum specified by our quotas. The largest discrepancy was 50 percent over the specified quota. Examination of the actual number of students sampled per cohort per institution indicated that the discrepancy between our instructions and the actual number of cases sampled was probably due to an error in the computer program for sampling the institutional files, which resulted in a higher rate per institution than had been intended. This is in no way serious, since our weighting procedures necessitated weighting by institution prior to making any other adjustments.

Professional Research Personnel The criteria used to define researchers in the Office of Education and *Industrial Research* studies must be interpreted in a "broad" sense to include, in addition to "full-fledged" researchers, many personnel having auxiliary or trainee status. For the purpose of this study, the following definition of researchers was used: "Persons appointed to perform research in positions other than regular 'ladder' faculty positions, who are capable of independent research or scholarly work as evidenced by their possession of the Ph.D. degree or equivalent research accomplishment."

Site visits were made to all but one of the 23 institutions in the researcher sample. Interviews were conducted with academic and other administrative personnel with a view to determining the best mode of identifying and collecting names and departmental addresses of persons in nonfaculty research positions. Four sources of such information were eventually used, some of them exclusively for some institutions; for other institutions, combinations of these sources were used. The sources were printouts from payroll tapes; printouts or listings from records in personnel offices; listings assembled from academic catalogs; and finally, in one institution, listings from the campus telephone book. The initial period of the enumeration thus gained the cooperation of administrative or research personnel in order to identify those researchers necessary to this study. Although in most cases information was easily obtained, some bias in the sample remains.

The most serious bias in the types of researchers that were enumerated is an undercount of the kind of postdoctoral fellows who come on fellowships, particularly to the large universities, without any formal appointments. It is safe to say that none of the large institutions had any regular administrative methods for keeping tabs on such people. The magnitude of the group thus missed may range up to 20 percent or so of the total at some institutions. Richard Curtis's study, *The Invisible University: Postdoctoral Education in the United States*, conducted by the National Academy of Sciences (1969), provides some clue as to the magnitude of this bias. The 1967 study identified some 13,300 postdoctoral appointments in universities, 25 percent of which were individuals on nationally competitive fellowships; the others were hired on project funds with various titles. Institutions seem to vary in the extent to which they press for appointing all their research personnel to research staff appointments and the extent to which they are willing to lend the title "fellow" to these people.

QUESTIONNAIRE DEVELOPMENT During the fall of 1968 work on questionnaire development was completed for the faculty and graduate students and pretesting was begun. Because the questionnaires were to be machine-readable, exacting care with the layout had to be taken, as well as concern with substantive issues. Although some small random error results from the use of an optical scanner to read this type of document, it is a more accurate and economical method than any other used in large-scale data collection.[7] Four versions of each questionnaire were ultimately constructed. Pretesting was carried out on the two final versions, but was somewhat limited because it was impossible to produce an interim machine-readable questionnaire. Most of the pretesting was done, therefore, by interview.

* * * * *

The second major period of work, February 1, 1969 to March 1, 1970, covered the completion of the enumeration of individuals in the sample for all the surveys, the mailing of the questionnaires, and limited preliminary analyses of data from all but the undergraduate survey. The work for this period was funded by the Office of Education and the Carnegie Commission. The Office of Education funds were used primarily for data collection, computer costs, and the intensive follow-up of nonrespondents. The initial grant was awarded February 1, 1969 to run for one year.

DATA COLLECTION Printing and mailing of the questionnaires for the four major studies was handled through National Computer Systems (NCS), Minneapolis, Minnesota.

Faculty and Graduate Students The layout and printing of the faculty and graduate questionnaires was accomplished during the early spring of 1969. Name

---

[7] The error is estimated at less than 0.5 of 1 percent.

and address files were given to NCS, and great care was taken to ensure the anonymity of all respondents. Faculty questionnaires were mailed the second week of March over a period of five days. Graduate questionnaires were mailed during three days in the third week of March. Follow-up postcards were mailed out approximately a week after the mailing of the questionnaires.

Considerable effort was taken to assure the highest possible response rate. Two weeks after the mailing of the postcards a follow-up letter was sent to all nonrespondents. Six weeks after the original mailing a second questionnaire was sent to the remaining nonrespondents (see Table A-3). As Table A-3 indicates, most people responded to the initial questionnaire. A total of 1,650 faculty members responded to the follow-up letter, and an additional 5,778 individuals responded after receiving the second questionnaire. After the follow-up letter, 1,350 graduate students responded, and 3,091 responded after receiving a second questionnaire. Slightly more than 8 percent of the faculty and graduate samples responded as a result of the three additional mailings.

Undergraduates and Professional Research Personnel Questionnaires were mailed to the researchers a little over a month after the original faculty and graduate mailings. Most of the respondents had returned their questionnaires by the first week in June, but follow-up letters were mailed to the nonrespondents the second week in July. Out of the 7,300 researchers sampled, we received 3,729 usable questionnaires, a response rate of 51 percent.

The layout and printing of the undergraduate questionnaire was completed in November 1969. The questionnaires were mailed out a month later to reach the students during the Christmas recess. Follow-up postcards urging the completion of the questionnaire were mailed out a week later to everyone in the 171,525-undergraduate sample. By our cutoff date we had received 70,772 usable questionnaires for a response rate of 41 percent (by cohort: 1966, 38 percent; 1967, 39 percent; 1968, 44 percent; 1969, 46 percent).

DATA PREPARATION ACTIVITIES The next step in the project was to design procedures for the use of the data, taking into consideration such problems as respondents' anonymity, quality control, response bias, and the development of an institutional file.

TABLE A-3 *Faculty and graduate participation in follow-up study*

	*Number of follow-up postcards sent**	*Number of respondents receiving follow-up letters*	*Number of respondents receiving second questionnaire*	*Total returned questionnaires*	*Response rate, %*
Faculty	100,290	47,580	45,930	60,028	60
Graduates	51,682	23,160	21,810	32,963	64

*Equals number of questionnaires first mailed.

SOURCE: Carnegie Commission survey files.

Protection of Respondents' Anonymity

This was accomplished by removing from the master tape the links between the names and addresses of the respondents and the serial numbers used for analytical identification. The names were wholly obliterated, preventing any inadvertent disclosure of individual responses. In the case of the faculty, their departmental addresses were sorted and recoded into the 69 departmental categories that were included in the questionnaire. The recoded addresses, in most cases the name of a department, were merged with the respondent's data record and used as a supplement for the respondent's self-reported teaching department, especially useful for those who failed to answer the whole of the question on that matter. At the same time, a master file was created for merging with the data files. These files contained the recoded departmental mailing address for the faculty only, indications of when each respondent returned the completed questionnaire, and a system for cross-referencing all the different serial numbers used for any respondent. Thus the study was able to accumulate information on nonrespondents and to eliminate duplicate responses.

The Quality Control of Data

Quality control of the data from NCS took several forms. After the coding specifications were sent to NCS, a sample of 200 questionnaires for each of the faculty and graduate studies was coded by hand in Berkeley and a tape was prepared to be checked against machine-coded NCS tapes for the same questionnaire. Several procedures were used to check the accuracy of the machine coding: marginal distributions were compared, contingencies built into the coding were checked, and finally a column-by-column check was carried out. Dummy questionnaires were created to check coding possibilities not covered in the 200 questionnaires. As a result of this, the proportion of errors in the final data tapes was very small. The same process was later used to check the quality of the undergraduate and researcher data.

Programs for contingency checking were developed for "cleaning" the data to ensure that instructions were followed by respondents and to assure that the analysis would at all times examine only those respondents to whom a particular question was intended to apply.

Study of Respondent Bias During this period an intensive study of faculty and graduate nonrespondents was undertaken to learn who they were in order to be able to properly weight for any response bias. After approximately 50 percent of the sample had responded, random samples of 2,000 cases (faculty) and 2,037 cases (graduate) were selected for an intensive follow-up. Of these, approximately half had responded by the time the follow-up began. The remainder were first sent an additional questionnaire and then telephoned. The phoning operation had three major functions: First, to identify respondents who were either no longer available or ineligible, and therefore not genuinely part of our survey; second, to encourage genuine respondents to return their completed questionnaires; and third, failing that, to elicit from them over the phone responses to seven questions that would give us valuable data that we could use to characterize nonrespondents for the subsequent weighting operation.

On the first call, telephone interviewers were instructed to encourage the respondent to complete and return the questionnaire. If the respondent agreed to do so, the interview was terminated. If the respondent indicated that he did not intend to complete the questionnaire, he was asked a brief list of questions identical to items on the questionnaire. After a lapse of some weeks, those respondents who had not completed the questionnaire but who had indicated willingness to do so were called again. On the second call, they were again encouraged to complete the questionnaire but were asked the brief list of questions, whether or not they agreed to complete the questionnaire.

Of those selected for the graduate telephone sample, 1,580 completed the graduate questionnaire, 190 others answered the brief list of questions, 128 refused to answer any questions, and

139 could not be located. Of those selected for the faculty telephone sample, 1,512 completed the questionnaire, 214 answered the brief list of questions, 128 refused to answer any questions, 87 could not be located, and 59 were not followed up because of a computer error. Over 85 percent of the people in both samples responded either to the full questionnaire or to the additional questions during the phone interview (see section on nonresponse bias, p. 329ff).

Development of an Institutional File

An institutional file for all colleges and universities in the United States was created. It is based on information gathered from the American Council on Education, from the Higher Education General Information Survey (HEGIS) tapes sent to us by the Office of Education, and from a variety of published sources not available on magnetic tape. This file is used for general descriptive purposes and some items from it have been added to the data tapes for use in data analysis. It was essential to the development of an accurate weighting scheme. A major part of the individual weight is a function of the institutional weight.

* * * * *

The third major period of work, March 1, 1970 to January 1, 1971, was taken up in the development of weighting schemes for the faculty and graduate studies, analysis of response bias, creation of data samples, and production of weighted and unweighted marginal tabulations.

WEIGHTING

Disproportionate sampling and the failure of some institutions to respond to the request for lists required that cooperating institutions be differentially weighted.

Faculty and Graduate Students

As a first step in the computation of these weights, all institutions were assigned to their 1966 cells on the basis of information supplied by ACE.[8] Table A-4 summarizes this procedure. It shows that all but 228 of the 2,843 institutions listed by the U.S. Office of Education (data tape on *Opening Fall Enrollment, 1968,* HEGIS, series 2) would have been eligible for inclusion and could be located within the 1966 scheme based either on institu-

---

[8] For its own surveys, ACE no longer relies on its 1966 stratification scheme. For a summary and justification of the various stratification dimensions used by ACE over the course of its research program, see Bayer, et al., 1969.

TABLE A-4A *Assignment of institutions to 1966 ACE cells with faculty institutional weights*

ACE 1966 cell	Enrollment	Universe Number of institutions	Universe Faculty number	Sample Number of institutions	Sample Faculty number	Faculty weight
Public two-year colleges						
1	Low enrollment	172	6,108	6	390	15.66
2	.	182	10,621	7	447	23.76
3	.	175	17,567	7	593	29.62
4	.	54	9,068	5	645	14.06
5	High	50	12,352	5	1,457	8.48
Private two-year colleges						
6	Low enrollment	229	6,824	10	353	19.33
7	.					
8	.	36	2,664	4	343	7.77
9	High					
	Affluence					
Universities						
10	Unknown	0	0	0	0	—
11	Low	15	6,780	4	2,691	2.52
12	.	10	3,715	5	2,418	1.54
13	.	47	18,079	5	5,815	3.11
14	.	52	20,306	12	9,401	2.16
15	.	18	13,382	5	4,362	3.07
16	.	69	36,638	13	19,060	1.92
17	.	32	22,036	23	18,512	1.19
18	.	44	19,177	8	8,146	2.35
19	High	76	67,775	26	36,316	1.87
Four-year colleges						
20	Unknown	449	37,497	30	2,818	13.31
21	Low					
22	.	248	34,436	20	3,010	11.44
23	.	250	34,435	22	2,241	15.37
24	.	175	30,891	26	4,769	6.48
25	.	84	11,747	19	2,091	5.62
26	.	56	8,753	25	3,799	2.30

TABLE A-4A *(continued)*

		Universe		Sample		
ACE 1966 cell	Affluence	Number of institutions	Faculty number	Number of institutions	Faculty number	Faculty weight
27	·	29	5,078	12	2,401	2.11
28	·	24	3,369	9	1,733	1.94
29	High	39	6,998	18	3,160	2.21
Total eligible		2,615	446,296*	326†	136,971	‡
Ineligible institutions						
No undergraduates		8	918	0	0	
Seminaries		123	3,137	0	0	
Professional schools		31	4,965	0	0	
Freshman class less than 30 students		66	1,302	0	0	
Total ineligible		228	10,322	0	0	
Grand total		2,843	456,618	326	136,971	

*97.74 percent of total.

†The number of institutions given here includes branch campuses counted as separate institutions by OE. This number includes the 303 institutions indicated in Table A-1 plus the branch campuses.

‡Average weight = 3.26.

SOURCE: Carnegie Commission survey files and published lists of faculty members

TABLE A-4B *Assignment of institutions to 1966 ACE cells with graduate student institutional weights*

		Universe		Sample		
ACE 1966 cell	Affluence	Number of institutions	Graduate numbers	Number of institutions	Graduate numbers	Graduate weight
Universities						
10	Unknown	0	0	0	0	—
11	Low	15	27,447	4	9,403	2.92
12	·	10	14,468	5	12,147	1.19
13	·	47	43,664	5	15,202	2.87
14	·	52	73,872	11	23,486	3.15
15	·	18	42,569	5	12,320	3.46
16	·	69	121,747	13	60,904	2.00
17	·	32	71,985	18	57,486	1.25
18	·	44	69,290	7	31,898	2.17
19	High	76	187,622	18	93,878	2.00

TABLE A-4B *Assignment of institutions to 1966 ACE cells with graduate student institutional weights*

ACE 1966 cell	Affluence	Universe		Sample		Graduate weight
		Number of institutions	Graduate numbers	Number of institutions	Graduate numbers	
Four-year colleges						
20	Unknown					
21	Low	697	119,903	18	6,446	18.60
22	.					
23	.	425	151,499	17	12,928	11.72
24	.					
25	.	84	23,235	6	2,116	10.98
26	.	56	20,119	15	4,932	4.08
27	.	29	13,240	7	8,803	1.50
28	.	24	8,178	6	3,794	2.16
29	High	39	13,853	10	6,246	2.22
Total eligible		1,717	1,002,691*	165[†]	361,989	‡
Two-year colleges						
1–9		898	0	0	0	
Ineligible institutions						
No undergraduates		8	4,432	0	0	
Seminaries		123	17,813	0	0	
Professional schools		31	13,257	0	0	
Freshman class less than 30 students		66	2,976	0	0	
Total ineligible		228	38,478	0	0	
Grand total		2,843	1,041,169	165	361,989	

*96.30 percent of total.

[†] Including branch campuses.

‡ Average weight = 2.77.

SOURCE: Carnegie Commission survey files and Office of Education enrollment data (see footnote 10).

tional type and affluence or on enrollment. The 228 ineligible institutions contain only slightly more than 2 percent of the faculty and less than 4 percent of the graduate students in American colleges and universities. The bulk of ineligible faculty and graduate students teach or are enrolled in 123 theological seminaries or in 31 independent graduate or professional schools.

Branch or satellite campuses of institutions included in the ACE sampling frame were assigned to the sampling cell occupied by the main campus. Although in some cases the branch campus lists were provided either directly or by the main campus, both faculty and graduate students at such branch campuses are in general underrepresented in the sample. Since we have no way of distinguishing between main and branch campus respondents, there is no way we can exclude them from the sample or adjust for their lesser likelihood of appearing in the sample by adjusting the magnitude of their weights. (The bias is not large. About 6 percent, or 61,000, of all graduate students are enrolled at such campuses. The names of 5,500 of these were on lists sent to the Carnegie Commission survey.)

Initial assignment of institutions to the 1966 ACE cells revealed that the "unknown" categories of affluence for both universities and colleges were greatly undersampled. Rather than assign very large weights to these undersampled institutions, we attempted to distribute them over the other sampling cells on the basis of affluence information not available to ACE in 1966. All universities were easily reassigned on the basis of current information. Although per-student expenditure information was still unavailable for many four-year colleges, colleges for which such information had become available were generally poor. We therefore combined the "unknown" category with the lowest category of affluence in the case of faculty and with the two lowest four-year college affluence cells in the case of graduate students.[9]

Finally, two faculty junior college cells and two graduate student four-year college cells were sufficiently undersampled

---

[9] "Faculty" institutions are of course more numerous than "graduate student" institutions in the four-year college category. Undersampling problems were thus less serious for the faculty than for the graduate student sample.

that we considered it necessary for purposes of weighting to combine them with adjacent cells that were more fully sampled.

Once these operations were performed, we determined the total number of graduate students in each cell from enrollment information provided by the Office of Education;[10] faculty numbers were obtained from the *College Blue Book* (1969), *World Almanac* (1969), and ACE's *American Universities and Colleges* (1968). Table A-4 shows the number of faculty and graduate students in each cell in the universe of colleges and universities and in sample institutions. It also shows the base institutional weight obtained by dividing the number in the universe by the number in the sample.

Once these institutional weights had been computed, we were in a position to check for possible bias in the sample. The first check was on institutional quality. The weights were first used to estimate the total number of faculty and graduate students in each of several quality strata. These estimates were then compared with the actual number derived from both published sources and data tapes provided by the Office of Education. The Office of Education projected that there were 841,622 graduate students registered in master's, doctoral, or first professional degree programs in 1968. The remaining graduate students are in nondegree or special programs. The projected total includes only graduate students in eligible institutions and does not include students in autonomous graduate institutions such as theological seminaries, independent medical or law schools, and graduate institutions that have no undergraduates. The results for graduate students are shown in Table A-5.

Table A-5 shows that high-quality institutions, both colleges and universities, were substantially overrepresented in the original ACE sample. Since, as noted in an earlier footnote, ACE departed from a strictly random procedure by including in the final sample 71 pilot-study institutions (many of which were initially selected by nonrandom means), and since this pilot study was known to overrepresent high-quality institutions, all pilot-study institutions were eliminated from the sample and institutional weights recomputed for only those institutions

10 Magnetic tapes from recent enrollment surveys were provided by the Office of Education.

TABLE A-5
Actual population of graduate students in quality strata and number of graduate students estimated from 1966 ACE cells

Quality ranking	Actual population	Estimates from ACE strata	Error,* %
Universities (total)	652,664	652,663	
High	172,330	226,983	(+) 31.7
Medium	258,232	231,134	(−) 10.5
Low	222,102	194,546	(−) 12.4
Colleges (total)	350,027	350,027	
High	60,791	78,190	(+) 28.6
Medium	120,682	114,927	(−) 4.8
Low	168,554	156,910	(−) 6.9

*Percent by which estimates exceed or fall short of actual population.
SOURCE: Carnegie Commission survey files and Office of Education/ACE data.

selected according to a strictly random procedure.

This approach did not reduce the variation in the weights: Elimination of pilot-study institutions reduced only slightly the overall bias toward high-quality institutions in the sample. Since the loss in sample breadth appeared to be greater than the gain in reduction of bias, we returned pilot-study institutions and adjusted for bias within the limits provided by the sample. After the extent of bias with respect to geographical location, size, public or private control, and quality had been determined, it was decided that it was both necessary and feasible to adjust the sample weights simultaneously for quality and type of control. These adjustments or correction factors for the various quality-control categories are shown in Table A-6. (Correction factors are the ratios of the actual cell population to the cell population estimated from 1966 ACE strata [see Table A-5]. The ratio adjustments were made within quality-control cells rather than original sampling cells. Although this facilitates the weighting procedure, it introduces minor distortion.) A correction factor of .500 indicates that the estimated number of faculty (or graduate students) in the cell is twice as large as the actual number of faculty and that responses of faculty in this cell were reduced by one-half in estimating the distribution of responses in the population as a whole.

The weights and corrections to this point adjusted the data for disproportionate sampling of institutions. The data were also

TABLE A-6
Correction
factors for quality
and control bias
in 1966 ACE
sample, faculty
and graduate
students

	Public institutions	
Quality ranking	Faculty	Graduate students
Universities		
High	.987	.793
Medium	1.273	1.190
Low	1.180	1.094
Four-year colleges		
High	.973	.708
Medium	1.001	2.078
Low	1.679	1.021
Junior colleges	.990	
	Private institutions	
	Faculty	Graduate students
Universities		
High	.695	.731
Medium	.781	.978
Low	1.129	1.222
Four-year colleges		
High	.872	.951
Medium	.511	.500
Low	1.059	1.220
Junior colleges	1.067	

SOURCE: Carnegie Commission survey files.

adjusted for three additional sources of variation: institutional nonresponse (the lists of faculty and graduate students sent to the Carnegie Commission survey were variably complete); sampling of individuals from the lists (in the case of faculty, a systematic sample of six-sevenths, secured by removing every seventh case from the list and retaining the remainder in the sample; in the case of graduate students, a systematic sample of one-sixth obtained by selecting every fourth case and subsequently removing every third case from those selected); and, finally, individual nonresponse. All these variations were taken into account when we divided the total number of faculty or graduate students in an institution (according to published, i.e., independent, information) by the number of faculty or graduate student *respondents* in the institution. This procedure assumed that the lists provided by the institution were representative of all persons in the institution; it also assumed that respondents within an institution were representative of nonrespondents within that institution.

Extreme graduate weights were reduced by combining low-response (or incomplete list) institutions with institutions similar with respect to quality, size, type of control, and geographical region. All in all, seven small institutions were combined with other institutions for this purpose.

The final weights used for the tabulations in this report are thus an attempt to take into account the sampling of institutions, bias with respect to quality and control, sampling of individuals, and two types of nonresponse. These weights range in magnitude from 1.34 to 103.09 for faculty and from 0.82 to 1,314.94 for graduate students. The actual distribution of weights is shown in Table A-7.

Of 51,682 questionnaires sent to graduate students enrolled in participating institutions, 32,963, or 64.0 percent, were eventually returned in usable form.[11] Of the 100,290 questionnaires sent to faculty, 60,028, or 59.8 percent, were returned. Although these return rates were excellent for a mail questionnaire, the problem of nonresponse bias remained. Several methods for estimating the extent of such bias were possible. We chose to compare the obtained sample with a smaller sample intensively followed up; this process is described in the section on nonresponse bias.

Undergraduates   The undergraduate data posed several weighting problems that were not found in the other studies. The first was the problem of defining the universe we were weighting toward. In the undergraduate study, the weighted sample predicts the number of students who entered institutions of higher education during the

---

[11] An additional 650 (or 1.3 percent of the total) questionnaires were returned to the Commission. Of these, 378 were determined to be undergraduates and thus ineligible for the survey. Ninety-three questionnaires were returned with the identification number so defaced that institutional affiliation could not be determined. The remaining usable questionnaires were duplicates of questionnaires already returned. One hundred and seventy graduate students returned blank questionnaires.

	Number of institutions	
Weight	Faculty	Graduate students
0.0–4.9*	111	3
5.0–9.9	52	3
10.0–14.9	25	22
15.0–19.9	22	20
20.0–24.9	26	15
25.0–29.9	15	11
30.0–34.9	19	9
35.0–39.9	10	11
40.0–49.9	11	3
50.0–99.9	11	27
100.0–199.9	1	16
200.0–299.9	—	4
300.0–399.9	—	3
400.0–499.9	—	—
500.0–999.9	—	4
1000.0 or greater[†]	—	4
TOTAL	303	155[‡]

TABLE A-7 Distribution of final weights adjusted for quality, control, and nonresponse—faculty and graduate students

*Minimum weight: faculty = 1.34; graduate students = .82.

[†] Maximum weight: faculty = 103.09; graduate students = 1,314.94.

[‡] Three four-year colleges (from which a total of eight graduate students were sampled) were eliminated at the last stage of weighting because of nonresponse.

SOURCE: Carnegie Commission survey files.

fall of years 1966, 1967, 1968, and 1969, with the following limitations:

1 All institutions included were accredited in 1966 and listed by the U.S. Office of Education in its publication *Opening Fall Enrollment in Higher Education* (part A, Summary Data, 1966). Thus, newly founded or recently accredited institutions were likely to be excluded.

2 Those institutions that had an opening fall enrollment of less than 30 students in 1966 were eliminated.

3 The enrollment data were derived from tapes supplied by the Office of Education to the Carnegie Commission. Inconsistencies in institution I.D. numbers, differences between the tape content and published data, errors in reading tapes by the computer, and the omission of newly founded or accredited institutions led to small differences between our

total enrollment figures and those published by the Office of Education (see Table A-8).

4 The Office of Education changed its definition of entering student during the four years for which we collected data. The figures given below are defined as follows:

1966 "First time students," both full-time and part-time

1967 "First time Freshmen students," both full-time and part-time

1968 "First time students working toward B.A. degree" and "First time students not working toward a B.A. degree," both part-time and full-time

1969 "First time Freshmen students," both full-time and part-time

TABLE A-8
Entering undergraduate enrollment data

	1966	1967	1968	1969
Our total	1,535,756	1,554,218	1,711,446	1,737,675
Office of Education total	1,565,564	1,652,317	1,907,938	1,983,525

SOURCE: Office of Education data and Carnegie Commission survey files

The weights do not account for the total number of students currently in American higher education, but rather for the number of students who *entered* during one of the four years. Because this is true, separate weights had to be calculated for each cohort of entering students. The method of calculating the weights was as follows:

1 Since we sampled a quota of students from each institution, and institutions differed in their response rate, we first calculated an *institutional response weight* that was the ratio of the number of students in the institution to the number who actually responded. This weight accounts for both different sampling rates and different response rates.

$$\text{Institutional response weight} = \frac{\text{total entering students}}{\text{students who responded}}$$

2 Since the sample of institutions was drawn from the universe according to 29 sampling strata, we next calculated a *stratum weight* that represents the ratio of the number of students in institutions included in the stratum to the number of students in sample institutions also in that stratum. Because private institutions were heavily oversampled and public institutions were heavily undersampled, we calculated strata weights separately for public and private institutions in each stratum (see Table A-9). Further, since all strata were not evenly represented by

TABLE A-9 *Strata weights*

ACE 1966 cell	Enrollment	1966 Public	1966 Private	1967 Public	1967 Private	1968 Public	1968 Private	1969 Public	1969 Private
Public two-year colleges									
1	Low	110.56		106.79		126.71		160.59	
2	.	110.56		106.79		126.71		160.59	
3	.	110.56		106.79		126.71		160.59	
4	.	13.45		15.95		18.17		22.66	
5	High	13.45		15.95		18.17		22.66	
Private two-year colleges									
6	Low		17.92		17.87		19.17		28.15
7	.		17.92		17.87		19.17		28.15
8	.		17.92		17.87		19.17		28.15
9	High		17.92		17.87		19.17		28.15
	Affluence								
Universities									
10	Unknown								
11	Low	9.43	3.09	8.38	3.42	13.92	2.32	9.02	4.48
12		9.43	1.23	8.38	1.15	13.92	1.15	9.02	1.18

13	·	7.55	1.61	8.85	1.67	10.52	1.74	9.26	2.07
14	·	4.51	3.08	5.17	2.85	5.35	1.12	6.29	12.72
15	·	3.01	6.41	3.42	6.58	3.72	6.97	6.29	6.90
16	·	3.58	6.41	3.32	6.58	4.44	6.97	3.52	6.90
17	·	3.61	4.21	3.55	3.42	3.10	3.74	3.14	6.90
18	·	15.90	3.67	12.54	3.83	17.68	3.48	16.94	4.46
19	High	15.90	3.67	12.54	3.83	17.68	3.48	16.94	4.46
Four-year colleges									
20	Unknown	80.60	16.57	87.67	15.61	86.27	15.20	133.59	16.31
21	Low	80.60	16.57	87.67	15.61	86.27	15.20	133.59	16.31
22	·	53.00	9.94	44.66	9.74	37.79	10.33	133.59	11.52
23	·	31.50	14.15	35.22	13.48	35.33	13.50	32.46	16.44
24	·	8.79	6.41	7.94	6.14	8.25	6.35	7.15	6.26
25	·	9.97	5.41	10.40	5.40	10.95	5.04	10.90	5.12
26	·	3.58	4.99	3.37	4.55	3.04	4.06	5.24	4.71
27	·	3.58	4.07	3.37	4.42	3.04	4.37	5.24	4.71
28	·	3.58	2.44	3.37	2.72	3.04	2.48	5.24	3.19
29	High	2.58	2.14	3.37	2.02	3.04	2.03	5.24	2.47

SOURCE: Carnegie Commission survey files.

institutions, we found it necessary to combine several neighboring strata to achieve more stable weights. The strata combined were: Public: (1, 2, and 3), (4 and 5), (11 and 12), (18 and 19), (20 and 21), (26, 27, 28, and 29); Private: (6, 7, 8, and 9), (15 and 16), (18 and 19), (20 and 21). In 1969 we also had to combine: Public: (14 and 15), (20, 21, and 22); Private: (15, 16, and 17).

$$\text{Stratum weight} = \frac{\text{total students in all institutions in stratum}}{\text{students in sample institutions in stratum}}$$

3 An individual student's weight was the product of his institution's response weight and the appropriate stratum weight. We found, however, that this weight, while it correctly predicted the distribution of students in the universe according to the sampling cells, failed to predict their distribution according to the quality of the institution. When we observed the distribution of students by the quality of their institution and compared this with the distribution of all the students who entered higher education, we found that there was need for an adjustment in the weight so that quality would be correctly predicted. The adjustments for quality (calculated separately for public and private institutions) are the ratio between the actual number of students in a quality cell and our estimate based on the previous weights. The adjustment factors are shown in Table A-10.

TABLE A-10 *Adjustment factors*

	1966		1967		1968		1969	
Type and quality	Public	Private	Public	Private	Public	Private	Public	Private
University								
High quality	2.46	0.63	2.52	0.63	1.89	0.66	2.32	0.79
Medium quality	0.74	1.00	0.75	1.07	0.77	1.07	0.76	0.75
Low quality	1.17	1.34	1.15	1.33	1.33	1.30	1.15	1.39
Four-year college								
High quality	0.85	0.73	0.91	0.79	0.95	0.79	0.98	0.76
Medium quality	0.58	0.77	0.59	0.78	0.58	0.75	0.32	0.69
Low quality	1.36	1.24	1.36	1.22	1.41	1.25	5.84	1.36
Junior college								
All qualities	1.00	1.00	1.00	1.00	1.00	1.00	1.00	1.00

SOURCE: Carnegie Commission survey files.

$$\text{Adjustment factor} = \frac{\text{actual students in quality cell}}{\text{estimated students in quality cell}}$$

4   The product of the earlier student's weight and the appropriate adjustment factor produces the final weight used in this study. Table A-11 shows the distribution of the weights by sampling strata and by institutional control, giving the highest and the lowest weight within each category of institutions.

Weight = institutional response × stratum weight × adjustment factor

5   In order to verify that the weights were computed correctly, we compared our estimates with figures for the total sample. Table A-12 shows our estimate for the type of institutional control, and Table A-13 shows our estimate for the institutional quality. The small differences are due to rounding error. The use of the adjustment factor successfully corrected for institutional quality, but it changed the distribution by original sampling strata. The extent of the strata error is shown in Table A-14. There is nothing we can do about this since we choose to sacrifice accuracy by strata to gain accuracy by quality, which is much more important to our analysis.

There is considerable variation in the size of the weights from a low of about 2 to a high of around 2,000. Although this much variation is technically satisfactory, care must be taken in analysis so that misleading results are not obtained from the analysis of a few students with very high weights. It should be noted that the weights do not totally eliminate the bias introduced by nonrandom institutional selection or by nonresponse bias. (A discussion of undergraduate nonresponse bias begins on p. 354).

NONRESPONSE BIAS   A random sample of graduate students and faculty was drawn for intensive follow-up. From the orginal samples, 2,000 faculty members and 2,037 graduate students were selected. At the time the samples were drawn, over 50 percent of these special samples had returned the appropriate questionnaire. Approximately 1,000 graduate students and 800 faculty members were thus left to follow up. The intention was to achieve a high rate of response, and then to compare these special samples with the respective full samples to determine the extent of the bias, if any, that results from response rates of 64 percent for the graduate students and 60 percent for the faculty.

TABLE A-11 Range of final weights, by year

ACE 1966 cell	Enrollment	1966 Public		Private		Number of institutions		1967 Public		Private		Number of institutions	
		Low	High	Low	High	Public	Private	Low	High	Low	High	Public	Private
Public two-year colleges													
1	Low	380	1,095			4	0	380	1,133			4	0
2	.	1,240	1,240			1	0	806	806			1	0
3	.					0	0					0	0
4	.	310	447			2	0	455	471			2	0
5	High	882	2,306			2	0	1,503	1,666			2	0
Private two-year colleges													
6	Low			39	107	0	5			41	112	0	5
7	.					0	0					0	0
8	.			169	241	0	3			152	224	0	3
9	High					0	0			123	123	0	1
	Affluence												
Universities													
10	Unknown					0	0					0	0
11	Low	138	138	11	51	1	2			10	46	0	2

#													Label
12	238	238	28	38	0	2	167	167	18	19	0	2	·
13	101	235	20	157	1	3	99	190	17	187	1	3	·
14	148	148	31	63	3	3	230	230	31	58	3	3	·
15	76	220	19	87	1	2	31	155	23	125	1	2	·
16	14	120	54	54	5	0	11	105	43	43	5	0	·
17			18	21	7	1			23	29	7	1	·
18			10	34	0	2			13	51	0	2	·
19	223	238				5	169	278			2	5	High

Four-year colleges

#													Label
20	874	874	58	85	0	5	959	959	34	88	0	5	Unknown
21	249	497	23	141	1	14	277	553	24	130	1	14	Low
22	205	296	18	105	2	10	199	368	20	92	2	10	·
23	62	109	23	86	2	14	69	108	24	98	2	14	·
24	20	118	11	58	5	16	18	79	10	44	5	17	·
25	17	24	8	32	3	13	11	29	9	28	3	13	·
26			6	20	4	14			7	14	5	14	·
27			7	24	0	5			6	15	0	5	·
28			4	35	0	8			7	28	0	8	·
29			2	7	0	13			2	9	0	13	High

TABLE A-11 (continued)

ACE 1966 cell	Enrollment	1968 Public Low	Public High	Private Low	Private High	Number of institutions Public	Private	1969 Public Low	Public High	Private Low	Private High	Number of institutions Public	Private
Public two-year colleges													
1	Low	439	1,766			4	0	856	2,129			3	0
2	.	841	841			1	0					0	0
3	.					0	0					0	0
4	.	395	1,651			2	0	514	514			1	0
5	High	1,061	1,855			2	0	1,763	2,458			2	0
Private two-year colleges													
6	Low			40	68	0	5			58	128	0	5
7	.					0	0					0	0
8	.			179	300	0	3			229	239	0	2
9	High					0	0					0	0
	Affluence												
Universities													
10	Unknown					0	0					0	0
11	Low	227	227	7	34	1	2	224	224	778	778	1	1

12			16	21	0	2			15	35	0	2
13	240	240	22	239	1	3	323	323	31	391	1	2
14	135	265	36	87	3	3	186	322	104	104	3	1
15	151	151	36	186	1	2			34	136	0	2
16	70	287	60	60	4	0	66	314			5	0
17	14	135	23	31	7	1	19	155			6	0
18					0	2	2,893	2,893			1	0
19 High	310	311	18	46	2	5	269	269	28	150	1	5
Four-year colleges												
20 Unknown	1,306	1,306	37	68	0	5			23	134	0	4
21 Low	377	596	21	145	1	14			27	124	0	13
22	182	423	24	83	2	10	635	635	18	153	1	9
23	77	123	19	93	2	14	233	612	23	106	2	13
24	23	94	11	86	5	17	70	920	11	54	5	17
25	14	43	9	23	3	13	12	49	9	21	3	13
26			4	19	5	14	11	93	5	35	3	13
27			7	14	0	5			7	15	0	4
28			5	27	0	8			7	46	0	7
29 High			3	12	0	13			3	14	0	12

SOURCE: Carnegie Commission survey files.

TABLE A-12 *Verification of weights, by control*

	1966		1967		1968		1969	
	Estimated	*Actual*	*Estimated*	*Actual*	*Estimated*	*Actual*	*Estimated*	*Actual*
Public	1,104,607	1,104,611	1,134,608	1,134,612	1,281,144	1,281,148	1,298,762	1,298,905
Private	431,137	431,145	419,602	419,606	430,293	430,298	438,905	438,910

SOURCE: Carnegie Commission survey files and Office of Education data.

TABLE A-13 *Verification of weights, by type and quality*

	1966		1967		1968		1969	
	Estimated	*Actual*	*Estimated*	*Actual*	*Estimated*	*Actual*	*Estimated*	*Actual*
University								
High quality	61,051	61,051	62,154	62,154	63,839	63,839	66,137	66,137
Medium quality	149,104	149,104	141,191	141,191	145,626	145,626	160,875	160,875
Low quality	197,645	197,645	182,544	182,544	208,815	208,815	215,964	215,964
Four-year colleges								
High quality	47,265	47,265	50,065	50,065	54,031	54,031	54,632	54,632
Medium quality	149,027	149,027	153,919	153,919	163,285	163,285	171,295	171,295
Low quality	393,420	393,424	379,220	379,219	394,809	394,808	407,140	407,142
Junior colleges								
All quality	538,240	538,240	585,124	585,126	681,039	681,041	661,630	661,630

SOURCE: Carnegie Commission survey files and Office of Education data.

Faculty   Six items thought to represent possible bias were chosen for the follow-up sample.[12] These will be examined in some detail below. Of those drawn in the special faculty sample, 1,512 respondents completed the faculty questionnaire, 214 answered the brief list of questions asked in the telephone interview providing information comparable with that on the questionnaire, 128 faculty members refused to answer any questions; 87 could not be located; 59 individuals were not contacted because of a computer error, which showed that the questionnaire had been returned when in fact it had not.

We have, then, a response rate in this special sample of 76 percent to the whole questionnaire and of 86 percent to the six items asked both in the questionnaire and in the telephone interview. This is a conservative estimate of response rate in this special sample, since it is likely that at least some of the 87 who could not be located had in fact left their jobs, and were therefore no longer part of the population we were sampling.

By comparing the sample of 2,000, the sample that best represents the population, with the total sample, we can discover the differences, if any, between a sample with a return rate of 60 percent and a sample with a return rate of 86 percent. In the following discussion we will, for the most part, be comparing distributions of characteristics in a sample of the "achieved" sample with distributions in the special or "criterion" sample of 2,000.[13] Several weighted distributions on the entire "achieved" sample are presented below for comparison with a sample of the achieved sample and the criterion sample. Because of the expense of using the entire achieved sample, most of the distributions are presented for a random sample of 8,500 drawn from the total sample of 60,000.

The most complete respondent information is available for sex and quality of institution. For both variables we have information

---

[12]   The six items asked in the telephone interview were rank, kind of appointment (tenure), highest degree, date of birth, research or teaching as primary interest, and political identification. Information on institutional quality and the respondent's sex was obtained from independent sources.

[13]   The "criterion" sample includes 1,197 people who responded before the phone survey, 542 who responded after being phoned, and 214 who answered only the telephone interview. The "telephone" sample includes only the latter two categories, i.e., only the respondents in the nonrespondent sample. Except where otherwise indicated, tables are presented with the not-answered category excluded.

TABLE A-14 *Verification of weighting cells*

ACE 1966 cell	Enrollment	Public 1966 Estimated	Public 1966 Actual	Percent (estimated/actual)	Private 1966 Estimated	Private 1966 Actual	Percent (estimated/actual)
Public two-year colleges							
1	Low	225,985	225,985⎫	100			
2	·						
3	·		⎬				
4	·	248,521	248,521⎫	100			
5	High		⎭				
Private two-year colleges							
6	Low				63,734	63,734⎫	100
7	·						
8	·					⎬	
9	High					⎭	
	Affluence						
Universities							
10	Unknown						
11		16,509	22,247⎫	74	6,808	6,233	109
12	·		⎭		4,436	3,307	134
13	·	34,850	29,515	117	26,263	21,500	122
14	·	41,595	35,502	117	17,978	16,205	111
15	·	15,221	12,991	117	13,186	15,391⎫	86
16	·	98,394	86,379	114		⎭	
17	·	45,947	43,904	105	4,792	3,572	134
18	·	62,464	84,173⎫	74	19,624	26,964⎫	73
19	High		⎭			⎭	
Four-year colleges							
20	Unknown	104,855	77,217⎫	136	75,133	62,179⎫	121
21	Low		⎭			⎭	
22	·	103,696	106,939	97	47,015	46,003	102
23	·	39,595	56,425	70	64,125	63,213	101
24	·	47,943	52,263	92	34,023	36,858	92
25	·	7,544	8,540	88	17,639	21,560	82
26	·	11,758	13,960⎫	84	17,899	22,470	80
27	·				3,902	4,353	90
28	·		⎬		8,000	8,733	92
29	High		⎭		6,580	8,870	74
TOTAL		1,104,607	1,104,611	100	431,137	431,145	100

Public 1967		Percent (estimated/ actual)	Private 1967		Percent (estimated/ actual)
Estimated	Actual		Estimated	Actual	
252,447	252,447⎤	100			
269,206	269,206⎤	100			
			63,473	63,473⎤	100
15,547	20,863⎤	75	7,231	6,322	114
			3,838	2,893	133
27,265	23,660	115	24,790	20,583	120
42,112	36,544	115	16,192	13,975	116
14,321	12,428	115	13,624	15,106⎤	90
90,660	76,785	118			
45,072	44,213	102	4,463	3,364	133
59,923	80,407⎤	75	20,849	28,830⎤	72
107,394	78,731⎤	136	68,763	58,117⎤	118
99,375	106,064	94	45,758	44,667	102
42,085	57,627	72	62,450	62,396	100
48,221	51,536	94	33,335	35,140	95
7,807	8,802	84	17,861	21,153	84
13,177	15,299⎤	86	16,560	20,264	82
			3,902	4,369	89
			9,204	9,852	93
			7,310	9,102	80
1,134,612	1,134,612	100	419,603	419,606	100

ACE 1966 cell	Enrollment	Public 1968		Percent (estimated/ actual)	Private 1968		Percent (estimated/ actual)
		Estimated	Actual		Estimated	Actual	
Public two-year colleges							
1	Low	313,096	313,096⎤	100			
2	.		⎬				
3	.		⎦				
4	.	301,434	301,434⎤	100			
5	High		⎦				
Private two-year colleges							
6	Low				66,511⎤	66,511	100
7	.				⎬		
8	.				⎬		
9	High				⎦		
	Affluence						
Universities							
10	Unknown						
11	Low	20,639	26,801⎤	77	4,857	4,379	111
12	.		⎦		3,617	2,777	130
13	.	32,112	28,330	113	26,561	22,193	120
14	.	48,290	42,603	113	18,099	15,641	116
15	.	14,480	12,775	113	15,081	16,564⎤	91
16	.	89,244	75,512	118		⎦	
17	.	49,241	47,607	103	4,536	3,482	130
18	.	68,253	88,632⎤	77	23,267	31,062⎤	75
19	High		⎦			⎦	
Four-year colleges							
20	Unknown	120,116	85,407⎤	141	72,047	59,311⎤	121
21	Low		⎦			⎦	
22	.	98,279	113,104	87	46,630	46,145	101
23	.	43,429	59,888	73	60,123	60,705	99
24	.	57,089	58,108	98	34,456	36,417	95
25	.	10,750	11,203	96	17,722	21,343	83
26	.	14,698	16,648⎤	88	16,996	21,000	81
27	.		⎬		3,830	4,320	89
28	.		⎬		8,452	9,039	94
29	High		⎦		7,511	9,409	80
TOTAL		1,281,146	1,281,148	100	430,296	430,298	100

SOURCE: Carnegie Commission survey files and Office of Education/ACE data.

| Public 1969 | | Percent (estimated/ actual) | Private 1969 | | Percent (estimated/ actual) |
Estimated	Actual		Estimated	Actual	
337,239	337,239	100			
264,094	264,094	100			
			60,297	60,297	100
17,447	22,825	76	9,261	6,653	139
			3,839	2,758	139
32,021	27,825	115	31,514	22,690	139
58,874	51,160	115	11,596	15,545	75
			14,972	19,725	76
103,110	91,036	113			
55,627	51,915	107			
72,407	94,724	76	32,307	36,239	89
66,461	206,260	32	73,097	56,367	130
			45,294	45,839·	99
72,040	60,046	120	62,788	63,031	100
180,997	62,724	289	35,736	37,422	95
28,426	11,484	248	18,154	22,892	79
9,842	17,433	56	18,740	29,211	77
			3,616	4,468	81
			10,050	10,819	93
			7,646	10,004	70
1,298,762	1,298,765	100	438,409	438,410	100

from independent sources. As we can see in Table A-15A, the criterion sample does not differ on sex from the achieved sample; Table A-15B indicates that although medium-quality universities are very slightly overrepresented and faculty in junior colleges slightly underrepresented, the achieved sample is remarkably close to the criterion sample.

Distributions in Table A-16 indicate that there are no major differences between the achieved sample and the criterion sample on rank, appointment, and field of highest degree. The only real difference appears in the distribution of advanced degrees. The achieved sample slightly overrepresents faculty members with Ph.D.'s and underrepresents faculty members with master's and doctor of arts degrees. It does not appear, however, that the criterion sample includes more younger men working toward advanced degrees. It is more likely that this is a function of the slight underrepresentation of junior college faculty in the achieved sample.

One further difference emerges in the item on research and teaching interests. Table A-17 indicates a 5 percent difference between the achieved and criterion sample in the number of

TABLE A-15A
Distribution of sex in the achieved and criterion samples (faculty)*

Sex	Total achieved sample	Achieved sample	Criterion sample
Male	80.0%	80.0%	79.9%
Female	20.0	20.0	20.1
	100.0%	100.0%	100.0%
Unweighted N	58,884	8,329	1,901
All other	1,183	171	99
Unweighted total	60,028	8,500	2,000
Weighted total	446,203	61,117†	

*Tables A-15–A-21 are presented in weighted form; for an explanation of the weighting scheme used, refer to p. 315. The weights for the criterion samples were constructed from the institutional base weight excluding institutional nonresponse and correcting for quality and type of control. The weighted total would not be meaningful for this sample, and is therefore omitted.

† The weighted total presented here is approximately one-seventh of the projected population total of 466,203. This is a function of using a sample that is approximately one-seventh of the obtained N of 60,028 for the faculty.

SOURCE: Full sample: N = 60,028; random sample: N = 8,500; criterion sample: see footnote 13.

TABLE A-15B
Distribution of
quality in the
achieved and
criterion samples
(faculty)

Quality	Total achieved sample	Achieved sample	Criterion sample
Universities			
High quality	12.6%	12.5%	11.4%
Medium quality	18.1	18.1	15.6
Low quality	15.8	15.7	15.5
Colleges			
High quality	5.7	5.6	6.0
Medium quality	10.9	10.9	11.7
Low quality	22.4	22.3	23.6
Junior colleges	14.6	14.6	16.2
	100.1%	99.7%	100.0%
Unweighted N	60,028	8,500	2,000
All other	0	0	0
Unweighted total	60,028	8,500	2,000
Weighted total	446,203	61,117	

SOURCE: Same as Table A-15A.

TABLE A-16
Distribution of
selected
characteristics in
the achieved
sample and the
criterion sample
(faculty)

	Total achieved sample	Achieved sample	Criterion sample
A. Rank			
Professor	22.8%	23.5%	22.0%
Associate professor	21.0	20.7	18.6
Assistant professor	27.6	27.8	27.3
Instructor	19.2	18.3	19.7
Lecturer	2.9	2.8	3.2
No rank designated	3.9	4.3	5.9
Other	2.5	2.5	3.3
	99.9%	99.9%	100.0%
Unweighted N	59,836	8,478	1,718
All other	192	22	282
Unweighted total	60,028	8,500	2,000
Weighted total	446,203	61,177	

TABLE A-16 (continued)		*Achieved sample*	*Criterion sample*
B. Kind of appointment			
	Regular with tenure	50.7%	48.7%
	Regular without tenure	44.8	45.2
	Acting	2.0	2.0
	Visiting	2.6	4.5
		100.1%	100.4%
Unweighted N		8,429	1,694
All other		71	306
Unweighted total		8,500	2,000
Weighted total		61,177	
C. Field of highest degree			
	Business, commerce, and management	4.0%	5.6%
	Biological sciences	7.3	6.7
	Education	15.0	14.2
	Engineering	5.8	5.4
	Fine arts	8.3	8.9
	Old professions—medicine and law	4.3	4.7
	Humanities	21.7	20.7
	Physical science, mathematics, and statistics	13.4	12.5
	Psychology and social science	12.5	12.2
	New and semiprofessions	7.7	8.9
		100.0%	99.8%
Unweighted N		7,418	1,462
All other		1,082	538
Unweighted total		8,500	2,000
Weighted total		61,177	
D. Highest degree			
	Ph.D.	41.5%	37.2%
	First professional—medical degree (e.g., M.D., D.D.S.)	4.1	4.5

TABLE A-16
(continued)

	Achieved sample	Criterion sample
First professional— law degree	1.2	1.8
Ed.D.	4.5	3.0
Other doctorate	1.4	1.5
Doctorate of arts or equivalent	1.9	2.3
Other first professional—beyond undergraduate bachelor's	7.7	6.6
Master's	32.1	35.6
Undergraduate bachelor's	4.8	6.0
Less than bachelor's	.6	.8
None	.2	.7
	100.0%	100.0%
Unweighted N	8,106	1,656
All other	394	344
Unweighted total	8,500	2,000
Weighted total	61,177	
E. Date of birth		
1908 or before	7.1%	8.1%
1909–1913	6.4	7.2
1914–1918	9.0	9.8
1919–1923	13.0	12.8
1924–1928	14.9	16.3
1929–1933	16.9	15.0
1934–1938	17.3	16.1
1939–1943	12.6	13.3
1944 or later	2.7	1.4
	99.9%	100.0%
Unweighted N	8,353	1,692
All other	147	308
Unweighted total	8,500	2,000
Weighted total	61,177	

SOURCE: Section A: full sample: ($N = 60,028$); random sample: ($N = 8,500$); criterion sample; Sections B through E: random sample and criterion sample.

TABLE A-17		Achieved sample	Criterion sample
Faculty—interests primarily in research or teaching (in percentages)	*Very heavily in research*	4.1%	3.6%
	In both—but leaning toward research	20.4	19.6
	In both—but leaning toward teaching	33.7	30.5
	Very heavily in teaching	41.4	46.2
		99.6%	99.9%
	Unweighted N	8,231	1,621
	All other	269	379
	Unweighted total	8,500	2,000
	Weighted total	61,117	

SOURCE: Same as section B, Table A-16.

respondents whose primary interest is "very heavily in teaching." It appears that the achieved sample somewhat over-represents individuals interested in research or research and teaching. This difference appears also in universities and is not a function only of the lack of a research choice in colleges and junior colleges (Table A-18).

There are reasons to expect the nonresponse rate among the political left to be somewhat high. Research focused on political activism is frequently condemned in radical literature; research itself is often the target for much debate and sometimes

TABLE A-18		Achieved sample	Criterion sample
Faculty—percent heavily interested in teaching by quality of institution	*Universities*		
	High quality	15.5 (1,905)*	22.6 (414)*
	Medium quality	22.2 (2,181)	23.8 (446)
	Low quality	31.7 (2,114)	38.2 (415)
	Colleges		
	High quality	32.5 (647)	36.9 (127)
	Medium quality	45.4 (728)	55.8 (126)
	Low quality	53.5 (632)	54.3 (128)
	Junior colleges	73.9 (293)	75.1 (62)
	All institutions	41.4 (8,500)	46.2 (1,718)

*Unweighted N: for weighted total see Tables A-20A and A-20B.
SOURCE: Same as section B, Table A-16.

TABLE A-19
Political self-
identification
(faculty)

	Achieved sample	*Criterion sample*
Left	4.8%	5.2%
Liberal	39.0	39.5
Middle of the road	26.3	25.7
Moderately conservative	24.4	20.8
Strongly conservative	2.5	2.6
Not answered (includes category "No answer" in mail questionnaire, and refusal to answer in telephone interview)	3.1	5.6
	100.1%	99.4%
Unweighted N	8,299	1,704
All other	201	296
Unweighted total	8,500	2,000
Weighted total	61,177	

SOURCE: Same as section B, Table A-16.

demonstration. Table A-19 indicates that there is little difference between the achieved sample and the criterion sample. The "not answered" category for both samples is slightly larger than in many attitudinal questions in the achieved sample. The number is too small to analyze in detail, but some preliminary tables indicate that respondents who refused to answer or who did not answer do not cluster in any particular age, department, or rank categories.

The similarity of the two samples holds up equally well if we turn from marginal to bivariate tabulations. Although there are some differences in particular cells, the distributions are quite similar. Tables A-20A and A-20B compare rank within categories of quality for the achieved and the criterion sample. Tables A-21A and A-21B compare age for both samples. The minor discrepancies in the joint distributions, e.g., the differences between the proportion holding the rank of professor in the achieved (34 percent) and the criterion (30 percent) sample, may be real deviations, or they may be a function of the small Ns in the criterion sample. The fit is close enough in both distributions to give us the same picture.

There is no apparent difference between the two samples

TABLE A-20A *Faculty rank, by quality of institution; achieved sample*

	Quality level							Total
	I	*II*	*III*	*IV*	*V*	*VI*	*VII*	
Professor	33.9%	30.0%	24.5%	28.0%	20.8%	23.2%	6.5%	23.5%
Associate professor	19.7	24.7	25.4	23.9	22.3	20.6	8.3	20.7
Assistant professor	25.3	31.0	30.0	32.0	31.8	27.6	18.8	27.8
Instructor	8.7	9.0	16.4	10.4	19.8	24.5	33.2	18.3
Lecturer	6.6	3.5	1.7	2.4	2.4	1.8	1.9	2.8
No rank	0.5	0.3	0.2	0.3	1.1	0.9	26.9	4.3
Other	5.3	1.5	1.8	2.9	1.8	1.5	4.4	2.5
	100.0%	100.0%	100.0%	99.9%	100.0%	100.1%	100.0%	99.9%
Unweighted N	1,901	2,175	2,109	646	724	630	293	8,478
All other	4	6	5	1	4	2	0	22
Unweighted total	1,905	2,181	2,114	647	728	632	293	8,500
Weighted total	7,614	11,379	10,492	3,590	7,536	13,444	9,031	63,087

SOURCE: Random sample.

TABLE A-20B *Faculty rank, by quality of institution; criterion sample*

	Quality level							Total
	I	*II*	*III*	*IV*	*V*	*VI*	*VII*	
Professor	29.7%	33.4%	25.1%	24.4%	16.7%	20.3%	4.8%	26.6%
Associate professor	21.0	22.9	20.7	18.9	21.4	20.3	11.3	20.9
Assistant professor	26.3	25.6	33.7	29.9	37.3	32.8	4.8	28.7
Instructor	10.1	12.6	16.9	15.0	19.8	16.4	41.9	15.1
Lecturer	7.2	2.7	1.4	6.3	1.6	5.5	0.0	3.8
No rank	1.0	.4	.2	1.6	1.6	1.6	29.0	1.8
Other	4.6	2.5	1.9	3.9	1.6	3.1	8.1	3.1
	99.9%	100.1%	99.9%	100.0%	100.0%	100.0%	99.9%	100.0%
Unweighted N	414	446	415	127	126	128	62	1,718
All other	99	74	51	18	16	14	10	282
Unweighted total	513	520	466	145	142	142	72	2,000

SOURCE: Criterion sample.

TABLE A-21A *Faculty date of birth, by quality of institution; achieved sample*

	Quality level							
	I	II	III	IV	V	VI	VII	Total
1908 and before	7.1%	7.7%	7.4%	6.1%	5.6%	9.0%	4.8%	7.1%
1909–13	7.7	5.8	6.2	6.0	7.6	6.8	5.2	6.4
1914–18	8.9	9.3	8.0	10.8	7.6	10.4	8.5	9.0
1919–23	11.2	13.1	12.2	10.0	11.2	14.2	16.2	13.0
1924–28	15.2	16.1	15.9	15.2	13.0	13.3	15.6	14.9
1929–33	17.9	16.6	18.3	19.6	18.0	16.0	14.5	16.9
1934–38	19.3	18.1	16.1	16.9	18.8	15.8	17.3	17.3
1939–43	10.1	12.6	13.7	14.3	15.0	10.2	14.3	12.6
1944 and after	2.6	.8	2.1	1.0	3.1	4.5	3.6	2.7
	100.0%	100.1%	99.9%	99.9%	100.0%	100.2%	100.0%	99.9%
Unweighted N	1,876	2,142	2,076	632	719	622	286	8,353
All other	29	39	38	15	9	10	7	147
Unweighted total	1,905	2,181	2,114	647	728	632	293	8,500
Weighted total	7,614	11,379	10,492	3,590	7,536	13,444	9,031	63,087

SOURCE: Random sample.

TABLE 21B *Faculty date of birth, by quality of institution; criterion sample*

	Quality level							
	I	II	III	IV	V	VI	VII	Total
1908 and before	7.6%	8.3%	6.7%	6.3%	7.1%	8.2%	10.0%	7.6%
1909–1913	5.6	9.0	7.2	4.8	6.3	13.1	13.3	8.5
1914–1918	8.1	8.8	6.4	9.5	7.9	13.1	13.3	8.5
1919–1923	12.7	12.8	14.6	11.1	13.4	9.0	18.3	13.1
1924–1928	14.2	15.8	14.6	19.0	18.9	13.9	20.0	15.6
1929–1933	18.9	15.3	16.0	7.9	13.4	14.8	11.7	15.5
1934–1938	17.9	17.6	18.5	19.0	18.9	10.7	11.7	17.4
1939–1943	11.8	11.7	14.6	20.6	14.2	16.4	10.0	13.5
1944 and after	3.2	.7	1.5	1.6	0.0	.8	1.7	1.5
	100.0%	100.0%	100.1%	99.8%	100.1%	100.0%	100.0%	100.0%
Unweighted N	408	444	405	126	127	122	60	1,692
All other	105	76	61	19	15	20	12	308
Unweighted total	513	520	466	145	142	142	72	2,000

SOURCE: Criterion sample.

that might indicate that the respondents to the faculty survey are significantly different from the nonrespondents. We conclude that the 60 percent (achieved) sample adequately represents the total population.

Graduates Of the 2,037 graduate students drawn in the special sample, 1,580 respondents completed the questionnaire, 190 answered the brief list of questions asked in the telephone interview, 128 refused to answer any questions, and 139 could not be located.

For the graduate special or criterion sample we have a response rate of 78 percent to the whole questionnaire and of 87 percent to the six items[14] asked both in the questionnaire and the telephone interview. This is, again, a conservative estimate, since some of the 139 students who could not be located had undoubtedly left academic life.

By comparing the distributions of characteristics of the achieved and criterion[15] samples, we can determine whether the achieved sample, with a response rate of 64 percent, is in fact representative of the population from which it is drawn.

The most complete respondent information is available for quality of the respondent's institution and sex. Tables A-22A and A-22B give the distributions for both samples. The distributions for both variables in the two samples are quite close. Table A-22A indicates that the achieved graduate sample somewhat underrepresents medium-quality universities and overrepresents low-quality colleges. Few graduate students are located in low-quality colleges. The largest number of graduate students are located in medium-quality universities; thus there is no serious bias in underrepresenting this category, given, as we shall see below, that the criterion and the achieved samples appear quite similar on all other variables.

The distributions of "year entered graduate school," "highest

[14] The six items asked in the telephone interview were as follows: year entered graduate school, highest degree working for, department, when degree expected, political identification and employment. Information on institutional quality and the respondent's sex was obtained from independent sources.

[15] Several weighted distributions on the entire achieved sample are presented below. Because of the cost involved in using full samples the remaining distributions are presented for a sample of 8,500 of the achieved sample. These are compared with the criterion sample. The criterion sample includes all 2,037 of the graduate students chosen for the special sample.

TABLE A-22A
*Distribution of quality in the achieved and criterion samples; graduates**

Quality of institution	Total achieved sample	Achieved sample	Criterion sample
Universities			
High quality	17.1	16.6	16.9
Medium quality	25.7	24.8	29.6
Low quality	22.1	22.2	23.5
Colleges			
High quality	6.0	6.0	5.3
Medium quality	12.0	11.7	10.7
Low quality	17.1	18.6	13.9
	100.0	99.9	99.9
Unweighted N	32,964	8,500	2,037
All other	0	0	0
Unweighted total	32,964	8,500	2,037
Weighted total	1,005,834	264,017[†]	

*Tables are presented in weighted form; for an explanation of the weighting scheme used, refer to p. 315. The weights for the criterion sample are constructed from the institutional base weight, excluding institutional nonresponse and correcting for quality and control. Weighted totals are not given for this sample (see above, Table A-15 note).

[†] The weighted total presented here is approximately a quarter of the projected population total of 1,005,834.

SOURCE: Full sample (*N* = 32,964); random sample (*N* = 8,500); criterion sample (see above, pp. 329, 348).

TABLE A-22B
Distribution of sex in the achieved and criterion samples; graduates

Sex	Total achieved sample	Achieved sample	Criterion sample
Male	68.8%	71.2%	69.3%
Female	31.2	28.8	30.5
	100.0%	100.0%	100.0%
Unweighted N	32,818	8,462	2,030
All other	145	38	7
Unweighted total	32,964	8,500	2,037
Weighted total	1,005,834	264,017	

SOURCE: Same as Table A-22A.

In what year did you first enter graduate school?	Achieved sample	Criterion sample
1955 or before	3.4%	5.2%
1956–1957	1.7	2.6
1958–1959	2.3	2.6
1960–1961	3.7	4.8
1962–1963	7.9	7.7
1964	7.6	6.0
1965	9.4	9.8
1966	13.1	13.4
1967	22.4 ⎱ 50.9	17.5 ⎱ 47.5
1968–1969	28.5 ⎰	30.0 ⎰
	100.0%	99.6%
Unweighted N	8,188	1,692
All other	312	345
Unweighted total	8,500	2,037
Weighted total	264,017	

SOURCE: Random sample and criterion sample.

degree working for," "when degree expected," and "department" are given in Tables A-23A to A-23D. There appear to be some minor differences between the two samples. Of the achieved sample, 51 percent entered graduate school between 1967 and 1969; 48 percent of the criterion sample entered in these years. Of the achieved sample, 55 percent are working for master's degrees as opposed to 51 percent in the criterion sample. Of the graduate students in the achieved sample, 39 percent expect their degree "this" (1969) year; 34 percent of those in the criterion sample expect their degree "this" year. The achieved sample, then, slightly undersamples long-term Ph.D. students. There do not appear to be any differences by field (Table A-23D).

Graduate students were also asked about their employment status. Table A-24 indicates that there are only minor differences between the two samples on this variable. As with the faculty samples, we anticipated the possibility of bias on political characterization. Again, the two distributions are virtually identical

(Table A-25). The distributions are also quite similar when quality is introduced (Table A-26). There are minor differences in particular cells, but the relationship in both samples is the same. For both the criterion and the achieved samples the proportion of left and liberal graduate students decreases as the quality of the institution decreases. The one substantial difference appears in the number of left graduate students in high-quality colleges. The discrepancy between the two samples is, no doubt, a function of the small N in the criterion sample. (The unweighted N for this cell is 6.)

The distributions of age by quality of institution are given in Table A-27. There are, again, minor differences, probably owing to the small N in the criterion sample. Overall, the distributions tell the same story. In general, we see that older students are slightly more likely to be found in lower-quality colleges but that the age distributions are quite similar regardless of quality.

TABLE A-23B
Distribution of selected characteristics in the achieved sample and the criterion sample; graduates

Highest degree working for	Achieved sample	Criterion sample
Ph.D.	22.6%	24.7%
First professional—medical	4.7	5.0
First professional—law	5.3	5.0
Ed.D.	2.2	2.0
Other doctorate	.5	.3
Doctorate of arts	.9	1.1
Other first professional	6.1	5.8
M.A.T.	3.8 }54.7	1.8 }50.6
M.A.	50.9	48.8
B.A.	—	.7
Less than B.A.	—	—
None	3.1	4.7
	100.1%	99.9%
Unweighted N	7,785	1,609
All other	715	428
Unweighted total	8,500	2,037
Weighted total	264,017	

SOURCE: Random sample and criterion sample.

TABLE A-23C
Distributions of selected characteristics in sample and the criterion sample; graduates

When do you expect to get the degree you are now working for?	Achieved sample		Criterion sample	
This year	39.1%	} 74.5	33.6%	} 68.2
Within two years	35.4		34.6	
Within three years	12.5		13.6	
Within four years	5.2		5.5	
Within five years	3.5		4.3	
Six or more years	1.7		2.9	
Don't expect to get	2.6		5.4	
	100.0%		99.9%	
Unweighted N	8,136		1,676	
All other	364		361	
Unweighted total	8,500		2,037	
Weighted total	264,017			

SOURCE: Random sample and criterion sample.

TABLE A-23D
Distributions of selected characteristics in the achieved sample and the criterion sample; graduates

Department in which you are studying	Achieved sample	Criterion sample
Business, commerce, management	8.8%	8.5%
Biological sciences	4.9	4.5
Education	22.3	22.7
Engineering	9.8	9.5
Fine arts	3.6	3.2
Medicine and law	8.2	8.4
Humanities	12.5	12.4
Physical sciences, math, statistics	11.1	9.6
Social sciences, psychology	9.0	9.6
New and semiprofessions	10.0	12.0
	100.2%	100.4%
Unweighted N	7,965	1,642
All other	535	385
Unweighted total	8,500	2,037
Weighted total	264,017	

SOURCE: Random sample and criterion sample.

TABLE A-24
Employment status in the achieved and criterion sample; graduates

Are you now employed for a term or more while a graduate student as a:	Achieved sample	Criterion sample
Part-time research assistant	8.3%⎫ 11.6	10.9%*
Full-time research assistant	3.3 ⎭	
Part-time teaching assistant	11.3 ⎫ 15.4	13.7
Full-time teaching assistant	4.1 ⎭	
Faculty position	4.9	5.2
Other academic position	8.4	7.2
None of these	59.8	62.9
	100.1%	99.9%
Unweighted N	6,977	1,451
All other	1,523	586
Unweighted total	8,500	2,037
Weighted total	264,017	

*The telephone respondents were not asked whether the position held was part- or full-time.

SOURCE: Random sample and criterion sample.

TABLE A-25
Political self-identification; graduates

	Achieved sample	Criterion sample
Left	5.8%	5.8%
Liberal	37.2	37.7
Middle of the road	27.7	27.1
Moderately conservative	25.5	25.8
Strongly conservative	3.9	3.7
	100.1%	100.1%
Unweighted N	8,350	1,707
All other	150	330
Unweighted total	8,500	2,037
Weighted total	264,017	

SOURCE: Random sample and criterion sample

TABLE A-26A *Political identification, by quality of institution (achieved sample): graduates*

Politics	Quality level and type						Total
	Universities			Colleges			
	High	Medium	Low	High	Medium	Low	
Left	12.1%	6.1%	4.1%	7.5%	1.1%	4.3%	5.8%
Liberal	48.4	40.7	35.3	35.0	33.1	28.1	37.2
Middle of the road	21.7	27.0	27.9	28.2	32.3	30.6	27.7
Moderately conservative	16.4	23.3	28.6	28.5	27.8	30.3	25.5
Strongly conservative	1.5	2.9	4.2	.8	5.7	6.7	3.9
	100.1%	100.0%	100.1%	100.0%	100.0%	100.0%	100.1%
Unweighted N	2,529	2,786	2,162	412	282	178	8,349
All other	42	46	42	11	7	3	151
Unweighted total	2,571	2,832	2,204	423	289	181	8,500
Weighted total	43,944	65,522	58,712	15,972	30,774	49,064	264,017

SOURCE: Random sample.

For graduate students as well as faculty we are confident that, with the minor exceptions indicated, the achieved samples represent the population from which they are drawn. We can also say that the differences between nonrespondents and respondents are not significant in ways that would be revealed by any substantial differences between the criterion and achieved samples.

Undergraduates A total of 70,694 questionnaires were returned in usable form out of 171,520 mailed on December 20, 1969. This represents a response rate of 41.2 percent. The only addresses available were parents' addresses, which, in many instances, were out of date. Parents were depended on to forward questionnaires to students who were not home for the Christmas break. No attempts were made to follow up nonrespondents.

A random sample of 10 percent of the entire sample of undergraduates to whom questionnaires were mailed was drawn for the nonresponse analysis. Our purpose here is to compare this criterion sample (which includes respondents and nonrespondents) with a sample of 20,000 respondents to see what differences, if any, exist between the two samples owing to the

TABLE A-26B *Political identification, by quality of institution (criterion sample): graduates*

	Quality level and type						
	Universities			Colleges			
Politics	High	Medium	Low	High	Medium	Low	Total
Left	15.1%	6.3%	5.0%	2.3%	1.0%	0.0%	8.2%
Liberal	45.7	41.3	34.6	39.7	37.7	24.4	39.5
Middle of the road	22.3	25.8	27.4	35.1	31.3	28.6	25.8
Moderately conservative	15.4	23.6	29.1	20.6	23.5	42.1	23.4
Strongly conservative	1.7	3.2	3.9	2.3	6.4	4.9	3.0
	100.2%	100.2%	100.0%	100.0%	99.9%	100.0%	99.9%
Unweighted N	510	593	441	91	54	42	1,731
All other	91	100	78	14	11	12	306
Unweighted total	601	693	519	105	65	54	2,037

SOURCE: Criterion sample.

TABLE A-27A *Age, by quality of institution (achieved sample): graduates*

	Quality level and type						
	Universities			Colleges			
Age	High	Medium	Low	High	Medium	Low	Total
21 or younger	2.4%	1.3%	0.6%	2.8%	0.2%	0.0%	1.0%
22	11.7	8.7	7.4	9.0	5.6	1.6	7.3
23	13.1	11.1	9.8	12.3	10.8	5.2	10.1
24	12.7	11.1	9.6	9.4	11.3	5.4	9.9
25	12.2	11.1	8.9	8.7	6.7	8.0	9.5
26–27	16.1	17.0	15.7	15.7	14.3	10.2	14.9
28–29	10.0	9.7	11.4	6.5	9.6	9.9	10.0
30–34	10.0	13.4	17.0	20.3	13.8	26.1	16.5
35–39	5.7	7.6	8.0	5.6	9.3	9.5	7.8
40 or older	6.2	9.0	11.8	9.7	18.4	24.1	13.1
	100.1%	100.0%	100.2%	100.0%	100.0%	100.0%	100.1%
Unweighted N	2,554	2,806	2,184	418	286	181	8,429
All other	17	26	20	5	3	0	71
Unweighted total	2,571	2,836	2,204	423	289	181	8,500
Weighted total	43,944	65,552	58,712	15,972	30,774	49,064	264,017

SOURCE: Random sample.

TABLE A-27B *Age, by quality of institution (criterion sample): graduates*

| | Quality level and type | | | | | | |
| | Universities | | | Colleges | | | |
	High	Medium	Low	High	Medium	Low	Total
21 or younger	1.9%	1.1%	0.4%	0.8%	1.2%	0.0%	0.9%
22	10.4	8.0	7.1	7.2	19.4	6.0	9.1
23	13.1	11.3	8.3	7.5	4.2	2.0	8.7
24	12.2	11.2	10.2	18.9	6.2	1.8	9.8
25	10.3	11.8	9.5	7.2	9.5	8.3	10.0
26–27	17.6	15.8	16.6	11.3	5.0	7.6	13.8
28–29	9.1	10.7	12.3	13.2	9.5	12.6	11.1
30–34	13.4	12.8	15.6	7.2	12.3	19.2	13.8
35–39	6.7	7.3	7.7	10.6	8.5	13.1	8.6
40 or older	5.3	10.0	12.4	16.2	24.2	29.6	14.2
	100.0%	100.0%	100.1%	100.1%	100.0%	100.2%	100.0%
Unweighted N	516	598	445	91	57	40	1,747
All other	85	95	74	14	8	14	290
Unweighted total	601	693	519	105	65	54	2,037

SOURCE: Criterion sample.

low rate of response. Because the entire sample responded to an ACE questionnaire in their freshman year, considerable data are available on all nonrespondents. By comparing the 10 percent criterion sample—the sample which best represents the population—with a random sample of the respondent questionnaires, we can determine the differences between the achieved sample and what would have been obtained if all sampled individuals had returned the questionnaires.

Table A-28 shows the number of questionnaires sent out by year of college entrance and the response rate for each cohort. The effect of having older addresses and a higher drop-out rate for the older cohorts is a lower response rate among seniors than among freshmen.

Tables A-29 to A-35 are presented in weighted form (for an explanation of the weighting scheme used for the undergraduate data, refer to p. 323). The weights for the achieved sample were constructed in the same manner as the final respondent weights

	1966 (seniors)	1967 (juniors)	1968 (sophomores)	1969 (freshmen)	Total
Number of questionnaires sent out	50,158	48,610	40,217	32,535	171,520*
Number undeliverable	3,756	2,545	1,992	1,103	9,396
Number returned	19,190	18,909	17,611	14,984	70,694*
Response rate	38.3	38.9	43.8	46.1	41.2*

*These figures include only those students included in the Carnegie study of under-graduates. ACE augmented the study with some additional students, which accounts for any differences in totals that may be published by ACE.

SOURCE: Carnegie Commission survey files.

excluding, of course, the institutional nonresponse factor. The weights for the criterion sample were constructed from the strata weight, correcting for quality and control. All the variables are presented in the following format: variable (e.g., father's education) for the criterion sample; variable for the respondent or achieved sample (currently and not currently enrolled students); variable for currently enrolled respondents; variable for respondents not currently enrolled.[16] Because of slight differences in the weights for the achieved and criterion samples and rounding error in the computation of the percentages for weighted tables, differences of up to two percentage points should be anticipated between categories of variables in the criterion and in the achieved samples. This poses no analytic problems, but it does pose a descriptive problem when considering a variable in which a significant category, such as the percentage of black undergraduates, is extremely small to begin with. Users are cautioned, therefore, to consider this when using the data descriptively.

Most studies of nonresponse bias have found that nonresponse is associated with lower social class and its correlates, such as nonwhite race and attendance at low-quality schools. Here we are not solely concerned with the differences between respondents and nonrespondents. Instead the focus is on the differences between a sample in which all the nonrespondents

---

[16] We refer, here, to currently and not currently enrolled entrants as "students," although those who are not currently enrolled are either temporarily or permanently not students.

TABLE A-29A
Socioeconomic status of undergraduates: father's educational attainment (in percentages)

	Criterion sample	Achieved sample	CE respondents	NCE respondents
1–3 years high school or less	25	22	22	28
High school graduate	29	28	28	29
1–3 years college	19	20	20	21
B.A. or postgraduate degree	27	29	30	22
	100	99	100	100

TABLE A-29B
Socioeconomic status of undergraduates: mother's educational attainment (in percentages)

	Criterion sample	Achieved sample	CE respondents	NCE respondents
1–3 years high school or less	18	16	16	20
High school graduate	44	43	43	44
1–3 years college	20	21	21	22
B.A. or postgraduate degree	18	19	20	15
	100	99	100	101

TABLE A-29C
Socioeconomic status of undergraduates: total family income (in percentages)

	Criterion sample	Achieved sample	CE respondents	NCE respondents
Less than $6,000	16 } 33	15 } 30	14 } 29	19 } 36
$6,000–$7,999	17	15	15	17
$8,000–$9,999	16	17	16	18
$10,000–$14,999	26	29	29	27
$15,000–$19,999	12	11	12	8
$20,000 and over	14	14	15	12
	101	101	101	101

TABLE A-30
Undergraduates,
by race (in
percentages)

Criterion sample

White	91

Nonwhite:

Blacks	49 ⎫	
Oriental	8 ⎬ 9	
Other (including Native American)	43 ⎭	
	100

Achieved sample

White	93

Nonwhite:

Blacks	44 ⎫	
Oriental	6 ⎬ 7	
Other (including Native American)	50 ⎭	
	100

Currently enrolled respondents

White	93

Nonwhite:

Blacks	43 ⎫	
Oriental	7 ⎬ 7	
Other (including Native American)	50 ⎭	
	100

Not currently enrolled respondents

White	93

Nonwhite:

Blacks	50 ⎫	
Oriental	10 ⎬ 7	
Other (including Native American)	39 ⎭	
	100

TABLE A-31
Undergraduates,
by sex (in
percentages)

	Criterion sample	Achieved sample	CE respondents	NCE respondents
Male	57	51	52	48
Female	43	49	48	52
	100	100	100	100

TABLE A-32
Undergraduates:
quality of
entering
institution (in
percentages)

	Criterion sample	Achieved sample	CE respondents	NCE respondents
High-quality universities	4	5	6	2
Medium-quality universities	9	10	11	7
Low-quality universities	12	14	14	12
High-quality colleges	3	4	4	1
Medium-quality colleges	10	12	12	8
Low-quality colleges	24	26	27	23
Junior colleges	38	28	26	47
	100	99	100	100

TABLE A-33A
High school
grade-point
average of
undergraduates
(in percentages)

High school grade-point average	Criterion sample	Achieved sample	CE respondents	NCE respondents
B+ or above	28	38	39	22
B	22	25	25	25
C+, B−	33	27	27	33
C	15	9	8	18
Below C	1	—	—	1
	99	99	99	99

TABLE A-33B
Degree goals of
undergraduates
(in percentages)

Highest degree intend to obtain	Criterion sample	Achieved sample	CE respondents	NCE respondents
None or A.A.	13 } 49	8 } 43	6 } 41	20 } 58
B.A.	36	35	35	38
M.A.	33	35	36	26
Ph.D. or Ed.D.	10	12	13	8
M.D., D.D.S., D.V.M.	4	6	6	4
LL.B. or J.D.	1	—	2	1
Other	3	2	2	3
	100	98	100	100

TABLE A-34 Undergraduates: control of institution: public or private (in percentages)	Control	Criterion sample	Achieved sample	CE respondents	NCE respondents
	Public	74	70	69	76
	Private	26	30	31	24
		100	100	100	100

TABLE A-35 Undergraduates' intended major field (in percentages)		Criterion sample	Achieved sample
	Agriculture	2	2
	Biology	3	4
	Business	16	11
	Education	10	12
	Engineering	10	9
	English	3	4
	Health	4	6
	History	6	7
	Humanities	4	4
	Fine arts	8	7
	Mathematics	3	5
	Physical sciences	2	3
	Preprofessional (L.L.B., M.D., D.V.M.)	7	8
	Social sciences	8	9
	Technical	3	2
	Nontechnical	3	3
	Undeclared	7	6
		99	102

are included and one in which they are not. In the analysis that follows we shall try to answer the following questions: What are the differences between the achieved sample (with a 40 percent response rate) and the criterion sample (with a 100 percent response rate)? To what degree are demographic variables responsible for these differences? And to what degree are variables associated with the academic careers of undergraduate

TABLE A-36A
Undergraduates: final weighted distribution—quality of entering institution (criterion and achieved samples) (in percentages)

Quality	Criterion sample	Achieved sample
High-quality universities	4	4
Medium-quality universities	9	9
Low-quality universities	12	12
High-quality colleges	3	3
Medium-quality colleges	10	10
Low-quality colleges	24	24
Junior colleges	38	38
	100	100
Weighted total	(6,513,516)	(6,537,869)

TABLE A-36B
Undergraduates: final weighted distribution—high school grade-point average (criterion and achieved samples) (in percentages)

	Criterion sample	Achieved sample
B+ or above	28	33
B	22	24
C+, B−	33	31
C	15	11
Below C	1	—
	99	99
Weighted total	(6,513,516)	(6,537,869)

TABLE A-36C
Undergraduates: final weighted distribution—sex (criterion and achieved samples) (in percentages)

	Criterion sample	Achieved sample
Male	57	53
Female	43	47
	100	100
Weighted total	(6,513,516)	(6,537,869)

students the cause of differences in response rates among particular subsets of the population? For the latter analysis we will look at quality of the institution entered as a freshman, high school grade-point average (GPA), intended major, and academic aspirations.

In the undergraduate study the largest potential source of bias is due to the low response rate among individuals who are not currently enrolled in college. The undergraduate sample is a sample of entrants to the nearly 200 institutions over a four-year period. The weighted projections are to the universe of entrants in the four-year period. Twelve percent of the achieved sample is made up of students who are not currently enrolled in college. Based on population projections and studies of attrition, we estimate that 30 percent to 35 percent of the criterion sample were no longer enrolled in college at the time the survey was conducted.[17] Using these estimates of attrition, the response rate among currently enrolled students would be approximately 52 percent; among students not currently enrolled it would be approximately 17 percent.

As we shall see, respondents who are not currently enrolled (NCE) differ considerably from currently enrolled (CE) students. NCE respondents are in lower-quality institutions; they are from families with lower socioeconomic status; and as entrants they had lower high school grades and lower academic aspirations than CE students. We would anticipate differences, then, between the criterion sample with many NCE nonrespondents and the achieved sample with fewer NCE respondents.

Because such a large component of nonresponse to this study (but by no means the only component) was probably due to enrollment status, we can infer certain important characteristics associated with attrition from the analysis of nonresponse. We can also identify here the kinds of students and institutions from which a low response rate can be expected in similar research.

As has been shown elsewhere, the most substantial impact of socioeconomic status on college attendance occurs prior to college entrance. Thus, relatively small differences between the criterion and achieved sample were found on most of the demographic variables related to SES and selected for nonresponse analysis. As Tables A-29A and A-29B indicate, there are small differences in parents' educational attainment between the criterion and achieved sample. The same is true for parents' income (Table A-29C). There are, as we can see, more substantial differences between the currently enrolled and not currently

---

[17] In a study of attrition among undergraduates, Astin and Panos (1968) report that "65 percent of the students in the population (of entrants from 1961) had completed four or more years of college at the time of the study (1965)." In the same study 44 percent reported that they had changed college or dropped out for some period since entering their first college.

enrolled respondents. Of the NCE respondents, 36 percent report total parents' income of less than $7,999; 29 percent of the currently enrolled report this income. These data suggest that nonrespondents and not currently enrolled respondents come from families with somewhat lower socioeconomic status than currently enrolled respondents but that these differences are reflected in rather small differences between the criterion and achieved sample.

As Table A-30 indicates, nonwhites make up a slightly larger proportion of the criterion than of the achieved sample. There is, however, no evidence that nonwhite students are *significantly* less likely than whites to respond. The criterion sample has 9 percent nonwhite entrants compared with 7 percent of the achieved sample. Because the percentage of nonwhite students is quite small, it is difficult to determine response rates for the various nonwhite groups. Table A-30 indicates that half of the not currently enrolled nonwhite respondents are black compared with 43 percent of the currently enrolled nonwhite respondents. This suggests that the achieved sample with a smaller proportion of NCE respondents may underrepresent blacks.

There is little evidence that women leave college more often than men.[18] Therefore, we would expect any difference between the achieved and criterion sample on this variable to be primarily a function of differential response rates among men and women. Table A-31 indicates that 57 percent of the criterion sample are men compared with 51 percent of the achieved sample. The underrepresentation of men among both CE and NCE suggests that independent of enrollment status men were less likely to respond to the questionnaire. Although there are no baseline statistics for students not currently enrolled, census figures indicate that 60 percent of currently enrolled undergraduates are men.

Attrition and nonresponse are both highly correlated with the quality of the institution, preparation for academic life (measured by high school grades), and academic aspirations. Of the criterion sample, 38 percent entered junior colleges compared with 28 percent of the achieved sample (see Table A-32). As we can see here, nearly half of the NCE respondents and only 24 percent of the CE respondents entered junior college as freshmen.

---

[18] Astin and Panos (1968) report no significant correlation between sex and attrition.

Both achievement in secondary school and level of aspiration affect the decision-making process leading to the choice of a college. Junior college students, overall, have lower grades and lower aspirations. Having less commitment to and preparation for the academic enterprise, they are more likely to leave college. Table A-33A and A-33B indicate substantial differences between the currently enrolled and not currently enrolled respondents in the proportion entering college with a B+ or better GPA and aspiring to no higher than a B.A. degree. These large differences are reflected in smaller, but significant, differences between the criterion and achieved sample. These data suggest that marginal students in lower-quality institutions are underrepresented in the achieved sample. The data are consistent with our inference that a substantial proportion of our nonrespondents and, therefore, of the criterion sample are no longer attending college.

There is a small, but significant, difference between the achieved and criterion sample on institutional control (see Table A-34). Of the criterion sample, 74 percent entered a public institution compared with 70 percent of the achieved sample. This is largely because the junior colleges in the sample are predominately public institutions and, as noted, a large proportion of the not currently enrolled entered junior colleges.

As shown in Table A-35, overall there are only small differences in intended major field for the criterion and achieved samples. The achieved sample underrepresents business majors, in particular. This, no doubt, is a function of the underrepresentation both of men and of junior college students. Among both groups a significant proportion are men. Corresponingly, the achieved sample slightly overrepresents education majors, a field made up predominantly of women.

It is important, at this point, to keep in mind that differences on *related* variables (nonrandom differences) between a criterion and achieved sample occur only in the case where a distinct subset of the population (in this case NCE students or men) is coincident with the subset of nonrespondents *and* where both subsets are large. The largest differences, therefore, occur on variables related to academic performance (a strong predictor of persistence in college and therefore of nonresponse) and sex (a strong predictor of nonresponse but not persistence). Thus, very small differences between respondents and nonrespondents will not be apparent using this method of analysis, nor are those differences likely to affect analysis of the data.

An 18 percent difference between CE and NCE respondents in the proportion of students with GPA of B+ or better is reflected in only a 10 percent difference between the achieved and criterion sample. This is the largest difference between the two samples among the variables examined here. If the quality of the entering institution is controlled, even these differences are greatly minimized. Referring back to Table A-32, we find that only 2 percent of the NCE respondents entered high-quality universities, whereas 47 percent entered junior colleges. Institutional quality, level of aspiration, and preparation for academic life appear to play a larger role than demographic variables in determining attrition, and, therefore, nonresponse.

The final weighting procedures for the achieved sample include a component to compensate for response bias. Because of different intercohort response rates, each cohort within an institution was weighted separately. Tables 36 A, B, and C indicate the final weighted distributions on institutional quality, high school grade-point average, and sex for the criterion and achieved samples. The final weights underrepresent men and poorly prepared students by less than 5 percent. On measures of SES (not shown) the differences between the criterion and achieved samples for any given category are less than 2 percent.

Our conclusion is that, at least on those variables that we have available, the weighted achieved sample of undergraduates represents the population from which it was drawn, with the exceptions noted, and that the magnitude of difference between the two samples is quite small.

QUALITY RANKING OF INSTITUTIONS Institutional quality has proven to be an important control variable. The initial marginals and many later cross-tabulations have used institutional quality as a stratifying variable.

The colleges and universities in the sample have been classified on the basis of quality into seven groups: three groups of universities, three groups of four-year colleges, and all junior colleges.

Institutional Type Our university, four-year college, and junior college classification is based on information supplied by the American Council on Education, which information is itself based on the classification scheme developed by the U.S. Office of Education. The Office of Education defines universities as "institutions which give considerable stress to graduate instruction, which confer advanced degrees as well as bachelor's degrees in a variety of liberal arts fields, and which have at least two professional schools that are not exclusively technological." "Four-year colleges" is an "all other" residual category (USOE, 1969, p. 3). As some users have noted, this definition is "not very precise," yet it is precise enough to exclude from the university category the California Institute of Technology and other technical institutes one expects to find in studies of graduate education (Berelson, 1960, pp. 280–281). Although we were tempted to move some specialized institutions from the four-year college to the university category, systematic reclassification of institutions would have required analysis of our data far beyond the scope of this report. For that matter, since many OE statistics provide reference points for the data presented here, there are obvious advantages to the use of identical definitions, regardless of how unsatisfactory these definitions may be on other grounds.

Quality   The basic source of information on quality is *The Gourman Report* (1967), which rates "the undergraduate programs of nearly all of the colleges and universities in the United States." Gourman provides three composite ratings for each institution: a rating of the academic departments in terms of such things as accreditation and the proportion of students receiving scholarships and fellowships; a rating of nondepartmental aspects of the institution, such as the administration's "commitment to excellence," the level of financial aid available to students, the quality of the board of trustees, and faculty morale (e.g., rank, tenure, salary scale, research facilities); and a total institutional rating (the arithmetic mean of the departmental and nondepartmental ratings). The correlation between the departmental and nondepartmental ratings is very high ($r = +.956$) (Abbott & Schmid, 1969). We decided, therefore, to use the institutional rating (which correlates $+.99$ with departmental rating). As Gourman points out, "the criteria for evaluation of the individual departments are quite complex and take into account many factors." Since the department is only one of many elements of the college or university to which Gourman applies a complex rating scheme, since his ranking criteria are at times idiosyncratic (e.g., "one of the basic criteria" for rating *method of instruction* is the following assertion: "It has been long established that a minimum of ten years after college graduation is necessary to produce an excellent teacher in the college classroom."), and since he does not tell us how he combines the rankings of the various elements to produce overall scores, our justification for using Gourman's scheme is largely pragmatic.

The Gourman method produces results much like those obtained by other, less ambitious, efforts to rank American institutions of higher education. Of the "top 22 universities" listed by Berelson (1960), we have 15 in our sample. All 15 of these institutions are found among the top 22 universities in the sample, when sample institutions are ranked according to Gourman scores. Edward Gross and Paul Grambsch (1968), using information supplied by Allen Cartter (1966), rate major universities in terms of the quality of their doctoral training programs. Although the Gross and Grambsch index ranks graduate schools, and Gourman ranks undergraduate instruction, the correlation between the two ranking systems, based on 79 universities, is .83.[19]

Abbott and Schmid provide further validation of the Gourman ratings as they apply to the 79 universities rated by Gross and Grambsch:

Average compensation of faculty, 1963–64	.78
Number of library volumes	.74
Selectivity	.73
Doctorates conferred, 1861–1962	.71
Percent foreign students	.66

TABLE A-37 **Correlations between selected measures of university quality and total Gourman ratings (79 institutions)**

SOURCE: Abbott and Schmid (1969, p. 21).

In short, then, the three categories we use for universities differ little from the gross categories of quality that might be obtained from other well-known quality rankings. Since the Gourman system applies to four-year colleges as well as to universities, we have used it here.

The high-quality universities score 580 or above on Gourman.

[19] Gross and Grambsch too have three indexes of quality. The correlation reported is between the Gourman total rating and the Gross and Grambsch index based on a "weighted mean of [Cartter] departmental ratings" (the simplest of the Gross and Grambsch indexes). See Abbott and Schmid (1969, p. 19).

In 1968–69 there were 35,118 faculty in these institutions; 13,924 responded to our questionnaire. Of the 114,093 graduate students in these institutions, 10,203 responded to our questionnaire.

The medium-quality universities score between 477 and 579 on Gourman. In 1968–69 there were 41,050 faculty in these institutions; 15,475 responded to to our questionnaire. Of the 119,486 graduate students, 11,131 responded to the questionnaire.

The low-quality universities score less than 477 on Gourman. In 1968–69 there were 30,407 faculty in these institutions; 14,382 responded to our questionnaire. Of the 90,863 graduate students in these universities, 8,230 responded to our questionnaire.

Four-Year Colleges Grouping of the four-year colleges in our sample is based on a combination of Gourman rankings and rankings provided by *College-Rater* (1967) with precedence given to the higher of the ratings available for each college. At first glance, *College-Rater* appears to base its rankings on a strategy very different from that employed by Gourman. In fact, *College-Rater* appears to have *The Gourman Report* in mind when it describes its own procedure:

COLLEGE-RATER does not attempt to evaluate the academic excellence of a college or university, the competency of its faculty and staff, or the scope and variety of its curricula. Neither does it profess to measure the efficacy of the operation of its various departments or the size of its physical plant and endowment. Guidelines used do not take into account the quality of the academic program, the intellectual environment, educational techniques, facilities, and other considerations. If such imponderables could be measured, the ratings would change considerably.

In the end, however, Gourman and *College-Rater* come out with criteria that are much alike and with roughly similar rankings (the correlation between the two sets of scores is +.75). The four major criteria upon which *College-Rater* scores are based are, in descending order: SAT/ACE scores of recently enrolled freshman, proportion of faculty with doctorate, faculty salaries, and library collection. As will be recalled from Table A-37, three of these variables are strongly correlated with total Gourman scores. (Information on the correlation with the fourth variable—proportion of faculty with doctorate—is not available.)

In terms of clarity and logic of method, the *College-Rater* system is decidedly superior to Gourman's. In terms of outcome, in our judgment, *College-Rater* does better than Gourman in the ranking of four-year colleges; it does less well in the ranking of universities. (As is to be expected: *College-Rater* explicitly avoids the subjective judgments that are the basis of most ratings of graduate schools, including our own.)

The top-quality colleges score 445 or above on Gourman or 719 and above on *College-Rater.* In 1968–69 there were 8,820 faculty in these institutions; 4,648 responded to our questionnaire. Of the 20,733 graduate students, 1,640 responded to the questionnaire.

The middle-quality colleges score between 378 and 444 on Gourman and between 550 and 718 on *College-Rater.* In 1968–69 there were 8,396 faculty in these institutions; 4,801 responded to our questionnaire. Of the 14,809 graduate students, 1,062 responded.

The low-quality colleges score less than 378 on Gourman and less than 550 on *College-Rater.* In 1968–69 there were 8,952 faculty in these institutions; 4,801 responded to the questionnaire. Of the 17,056 graduate students, 699 responded to the questionnaire.

All junior colleges were treated as one category. In 1968–69 there were 4,228 faculty in these institutions; 2,140 responded to the questionnaire.

References

Abbott, Walter F., and Calvin F. Schmid: "Toward an Organizational Theory of Migration: University Prestige and First-Time Undergraduate Student Migration in the United States," paper presented before the 1969 meetings of the Population Association of America, Atlantic City, N.J., 1969.

American Council on Education: *American Universities and Colleges,* 10th ed., Washington, 1968.

American Council on Education: *An Assessment of Quality in Graduate Education,* Washington, 1966.

American Council on Education: *National Norms for Entering College Freshmen,* Research Reports (annual), Washington, 1967–1970.

Astin, Alexander W., and Robert J. Panos: "A National Research Data Bank for Higher Education," *Educational Record,* pp. 5–17, Winter 1966.

Astin, Alexander W., and Robert W. Panos: "Attrition Among College Students," *American Education Research Journal,* vol. 5, no. 1, January 1968.

Astin, Alexander W., Robert J. Panos, and John A. Creager: *A Program of Longitudinal Research on the Higher Education System,* ACE Research Reports, vol. 1, no. 1, 1966.

Bayer, Allan E., et al.: *Users' Manual: ACE Higher Education Data Bank,* American Council on Education, Washington, 1969.

Berelson, Bernard: *Graduate Education in the United States,* McGraw-Hill Book Company, New York, 1960.

CCMI Information Corporation: *The College Blue Book 1969-70,* 13th ed., New York, 1969.

Curtis, Richard: *The Invisible University: Postdoctoral Education in the United States,* National Academy of Sciences, Washington, 1969.

Gourman, John: *The Gourman Report,* The Continuing Education Institute, Phoenix, Ariz., 1967.

Gross, Edward, and Paul V. Grambsch: *University Goals and Academic Power,* American Council on Education, Washington, 1968.

U.S. Department of Health, Education, and Welfare: *Digest of Educational Statistics,* 1969 ed., September 1969.

U.S. Office of Education: *Opening Fall Enrollment in Higher Education (Part A - Summary Data),* 1966.

U.S. Office of Education: *Opening Fall Enrollment in Higher Education (Part A - Summary Data),* 1969.

U.S. Office of Education: *Faculty and Other Professional Staff in Institutions of Higher Education, 1963-64,* 1964.

U.S. Office of Education: *1965-66 Education Directory, Part 3,* 1966.

World Almanac 1969: Newspaper Enterprise Association, New York, 1969.

Faculty Questionnaire

THE CARNEGIE COMMISSION ON HIGHER EDUCATION

THE AMERICAN COUNCIL ON EDUCATION

Dear Colleague:

American higher education is currently undergoing its greatest changes in a hundred years. The extent and rapidity of these changes are causing severe strains and grave problems in our colleges and universities. But while we can see the broad outlines of these problems in over-crowded classrooms, rising costs, student rebellions, and threats to academic feeedom from several quarters, there is very little detailed information on the form they take in different kinds of institutions, or in different disciplines and professions. Nor do we have firm knowledge of how the people most directly affected, the students and faculty, feel about these problems and issues.

To meet this need for more and better knowledge, the Carnegie Commission on Higher Education, in cooperation with the American Council on Education, is conducting a national survey of students and faculty in a broad sample of colleges and universities. The information we are gathering will be of help to the Carnegie Commission and to other bodies concerned with public policy in this area, as well as to scholars who are studying current problems and developments in American higher education. Our findings will be published in books and reports; the data we collect will be made available in an anonymous form to other scholars and students of higher education.

We have no illusion that even a broad survey of this kind will answer all our questions. We know the limits of questionnaires, and are conducting other studies, in other ways, to supplement this survey. Nevertheless, a broad survey such as this provides information that can be obtained in no other way. We know how busy faculty members and administrators are. And we know also that other surveys may have made similar demands on your time. But the present survey is unique in its scope and purposes: it is the first to ask similar questions of students and faculty in the same institutions, and it is the first to explore a variety of these issues on a national scale. The accuracy of the survey and the worth of its findings are dependent on your willingness to answer our questions. We believe the importance of the study will justify the time you give it.

One other matter. It is impossible to frame questions all of which are equally relevant to faculty members in many different fields and kinds of institutions; you may find some that seem inappropriate to your situation. We urge you to answer all the questions as well as you can; in our analysis we will be able to take into account special circumstances that affect replies to some questions.

Finally, we assure you that your answers will be held in strictest confidence. We are interested only in statistical relationships and will under no circumstances report responses on an individual or departmental basis. Any special markings on your form are used solely for internal data processing.

We hope you will find the questionnaire interesting to answer, and that you will complete and return it to us while you have it at hand.

With our thanks for your cooperation.

Sincerely,

Logan Wilson   Clark Kerr

Logan Wilson
President
American Council
on Education

Clark Kerr
Chairman
Carnegie Commission
on Higher Education

MARKING INSTRUCTIONS:

This questionnaire will be read by an automatic scanning device. Certain marking requirements are essential to this process. Your careful observance of these few simple rules will be most appreciated.

Use soft black lead pencil only. (No. 2½ or softer)

Make heavy black marks that completely fill the circle.

Erase completely any answers you wish to change.

Avoid making any stray marks in this booklet.

1. What is your present rank?

Instructor ....O
Assistant Professor ....O
Associate Professor ....O
Professor ....O
Lecturer ....O
No ranks designated ....O
Other ....O

2. What kind of appointment do you have here?

Regular with tenure....................O
Regular without tenure ....O
Acting ....O
Visiting.............................O

3. During the spring term*, how many hours per week are you spending in formal instruction in class? (Give actual, not credit hours)

None.. O   7-8 ....O   13-16........O
1-4 ...O   9-10 ......O   17-20.......O
5-6 ...O   11-12 .....O   21 or more...O

4. Are your teaching responsibilities this academic year

Entirely undergraduate ....O
Some undergraduate, some graduate ..O ⌐Skip to
Entirely graduate..................O ⌐ No. 7
Not teaching this year ....O →Skip to
No. 8

5. How much do you control the content of your undergraduate courses?

Almost completely.. O   Somewhat ......O
Substantially ......O   Hardly at all...O

6. In about how many of the undergraduate courses you teach do you use the following?

	Most	Some	None
Term papers	O	O	O
Frequent quizzes..............	O	O	O
Graduate teaching assistants ..	O	O	O
Closed-circuit television	O	O	O
Computer or machine-aided instruction.................	O	O	O

* Quarter, semester, trimester, etc.

7. About how many students, at all levels, are enrolled in your courses this term?

None....O   Under 25 ..O   100-249 .....O
25-49 .....O   250-399 .....O
50-99 .....O   400 or more ..O

8. Do you discourage undergraduates from seeing you outside your regular office hours?

Yes, almost always ....O
Yes, but with many exceptions...........O
No ....O

9. Please indicate your agreement or disagreement with each of the following statements.

1. Strongly Agree
2. Agree With Reservations
3. Disagree With Reservations
4. Strongly Disagree

①②③④

Most undergraduates are mature enough to be given more responsibility for their own education .....①②③④
Graduate students in my subject do best if their undergraduate major was in the same general field.....①②③④
Most graduate students in my department*are basically satisfied with the education they are getting ....①②③④
Most Ph.D. holders in my field get their degrees without showing much real scholarly ability ....①②③④
My department* has taken steps to increase graduate student participation in its decisions...........①②③④
The graduate program in my department*favors the bright, imaginative student ....①②③④
Many of the best graduate students can no longer find meaning in science and scholarship ....①②③④
Graduate education in my subject is doing a good job of training students ....①②③④
Some of the best graduate students drop out because they do not want to "play the game" or "beat the system"........................①②③④
The female graduate students in my department*are not as dedicated as the males....................①②③④
The typical undergraduate curriculum has suffered from the specialization of faculty members ....①②③④
This institution should be as concerned about students' personal values as it is with their intellectual development ....①②③④

*If no graduate program in your department, leave blank.

9 Continued.

Most undergraduates here are basically satisfied with the education
they are getting . . . . ①②③④

A man can be an effective teacher
without personally involving him-
self with his students . . . . ①②③④

Most faculty here are strongly interested in the academic problems of
undergraduates . . . . ①②③④

Most American colleges reward
conformity and crush student
creativity . . . . ①②③④

This institution should be actively
engaged in solving social prob-
lems . . . . ①②③④

More minority group undergraduates
should be admitted here even if
it means relaxing normal academic standards of admission . . . . ①②③④

Any institution with a substantial
number of black students should
offer a program of Black Studies
if they wish it . . . . ①②③④

Any special academic program for
black students should be administered and controlled by black
people . . . . ①②③④

Undergraduate education in America would be improved if:

a) All courses were elective . . . . . ①②③④

b) Grades were abolished . . . . ①②③④

c) Course work were more relevant
to contemporary life and prob-
lems . . . . ①②③④

d) More attention were paid to the
emotional growth of students . . ①②③④

e) Students were required to
spend a year in community
service at home or abroad . . . . ①②③④

f) Colleges and universities were
governed completely by their
faculty and students . . . . ①②③④

g) There were less emphasis on
specialized training and more
on broad liberal education . . . . . ①②③④

10. For each of these areas, **should** present academic
standards in your institution (a,b) and your graduate department (c,d) be--
(Mark one in each row)

```
                            1. Much higher
                            2. Somewhat higher
                            3. Left as they are
                            4. Somewhat lower
                            5. Much lower
    ①②③④⑤⑥—— 6. No graduate department
```
a) Undergraduate admissions . . ①②③④⑤
b) Bachelor's degrees . . . . ①②③④⑤
c) Graduate admissions . . . . ①②③④⑤⑥
d) Advanced degrees . . . . ①②③④⑤⑥

11. Do you feel that the administration of your
department*is:

Very autocratic . . . . O
Somewhat autocratic . . . . O
Somewhat democratic . . . . O
Very democratic . . . . O

*Here and hereafter, if you have a joint appoint-
ment, answer for your main department. If your
institution has no departments, answer for the
equivalent administrative unit (e.g., division
for junior colleges).

12. Is the chairman of your department appointed
for a fixed short term (3 years or less) or for a
long or indefinite period?

Long/Indefinite . . . O   Short term . . . . . . O

13. Roughly how many regular members (at the rank
of instructor or above) does your department
have this year?

3 or fewer . . . . O	16 - 20 . . . . O
4 - 5 . . . . O	21 - 25 . . . . O
6 - 7 . . . . O	26 - 30 . . . . O
8 - 10 . . . . O	31 - 40 . . . . O
11 - 15 . . . . O	41 or more . . . . . O

14. How much has your department changed in size
in the last 3 years? Is it:

Much larger . . . . O
Somewhat larger . . . . O
About the same . . . . O
Smaller . . . . O

15a Do you think your department is now

Too big . . . . O
About right . . . . O
Too small . . . . O

b Do you think your institution is now

Too big . . . . O
About right . . . . O
Too small . . . . O

16. How active are you (a) in your own department's affairs? (b) in the faculty government
of your institution (committee memberships, etc,)?
(Mark one in each column)

	Department	Institution
Much more than average	O	O
Somewhat more than average . .	O	O
About average	O	O
Somewhat less than average . .	O	O
Much less than average	O	O

17. How much opportunity do you feel you have to influence the policies (a) of your department? (b) of your institution?

(Mark one in each column)

Department *Institution*

A great deal.................O...O
Quite a bit...............O...O
Some.....................O...O
None......................O...O

18. How many of the people you see socially are:
(a) members of the faculty here?

Almost all ......O   Some........O
Most ....O   Almost none ..O
About half ......O

(b) members of your department?

Almost all ......O   Some ....O
Most ....O   Almost none ..O
About half ......O

19. What do you think of the emergence of radical student activism in recent years?

Unreservedly approve...................O
Approve with reservations..............O
Disapprove with reservations ....O
Unreservedly disapprove ....O

20. With respect to the student revolt at Columbia last year, were you in sympathy with

the students' aims and their methods ....O
their aims but not their methods.........O
neither their aims nor their methods .....O
I don't know enough about it to judge ....O

21. Have any of your children been active in civil rights, anti-Vietnam, or other demonstrations?

Yes.....................................O
None active ....O
None of that age ....O

22. Has your campus experienced any student protests or demonstrations during the current academic year?

Yes...O   No....O (if no, skip to No. 25)

23. How would you characterize your attitude toward the most recent demonstration?

Approved of the demonstrators' aims and methods ....O
Approved of their aims but not their methods ....O
Disapproved of their aims ....O
Uncertain or mixed feelings ....O
Indifferent ....O

24. What was your role in this demonstration?
(Mark all that apply)

Helped to plan, organize, or lead the protest ....O
Joined in active protest with the demonstrators ....O
Openly supported the goals of the protestors................................O
Openly opposed the goals of the protestors...O
Tried to mediate in the protest ....O
Was not involved actively in any way ......O

25. What effect have student demonstrations (on your campus or elsewhere) had on each of the following? (Mark one in each row)

1. Very favorable
2. Fairly favorable
3. Fairly harmful
4. Very harmful
①②③④⑤ — 5. No effect

Your research.................①②③④⑤
Your teaching................①②③④⑤
Your relations with departmental colleagues ....①②③④⑤
Your relations with other colleagues ....①②③④⑤
Your relations with students .....①②③④⑤
Your view of your campus administration ....①②③④⑤
Your institution's relations with the local community ....①②③④⑤

26a. What role do you believe undergraduates should play in decisions on the following?

1. Control
2. Voting power on committees
3. Formal consultation
4. Informal consultation
①②③④⑤ — 5. Little or no role

Faculty appointment and promotion ....①②③④⑤
Undergraduate admissions policy .①②③④⑤
Provision and content of courses .①②③④⑤
Student discipline.............①②③④⑤
Bachelor's degree requirements ..①②③④⑤

b. What role do you believe graduate students should play in decisions on the following?

Faculty appointment and promotion ....①②③④⑤
Departmental graduate admissions policy ....①②③④⑤
Provision and content of graduate courses ....①②③④⑤
Student discipline.............①②③④⑤
Advanced degree requirements ...①②③④⑤

27. Please indicate your agreement or disagreement with each of the following statements.

```
┌──── 1. Strongly agree
│┌─── 2. Agree with reservations
││┌── 3. Disagree with reservations
①②③④ ─ 4. Strongly disagree
```

The normal academic requirements should be relaxed in appointing members of minority groups to the faculty here .... ①②③④

Opportunities for higher education should be available to all high school graduates who want it .... ①②③④

Most American colleges and universities are racist whether they mean to be or not .... ①②③④

Public colleges and universities must be more responsive to public demands than are private institutions .... ①②③④

Junior faculty members have too little say in the running of my department .... ①②③④

A small group of senior professors has disproportionate power in decision-making in this institution. ①②③④

This institution would be better off with fewer administrators .... ①②③④

There should be faculty representation on the governing board of this institution. .... ①②③④

Trustees' only responsibilities should be to raise money and gain community support. .... ①②③④

The administration here has taken a clear stand in support of academic freedom .... ①②③④

Faculty unions have a divisive effect on academic life .... ①②③④

Teaching assistants' unions have a divisive effect on academic life ... ①②③④

Faculty members should be more militant in defending their interests .... ①②③④

Collective bargaining by faculty members has no place in a college or university .... ①②③④

Most rules governing student behavior here are sensible .... ①②③④

Campus rules here are generally administered in a reasonable way.. ①②③④

Undergraduates known to use marijuana regularly should be suspended or dismissed .... ①②③④

Political activities by students have no place on a college campus ①②③④

27 Continued.

Student demonstrations have no place on a college campus .... ①②③④

Students who disrupt the functioning of a college should be expelled or suspended .... ①②③④

Most campus demonstrations are created by far left groups trying to cause trouble................... ①②③④

College officials have the right to regulate student behavior off campus .... ①②③④

Respect for the academic profession has declined over the past 20 years. ①②③④

A student's grades should not be revealed to anyone off campus without his consent .... ①②③④

Faculty members should be free on campus to advocate violent resistance to public authority .... ①②③④

Faculty members should be free to present in class any idea that they consider relevant .... ①②③④

Campus disruptions by militant students are a threat to academic freedom........................ ①②③④

28. Have you known of a case here within the past two years in which a man's politics affected his chances for retention or promotion?

I know definitely of a case .... ○

I've heard of a case .... ○

I don't know of a case .... ○

I'm sure it hasn't happened .... ○

29. In recent years, have you ever felt intimidated in your classes by students with strong political or racial views?

Yes .... ○   No ...... ○

30. In what year did you obtain your highest degree?

1928 or before .. ○	1949-1953 ...... ○
1929-1933 ...... ○	1954-1958 ...... ○
1934-1938 ...... ○	1959-1963 ...... ○
1939-1943 ...... ○	1964-1966 ...... ○
1944-1948 ...... ○	1967 or later.... ○

31. How many years elapsed between your obtaining your bachelor's degree and your highest degree?

No degree higher than bachelor's.......... ○

I am still working for a higher degree ...... ○

1 - 2 years .... ○

3 - 4 years .... ○

5 - 7 years .... ○

8 - 10 years .... ○

11 - 15 years .... ○

Over 15 years .... ○

32. On the following list, please mark
1. (If any) the degree(s) for which you are currently working
2. <u>All</u> degrees that you have earned
3. <u>All</u> degrees you have earned at <u>this</u> institution

Working Toward
Now hold
Earned here

Less than Bachelor's (A.A., etc.)	①②③
Undergraduate Bachelor's	①②③
First professional law degree	①②③
First professional medical degree (e.g. M.D., D.D.S.)	①②③
Other first professional beyond under- graduate bachelor's	①②③
Master's (except first professional) ...	①②③
Doctor of Arts or equivalent for doc- torate degree without dissertation ...	①②③
Ph.D	①②③
Ed.D..............................	①②③
Other doctorate (except first profes- sional)...........................	①②③
None	①②③

33. From the following list, mark <u>one</u> subject in each column; mark the most appropriate <u>fine</u> categories, if applicable; where your precise field does not appear, mark the most similar category.

1. **Undergraduate major**
2. **Highest postgraduate degree**
3. **Present principal teaching field**
4. **Present primary field of research, scholarship, creativity**
5. **Department*of teaching appointment**

①②③④⑤

NONE	①②③④⑤
Agriculture and/or Forestry.....	①②③④⑤
Architecture and/or Design	①②③④⑤
Biological Sciences (General Biology)	①②③④⑤
Bacteriology, Molecular biology, Virology, Micro- biology	①②③④⑤
Biochemistry	①②③④⑤
General Botany	①②③④⑤
Physiology, Anatomy	①②③④⑤
General Zoology	①②③④⑤
Other Biological Sciences	①②③④⑤
Business, Commerce and Management	①②③④⑤
Education....................	①②③④⑤
Elementary and/or Secondary ..	①②③④⑤
Foundations	①②③④⑤
Educational Psychology and Counseling	①②③④⑤
Educational Administration	①②③④⑤
Other Education fields	①②③④⑤

Engineering	①②③④⑤
Chemical.....................	①②③④⑤
Civil	①②③④⑤
Electrical	①②③④⑤
Mechanical	①②③④⑤
Other Engineering fields	①②③④⑤
Fine Arts	①②③④⑤
Art	①②③④⑤
Dramatics and Speech	①②③④⑤
Music.......................	①②③④⑤
Other Fine Arts	①②③④⑤
Geography....................	①②③④⑤
Health Fields.................	①②③④⑤
Medicine	①②③④⑤
Nursing	①②③④⑤
Other Health fields	①②③④⑤
Home Economics	①②③④⑤
Humanities	①②③④⑤
English language & literature..	①②③④⑤
Foreign languages & literature ..	①②③④⑤
French.....................	①②③④⑤
German	①②③④⑤
Spanish....................	①②③④⑤
Other foreign languages (in- cluding linguistics).........	①②③④⑤
History	①②③④⑤
Philosophy	①②③④⑤
Religion & Theology	①②③④⑤
Other Humanities fields	①②③④⑤
Industrial Arts	①②③④⑤
Journalism	①②③④⑤
Law.......................	①②③④⑤
Library Science	①②③④⑤
Mathematics and Statistics	①②③④⑤
Physical & Health Education	①②③④⑤
Physical Sciences..............	①②③④⑤
Chemistry...................	①②③④⑤
Earth Sciences (incl. Geology)..	①②③④⑤
Physics.....................	①②③④⑤
Other Physical Sciences	①②③④⑤
Psychology...................	①②③④⑤
Clinical.....................	①②③④⑤
Experimental	①②③④⑤
Social	①②③④⑤
Counseling and Guidance......	①②③④⑤
Other Psychology fields	①②③④⑤
Social Sciences	①②③④⑤
Anthropology & Archaeology	①②③④⑤
Economics	①②③④⑤
Political Science, Government ..	①②③④⑤
Sociology	①②③④⑤
Other Social Sciences.........	①②③④⑤
Social Work, Social Welfare......	①②③④⑤
ALL OTHER FIELDS..........	①②③④⑤

* Mark main department, if you have a joint appointment.

34. On the following list of large American universities, mark one in each column; if the names of your institutions do not appear, mark appropriate "other" categories.

```
       ┌──── 1. Bachelor's degree
     ┌──── 2. Highest degree
 ①②③ ── 3. First regular teaching job
```

NONE or not appropriate . . . . ①②③
Boston University . . . . ①②③
Brown University, R.I. . . . . ①②③
California Institute of Technology . . . ①②③
California, University of, at Berkeley ①②③
California, University of, at Los
  Angeles . . . . ①②③
Carnegie Institute of Technology, Pa. ①②③
Catholic University of America, D.C. . ①②③
Chicago, University of . . . . ①②③
Colorado, University of . . . . ①②③
Columbia University Teachers'
  College, N.Y. ①②③
Columbia University, N.Y. . . . . ①②③
Cornell University, N.Y. . . . . ①②③
Duke University, N.C. . . . . ①②③
Florida, University of . . . . ①②③
Fordham University, N.Y. . . . . ①②③
Harvard University, Mass . . . . ①②③
Illinois, University of . . . . ①②③
Indiana University at Bloomington . . . ①②③
Iowa State University . . . . ①②③
Iowa, University of . . . . ①②③
Johns Hopkins University . . . . ①②③
Kansas, University of . . . . ①②③
Louisiana State University . . . . ①②③
Maryland, University of . . . . ①②③
Massachusetts Institute of Technology ①②③
Michigan State University . . . . ①②③
Michigan, University of . . . . ①②③
Minnesota, University of . . . . ①②③
Missouri, University of, at Columbia . ①②③
Nebraska, University of . . . . ①②③
New York University . . . . ①②③
North Carolina, University of . . . . ①②③
Northwestern University, Ill. . . . . ①②③
Notre Dame University, Ind . . . . ①②③
Ohio State University . . . . ①②③
Oklahoma, University of . . . . ①②③
Oregon State University . . . . ①②③
Oregon, University of . . . . ①②③
Pennsylvania State University . . . . . . ①②③
Pennsylvania, University of . . . . ①②③
Pittsburgh, University of . . . . ①②③
Princeton University, N.J. . . . . ①②③
Purdue University . . . . ①②③
Rochester, University of . . . . ①②③
Rutgers University, N.J. . . . . ①②③
Southern California, University of . . . . ①②③
Stanford University, Calif. . . . . ①②③

34 Continued

Syracuse University, N.Y. . . . . ①②③
Texas, University of . . . . ①②③
Utah, University of . . . . ①②③
Virginia, University of . . . . ①②③
Washington University, Mo. . . . . ①②③
Washington, University of, Wash . . . . . ①②③
Western Reserve University, Ohio . . . . ①②③
Wisconsin, University of . . . . ①②③
Yale University, Conn . . . . ①②③
Other private Ph.D.-granting univer-
  sity . . . . ①②③
Other state Ph.D.-granting university . . ①②③
Other private college (no Ph.D.
  program) . . . . ①②③
Other public college (no Ph.D.
  program) . . . . ①②③
A foreign institution . . . . ①②③
A junior or community college . . . . ①②③

35. How long have you been employed (beyond the level of teaching or research assistant):
a. in colleges or universities?

1 year or less . . . . . ◯	10-14 years . . . . . . ◯
2-3 years . . . . ◯	15-19 years . . . . . . ◯
4-6 years . . . . ◯	20-29 years . . . . . . ◯
7-9 years . . . . ◯	30 years or more . . ◯

b. at this institution?

1 year or less . . . . . ◯	10-14 years . . . . . . ◯
2-3 years . . . . ◯	15-19 years . . . . . . ◯
4-6 years . . . . ◯	20-29 years . . . . . . ◯
7-9 years . . . . ◯	30 years or more . . ◯

36. At how many different colleges or universities have you been employed full-time (beyond the level of teaching or research assistant)?

None . . . . ◯	Four . . . . ◯
One . . . . ◯	Five . . . . ◯
Two . . . . ◯	Six . . . . ◯
Three . . . . ◯	Seven or more . . . . ◯

37. Comparing yourself with other academic men of your age and qualifications, how successful do you consider yourself in your career?
Very successful . . . ◯
Fairly successful . . ◯
Fairly unsuccessful . ◯
Very unsuccessful . . ◯

38. In general, how do you feel about this institution?
It is a very good place for me . . . . ◯
It is fairly good for me . . . . ◯
It is not the place for me . . . . ◯

39. Do you think you could be equally or more satisfied with life in any other college or university?

Definitely yes .... O
Probably yes .... O
Probably no .... O
Definitely no .... O

40. If you were to begin your career again, would you still want to be a college professor?

Definitely yes .... O
Probably yes .... O
Probably no .... O
Definitely no .... O

41. (a) Mark all types of work that you have engaged in for a year or more since earning your bachelor's degree (not counting part-time work while in graduate school). (b) What were you doing immediately prior to taking a job at this institution? (Mark one)

	Have Done	Did Last
Teaching in a university	O	O
Teaching in a 4-year college........	O	O
Teaching in a junior or community college	O	O
Full-time non-teaching research position in a college or university ..	O	O
Post-doctoral fellowship or traineeship in a university..............	O	O
Full-time college or university administration	O	O
Teaching or administration in an elementary or secondary school	O	O
Research and development outside educational institutions	O	O
Executive or administrative post outside educational institutions	O	O
Other professional position	O	O
Student	O	O
Other	O	O

42. Please indicate your agreement or disagreement with each of the following statements.

1. **Strongly agree**
2. **Agree with reservations**
3. **Disagree with reservations**
① ② ③ ④ — 4. **Strongly disagree**

My field is too research oriented . ① ② ③ ④
I prefer teaching courses which focus on limited specialties to those which cover wide varieties of material .... ① ② ③ ④

42 Continued

I consider myself an intellectual ..... ① ② ③ ④
I hardly ever get the time to give a piece of work the attention it deserves........................ ① ② ③ ④
I tend to subordinate all aspects of my life to my work.................... ① ② ③ ④
A man's teaching and research inevitably reflect his political values ..... ① ② ③ ④
My commitments to different aspects of my job are the source of considerable personal strain .... ① ② ③ ④
I am in frequent communication with people in my own academic specialty in other institutions........ ① ② ③ ④
Many of the highest-paid university professors get where they are by being "operators", rather than by their scholarly or scientific contributions .... ① ② ③ ④
By and large, full-time professional researchers in universities are people who couldn't quite make it on the faculty........................... ① ② ③ ④
Genuine scholarship is threatened in universities by the proliferation of big research centers .... ① ② ③ ④
The concentration of federal and foundation research grants in the big institutions (Mark each line)
1) is unfair to other institutions ..... ① ② ③ ④
2) is corrupting to the institutions and men that get them .... ① ② ③ ④
3) contributes substantially to the advancement of knowledge .... ① ② ③ ④
Many professors in graduate departments exploit their students to advance their own research .... ① ② ③ ④
In my department it is very difficult for a man to achieve tenure if he does not publish....................... ① ② ③ ④
Teaching effectiveness, not publications, should be the primary criterion for promotion of faculty .... ① ② ③ ④
Faculty promotions should be based in part on formal student evaluations of their teachers..................... ① ② ③ ④
A professor at a junior college or state college ought to get the same pay as a university professor of equal seniority......................... ① ② ③ ④
Classified weapons research is a legitimate activity on college and university campuses .... ① ② ③ ④
Big contract research has become more a source of money and prestige for researchers than an effective way of advancing knowledge .... ① ② ③ ④

43. Given the following four possible activities of academic men, please mark the first three in order:
    1. According to their importance to you personally
    2. According to your understanding of what your institution expects of you
    (Mark one in each column)

	Importance to Me			Institution's Expectation		
	First	Second	Third	First	Second	Third
Provide undergraduates with a broad liberal education	O	O	O	O	O	O
Prepare undergraduates for their chosen occupation	O	O	O	O	O	O
Train graduate or professional students	O	O	O	O	O	O
Engage in research	O	O	O	O	O	O

44. Within the past two years have you received an offer of another job or a serious inquiry about your availability for another position?
    An offer................................ O
    Not an offer, but a serious inquiry........ O
    Neither .... O

45. In a normal week, what proportion of your work time is devoted to the following activities:
    a. Administration (departmental or institutional, including committee work)

    None .....O   1-10% ...O   41-60% ......O
              11-20%...O   61-80% ......O
              21-40%...O   81-100% .....O

    b. Consulting (with or without pay)
    None .....O   1-10% ....O   41-60% ......O
              11-20% ...O   61-80% ......O
              21-40% ...O   81-100% .....O

    c. Outside professional practice
    None .....O   1-10% ....O   41-60% ......O
              11-20% ...O   61-80% ......O
              21-40% ...O   81-100% .....O

46. To how many academic or professional journals do you subscribe?
    None .....O 3-4 .....O   11-20........O
    1-2.......O 5-10 .....O More than 20 .O

47. How many articles have you published in academic or professional journals?
    None .....O 3-4 ......O   11-20........O
    1-2.......O 5-10 .....O More than 20 .O

48. How many books or monographs have you published or edited, alone or in collaboration?
    None ....O   3-4 ....O
    1-2............O   5 or more ....O

49. How many of your professional writings have been published or accepted for publication in the last two years?
    None ..O   3-4 ....O   More than 10 .O
    1-2.....O 5-10 ......O

50. Do your interests lie primarily in teaching or in research?
    Very heavily in research.................. O
    In both, but leaning toward research........ O
    In both, but leaning toward teaching........ O
    Very heavily in teaching.................. O

51. Are you currently engaged in any scholarly or research work which you expect to lead to publication?
    Yes.....O   No.....O (If no, skip to No. 55)

52. Which of these statements applies to your current major piece of research or scholarship?
    I am essentially working alone .... O
    I am working with one or two colleagues ....O
    I am a member of a larger group........... O

53. Are any of the following working with you on any research project? (Mark all that apply)
    Graduate research assistants.............. O
    Post-doctoral fellows or trainees .... O
    Full-time professional level research personnel............................. O

54. In the past 12 months, did you receive research support from: (Mark all sources that apply)
    Institutional or departmental funds .... O
    Federal agencies .... O
    State or local government agencies......... O
    Private foundations .... O
    Private industry .... O
    Other .... O
    None................................... O

55. During the past two years, have you served as a paid consultant to: (Mark all that apply)
    Local business, government or schools .....O
    A national corporation................... O
    A non-profit foundation .... O
    Federal or foreign government .... O
    A research project .... O
    Other .... O
    No paid consulting...................... O

56. **Are you a member of any of the following organi-sations? (Mark all that apply)**

American Association of University
Professors...........................O
American Federation of Teachers.......O
A National Education Association
affiliate............................O
A local or state association or union of
college teachers.....................O
A state, county or city employees' associa-
tion or other association not confined to
college teachers.....................O
An association limited to teachers at your
institution (other than the Academic
Senate).............................O

57. **Do you feel that there are circumstances in which a strike would be a legitimate means of collective action:**

a. **for faculty members**
Definitely yes........................O
Probably yes.........................O
Probably not.........................O
Definitely not........................O

b. **for teaching assistants**
Definitely yes........................O
Probably yes.........................O
Probably not.........................O
Definitely not........................O

58. **Please indicate your agreement or disagreement with each of the following statements.**

1. Strongly agree
2. Agree with reservations
3. Disagree with reservations
①②③④ — 4. Strongly disagree

Where de facto segregation exists,
black people should be assured
control over their own schools..①②③④
Racial integration of the public
elementary schools should be
achieved even if it requires
busing...........................①②③④
Meaningful social change cannot be
achieved through traditional
American politics.............①②③④
With a few exceptions, the Chicago
police acted reasonably in curbing
the demonstrations at the Democratic National Convention.....①②③④
Hippies represent an important
criticism of American culture...①②③④
Marijuana should be legalized...①②③④

58 Continued

Some form of Communist regime is
probably necessary for progress
in underdeveloped countries......①②③④
In the USA today there can be no
justification for using violence to
achieve political goals..........①②③④
The main cause of Negro riots in
the cities is white racism........①②③④

59. **Which of these positions on Vietnam is closest to your own?**

The U.S. should withdraw from Vietnam
immediately........................O
The U.S. should reduce its involvement,
and encourage the emergence of a coali-
tion government in South Vietnam......O
The U.S. should try to reduce its involvement, while being sure to prevent a
Communist takeover in the South.......O
The U.S. should commit whatever forces
are necessary to defeat the Communists O

60. **How active were you in last year's political campaigns:**

a. **before the conventions?**
Very active..........................O
Fairly active........................O
Not very active......................O
Not active at all.....................O

b. **after the conventions?**
Very active..........................O
Fairly active........................O
Not very active......................O
Not active at all.....................O

61.
1. Left
2. Liberal
3. Middle-of-the-road
4. Moderately conservative
①②③④⑤ — 5. Strongly conservative

a. How would you characterize
yourself politically at the
present time?................①②③④⑤

b. What were your politics as a
college senior?..............①②③④⑤

c. What were your father's politics
while you were growing up?.....①②③④⑤

d. How would you describe the prevailing political sentiments of
undergraduates here?..........①②③④⑤

62. Whom would you have favored:
   a. At the Republican convention:
   Nixon.........O   Rockefeller......O

   b. At the Democratic convention:
   Humphrey......O   McCarthy........O

63. Whom did you vote for in November?
   Humphrey...O   Another candidate.....O
   Nixon......O   Did not vote..........O
   Wallace ....O   No answer ....O

64. Whom did you vote for in 1964?
   Johnson....O   Another candidate.....O
   Goldwater ..O   Did not vote..........O
   No answer ....O

	Yes	No
65. a. Are you a United States citizen?...	O	O
b. IF YES: Have you ever been a	Yes	No
citizen of another country?.......	O	O

66. Have you ever been a member of a   Yes No
student political club or group?.......O   O

67. Have you ever attended a junior or   Yes No
community college as a student? ......O   O

68. During your career as a graduate student:
   Were you ever a teaching assis-   Yes No
   tant ?...........................O   O
   Were you ever a research   Yes No
   assistant?......................O   O
   Were you ever awarded a fellowship or scholarship worth $1,000   Yes No
   per year or more?................O   O
   Was there a faculty member who acted
   as your "sponsor" when you were   Yes No
   looking for your first job? ....O   O

69. Do you have a working association
   with any research institute or center   Yes No
   within your institution?.............O   O

70. In your department, are decisions other
   than personnel matters normally made
   by the vote of the whole department,   Yes No
   including junior members?...........O   O

71. a. Are you now chairman or head of   Yes No
   your department?................O   O
   b. IF NO: Have you ever been chairman or head of a university or   Yes No
   college department?.............O   O

72. a. Do you hold a full-time administrative position outside your own   Yes No
   department?.....................O   O
   b. IF NO: Do you hold a part-time
   administrative position outside   Yes No
   your own department?............O   O

73. a. Are you now negotiating for, or
   have you already found or accepted, another position for   Yes No
   the fall of 1969 ?................O   O
   b. IF NO: Are you looking for   Yes No
   another position?................O   O
   c. IF NO: Would you seriously
   consider a reasonable offer of   Yes No
   another position?................O   O

74. Would you describe yourself as con-   Yes No
   servative in your religious beliefs?....O   O

75. How would you rate each of the following?

```
          1. Excellent
          2. Good
          3. Fair
①②③④ — 4. Poor
```

Your own salary ....①②③④
Your own graduate education ......①②③④
The academic reputation of your de-
partment outside your institution..①②③④
At your institution--
The intellectual environment ......①②③④
Faculty salary levels.............①②③④
Teaching load ....①②③④
Ratio of teaching faculty to students①②③④
The administration...............①②③④
The effectiveness of your campus
senate or faculty council ....①②③④
General research resources (e.g.,
library, labs, computers, space,
etc.) ....①②③④
Availability of research funds from
all sources.....................①②③④
Cultural resources ....①②③④
In your department--
The intellectual environment ......①②③④
Personal relations among faculty...①②③④
Faculty/student relations ....①②③④

76. How often, on average, do you

```
          1. Once a week or more
          2. Two or three times a month
          3. About once a month
          4. A few times a year
①②③④⑤— 5. Once a year or less
```

See undergraduates informally
(for meals, parties, informal
gatherings)?..................①②③④⑤
Spend 4 hours uninterruptedly on
professional reading, writing or
research?.....................①②③④⑤
Attend:
1. A religious service ....①②③④⑤
2. A concert ....①②③④⑤
3. An "art" film ....①②③④⑤
4. A play....................①②③④⑤
5. An art exhibition...........①②③④⑤
6. An athletic event...........①②③④⑤

77. **Do you consider yourself**
    Deeply religious .... O
    Moderately religious .... O
    Largely indifferent to religion .... O
    Basically opposed to religion .... O

78. **a. In what religion were you raised?**
    Protestant .... O   Other .... O
    Catholic .... O   None .... O
    Jewish .... O   No answer ...... O

    b. What is your present religion?
    Protestant .... O   Other .... O
    Catholic .... O   None .... O
    Jewish .... O   No answer .... O

79. **What is the highest level of formal education reached by your spouse? Your father? Your mother? (Mark one in each column)**

    Spouse Father Mother

    No spouse .... O
    8th grade or less .... O O O
    Some high school .... O O O
    Completed high school .... O O O
    Some college .... O O O
    Graduated from college .... O O O
    Attended graduate or professional
       school .... O O O
    Attained advanced degree .... O O O

80. **What is (was) your father's principal occupation? (Mark one)**
    College or university teaching, research or
       administration .... O
    Elementary or secondary school teaching
       or administration .... O
    Other professional .... O
    Managerial, administrative, semiprofes-
       sional .... O
    Owner, large business .... O
    Owner, small business .... O
    Other white collar: clerical, retail sales ... O
    Skilled wage worker .... O
    Semi- and unskilled wage worker, farm
       laborer .... O
    Armed forces .... O
    Farm owner or manager .... O

81. **What is your basic institutional salary, before tax and deductions, for the current academic year?**
    Below $7,000 ..... O $17,000-$19,999 .. O
    $7,000-$9,999 ..... O $20,000-$24,999 .. O
    $10,000-$11,999 .. O $25,000-$29,999 .. O
    $12,000-$13,999 .. O $30,000 and over . O
    $14,000-$16,999 .. O

82. **Is this based on**
    9/10 months .... O 11/12 months ...... O

83. **In recent years, roughly how much have you earned over and above your basic salary? (Please estimate as a percentage of your basic salary.)**
    0% ..... O   Under 10% . O   30%-39% .... O
                 10%-19% .. O   40%-49% .... O
                 20%-29% .. O   50% and over . O

84. **What are the two largest sources of your supplementary earnings? (Mark one in each column)**

	Largest	Second Largest
Summer teaching	O	O
Teaching elsewhere (extension, etc.) other than summer teaching	O	O
Consulting	O	O
Private practice	O	O
Royalties (from publications, patents)	O	O
Fees for speeches and lectures	O	O
Research salaries and payments	O	O
Other	O	O
None	O	O

85. **What is your marital status?**
    Married (once only) .... O
    Married (remarried) .... O
    Separated .... O
    Single (never married) .... O
    Single (divorced) .... O
    Single (widowed) .... O

86. **How many dependent children do you have?**
    None .... O   Two .... O
    One .... O   Three or more ..... O

87. **What is your date of birth?**
    1903 or before ..... O   1924-1928 .... O
    1904-1908 .... O   1929-1933 .... O
    1909-1913 .... O   1934-1938 .... O
    1914-1918 .... O   1939-1943 .... O
    1919-1923 .... O   1944 or later ...... O

88. **Your sex:**   Male .... O   Female ...... O

Graduate Student Questionnaire

THE CARNEGIE COMMISSION ON HIGHER EDUCATION
THE AMERICAN COUNCIL ON EDUCATION

Dear Colleague:

American higher education is currently faced with grave problems. While we can see the broad outlines of these problems in over-crowded classrooms, rising costs, student rebellions, and threats to academic freedom, there is very little detailed information on the form they take in different institutions, or in different disciplines and professions. Nor do we have firm knowledge of how the people most directly affected, the students and the faculty, feel about them.

To provide such knowledge, the Carnegie Commission on the Future of Higher Education, in cooperation with the American Council on Education, is conducting a national survey of students and faculty in a broad sample of colleges and universities. The information we are gathering will be of help to the Carnegie Commission and to other bodies concerned with public policy in this area, as well as to scholars who are studying current problems and developments in American higher education.

We have no illusion that even a broad survey such as this will answer all our questions. We know the limits of questionnaires, and are conducting other studies, in other ways, to supplement this survey. Nevertheless, this survey will provide information that can be obtained in no other way. We know that you have much to do, and we know also that other surveys may have made similar demands on your time. But the present survey is unique in its scope and purposes: it is the first to ask similar questions of students and faculty in the same institutions, and it is the first to explore a variety of these issues on a national scale. The accuracy of the survey and the worth of its findings are dependent on your willingness to answer our questions. We believe the importance of the study will justify the time you give it.

One other matter. It is impossible to frame questions all of which are equally relevant to students in different fields and institutions; you may find some that seem inappropriate to your situation. We urge you to answer all the questions as well as you can; in our analysis we will be able to take into account the special circumstances that affect replies to some questions.

Finally, we assure you that your answers will be held in strictest confidence. We are interested only in statistical relationships and will under no circumstances report responses on an individual or departmental basis. Any special markings on your form are used solely for internal data processing.

We hope you will find the questionnaire interesting to answer, and that you will complete and return it to us while you have it at hand.

With our thanks for your cooperation.

Sincerely,

Logan Wilson *Clark Kerr*

Logan Wilson
President
American Council
on Education

Clark Kerr
Chairman
Carnegie Commission on
Higher Education

1. **Your sex:**

Male....... O   Female .... O

2. **What is your marital status?**

Engaged............................ O
Married (once only) .... O
Married (remarried)..................... O
Separated .... O
Single (never married)................. O
Single (divorced) .... O
Single (widowed) .... O

3. **Number of children:**

None....... O   Two .... O
One........ O   Three or more ...... O

4. **On the following list, please mark (1) all the degrees you now hold, (2) the degree(s) you are now working for, (3) the highest degree you expect to obtain.**
   (Mark each column)

   ┌───── 1. Now Hold
   ┌──── 2. Working For
   ① ② ③ ── 3. Highest Expect to Obtain

Less than Bachelor's (A.A., etc.)....① ② ③
Undergraduate Bachelor's...........① ② ③
First professional law degree ......① ② ③
First professional medical degree
  (e.g., M.D., D.D.S.)..............① ② ③
M.A.T..............................① ② ③
Other first professional beyond
  undergraduate bachelor's ....① ② ③
Master's (except first professional)..① ② ③
Doctor of Arts or equivalent for doc-
  torate degree without dissertation...① ② ③
Ph.D..............................① ② ③
Ed.D. ....① ② ③
Other doctorate (except first profes-
  sional)..........................① ② ③
None..............................① ② ③

5. **When do you expect to get the degree you are now working for?**

This year...................... O
Within two years................ O
Within three years .... O
Within four years .... O
Within five years .... O
Six or more years .... O
I don't expect to get the degree......... O

6. **Are you now thinking about a job after finishing graduate school?** *

I already have a job.................. O
Yes, I am now looking................ O
Yes, I'm thinking seriously about where to
go................................ O
Yes, but not seriously............... O
No................................ O
* "Graduate school" means any program of instruction beyond the undergraduate bachelor's, including professional schools such as law and medicine.

7. **In what year did you (1) obtain your bachelor's degree, (2) first enter graduate school, (3) first enter this department** * **as a graduate student? (Mark one in each column)**

   ┌───── 1. Bachelor's Degree
   ┌──── 2. Entered Graduate School
   ① ② ③ ── 3. Entered Department

1955 or before..................... ① ② ③
1956-57 .... ① ② ③
1958-59 .... ① ② ③
1960-61 .... ① ② ③
1962-63 .... ① ② ③
1964 .... ① ② ③
1965 .... ① ② ③
1966 .... ① ② ③
1967 .... ① ② ③
1968-69 .... ① ② ③
* "Department" includes professional schools such as law, medicine, and social work.

7A. **Are you currently enrolled as a student?**

Yes, full time....................... O
Yes, part time .... O
No, I am not enrolled................. O

8. **How many colleges and universities have you attended?**

	As an Undergraduate	As A Graduate Student
One	O	O
Two	O	O
Three	O	O
Four	O	O
Five or more	O	O

9. Mark institutions attended in following list of large institutions; or if your institution does not appear, mark appropriate "other" category. (Mark one in each column)

    1. Institution Entered as Freshman
    2. Bachelor's Degree
    3. Institution (other than your present one) last attended as graduate student

    ① ② ③

None or not Applicable	① ② ③
Alabama, University of	① ② ③
Boston University	① ② ③
Brigham Young University, Utah	① ② ③
Brooklyn College	① ② ③
California Institute of Technology	① ② ③
California, University of, at Berkeley	① ② ③
California, University of, at Los Angeles	① ② ③
Carnegie Institute of Technology, Pa	① ② ③
Catholic University of America, D.C.	① ② ③
Chicago, University of	① ② ③
City College of New York	① ② ③
Colorado, University of	① ② ③
Columbia University, New York	① ② ③
Cornell University	① ② ③
Dartmouth College, New Hampshire	① ② ③
Florida, University of	① ② ③
Georgia, University of	① ② ③
Harvard University	① ② ③
Hunter College, New York	① ② ③
Illinois, University of	① ② ③
Indiana University, Bloomington	① ② ③
Iowa State University	① ② ③
Iowa, University of	① ② ③
Kansas, University of	① ② ③
Kentucky, University of	① ② ③
Louisiana State University	① ② ③
Maryland, University of	① ② ③
Massachusetts Institute of Technology	① ② ③
Michigan State University	① ② ③
Michigan, University of	① ② ③
Minnesota, University of	① ② ③
Missouri, University of, Columbia	① ② ③
Nebraska, University of	① ② ③
New York University	① ② ③
North Carolina, University of	① ② ③
Northwestern University, Illinois	① ② ③
Notre Dame, University of, Indiana	① ② ③
Oberlin College, Ohio	① ② ③
Ohio State University	① ② ③
Oklahoma State University	① ② ③
Oklahoma, University of	① ② ③
Oregon State University	① ② ③
Pennsylvania State University	① ② ③
Pennsylvania, University of	① ② ③
Pittsburgh, University of	① ② ③
Princeton University	① ② ③
Purdue University	① ② ③
Rensselaer Poly, New York	① ② ③

9 (Continued)

Rochester, University of	① ② ③
Rutgers, The State University, New Jersey	① ② ③
Southern California, University of	① ② ③
Stanford University, California	① ② ③
Swarthmore College, Pennsylvania	① ② ③
Syracuse University	① ② ③
Temple University, Pennsylvania	① ② ③
Tennessee, University of	① ② ③
Texas, University of	① ② ③
Utah, University of	① ② ③
Washington, University of, Seattle	① ② ③
Wayne State University, Michigan	① ② ③
Wisconsin, University of	① ② ③
Yale University	① ② ③
Other private Ph.D.-granting university	① ② ③
Other public Ph.D.-granting university	① ② ③
Other private college (no Ph.D. program)	① ② ③
Other public college (no Ph.D. program)	① ② ③
A junior or community college	①
A foreign institution	① ② ③

10. Is the institution in which you are now enrolled the institution in which you took (a) your bachelor's (b) your master's degree (if any)?

	Bachelor's	Master's
Yes	O	O
No	O	O
Not applicable	O	O

11. In general, how do you feel about this institution?

It is a very good place for me	O
It is fairly good for me	O
It is not the place for me	O

12. In my department, the academic standards for (a) admission to graduate work (b) advanced degrees should be--

	Graduate Admissions	Advanced Degrees
Much higher	O	O
Somewhat higher	O	O
Left as they are	O	O
Somewhat lower	O	O
Much lower	O	O

13. From the following list, mark <u>one</u> subject in each column; mark the most appropriate <u>fine</u> categories, if applicable; where your precise field does not appear, mark the most similar category.

- 1. Intended Undergraduate Major as Entering Freshman
- 2. Actual Undergraduate Major
- 3. Department in which you are studying *
- 4. Intended or Actual Master's Degree
- ① ② ③ ④ ⑤ — 5. Intended Doctor's Degree

NONE OR NOT APPLICABLE . ① ② ③ ④ ⑤
Agriculture and/or Forestry ... ① ② ③ ④ ⑤
Architecture and/or Design .... ① ② ③ ④ ⑤
Biological Sciences (General Biology) .... ① ② ③ ④ ⑤
　Bacteriology, Molecular Biology, Virology, Microbiology .. ① ② ③ ④ ⑤
　Biochemistry .... ① ② ③ ④ ⑤
　General Botany .... ① ② ③ ④ ⑤
　Physiology, Anatomy .... ① ② ③ ④ ⑤
　General Zoology .... ① ② ③ ④ ⑤
　Other Biological Sciences .... ① ② ③ ④ ⑤
Business, Commerce and Management .... ① ② ③ ④ ⑤
Education .... ① ② ③ ④ ⑤
　Elementary and/or Secondary .. ① ② ③ ④ ⑤
　Foundations .... ① ② ③ ④ ⑤
　Educational Psychology and Counseling .... ① ② ③ ④ ⑤
　Educational Administration ... ① ② ③ ④ ⑤
　Other Education fields .... ① ② ③ ④ ⑤
Engineering .... ① ② ③ ④ ⑤
　Chemical .... ① ② ③ ④ ⑤
　Civil .... ① ② ③ ④ ⑤
　Electrical .... ① ② ③ ④ ⑤
　Mechanical .... ① ② ③ ④ ⑤
　Other Engineering fields ..... ① ② ③ ④ ⑤
Fine Arts .... ① ② ③ ④ ⑤
　Art .... ① ② ③ ④ ⑤
　Dramatics .... ① ② ③ ④ ⑤
　Speech .... ① ② ③ ④ ⑤
　Music .... ① ② ③ ④ ⑤
　Other Fine Arts .... ① ② ③ ④ ⑤
Geography .... ① ② ③ ④ ⑤
Health Fields .... ① ② ③ ④ ⑤
　Dentistry .... ① ② ③ ④ ⑤
　Medicine .... ① ② ③ ④ ⑤
　Nursing .... ① ② ③ ④ ⑤
　Other Health fields .... ① ② ③ ④ ⑤
Home Economics .... ① ② ③ ④ ⑤

* Mark main department, if you are studying in more than one.

13 Continued.
　Humanities .... ① ② ③ ④ ⑤
　English language & literature . ① ② ③ ④ ⑤
　Foreign languages & literature ① ② ③ ④ ⑤
　　French .... ① ② ③ ④ ⑤
　　German .... ① ② ③ ④ ⑤
　　Spanish .... ① ② ③ ④ ⑤
　　Other foreign languages (including linguistics) .... ① ② ③ ④ ⑤
　History .... ① ② ③ ④ ⑤
　Philosophy .... ① ② ③ ④ ⑤
　Religion & Theology .... ① ② ③ ④ ⑤
　Other Humanities fields ..... ① ② ③ ④ ⑤
Journalism .... ① ② ③ ④ ⑤
Law .... ① ② ③ ④ ⑤
Library Science .... ① ② ③ ④ ⑤
Mathematics and Statistics .... ① ② ③ ④ ⑤
Physical & Health Education ... ① ② ③ ④ ⑤
Physical Sciences .... ① ② ③ ④ ⑤
　Chemistry .... ① ② ③ ④ ⑤
　Earth Sciences (incl. Geology) ① ② ③ ④ ⑤
　Physics .... ① ② ③ ④ ⑤
　Other Physical Sciences ...... ① ② ③ ④ ⑤
Psychology .... ① ② ③ ④ ⑤
　Clinical .... ① ② ③ ④ ⑤
　Experimental .... ① ② ③ ④ ⑤
　Social .... ① ② ③ ④ ⑤
　Counseling and Guidance ..... ① ② ③ ④ ⑤
　Other Psychology fields ..... ① ② ③ ④ ⑤
Social Sciences .... ① ② ③ ④ ⑤
　Anthropology .... ① ② ③ ④ ⑤
　Economics .... ① ② ③ ④ ⑤
　Political Science, Government . ① ② ③ ④ ⑤
　Sociology .... ① ② ③ ④ ⑤
　Other Social Sciences .... ① ② ③ ④ ⑤
Social Work, Social Welfare .... ① ② ③ ④ ⑤
ALL OTHER FIELDS .... ① ② ③ ④ ⑤

14. Please indicate the extent of your agreement or disagreement with each of the following statements. Mark one circle for each item.

- 1. Strongly Agree
- 2. Agree With Reservations
- 3. Disagree With Reservations
- ① ② ③ ④ — 4. Strongly Disagree

Opportunities for higher education should be available to all high school graduates who want it .... ① ② ③ ④
Most American colleges and universities are racist whether they mean to be or not .... ① ② ③ ④
American colleges and universities must be destroyed before they can be reformed .... ① ② ③ ④
The normal academic requirements should be relaxed in appointing members of minority groups to the faculty here .... ① ② ③ ④

14 Continued.

More minority group undergraduates should be admitted here
even if it means relaxing normal
academic standards of admission . ①②③④

Student demonstrations have no
place on a college campus........ ①②③④

Students who disrupt the functioning of a college should be
expelled or suspended.......... ①②③④

Most college officials have been
too lax in dealing with student
protests on campus .... ①②③④

College officials have the right
to regulate student behavior off
campus...................... ①②③④

Faculty unions have a divisive
effect on academic life .... ①②③④

Teaching assistants' unions have
a divisive effect on academic
life.......................... ①②③④

College professors deserve more
respect from the public than they
now receive.................. ①②③④

**15. Do you subscribe to any academic or profes-
sional journals?**

None........○   Three ....○

One.........○   Four or more ....○

Two ....○

16. Have you:

                                          Yes   No

Attended a meeting of an academic
or professional society ?...........○   ○

Presented a paper at a meeting of an
academic or professional society? ..○   ○

Published an article in an academic
or professional journal? ....○   ○

**17. Are you currently engaged in any scholarly or
research work which you expect to lead to
publication under your name?**

Yes...........○   No ....○

**18. Have you decided on an area or areas of spec-
ialization within your field?**

I don't intend to specialize .... ○

No, not yet .... ○

Yes, tentatively .... ○

Yes, definitely .... ○

**19. How do you rate yourself among the graduate
students in your department?**

Among the best....................... ○

Above average .... ○

About average....................... ○

Below average .... ○

**20. How would you describe the following in your
<u>department</u>?** (Mark one in each row)

1. Excellent
2. Good
3. Fair
4. Poor
①②③④⑤— 5. Don't Know

The academic ability of your
fellow graduate students .....①②③④⑤

The academic achievements of
the faculty ....①②③④⑤

The variety of graduate level
course offerings............①②③④⑤

The availability of faculty to
graduate students ....①②③④⑤

The quality of classroom instruction...................①②③④⑤

The relevance of course content to your future occupation.①②③④⑤

The intellectual environment...①②③④⑤

The academic reputation of
your department outside your
institution.................①②③④⑤

Your personal relations with
other graduate students .....①②③④⑤

**21. Please mark the extent of your agreement or
disagreement with each of the following
statements. Mark one circle for each item.**

1. Strongly Agree
2. Agree With Reservations
3. Disagree With Reservations
①②③④— 4. Strongly Disagree

I am in graduate school in order to:

Satisfy job requirements........①②③④

Continue my intellectual
growth......................①②③④

Avoid the draft................①②③④

Obtain an occupation with
high prestige ....①②③④

Increase my earning power......①②③④

Prepare for an academic
career ....①②③④

Find myself ....①②③④

See whether I really like a
particular field of study ....①②③④

Contribute to my ability to
change society...............①②③④

Get a teaching credential.......①②③④

Study my field for its intrinsic
interest ....①②③④

Better serve mankind ....①②③④

Engage in political activities ....①②③④

22. Please indicate the extent of your agreement or disagreement with each of the following statements. Mark one circle for each item.

1. Strongly Agree
2. Agree With Reservations
3. Disagree With Reservations
① ② ③ ④ — 4. Strongly Disagree

My field is too research oriented. . ① ② ③ ④
I consider myself an intellectual. . ① ② ③ ④
Much of what is taught in my department is irrelevant to what is going on in the outside world. . . . ① ② ③ ④
I hope to make significant contributions to knowledge in my field . . . . ① ② ③ ④
My department has taken steps to increase graduate student participation in its decisions. . . . . ① ② ③ ④
I am basically satisfied with the education I am getting. . . . . ① ② ③ ④
Most Ph.D. holders in my field get their degrees without showing much real scholarly ability . . ① ② ③ ④
The typical undergraduate curriculum has suffered from the specialization of faculty members . . ① ② ③ ④
Any institution with a substantial number of black students should offer a program of Black Studies if they wish it. . . . . ① ② ③ ④
Any special academic program for black students should be administered and controlled by black people . . . . ① ② ③ ④
Professors in my department don't really take female graduate students seriously. . . . . ① ② ③ ④
I see professors outside the classroom about as often as I would like. . . . . ① ② ③ ④
Professors here don't pay much attention to the graduate students . . . . ① ② ③ ④
The female graduate students in my department are not as dedicated to the field as the males . . ① ② ③ ④
Teaching effectiveness, not publications, should be the primary criterion for the promotion of faculty . . . . ① ② ③ ④
In my department it is very difficult for a man to achieve tenure if he does not publish . . . . ① ② ③ ④
I tend to subordinate all aspects of my life to my work. . . . . ① ② ③ ④
Classified weapons research is a legitimate activity on college and university campuses. . . . . ① ② ③ ④

22 Continued.

Big contract research has become more a source of money and prestige for researchers than an effective way of advancing knowledge. ① ② ③ ④
Many of the highest-paid university professors get where they are by being "operators," rather than by their scholarly or scientific contributions . . . . ① ② ③ ④
Genuine scholarship is threatened in universities by the proliferation of big research centers . . . . . ① ② ③ ④
Part of my graduate education has been essentially a wasteful repetition of what I had already covered at the undergraduate level. . . . ① ② ③ ④
Scientists should publish their findings regardless of the possible consequences. . . . . ① ② ③ ④
My career will take second place behind my family obligations . . . . ① ② ③ ④
Exciting developments are taking place in my field . . . . ① ② ③ ④
My field is among the most respected academic disciplines. . . . . ① ② ③ ④
My field gets a good share of the best students . . . . ① ② ③ ④
Graduate students should be more militant in defending their interests . . . . ① ② ③ ④
Faculty members should be free on campus to advocate violent resistance to public authority. . . . . . . ① ② ③ ④
Faculty members should be free to present in class any idea they consider relevant . . . . ① ② ③ ④
One should attempt to insulate one's academic work from one's personal values . . . . ① ② ③ ④
Some of the best graduate students in my department drop out because they do not want to "play the game" or "beat the system." . . . ① ② ③ ④
The doctorate is mainly a "union card," enabling one to get the kind of job he wants . . . . ① ② ③ ④
The graduate program in my department favors the bright, imaginative student. . . . . ① ② ③ ④

23. Do you find yourself bored in class these days?

Almost all the time . . . . ○
Fairly often. . . . . ○
Occasionally. . . . . ○
Almost never. . . . . ○
I don't take classes. ○

24. How important to you are each of the following?
(Mark one in each row)

- 1. Very Important
- 2. Fairly Important
①②③— 3. Not Important

Recognition as a good student by my
professors.........................①②③
Respect for my academic abilities
from my fellow students..........①②③
Approval by my parents of what I am
studying ....①②③

25. Do you think the following are likely to prevent
you from completing your graduate work?
(Mark one in each row)

Yes Maybe No

Lack of interest ....OOO
Lack of finances ....OOO
A job offer ....OOO
Inability to do the academic work....OOO
Too much emotional strain.........OOO
The draft.......................OOO
Pressure from my wife or husband ...OOO

26. On the average, how often do you meet informally (that is, for meals, parties, etc.) either
on or off campus with graduate students in
your department? With professors in your department? With people not connected with the
university? (Mark one in each column)

- 1. Students
- 2. Professors
- 3. People Not Connected With
①②③ University

Once a week or more...............①②③
Two or three times a month.........①②③
About once a month...............①②③
A few times a year ....①②③
Once a year or less...............①②③

27. About how many of the people you see socially
are also graduate students in your department?

Almost all.......O   Some............O
Most............O   Almost none ......O
About half.......O

28. Is there a professor in your department

Yes   No

You feel free to turn to for advice on
personal matters? ....O   O
Who is taking or will take a special
interest in helping you get a job
when you finish graduate school?...O   O

29. Does the professor with whom you have
most academic contact outside the class-
room regard you primarily as
A colleague..........................O
An apprentice ....O
An employee ....O
A student...........................O
No contact outside the classroom........O

30. As a graduate student, have there been times
when you felt you did not know where you stood,
i.e., how far along you really were or how well
you were doing?
Yes, very often........................O
Yes, often...........................O
Yes, occasionally ....O
No................................O

31. At present how much attention are you giving to
each of the following? (Mark one in each row)

- 1. Have Completed
- 2. Very Much
- 3. Some
- 4. Not Much
①②③④⑤— 5. None

Required courses ....①②③④⑤
Preparation for preliminary exams
(master's or doctoral) ....①②③④⑤
Preparation for language exams.①②③④⑤
Dissertation research ....①②③④⑤
Dissertation writing..........①②③④⑤

32. If you were to begin your academic training
again, would you still choose your present
discipline for specialization?
Definitely yes....O   Probably no.....O
Probably yes.....O   Definitely no....O

33. If no, would you choose another field
Very close to your own ....O
Not close, but related ....O
Quite different ....O

34. During the past year have you considered
changing to another institution to finish your
graduate training? Have you considered
changing your field of study?

Institution Field of Study

I am changing ....OO
I have considered it seriously ....OO
I have considered it, but not
seriously ....OO
I haven't considered it ....OO

35. During the past year have you considered quitting graduate school for good?

Yes, and I have definitely decided to quit. ..O
Yes, I have given it serious consideration .O
Yes, I have considered it, but not seriously ....O
No. ....O

36. What was your undergraduate grade point average?

A or A+ ..O   B.......O   C or below ..O
A-.......O   B-.....O
B+.......O   C+.....O

37. As an undergraduate were you ever a member of a social fraternity or sorority?

No. ....O
One year ....O
Two years ....O
Three years.........................O
Four or more years...................O

38. How important do you think it is that a student in your field get a firm grounding in the following during his underGraduate years?
(Mark one in each row)

1. Extremely Important
2. Fairly Important
3. Fairly Unimportant
①②③④— 4. Extremely Unimportant

English ....①②③④
Mathematics ....①②③④
Physical science ....①②③④
Life science ....①②③④
Social science ....①②③④
The humanities..................①②③④
Art and music ....①②③④
A foreign language..............①②③④

39. How satisfied are you with each of the following aspects of your underGraduate education?
(Mark one in each row)

1. Very Satisfied
2. Satisfied
3. Dissatisfied
①②③④— 4. Very Dissatisfied

Foreign languages ....①②③④
Ability to write and organize material......................①②③④
Preparation in my subject field ....①②③④
General background of liberal education.......................①②③④
Ability to work on my own ....①②③④
Ability to do original work........①②③④
General preparation for graduate school ....①②③④

40. a. What role do you believe underGraduates should play in decisions on the following?
(Mark one in each row)

1. Control
2. Voting Power On Committees
3. Formal Consultation
4. Informal Consultation
①②③④⑤— 5. Little or no Role

Faculty appointment and promotion....................①②③④⑤
Undergraduate admissions policy.....................①②③④⑤
Provision and content of courses....................①②③④⑤
Student discipline............①②③④⑤
Bachelor's degree requirements .①②③④⑤

b. What role do you believe graduate students should play in decisions on the following?

Faculty appointment and promotion.....................①②③④⑤
Departmental graduate admissions policy..............①②③④⑤
Provision and content of graduate courses ....①②③④⑤
Student discipline............①②③④⑤
Advanced degree requirements ..①②③④⑤

41. Has your campus experienced any student protests or demonstrations during the current academic year?

Yes .....O   No ....O
(If no, skip to No. 44 on page 9)

42. How would you characterize your attitude toward the most recent demonstration?

Approved of the demonstrators' aims and methods ....O
Approved of their aims but not their methods ....O
Disapproved of their aims ....O
Uncertain or mixed feelings ....O
Indifferent ....O

43. What was your role in this demonstration?
(Mark all that apply)

Helped to plan, organize, or lead the protest....................................O
Joined in active protest with the demonstrators................................O
Openly supported the goals of the protestors.................................O
Openly opposed the goals of the protestors O
Tried to mediate in the protest...........O
Was not involved actively in any way .....O

44. (a) Are you now employed (b) have you ever been employed for a term* or more while a graduate student as

	Am Now	Have Been
Part-time Research Assistant	○	○
Full-time Research position	○	○
Part-time Teaching Assistant	○	○
Full-time position as Teaching Associate or Teaching Fellow	○	○
Full or part-time faculty position as lecturer, instructor, acting assistant professor, etc.	○	○
Other academic position	○	○
None of these	○	○

* Quarter, semester, trimester, etc.

45. Would you yourself be inclined to join a union for employed graduate students if one were organized?

There is one; I am a member............○
There is one; I am not a member ....○
There isn't one; I almost certainly would
  join...............................○
There isn't one; I probably would join ....○
There isn't one; I probably would not join.○
There isn't one; I almost certainly would
  not join..........................○

46. If a large group of employed graduate students were to call for a strike over a campus issue, and you agreed with their position on the issue, do you think you would participate in the strike?

Definitely yes ...○   Probably not......○
Probably yes ....○   Definitely not.....○

47. Do you feel that there are circumstances in which a strike would be a legitimate means of collective action

┌─── 1. **Definitely yes**
│ ┌─── 2. **Probably yes**
│ │ ┌─── 3. **Probably not**
① ② ③ ④ — 4. **Definitely not**

For faculty members ....① ② ③ ④
For teaching assistants ....① ② ③ ④

48. What do you think of the emergence of radical student activism in recent years?

Unreservedly approve ....○
Approve with reservations ....○
Disapprove with reservations ....○
Unreservedly disapprove ....○

49. About how many hours a week do you devote to each of the following?
(Mark one in each row)

	None	1-4	5-8	9-12	13-20	21-30	31-40	Over 40
Studying	○	○	○	○	○	○	○	○
Hours in class or required laboratories (Give actual, not credit hours and exclude teaching, if any)	○	○	○	○	○	○	○	○
Employment connected with your field of study	○	○	○	○	○	○	○	○
Employment not connected with your field of study	○	○	○	○	○	○	○	○

50. Which of the following occupations* have you engaged in continously for six months or more? Which **one** do you realistically expect to enter when you complete your graduate training?

* Do **not** include apprenticeship, internship, or teaching/research assistantship.

┌─── 1. **Have Done**
① ② — 2. **Expect to enter**

Teaching at the elementary or secondary
  level............................① ②
Teaching at the junior college level....① ②
Teaching at the college or university
  level............................① ②
Full-time research at a university ......① ②
Research with a non-profit organization
  or institute not affiliated with a univer-
  sity ....① ②
Research in industry ....① ②
Self-employed professional practice
  alone............................① ②
Self-employed professional practice
  with partner(s)....................① ②
Employed professional practice ....① ②
Self-employed, business ....① ②
Executive or administrator in govern-
  ment ....① ②
Executive or administrator in education.① ②
Executive or administrator in private
  industry ....① ②
Manual labor or factory work..........① ②
Military service......................① ②
Clerical or sales work ....① ②
Other.............................① ②

51. Are you interested in an academic career?

Very interested ....○
Fairly interested.........○
Fairly uninterested.......○
Very uninterested ....○ (Skip to No. 53)

52. Are you interested primarily in teaching or in research?

Very heavily in research ....○
In both, but leaning toward research......○
In both, but leaning toward teaching......○
Very heavily in teaching...............○

53. Have you ever spent any time in programs such as VISTA or the Peace Corps?

Yes...................................○
No, but I plan to.......................○
No, but I'd like to ....○
No, and I wouldn't like to...............○

54. Please indicate the extent of your agreement or disagreement with each of the following statements. Mark one circle for each statement.

1. Strongly agree
2. Agree with reservations
3. Disagree with reservations
①②③④ — 4. Strongly disagree

There are many things that can
never possibly be understood by
the techniques of science........①②③④
It is all right to get around the law
if you don't actually break it......①②③④
I am as strict about right and
wrong as most people ....①②③④
I enjoy reading poetry ....①②③④
I enjoy classical music..........①②③④
I do a lot of serious reading outside my field of study ....①②③④
Persons with a graduate education
are no better than anyone else...①②③④
There is too much concern in the
courts for the rights of criminals. ①②③④
Most people who live in poverty
could do something about their
situation if they really wanted to .①②③④
I basically dislike large cities ...①②③④
I have a pretty good idea when I
will finish my graduate education .①②③④
When I'm with other graduate students, we usually talk about our
field of study ....①②③④
I think I would be happier if I
hadn't entered graduate school .①②③④
I intend to remain in this state
after I complete my graduate
education.....................①②③④
I am basically conservative in my
religious beliefs...............①②③④
I think of myself primarily as a
scholar or scientist and not as a
student......................①②③④

54 Continued.

These days you hear too much
about the rights of minorities and
not enough about the rights of the
majority ....①②③④
Where de facto segregation exists,
black people should be assured
control over their own schools....①②③④
Racial integration of the public
elementary schools should be
achieved even if it requires
busing ....①②③④
Meaningful social change cannot
be achieved through traditional
American politics...............①②③④
The main cause of Negro riots in
the cities is white racism.......①②③④
Communist China should be recognized immediately by the U.S. ①②③④
Hippies represent an important
criticism of American culture....①②③④
Marijuana should be legalized ....①②③④
Realistically, an individual person can do little to bring about
changes in our society ....①②③④
The decline in moral standards
among youth is a major problem
in America today ....①②③④

55. How adequate are your finances to your present needs?

Very adequate......................○
Adequate ....○
Inadequate.........................○
Very inadequate ....○

56. What was your total (family) income last year from all sources?

Less than $2,500 .○ $5,000 - $5,999.....○
$2,500 - $2,999...○ $6,000 - $6,999.....○
$3,000 - $3,499...○ $7,000 - $7,999.....○
$3,500 - $3,999...○ $8,000 - $9,999.....○
$4,000 - $4,499...○ $10,000 - $11,999..○
$4,500 - $4,999...○ $12,000 and over ..○

57. Apart from room and board, roughly what were your total educational expenses this term? (Include tuition, registration, other fees, books, lab supplies, etc.)

Under $50........○ $400 - $499.......○
$50 - $99 ....○ $500 - $699.......○
$100 - $199......○ $700 - $999.......○
$200 - $299......○ $1,000 or over ....○
$300 - $399......○

58. Which of the following have been sources of income for you during the current academic year? (Please check all that apply.) Which one of the following has been your <u>primary</u> source of income during the current year? Which has been your <u>primary</u> source of income since entering graduate school?

    1. A Source of Income This Year
    2. Primary Source This Year
    3. Primary Source Since Entering
①②③   Graduate School

Fellowship .... ①②③
Teaching/research assistantship, internship .... ①②③
Non-academic job................ ①②③
Spouse's job..................... ①②③
Savings .... ①②③
Investments..................... ①②③
Aid from family................. ①②③
Loans from family or friends .... ①②③
Government or institutional loans .... ①②③
Other .... ①②③

59. How interested are you in local and national politics? How interested would you be in politics as a career? (Mark one in each column)

	Local	National	Career
Extremely interested	○	○	○
Moderately interested	○	○	○
Only slightly interested..........	○	○	○
Not interested at all.............	○	○	○

60.
    1. **Left**
    2. **Liberal**
    3. **Middle-of-the-Road**
    4. **Moderately Conservative**
①②③④⑤— 5. **Strongly Conservative**

a. How would you characterize yourself politically at the present time? .... ①②③④⑤

b. What were your father's politics while you were growing up?..................... ①②③④⑤

61. Whom would you have favored
a. At the Republican convention?
Nixon .... ○   Rockefeller .... ○

b. At the Democratic convention?
Humphrey ...... ○   McCarthy .... ○

62. Whom did you vote for in November?
Nixon .... ○   Another candidate .. ○
Humphrey ...... ○   Did not vote .... ○
Wallace........ ○   No answer .... ○

63. In what religion were you raised? What is your present religious preference?

    1. Religion in which raised
①②— 2. Present religion

Baptist .... ①②
Baptist (Southern).................. ①②
Congregational (United Church of Christ) .... ①②
Episcopal.......................... ①②
Jewish .... ①②
Latter Day Saints (Mormon)........... ①②
Lutheran.......................... ①②
Lutheran (Missouri Synod)............ ①②
Methodist .... ①②
Presbyterian .... ①②
Quaker (Society of Friends) .... ①②
Roman Catholic.................... ①②
Unitarian-Universalist .... ①②
Other Protestant .... ①②
Other religions .... ①②
None .... ①②
No answer .... ①②

64. Do you consider yourself
Deeply religious .... ○
Moderately religious.................... ○
Largely indifferent to religion........... ○
Basically opposed to religion........... ○

65. Where did you live for most of the time while you were growing up? Where would you prefer to live after finishing graduate school?

	Lived	Would Prefer
On a farm	○	○
In a small town	○	○
In a moderate size town or city	○	○
In a suburb of a large city.....	○	○
In a large city	○	○

66. Do any of the following statements apply to you?

	Yes	No
I grew up in this state.............	○	○
I first came to this state as an undergraduate	○	○
I first came to this state as a graduate student.................	○	○

67. Since first entering graduate school, how many academic years have you not been enrolled in a college or university? (Do not count summer vacations.)
None.............. ○   Three years .... ○
Less than one year . ○   Four years..... ○
About 1 year....... ○   Five or more
Two years .... ○   years .... ○

68. What is the <u>highest</u> level of formal education reached by your spouse? Your father? Your mother? (Mark one in each column)

	Spouse	Father	Mother
No spouse	O		
8th grade or less	O	O	O
Some high school	O	O	O
Completed high school	O	O	O
Some college	O	O	O
Graduated from college	O	O	O
Attended graduate or professional school	O	O	O
Attained advanced degree	O	O	O

69. What is (was) your father's principal occupation? (Mark one)

College or university teaching, research or administration .... O
Elementary or secondary school teaching, administration .... O
Physician .... O
Lawyer............................. O
Other professional .... O
Managerial, administrative, semiprofessional .... O
Owner, large business................. O
Owner, small business .... O
Other white collar: clerical or retail sales. O
Skilled wage worker.................... O
Semi- and unskilled wage worker, farm laborer .... O
Armed forces......................... O
Farm owner or manager .... O
Other .... O

70. In general, I would characterize my parents as: Mark one circle for each item.

1. Strongly Agree
2. Agree
3. Disagree
① ② ③ ④ — 4. Strongly Disagree

Interested in intellectual pursuits........................① ② ③ ④
Interested in cultural pursuits ....① ② ③ ④
Deeply religious................① ② ③ ④
Interested in politics............① ② ③ ④
Deeply concerned about their children....................① ② ③ ④
Financially comfortable ....① ② ③ ④
Having high aspirations for me ...① ② ③ ④

71. How often do you now have contacts with your parents either through letters, phone calls, or personal visits?

Both parents deceased................... O
Am living with parents.................. O
Once a week or more .... O
Two or three times a month .... O
About once a month.................... O
A few times a year.................... O
Once a year or less .... O

72. How often, on the average, do you attend: (Mark one in each row)

1. Once a week or more
2. Two or three times a month
3. About once a month
4. A few times a year
① ② ③ ④ ⑤ — 5. Once a year or less

A religious service...........① ② ③ ④ ⑤
A concert ....① ② ③ ④ ⑤
An "art" film ....① ② ③ ④ ⑤
A play.....................① ② ③ ④ ⑤
An art exhibition...........① ② ③ ④ ⑤
An athletic event ....① ② ③ ④ ⑤

73. How many hours a day, on the average, do you spend watching television?

None .... O　　About 2 .... O
About ½ or less.. O　　About 3 .... O
About 1......... O　　Four or more...... O
About 1½ .... O

74. Your race:

Caucasian ...... O　　Oriental.......... O
Negro .... O　　Other .... O

75. Your age:

21 or younger.... O　　26-27 .... O
22 .... O　　28-29 .... O
23 .... O　　30-34 .... O
24 .... O　　35-39 .... O
25 .... O　　40 or older ...... O

	Yes	No
76. a. Are you a United States citizen?	O	O
b. (If yes) Have you ever been a citizen of another country?	O	O

Undergraduate Questionnaire

THE CARNEGIE COMMISSION ON HIGHER EDUCATION
THE AMERICAN COUNCIL ON EDUCATION

Dear Friend:

The Carnegie Commission on Higher Education and The American Council on Education are conducting several surveys of students, former students, and faculty members throughout the United States. The information gathered in the present study will be used to reveal young adults' views on aspects of American higher education, so that the qualities and relevance of our colleges and universities may be assessed and, hopefully, improved.

You have been selected to receive this questionnaire because you completed a brief information form when you first entered college, in which you indicated your educational and career plans. Your participation in this study is therefore of great value, because it will permit an assessment of changes over time. We are interested in your responses even if you are not now attending college.

We should greatly appreciate your help in this study by completing the questionnaire and returning it in the enclosed envelope. All of the information will be coded and used in group comparisons for research purposes only. Under no circumstances will individual responses be reported. Your name appears below in order to assure that the recipient is the same person who filled out the original freshman information form.

We realize that not all questions will be equally applicable to your particular situation. Please try to answer each question if there is any basis at all for answering. If you do not wish to answer a question, omit it and go on to the next.

We hope that you will find the questionnaire interesting to answer, and that you will complete it and return it to us immediately.

With thanks for your cooperation.

Sincerely,

Clark Kerr

Clark Kerr
Chairman
Carnegie Commission
 on Higher Education

Logan Wilson

Logan Wilson
President
American Council
 on Education

FOR NCS USE ONLY

NOTE: In some of the questions which follow, you will encounter the terms "your college," "my college," etc. In each case we are referring to the institution whose name you wrote in answer to question number 1.

In some questions you will encounter the terms "professors," or "instructors." These refer to faculty members who have the primary responsibility for the conduct of a course, whatever their titles. We do <u>not</u> mean those who assist the person primarily responsible for the course, such as teaching assistants, laboratory assistants, readers, etc.

MARKING INSTRUCTIONS

This questionnaire will be read by an automatic scanning device. Certain marking requirements are essential to this process. Your careful observance of these few simple rules will be most appreciated.

Use soft black lead pencil only (No. 2½ or softer). Do not use pen.

Make heavy black marks that completely fill the circle.

Erase completely any answers you wish to change.

Avoid making any stray marks in this booklet.

---

1. **Did you attend college (full or part time) during this past fall?**

   Yes . . . ○   No . . . ○

   IF YES, print the name of the college
   IF NO, print the name of the last college you attended. *

   _____   _____
   COLLEGE   CITY, STATE

2. **Did you enroll in college immediately after high school? (disregard summers)**

   Yes . . . ○   No . . . ○

3. **Since first entering college, have you ever dropped out for a term or longer? (disregard summers)**

   Yes . . . ○   No . . . ○

4. **In total, how many different colleges have you enrolled in (disregard temporary summer attendance)?**

   One . . ○   Four or
   Two . . ○   more . . ○
   Three . ○

5. **Have you ever enrolled in a junior college?**

   Yes . . . ○   No . . . ○

   IF YES, have you ever transferred to a four year college?

   Yes . . . ○   No . . . ○

   * *If you have <u>never</u> attended a college, print "none" on the blank, then stop, place questionnaire in return envelope, and return it.*

---

6. **Indicate what you were doing: (mark all that apply)**

   — 1. **During this past fall**
   — 2. **During the time you dropped out of college (if YES in Q. 3)**
   — 3. **Between high school and starting college (if NO in Q. 2)**
   ① ② ③

   College, full time . . . . ①
   College, part time . . . . ①
   Graduate school . . . . ①
   Temporary college interruption (illness, etc.) . . . . ① ② ③
   Night school, adult education . . . . ① ② ③
   Work, part time . . . . ① ② ③
   Work, full time . . . . ① ② ③
   Military service, active duty . . . . ① ② ③
   Housewife . . . . ① ② ③
   Unemployed, looking for a job . . . . . . ① ② ③

7. **When will you most likely graduate with your Bachelor's degree? (Mark one)**

   I do not expect to get a Bachelor's degree . . ○
   I have a Bachelor's degree already . . . . ○
   June 1970 or earlier . . . . ○
   July 1970 - June 1971 . . . . ○
   July 1971 - June 1972 . . . . ○
   July 1972 - June 1973 . . . . ○
   After June 1973 . . . . ○
   Highly uncertain . . . . ○

8. **Please indicate your agreement or disagreement with each of the following statements.**

   — 1. **Strongly Agree**
   — 2. **Agree With Reservations**
   — 3. **Disagree With Reservations**
   ① ② ③ ④ — 4. **Strongly Disagree**

   Opportunities for higher education should be available to all high school graduates who want it . . . ① ② ③ ④
   Classified weapons research is a legitimate activity on college and university campuses . . . . ① ② ③ ④
   A man can be an effective teacher without personally involving himself with his students . . . . ① ② ③ ④
   A professor's teaching inevitably reflects his political values . . . . . . ① ② ③ ④
   Teaching effectiveness, not publications, should be the primary criterion for promotion of faculty ① ② ③ ④
   A strike would be a legitimate means of collective action for faculty members under some circumstances . . . . ① ② ③ ④

8. Continued

Faculty members should be free on campus to advocate violent resistance to public authority .... ①②③④

Faculty members should be free to present in class any idea they consider relevant .... ①②③④

Most American colleges reward conformity and crush student creativity .... ①②③④

Most American colleges and universities are racist whether they mean to be or not .... ①②③④

Any special academic program for black students should be administered and controlled by black people .... ①②③④

Any institution with a substantial number of black students should offer a program of Black Studies if they wish it .... ①②③④

Student demonstrations have no place on a college campus ..... ①②③④

Students should be more militant in defending their interests ...... ①②③④

Students who disrupt the functioning of a college should be expelled or suspended .... ①②③④

Political activities by students have no place on a college campus ... ①②③④

Most college officials have been too lax in dealing with student protests on campus .... ①②③④

College officials have the right to regulate student behavior off campus .... ①②③④

Student publications should be cleared by college officials ..... ①②③④

Undergraduate education in America would be improved if:

All courses were elective ...... ①②③④

Grades were abolished .... ①②③④

Course work were more relevant to contemporary life and problems .... ①②③④

More attention were paid to the emotional growth of students . ①②③④

Students were required to spend a year in community service in the U.S. or abroad .... ①②③④

The college were governed completely by its faculty and students .... ①②③④

There were less emphasis on specialized training and more on broad liberal education ..... ①②③④

9. For each of these statements, indicate whether it is true or false at your college (if not now attending, indicate if it was true at your college).

```
        ┌──── 1. Almost Always True
      ┌─┴─── 2. Usually True
     ╱ ┌──── 3. Usually False
 ①②③④ ─ 4. Almost Always False
```

My grades understate the true quality of my work .... ①②③④

Professors in my major field give my work the attention it deserves ... ①②③④

Professors give my work too much attention .... ①②③④

I work hard at my studies .... ①②③④

I find myself bored in class ...... ①②③④

I really don't care what grades I get . ①②③④

It is possible to get good grades without really understanding the material .... ①②③④

Some forms of cheating are necessary to get the grade I want .... ①②③④

I think I would be happier if I hadn't entered college .... ①②③④

Getting a degree is more important to me than the content of my courses .... ①②③④

Professors tend to reward nonconformity .... ①②③④

The best way to make it is to tell professors what they want to hear .... ①②③④

10. People want different things from college.
A) Indicate how important it is for you to get each of the following at college. B) Indicate how much of each you have received at your college.

```
   IMPORTANCE                    RECEIVED
 ┌──── 1. Essential            ┌──── 7. Much
 ┌─┴── 2. Fairly Important     ┌─┴── 8. Some
①②③─ 3. Not Important        ⑦⑧⑨─ 9. None
```

	Importance	Received
A detailed grasp of a special field	①②③	⑦⑧⑨
A well-rounded general education	①②③	⑦⑧⑨
Training and skills for an occupation	①②③	⑦⑧⑨
Learning to get along with people	①②③	⑦⑧⑨
Preparation for marriage ...	①②③	⑦⑧⑨
Formulating the values and goals of my life	①②③	⑦⑧⑨

11. For each of these statements, indicate whether it is true or false at your college (if not now attending, indicate if it was true at your college). IF TRUE, indicate whether it bother(s)(ed) you.

	True	False	Bothers Yes	No
I am not interested in most of my courses	O	O	O	O
I am not really learning anything new	O	O	O	O
I am not really learning anything important	O	O	O	O
I am not doing as well as I wish academically	O	O	O	O
I often don't know what professors want	O	O	O	O
It is difficult both to get good grades and really learn something	O	O	O	O
Many successful students at my college make it by "beating the system" rather than by studying	O	O	O	O
I am often lonely	O	O	O	O
My college is much like high school	O	O	O	O
I am under much pressure and strain	O	O	O	O
I find it hard to meet my college expenses	O	O	O	O
I don't discuss personal matters with professors	O	O	O	O
I am often in low spirits	O	O	O	O

12. How hard would you work in a class in which:

┌──────── 1. Harder Than Usual
│ ┌────── 2. As Much As Usual
① ② ③ ─ 3. Less Than Usual

The instructor is very stimulating	① ② ③
The subject is essential to your career	① ② ③
A good grade is very hard to get	① ② ③
You are not at all interested in the course	① ② ③
Your parents really want you to do well	① ② ③
A pass-fail grade (or equivalent) is used	① ② ③

13. Did any of your courses during your most recent college term have the following?

	Yes	No
Term papers	O	O
Take-home examinations	O	O
Frequent quizzes in class	O	O
Computer or machine-aided instruction	O	O

13. Continued

	Yes	No
Closed-circuit television	O	O
100 or more students	O	O
Small discussion meetings	O	O
Laboratory assistants	O	O
Teaching assistants	O	O
Some class meetings at the professor's home	O	O

14. How satisfied are you with the following at your college?

┌──────── 1. Very Satisfied
│ ┌────── 2. Satisfied
│ │ ┌──── 3. Dissatisfied
① ② ③ ④ ─ 4. Very dissatisfied

The college's academic reputation	① ② ③ ④
The intellectual environment	① ② ③ ④
Faculty/student relations	① ② ③ ④
The quality of classroom instruction	① ② ③ ④
The variety of courses I can take	① ② ③ ④
Friendships with other students	① ② ③ ④
The administration	① ② ③ ④

15. Do you think you will:

┌──────── 1. Definitely
│ ┌────── 2. Probably
│ │ ┌──── 3. Probably Not
① ② ③ ④ ─ 4. Definitely Not

Change to another college before receiving a Bachelor's degree	① ② ③ ④
Return to college (if not now attending)	① ② ③ ④
Drop out before getting a Bachelor's degree	① ② ③ ④
Graduate without a specific career in mind	① ② ③ ④
Never have a career at all	① ② ③ ④

16. Please indicate your agreement or disagreement with each of the following statements.

┌──────── 1. Strongly Agree
│ ┌────── 2. Agree With Reservations
│ │ ┌──── 3. Disagree With Reservations
① ② ③ ④ ─ 4. Strongly Disagree

Most undergraduates at my college are satisfied with the education they are getting	① ② ③ ④
Much of what is taught at my college is irrelevant to what is going on in the outside world	① ② ③ ④
Most faculty at my college are strongly interested in the academic problems of undergraduates	① ② ③ ④

16. Continued

Professors and administrators at my
college show too much interest
in students' personal lives ...... ①②③④

The normal academic requirements
should be relaxed in appointing
members of minority groups to
the faculty at my college ...... ①②③④

My college should be actively engaged in solving social problems . ①②③④

Most rules governing student behavior at my college are sensible . ①②③④

Most professors at my college don't
do much to earn their pay ..... ①②③④

More minority group undergraduates
should be admitted to my college
even if it means relaxing normal
academic standards of admission . ①②③④

I cannot imagine being happy in
any of the careers available to
me .... ①②③④

I consider myself an intellectual ... ①②③④

I consider myself religious ...... ①②③④

I believe there is a God who judges
men .... ①②③④

I would rather be going to college
now than doing anything else ... ①②③④

My beliefs and attitudes are similar
to those of most students ..... ①②③④

Striving for occupational success
would require me to compromise
important ethical principles .... ①②③④

The military draft has influenced
my decisions about college
attendance .... ①②③④

My finances are adequate to my
needs .... ①②③④

American colleges and universities
must sever all ties with the
military-industrial complex ..... ①②③④

College officials have the right to
ban persons with extreme views
from speaking on campus ...... ①②③④

**17. What role do you believe <u>undergraduates</u>
should play in decisions on the following?**
(Mark one in each row)

┌──────1. **Control**
│ ┌────2. **Voting Power on Committees**
│ │ ┌──3. **Formal Consultation**
│ │ │ ┌─4. **Informal Consultation**
①②③④⑤—5. **Little or No Role**

Faculty appointment and promotion .... ①②③④⑤

Undergraduate admissions policy . ①②③④⑤

Bachelor's degree requirements . ①②③④⑤

Provision and content of courses . ①②③④⑤

Residence hall regulations ..... ①②③④⑤

Student discipline .... ①②③④⑤

**18. All in all, in terms of your own needs and
desires, how much of the following have you
had at college?**(Mark one in each row)

┌──────1. **Too Much or Too Many**
│ ┌────2. **About the Right Amount**
①②③—3. **Not Enough**

Freedom in course selection .... ①②③

Social life .... ①②③

Personal contacts with classmates .... ①②③

Work required of you in courses ..... ①②③

Outlets for creative activities .... ①②③

Sleep .... ①②③

Exercise .... ①②③

Personal contacts with faculty ...... ①②③

Personal contacts with family ...... ①②③

Advice and guidance from faculty and
staff .... ①②③

**19. How important are each of the following to
you for your future?**

┌──────1. **Essential**
│ ┌────2. **Desirable**
①②③—3. **Not Important**

Opportunities to be original and
creative .... ①②③

A stable, secure future .... ①②③

Freedom from supervision in my work . ①②③

Opportunities to be useful to society .. ①②③

A chance to exercise leadership ...... ①②③

Living and working in the world of
ideas .... ①②③

Work with people rather than things .. ①②③

Avoiding a high-pressure job .... ①②③

**20. Answer each of the following as you think it
applies to your college:**

	Yes	No
The students are under a great deal of pressure to get high grades	O	O
The student body is apathetic and has little "school spirit"	O	O
Most of the students are of a very high calibre academically	O	O
There is a keen competition among most of the students for high grades .	O	O
Freshmen have to take orders from upperclassmen for a period of time .	O	O
There isn't much to do except to go to class and study	O	O
I felt "lost" when I first came to the campus	O	O
Being in this college builds poise and maturity	O	O
Athletics are overemphasized	O	O
The classes are usually run in a very informal manner	O	O
Most students are treated like "numbers in a book"	O	O

21. **Which of the following experiences applies to you since entering college? (Mark all that apply)**

	Yes
Elected to a student office	○
Played on a varsity athletic team	○
Changed your long-term career plans	○
Flunked a course	○
Changed your major field	○
Fell in love	○
Had a lead in a college play	○
Wrote an article for the school paper or magazine	○
Joined a social fraternity or sorority	○
Received treatment in the Student Health Center	○
Participated in an honors program	○
Was enrolled in a program for disadvantaged students	○
Took pass-fail course (or equivalent)	○
Participated in ROTC	○
Was ever on academic probation	○
Voted in a student election	○
Worked in a college political campaign	○
Worked in a local, state or national political campaign	○

22. **To what extent do you think each of the following describes the psychological climate or atmosphere at your college? (Mark one for each item)**

① ② ③ —
— 1. Very Descriptive
— 2. In Between
— 3. Not At All Descriptive

Intellectual	① ② ③
Snobbish	① ② ③
Social	① ② ③
Victorian	① ② ③
Practical-minded	① ② ③
Warm	① ② ③
Realistic	① ② ③
Liberal	① ② ③

23. **Is there any Professor at your college with whom you:**

	Major Field Professors		Other Professors	
	Yes	No	Yes	No
Often discuss topics in his field	○	○	○	○
Often discuss other topics of intellectual interest	○	○	○	○
Sometimes engage in social conversation .	○	○	○	○
Ever talk about personal matters	○	○	○	○

24. **Think about the course you took during your most recent college term which was most closely related to your primary field of interest. Please mark "yes" for all the following statements which apply to this course. (if the course had a lab portion, mark "yes" only for those items which apply to the lecture portion.)**

	Yes
The class met only at a regularly scheduled time and place	○
Students had assigned seating	○
The lectures followed the textbook closely . .	○
The instructor called students by their first names	○
The instructor encouraged a lot of class discussion	○
I knew the instructor's first name	○
I was in the instructor's office one or more times	○
The instructor was enthusiastic	○
The instructor had a good sense of humor	○
The instructor was often dull and uninteresting .	○
The instructor knew me by name	○
I sometimes argued openly with the instructor	○
I usually typed my written assignments	○
I was a guest in the instructor's home one or more times	○

25. **What action would be taken at your college if a student were known to have done the following? (Mark one for each item.)**

① ② ③ ④ —
— 1. No action would be taken
— 2. Reprimand or minor disciplinary action
— 3. Major disciplinary action (possible expulsion from college)
— 4. Sure expulsion from college

Coming in from a date two hours late .	① ② ③ ④
Cheating on exams	① ② ③ ④
Drinking in living quarters	① ② ③ ④
Being drunk	① ② ③ ④
Being alone with a date in your room during the day	① ② ③ ④
Being alone with a date in your room at night	① ② ③ ④
Staying off campus overnight without permission	① ② ③ ④
Organizing a student demonstration against some administrative policy .	① ② ③ ④
Writing off-color stories in a student publication	① ② ③ ④
Participating in a water fight or dormitory raid	① ② ③ ④
Using LSD or speed	① ② ③ ④
Using marijuana	① ② ③ ④

26. What is your over-all evaluation of your college? (mark one)

Very satisfied with my college . . . .○
Satisfied with my college . . . .○
On the fence . . . .○
Dissatisfied with my college . . . .○
Very dissatisfied with my college . . . .○

27. Indicate the importance to you personally of each of the following (mark one for each item).

┌─────Essential
│ ┌────Very Important
│ │ ┌───Somewhat Important
Ⓔ Ⓥ Ⓢ Ⓝ —Not Important

Becoming accomplished in one of
the performing arts (acting,
dancing, etc.) . . . . Ⓔ Ⓥ Ⓢ Ⓝ
Becoming an authority on a special
subject in my subject field . . . . . . Ⓔ Ⓥ Ⓢ Ⓝ
Obtaining recognition from my
colleagues for contributions
in my special field . . . . Ⓔ Ⓥ Ⓢ Ⓝ
Influencing the political structure . . . . Ⓔ Ⓥ Ⓢ Ⓝ
Influencing social values. . . . . Ⓔ Ⓥ Ⓢ Ⓝ
Raising a family . . . . Ⓔ Ⓥ Ⓢ Ⓝ
Having an active social life . . . . Ⓔ Ⓥ Ⓢ Ⓝ
Having friends with different back-
grounds and interests from mine . . Ⓔ Ⓥ Ⓢ Ⓝ
Becoming an expert in finance and
commerce . . . . Ⓔ Ⓥ Ⓢ Ⓝ
Having administrative responsibility
for the work of others. . . . . Ⓔ Ⓥ Ⓢ Ⓝ
Being very well-off financially . . . . . . Ⓔ Ⓥ Ⓢ Ⓝ
Helping others who are in difficulty . . Ⓔ Ⓥ Ⓢ Ⓝ
Becoming a community leader . . . . . . Ⓔ Ⓥ Ⓢ Ⓝ
Making a theoretical contribution
to science . . . . Ⓔ Ⓥ Ⓢ Ⓝ
Writing original works (poems,
novels, short stories, etc.) . . . . Ⓔ Ⓥ Ⓢ Ⓝ
Never being obligated to people . . . . . Ⓔ Ⓥ Ⓢ Ⓝ
Creating artistic work (painting,
sculpture, decorating, etc.) . . . . . . Ⓔ Ⓥ Ⓢ Ⓝ
Keeping up to date with political
affairs . . . . Ⓔ Ⓥ Ⓢ Ⓝ
Being successful in a business of
my own . . . . Ⓔ Ⓥ Ⓢ Ⓝ
Developing a meaningful
philosophy of life . . . . Ⓔ Ⓥ Ⓢ Ⓝ

28. Please indicate your agreement or disagreement with each of the following statements.

┌──────1. Strongly Agree
│ ┌─────2. Agree With Reservations
│ │ ┌────3. Disagree With Reservations
① ② ③ ④ — 4. Strongly Disagree

Communist China should be
recognized immediately by
the U.S. . . . . ① ② ③ ④

28. Continued

These days you hear too much
about the rights of minorities
and not enough about the
rights of the majority . . . . ① ② ③ ④
Most people who live in poverty
could do something about
their situation if they really
wanted to . . . . ① ② ③ ④
Some form of Communist regime
is probably necessary for
progress in underdeveloped
countries . . . . ① ② ③ ④
In the USA today there can be
no justification for using
violence to achieve political goals . ① ② ③ ④
The main cause of Negro riots in
the cities is white racism . . . . ① ② ③ ④
Meaningful social change cannot
be achieved through tradi-
tional American politics . . . . ① ② ③ ④
I am very interested in national politics ① ② ③ ④
However acute our domestic
problems, we cannot afford
to suspend our space effort . . . . . . ① ② ③ ④
In the Arab-Israeli dispute, my
sympathies are with the Israelis . . . ① ② ③ ④
The U.S. should withdraw from
Vietnam immediately . . . . ① ② ③ ④
Racial integration of the public
elementary schools should be
achieved even if it requires busing . ① ② ③ ④
Where de facto segregation exists,
black people should be assured
control over their own schools . . . . ① ② ③ ④
Only volunteers should serve in
the armed forces . . . . ① ② ③ ④
Undergraduates known to use
marijuana regularly should
be suspended or dismissed . . . . . . ① ② ③ ④
A student's grades should not
be revealed to anyone off
campus without his consent . . . . . ① ② ③ ④
The chief benefit of a college
education is that it increases
one's earning power . . . . ① ② ③ ④

29. Of your close friends at your college only, what proportion are/were: (answer for your most recent college term)

┌──────1. All
│ ┌─────2. Most
│ │ ┌────3. A few
① ② ③ ④ — 4. None

In your major field . . . . ① ② ③ ④
Of the same sex as you . . . . ① ② ③ ④
In your same class (year) in college . . ① ② ③ ④
Living in the same building as you . . . ① ② ③ ④

30. a. Where did you live most of the time during your most recent college term?

b. Where would you have preferred to live?

	Lived	Preferred
	(Mark One)	(Mark One)
College dormitory or other college-run housing	○	○
Fraternity or sorority house	○	○
Rooming house or rented room	○	○
Apartment (not with parents or relatives)	○	○
With parents or relatives	○	○
Other	○	○

31. In regard to <u>each</u> of the following activities:

a. Did you ever engage in the activity?

b. If not, would you like to do it?

	Did		Would like to	
	Yes	No	Yes	No
Work in the Peace Corps or Vista	○	○	○	○
Tutor minority group children	○	○	○	○
Community organizing for social action	○	○	○	○
Work in a political campaign	○	○	○	○
Work as a hospital volunteer	○	○	○	○
Participate in an encounter group (sensitivity training)	○	○	○	○

32. a. Mark the number of courses you took in <u>each</u> of the fields listed, during your most recent college term. (If you took no courses in a given field, leave it blank.)

b. If now attending, mark your major field of study. (If you have not formally selected a major field, mark your <u>intended</u> or <u>most probable</u> field.)

c. If planning graduate study, mark your most probable field of study.

```
            ⟨ Number of Courses
            ⟨   (4 = 4 or more)
            ⟨── Major (Mark one)
①②③④ⓂⒼ── Graduate Field (Mark one)
```

Architecture, Environmental Design	①②③④ⓂⒼ
Art and Art History	①②③④ⓂⒼ
English Literature	①②③④ⓂⒼ
Journalism (writing)	①②③④ⓂⒼ
Languages, Modern	①②③④ⓂⒼ
Languages, Other, and Classics	①②③④ⓂⒼ
Music	①②③④ⓂⒼ
Philosophy	①②③④ⓂⒼ

32. Continued

Speech and Drama	①②③④ⓂⒼ
Theology	①②③④ⓂⒼ
Other/General: Arts & Humanities	①②③④ⓂⒼ
Biochemistry, Biophysics	①②③④ⓂⒼ
Botany	①②③④ⓂⒼ
Zoology	①②③④ⓂⒼ
Other/General: Biological Science	①②③④ⓂⒼ
Accounting	①②③④ⓂⒼ
Business Administration	①②③④ⓂⒼ
Secretarial	①②③④ⓂⒼ
Other/General: Business	①②③④ⓂⒼ
Engineering	①②③④ⓂⒼ
Chemistry	①②③④ⓂⒼ
Computer Science	①②③④ⓂⒼ
Geology, Astronomy	①②③④ⓂⒼ
Mathematics	①②③④ⓂⒼ
Statistics	①②③④ⓂⒼ
Physics	①②③④ⓂⒼ
Other/General: Physical Science	①②③④ⓂⒼ
Anthropology	①②③④ⓂⒼ
Economics	①②③④ⓂⒼ
Geography	①②③④ⓂⒼ
History	①②③④ⓂⒼ
Political Science	①②③④ⓂⒼ
Psychology	①②③④ⓂⒼ
Social Work, Welfare, Criminology	①②③④ⓂⒼ
Sociology	①②③④ⓂⒼ
Other/General: Social Science	①②③④ⓂⒼ
Education	①②③④ⓂⒼ
Health Technology (medical, physical, etc.)	①②③④ⓂⒼ
Nursing	①②③④ⓂⒼ
Pharmacy	①②③④ⓂⒼ
Therapy (occupational, physical, etc.)	①②③④ⓂⒼ
Other Professional (Law, Medicine, etc.)	①②③④ⓂⒼ
Agriculture	①②③④ⓂⒼ
Ethnic Studies (e.g., Black Studies)	①②③④ⓂⒼ
Electronic Technology, Communications	①②③④ⓂⒼ
Forestry	①②③④ⓂⒼ
Home Economics	①②③④ⓂⒼ
Industrial Arts	①②③④ⓂⒼ
Library Science	①②③④ⓂⒼ

33. From the following list of employers, please mark:

   A. your probable <u>first</u> employer after you complete your education, or your present employer if you are not attending school.

   B. your expected long-run <u>career</u> employer

   C. the employer you would most <u>prefer</u> if you were free to choose

   D. your father's primary employer during most of his working years.

Mark one in
each column

	A	B	C	D
Self-employed professional practice	Ⓐ	Ⓑ	Ⓒ	Ⓓ
Partner or associate in professional practice	Ⓐ	Ⓑ	Ⓒ	Ⓓ
Self-employed or family business	Ⓐ	Ⓑ	Ⓒ	Ⓓ
Business or industry	Ⓐ	Ⓑ	Ⓒ	Ⓓ
Federal Government (U.S. incl. military)	Ⓐ	Ⓑ	Ⓒ	Ⓓ
State or local government	Ⓐ	Ⓑ	Ⓒ	Ⓓ
Elementary or secondary school system	Ⓐ	Ⓑ	Ⓒ	Ⓓ
Junior college	Ⓐ	Ⓑ	Ⓒ	Ⓓ
College or university	Ⓐ	Ⓑ	Ⓒ	Ⓓ
Research organization or institute	Ⓐ	Ⓑ	Ⓒ	Ⓓ
Hospital or clinic	Ⓐ	Ⓑ	Ⓒ	Ⓓ
Other non-profit organization (e.g., church, welfare agency)	Ⓐ	Ⓑ	Ⓒ	Ⓓ
Other	Ⓐ	Ⓑ	Ⓒ	Ⓓ

34. From the following list of occupations, please mark:

   A. your probable <u>first</u> job after you complete your education, or your present job if you are not presently attending school

   B. your expected long-run <u>career</u> occupation

   C. the career you would most <u>prefer</u> if you were free to choose any from the list

   D. your father's primary occupation during most of his working years.

Mark One
In Each Column

	A	B	C	D
Physician or Surgeon	Ⓐ	Ⓑ	Ⓒ	Ⓓ
Dentist	Ⓐ	Ⓑ	Ⓒ	Ⓓ
Nurse	Ⓐ	Ⓑ	Ⓒ	Ⓓ
Therapist, Lab Technician, Hygienist	Ⓐ	Ⓑ	Ⓒ	Ⓓ
Dietitian or Home Economist	Ⓐ	Ⓑ	Ⓒ	Ⓓ
Pharmacist, Optometrist	Ⓐ	Ⓑ	Ⓒ	Ⓓ
Other/Medical and Health Professions	Ⓐ	Ⓑ	Ⓒ	Ⓓ
Lawyer (Attorney)	Ⓐ	Ⓑ	Ⓒ	Ⓓ

34. Continued

	A	B	C	D
Public Administrator, Official, Politician	Ⓐ	Ⓑ	Ⓒ	Ⓓ
Military Service (career)	Ⓐ	Ⓑ	Ⓒ	Ⓓ
Law Enforcement Officer	Ⓐ	Ⓑ	Ⓒ	Ⓓ
Librarian	Ⓐ	Ⓑ	Ⓒ	Ⓓ
Social Welfare, Group Worker	Ⓐ	Ⓑ	Ⓒ	Ⓓ
Counselor, Psychologist	Ⓐ	Ⓑ	Ⓒ	Ⓓ
Clergy	Ⓐ	Ⓑ	Ⓒ	Ⓓ
Other/Public and Social Services	Ⓐ	Ⓑ	Ⓒ	Ⓓ
Architect, Designer, City Planner	Ⓐ	Ⓑ	Ⓒ	Ⓓ
Artist, Actor, Musician, Entertainer	Ⓐ	Ⓑ	Ⓒ	Ⓓ
Writer, Journalist	Ⓐ	Ⓑ	Ⓒ	Ⓓ
Other/Design, Arts and Writing	Ⓐ	Ⓑ	Ⓒ	Ⓓ
Teacher, elementary	Ⓐ	Ⓑ	Ⓒ	Ⓓ
Teacher, secondary	Ⓐ	Ⓑ	Ⓒ	Ⓓ
College Teacher, Professor	Ⓐ	Ⓑ	Ⓒ	Ⓓ
Other/Education	Ⓐ	Ⓑ	Ⓒ	Ⓓ
Engineer	Ⓐ	Ⓑ	Ⓒ	Ⓓ
Scientific Technician, Programmer	Ⓐ	Ⓑ	Ⓒ	Ⓓ
Scientist, Researcher	Ⓐ	Ⓑ	Ⓒ	Ⓓ
Business Executive, Official, Owner	Ⓐ	Ⓑ	Ⓒ	Ⓓ
Accountant	Ⓐ	Ⓑ	Ⓒ	Ⓓ
Secretary, Clerk	Ⓐ	Ⓑ	Ⓒ	Ⓓ
Salesman or Buyer	Ⓐ	Ⓑ	Ⓒ	Ⓓ
Other/Business, Industry--Non-manual.	Ⓐ	Ⓑ	Ⓒ	Ⓓ
Farmer, Rancher, Other Agricultural	Ⓐ	Ⓑ	Ⓒ	Ⓓ
Skilled Worker, Craftsman	Ⓐ	Ⓑ	Ⓒ	Ⓓ
Foreman, Inspector	Ⓐ	Ⓑ	Ⓒ	Ⓓ
Semiskilled Worker, Operator, Driver	Ⓐ	Ⓑ	Ⓒ	Ⓓ
Laborer (unskilled)	Ⓐ	Ⓑ	Ⓒ	Ⓓ
Housewife	Ⓐ	Ⓑ	Ⓒ	

35. Some jobs involve the following activities.

   a. Which, if any, will <u>probably</u> be part of your work?

   b. Which would you <u>most prefer</u> to do, if you had your choice?

	Will Probably Do		Would Prefer	
	Yes	No	Yes	No
Teaching	O	O	O	O
Research	O	O	O	O
Administration	O	O	O	O
Service to clients or patients	O	O	O	O

36. What is the highest academic degree you intend to obtain? (Mark one)

None	O
Associate (or equivalent)	O
Bachelor's degree (B.A., B.S., etc.)	O
LL.B. or J.D.	O
M.D., D.D.S., or D.V.M.	O
Other professional (M.B.A., M.S.W., B.D., etc.)	O
Master's degree (M.A., M.S., etc.)	O
Ed.D.	O
Ph.D.	O
Other	O

37. What is your cumulative college grade point average?

A or A+ .... O   B− .... O
A− .... O   C+ .... O
B+ .... O   C .... O
B .... O   C− or below .. O

38. Indicate the political leaning which best describes:

     1. Left
     2. Liberal
     3. Middle-of-the-Road
     4. Moderately Conservative
① ② ③ ④ ⑤ — 5. Strongly Conservative

Yourself .... ① ② ③ ④ ⑤
Your parents .... ① ② ③ ④ ⑤
Your friends .... ① ② ③ ④ ⑤
Most other students at your
    college .... ① ② ③ ④ ⑤
Most professors at your college .. ① ② ③ ④ ⑤

39. Please indicate your agreement or disagreement with each of the following statements.

     1. Strongly Agree
     2. Agree With Reservations
     3. Disagree With Reservations
① ② ③ ④ — 4. Strongly Disagree

Students should have a major role
    in specifying the college cur-
    riculum .... ① ② ③ ④
Scientists should publish their
    findings regardless of the
    possible consequences .... ① ② ③ ④
Realistically an individual person
    can do little to bring about
    changes in our society .... ① ② ③ ④
Man will never realize his full
    potential until he is freed from
    the laws and conventions of
    society .... ① ② ③ ④
Striving for occupational success is
    incompatible with contributing
    to the long-run good of mankind . ① ② ③ ④
Faculty promotions should be
    based on student
    evaluations .... ① ② ③ ④
Marijuana should be legalized ..... ① ② ③ ④
Divorce laws should be liberalized .. ① ② ③ ④
Under some conditions, abortions
    should be legalized .... ① ② ③ ④
There is too much concern in the
    courts for the rights of criminals . ① ② ③ ④
Capital punishment (the death
    penalty) should be abolished .... ① ② ③ ④
Current levels of air pollution in
    large cities justify the use of
    drastic measures to limit the
    use of motor vehicles .... ① ② ③ ④

39. Continued

Urban problems cannot be solved
    without huge investments of
    Federal money .... ① ② ③ ④
Cigarette advertising should be
    outlawed .... ① ② ③ ④
Women are at least the intellectual
    equals of men .... ① ② ③ ④
There are dimensions of life that
    cannot be grasped rationally .... ① ② ③ ④

40. How often, on average, do you:

     1. Nearly Every Day
     2. Once or Twice a Week
     3. A Few Times a Month
     4. A Few Times a Year
① ② ③ ④ ⑤ — 5. Never

Attend a concert or play ...... ① ② ③ ④ ⑤
Listen to classical music ...... ① ② ③ ④ ⑤
Read books not required for
    courses .... ① ② ③ ④ ⑤
Attend an "art" film .... ① ② ③ ④ ⑤
Watch TV more than one hour ... ① ② ③ ④ ⑤
Listen to rock, folk, or soul
    music .... ① ② ③ ④ ⑤
Go out on a date .... ① ② ③ ④ ⑤
Attend a party .... ① ② ③ ④ ⑤
Spend time in a cafeteria or
    other student hang-out ...... ① ② ③ ④ ⑤
Visit in friends' rooms or
    apartments .... ① ② ③ ④ ⑤
Attend a meeting of some
    College organization .... ① ② ③ ④ ⑤
Attend an athletic event ...... ① ② ③ ④ ⑤
Play a sport (non-varsity) ...... ① ② ③ ④ ⑤
Discuss schoolwork with your
    friends .... ① ② ③ ④ ⑤
Attend political meetings,
    lectures, etc. .... ① ② ③ ④ ⑤
Have contact with your parents
    by letter, phone, or visit ..... ① ② ③ ④ ⑤
Visit with other relatives ...... ① ② ③ ④ ⑤
Participate in student govern-
    ment (if now attending) ..... ① ② ③ ④ ⑤

41. What is your present religious preference?

Protestant .... O   Other .... O
Catholic .... O   None .... O
Jewish .... O

42. Of all the people you know, how many do you count as close friends?

None .... O   3 - 5 .... O   11 - 15 ... O
1 - 2 .... O   6 - 10 .... O   16 or more . O

43. Of your close friends, what proportion are/were: (answer for your most recent college term)

1. All
2. Most
3. A Few
①②③④— 4. None

Students at your college . . . . ①②③④
Students at another college . . . . . . ①②③④
Not college students . . . . ①②③④

44. With regard to demonstrations or protests on each of the following issues, have you, since entering college: (mark all that apply)

1. Helped Organize or Lead
2. Participated In
3. Observed at First Hand
①②③④— 4. None of These

	At My College	Elsewhere
A demonstration against U.S. military policy	①②③④	①②③④
A demonstration against existing ethnic or racial policies	①②③④	①②③④
A demonstration against administrative policies of a college	①②③④	①②③④
A demonstration against college demonstrators	①②③④	①②③④

45. How often did you do each of the following during your most recent college term? (Mark one for each item)

Frequently
Occasionally
Ⓕ Ⓞ Ⓝ— Not At All

Came late to class . . . . Ⓕ Ⓞ Ⓝ
Played a musical instrument . . . . . . Ⓕ Ⓞ Ⓝ
Studied in the library . . . . Ⓕ Ⓞ Ⓝ
Checked out a book or journal from the college library . . . . Ⓕ Ⓞ Ⓝ
Arranged a date for another student . Ⓕ Ⓞ Ⓝ
Overslept and missed a class or appointment . . . . Ⓕ Ⓞ Ⓝ
Typed a homework assignment . . . . Ⓕ Ⓞ Ⓝ
Discussed my future with my parents . Ⓕ Ⓞ Ⓝ
Failed to complete an assignment on time . . . . Ⓕ Ⓞ Ⓝ
Argued with an instructor in class . . Ⓕ Ⓞ Ⓝ
Attended a religious service . . . . . . Ⓕ Ⓞ Ⓝ
Did extra (unassigned) reading for a course . . . . Ⓕ Ⓞ Ⓝ
Took sleeping pills . . . . Ⓕ Ⓞ Ⓝ
Tutored another student . . . . Ⓕ Ⓞ Ⓝ

45. Continued

Played chess . . . . Ⓕ Ⓞ Ⓝ
Read poetry not connected with a course . . . . Ⓕ Ⓞ Ⓝ
Took a tranquilizing pill . . . . Ⓕ Ⓞ Ⓝ
Discussed religion . . . . Ⓕ Ⓞ Ⓝ
Took vitamins . . . . Ⓕ Ⓞ Ⓝ
Visited an art gallery or museum . . . . . Ⓕ Ⓞ Ⓝ
Missed classes because of illness . . . . . Ⓕ Ⓞ Ⓝ
Smoked cigarettes . . . . Ⓕ Ⓞ Ⓝ
Discussed politics . . . . Ⓕ Ⓞ Ⓝ
Drank beer . . . . Ⓕ Ⓞ Ⓝ
Discussed sports . . . . Ⓕ Ⓞ Ⓝ
Asked an instructor for advice after class . . . . Ⓕ Ⓞ Ⓝ
Had vocational counseling . . . . Ⓕ Ⓞ Ⓝ
Stayed up all night . . . . Ⓕ Ⓞ Ⓝ
Studied less than 5 hours in any given week . . . . Ⓕ Ⓞ Ⓝ
Studied more than 30 hours in any given week . . . . Ⓕ Ⓞ Ⓝ

46. Indicate below the actual or probable source(s) you are using to finance your college and living expenses this academic year. (If not attending this year, answer for the last year you did attend.)

1. Not a Source
2. Minor Source 1% - 25%
3. Minor Source 26% - 50%
①②③④— 4. Major Source - Over 50%

Support from family . . . . ①②③④
Employment during college year . . . ①②③④
Employment during summer . . . . . ①②③④
Spouse's employment . . . . ①②③④
Scholarship, fellowship, grant, gift, etc. . . . . ①②③④
Repayable loan taken by yourself . . ①②③④
Your own savings or investments . . . ①②③④
Other . . . . ①②③④

47. If your annual costs at your college were increased $300.00, would you . . . (Mark one for each item. If not attending this year, skip this question.)

Yes
Maybe
Ⓨ Ⓜ Ⓝ— No

Get it from your parents . . . . Ⓨ Ⓜ Ⓝ
Earn it during the summer . . . . Ⓨ Ⓜ Ⓝ
Have to work (more) during the school year . . . . Ⓨ Ⓜ Ⓝ
Borrow it . . . . Ⓨ Ⓜ Ⓝ
Try to live on less money . . . . Ⓨ Ⓜ Ⓝ
Go to a less expensive college . . . . Ⓨ Ⓜ Ⓝ
Quit school . . . . Ⓨ Ⓜ Ⓝ
Get more scholarship aid . . . . Ⓨ Ⓜ Ⓝ

48. Did you live with each of your parents during most of the periods indicated? (Disregard attendance at boarding school.)

	Father (Step-Father)		Mother (Step-Mother)	
	Yes	No	Yes	No
During your grade school years	○	○	○	○
During your high school years	○	○	○	○

49. The following are descriptions of how some parents raise their children. Mark the response which best describes your mother and father as they were most of your life up to the time you graduated from high school.

Ⓥ — Very True
Ⓢ — Somewhat True
Ⓝ — Not True At All

	Father	Mother
If I had some kind of problem I could count on them to help me out	Ⓥ Ⓢ Ⓝ	Ⓥ Ⓢ Ⓝ
They kept after me to do well in school	Ⓥ Ⓢ Ⓝ	Ⓥ Ⓢ Ⓝ
If I didn't do what was expected of me, they were very strict about it	Ⓥ Ⓢ Ⓝ	Ⓥ Ⓢ Ⓝ
They comforted and helped me when I had troubles	Ⓥ Ⓢ Ⓝ	Ⓥ Ⓢ Ⓝ
They kept after me to do better than other children	Ⓥ Ⓢ Ⓝ	Ⓥ Ⓢ Ⓝ
They expected me to keep my things in good order	Ⓥ Ⓢ Ⓝ	Ⓥ Ⓢ Ⓝ
They taught me things I wanted to learn	Ⓥ Ⓢ Ⓝ	Ⓥ Ⓢ Ⓝ
They kept pushing me to do my best in everything	Ⓥ Ⓢ Ⓝ	Ⓥ Ⓢ Ⓝ
They made me feel I could talk with them about everything	Ⓥ Ⓢ Ⓝ	Ⓥ Ⓢ Ⓝ
When they wanted me to do something, they explained why	Ⓥ Ⓢ Ⓝ	Ⓥ Ⓢ Ⓝ

50. In general, I would characterize my parents as: (Mark one number for each item.)

Ⓥ — Very Much So
Ⓢ — Somewhat
Ⓝ — Not At All

Interested in intellectual pursuits	Ⓥ Ⓢ Ⓝ
Interested in cultural pursuits	Ⓥ Ⓢ Ⓝ
Religious	Ⓥ Ⓢ Ⓝ
Interested in politics	Ⓥ Ⓢ Ⓝ
Financially comfortable	Ⓥ Ⓢ Ⓝ

51. From what kind of secondary school did you graduate? (Mark one)

Public school ○
Non-public, Catholic ○
Non-public, other religiously affiliated ○
Non-public, non-religiously affiliated ○
Bureau of Indian Affairs School ○
Other Federal Government school ○

52. Of the students in your high school graduating class, about what percentage went to college?

Less than 10% ○   51 - 75% ○
10 - 25% ○   76 - 90% ○
26 - 50% ○   More than 90% ○

53. Are you:

Single ○
Engaged ○
Married ○
Separated, divorced, widowed ○

54. How old do you expect to be when you get married? (If you are already married, please mark the age at which you married.) Mark one.

Age 20 or younger ○
Age 21 - 22 ○
Age 23 - 24 ○
Age 25 - 26 ○
Age 27 - 28 ○
Age 29 - 30 ○
Age 31 - 35 ○
Over age 35 ○
I do not expect to marry ○

55. Are you: (Mark all that apply.)

White/Caucasian ○
Black/Negro/Afro-American ○
American Indian ○
Spanish-American/Mexican-American ○
Puerto-Rican ○
Oriental ○
None of these ○

Index

Carnegie Commission on Higher Education

Commission Reports

*The following Commission Reports may be ordered from
McGraw-Hill Book Company, Hightstown, New Jersey 08520;
Manchester, Missouri 63011; Novato, California 94947.*

TOWARD A LEARNING SOCIETY:
ALTERNATIVE CHANNELS TO LIFE,
WORK, AND SERVICE

OPPORTUNITIES FOR WOMEN
IN HIGHER EDUCATION:
THEIR CURRENT PARTICIPATION,
PROSPECTS FOR THE FUTURE, AND
RECOMMENDATIONS FOR ACTION

CONTINUITY AND DISCONTINUITY:
HIGHER EDUCATION AND
THE SCHOOLS

HIGHER EDUCATION:
WHO PAYS? WHO BENEFITS?
WHO SHOULD PAY?

THE PURPOSES AND THE
PERFORMANCE OF HIGHER
EDUCATION IN THE UNITED STATES:
APPROACHING THE YEAR 2000

GOVERNANCE OF HIGHER
EDUCATION:
SIX PRIORITY PROBLEMS

COLLEGE GRADUATES AND JOBS:
ADJUSTING TO A NEW LABOR
MARKET SITUATION

THE CAMPUS AND THE CITY:
MAXIMIZING ASSETS AND
REDUCING LIABILITIES

REFORM ON CAMPUS:
CHANGING STUDENTS, CHANGING
ACADEMIC PROGRAMS

THE MORE EFFECTIVE USE OF
RESOURCES:
AN IMPERATIVE FOR HIGHER EDUCATION

THE FOURTH REVOLUTION:
INSTRUCTIONAL TECHNOLOGY IN
HIGHER EDUCATION

INSTITUTIONAL AID:
FEDERAL SUPPORT TO COLLEGES
AND UNIVERSITIES

NEW STUDENTS AND NEW PLACES:
POLICIES FOR THE FUTURE GROWTH AND
DEVELOPMENT OF AMERICAN
HIGHER EDUCATION

DISSENT AND DISRUPTION:
PROPOSALS FOR CONSIDERATION
BY THE CAMPUS

THE CAPITOL AND THE CAMPUS:
STATE RESPONSIBILITY FOR
POSTSECONDARY EDUCATION

FROM ISOLATION TO MAINSTREAM:
PROBLEMS OF THE COLLEGES
FOUNDED FOR NEGROES

LESS TIME, MORE OPTIONS:
EDUCATION BEYOND THE HIGH SCHOOL

HIGHER EDUCATION AND
THE NATION'S HEALTH:
POLICIES FOR MEDICAL AND
DENTAL EDUCATION

THE OPEN-DOOR COLLEGES:
POLICIES FOR COMMUNITY COLLEGES

QUALITY AND EQUALITY:
REVISED RECOMMENDATIONS
NEW LEVELS OF FEDERAL RESPONSIBILITY
FOR HIGHER EDUCATION
*a supplement to the 1968 special report
by the Commission*

A CHANCE TO LEARN:
AN ACTION AGENDA FOR EQUAL
OPPORTUNITY IN HIGHER EDUCATION

QUALITY AND EQUALITY:
NEW LEVELS OF FEDERAL RESPONSIBILITY
FOR HIGHER EDUCATION
*a special report and recommendations by
the Commission, with 1970 revisions*